WELCOME TO HELL?

JOHN McMANUS

WELCOME TO HELL?

IN SEARCH OF THE REAL TURKISH FOOTBALL

First published in Great Britain in 2018 by Weidenfeld & Nicolson
an imprint of The Orion Publishing Group Ltd
Carmelite House, 50 Victoria Embankment
London EC4Y 0DZ

An Hachette UK Company

1 3 5 7 9 10 8 6 4 2

A CIP catalogue record for this book is available from the British Library.

ISBN 978-1-4746-0476-5

Typeset by Input Data Services Ltd, Somerset

Printed and bound by CPI Group (UK) Ltd, Croydon, CR0 4YY

www.orionbooks.co.uk

For Laura

Contents

Guide to Turkish Pronunciation x
Map of Turkey xii

Introduction 1

1. Welcome to Hell 15
2. Istanbul 37
3. Reis 67
4. Izmir 91
5. Ankara 109
6. Arda 133
7. Ordinaryüs 147
8. Yabanja 161
9. The Emperor 185
10. Amazons 209
11. Manchester 231
12. Trabzon 251
13. Gezi 273
14. Gaziantep 295
15. Diyarbakır 311
16. Inferno 335

Postscript 355

Select Bibliography 359
Acknowledgements 368
Picture Credits 371
Index 373

Guide to Turkish Pronunciation

Turkish uses the Latin alphabet and is highly phonetic. For English-speakers, it means that most of the letters sound roughly the same as in English and words are pronounced pretty much as written. But it also has six extra letters that don't exist in English. Unfortunately these crop up frequently in the names of football teams, so it's better to learn them now.

Ç pronounced 'ch' as in China, making the name of Turkey's most-supported club *Fenerbah-che*

Ğ This letter is silent, simply causing the letter before to be elongated. Hence the name of Turkey's president Erdoğan is *Er-doh-wan.*

İ Turkish is odd in that it has two letter 'I's, one dotted the other undotted. The dotted i is similar to its English equivalent ('i' as in 'pin'). The capitalised version has a dot on top (İ). With place names familiar in English, such as Istanbul and Izmir, I have omitted the dot to avoid distraction.

I A dull sound pronounced 'uh', as in the first syllable of the word 'among'. So Aziz Yıldırım, the long-serving Fenerbahçe president, is *Aziz Yul-duh-rum.*

Ö The same as its German equivalent. Sounds a bit like an expression of disgust – 'eugh'. So Mesut Özil is *Mes-ut Eugh-zil.*

Ş Pronounced 'şh' as in shower. There are two of these letters in the name of Turkey's 'third' biggest team, Beşiktaş – *Besh-ik-tash.*

Ü Purse the lips to make an 'ooh' sound, as in French 'tu'. So the founder of the Turkish Republic, Atatürk, is pronounced *Ata-toork.*

The one pronunciation difference is 'c', which is pronounced 'j' as in 'jam'. So the name of Liverpool midfielder Emre Can is pronounced 'Emre Jan'. Commentators frequently mix this up with the

Ç – che sound, making him sound Chinese. Don't make the same mistake.

Bonus tip

Like the Irish or Scottish prefix 'Mc-' or 'Mac-', Turkish has its own suffix for 'son of . . .': -oğlu (pronounced oh-lu). But this being Turkish, it comes at the end of the word. So the former Blackburn midfielder Tugay Kerimoğlu is pronounced Tu-gai Kerim-oh-lu. And Newcastle player turned Başakşehir star Emre Belözoğlu is Em-reh Bel-eurghz-oh-lu.

ROMANIA
BULGARIA
BLACK SEA
Edirne
Bosphorus
Istanbul
Sea of Marmara
Izmit
Adapazarı
Bursa
Ankara
Eskişehir
TURKEY
Izmir
Aegean Sea
Konya
Bodrum
Antalya
Mersin
GREECE
CYPRUS
MEDITERRANEAN SEA

RUSSIA
N
GEORGIA
Samsun
Trabzon
Rize
ARMENIA
Erzurum
Sivas
Tunceli
Lake Van
IRAN
ıyseri
Van
Malatya
Tigris
Diyarbakır
Gaziantep
Şanlıurfa
Mardin
Cizre
ana
takya
Euphrates
IRAQ
SYRIA

Introduction

I first began to think about Turkish football on Champions League evenings, as I sat in the dormitory television room at Ankara Science High School, watching the boys scream at the screen in paroxysms of grief and joy.

Every evening at eight, the door to the dormitory would be locked. From then until lights out, the four-storey building would throb with chatter, laughter and testosterone. Over a hundred boys aged fifteen to nineteen would pile into its sparsely furnished bedrooms and push their way play-fighting through its halls.

But on Champions League nights it was different. The corridors and bedrooms would stand eerily quiet as everyone squeezed into the television room. The room had a tiled floor and was painted with a whitewash that would transfer itself to any hand, sleeve or leg with which it came into contact. There was no furniture save thirty or so uncomfortable wooden and plastic chairs, which would be arranged to face the television, a battered set sitting uneasily on a bracket on the wall.

There were never enough chairs to go around. Everyone would share, lacing their arms around each other's shoulders to stop them from falling off. Following a match did not seem to involve the eyes as much as the hands and legs. Arms would be thrust towards the television, imploring, criticising or dismissing the men on the screen. Boys would continually stand up, making the screen only ever visible for a few seconds at a time. The football arrived chopped into a million discrete events, like viewing the pages of a badly drawn flick-book. At the back of the room was a small tuckshop, manned by a weary retired man called Necati, who rushed to fulfil the endless requests for tea, biscuits and toasted sandwiches.

I arrived at the school as a teaching assistant in 2008, the year Fenerbahçe reached the quarter-finals of the Champions League. If the team scored, the room would disassemble. Students would jump to their feet, grabbing one another and knocking over chairs as they hugged and jumped up and down. When the mass would subside, one student, a Fenerbahçe fan called Onur, would climb onto his chair. Facing the crowd, he would raise his hands and address them in a voice that belied his small appearance: 'FE-NER-BAH-ÇE!'

When Sevilla were beaten on penalties in the round of 16, I remember being unable to sleep for hours after the game. Grown wild on the drama, the students went off to bed reluctantly. Outside my window, the cacophony of car horns continued in a constant wave until morning. The victory had stirred life both inside and outside the dormitory. But this was *Ankara*, I remember thinking to myself, 250 miles from Istanbul, where Fenerbahçe were from. And it was only the round of 16.

It was on Champions League nights in the television room that I first began to realise that football in Turkey was bigger and more important than I could ever have imagined.

I had been brought to Ankara and the school not by conscious choice but by a tick in a box. Just out of university and craving an adventure, I applied to a European Union scheme to work abroad as a language assistant. My target was France – a country I had visited frequently and thought I liked. I filled in a form, sent it off and promptly forgot about it.

Months later, I received a call. It was the organisers of the scheme. They liked my application and wanted to have me. Fist punching. Silent celebration. There then followed a pause on the other end of the line.

'We saw you put Turkey down,' the caller continued. 'Would you still be interested in going there?'

I groped back in my mind to filling in the form. France was first,

Spain second. Turkey, I dimly recalled, was my third choice. But did I actually want to go?

'Yes. Sure,' I said, my feelings on the matter far less certain than my words.

In the immediate aftermath of the call, however, the uncertainty broadened into excitement. Turkey was a country I had never visited. I knew next to nothing about the place. It would be a far more interesting prospect.

I had been paired with a school in Ankara, the Turkish capital – a science high school, one of the most prestigious in the country, and a boarding school. On the bus from Ankara airport on a cold February evening, I remember peering out into the darkness at the wide avenues and unfamiliar buildings, curious about the city in which I had committed to living for the next six months.

The English teachers picked me up from the bus station, friendly and welcoming as we sped away. Upon arriving at the school we got out of the car and walked across the yard, the snow piled on the edge of the paths. Buildings loomed in the dark on three sides. The teachers gestured for me to follow them into one of them. As soon as I stepped inside I was hit by a cacophony of shouting and cheering.

We had entered an atrium with stairs snaking up three storeys. Boys were lining the balconies and steps. More boys were crowded around the door. They pushed closer to greet me. I wasn't really sure what was going on. I remember feeling someone put something around my neck but I didn't have the time to see what it was. The teachers introduced me to students, face after face blurring into a frantic whirl, and showed me to my room – a small, sparse space with four beds but only used by me. The headmaster of the school took particular delight in showing me how to turn the television they'd acquired on and off via the remote control.

It was only after everyone had left and I sat down on the bed, exhausted and overloaded, that I realised I still had something round my neck. I took it off and inspected what it was that I was wearing. It was a Galatasaray scarf.

*

In Turkish the word for 'fan' is *taraftar. Taraf*, from the Arabic for side, and *dar*, the Farsi preposition that means 'at'. *Taraftar.* At one side. This is quite different from the words we use in English. 'Supporter' connotes structures and foundations. 'Fanatic' is closer, stemming from ideas of divine inspiration, but remains broad and needs qualifiers ('an *Arsenal* fanatic'). By contrast, *taraftar* seems to have inscribed into its very etymology overtones of partisanship. At the side. Or perhaps I'm projecting too much from my experience. For if football in Turkey is defined by one characteristic, it is intense partisanship.

One of the first things my new roommates wanted to know was which team I would support: Galatasaray or Fenerbahçe? These, I knew, were the big teams. I recognised their names from nights of European football on British television. I knew vaguely that they had a reputation for intense fans and even violent clashes, but that was as far as my knowledge of Turkish football stretched.

During breaks and after class, students would slip football tops over their school shirts – the cherry red and gold of Galatasaray ('the Lions'), or buttercup yellow and navy of Fenerbahçe ('the Canaries'). They would run around on the school playground, pinging a ball at the flimsy wooden goals set up at either end. The games would involve a lot of skilful dribbling, infrequent passing and long breaks in which the students would argue about decisions. Matches always concluded in rancour and acrimony, sometimes with a physical fight thrown in for good measure.

One Sunday a couple of months after I arrived, half a dozen students invited me to watch the Galatasaray v. Fenerbahçe derby on television. We left the school on a blustery spring day, walking down the precipitous Ankara hills, past apartment blocks to a local sports club. It was empty. The students were so nervous and excited that we had arrived two hours in advance. When I looked at them before kick-off, they were praying. I remember being disgusted at how little football took place, the players preferring to spend the entire game fouling and arguing.

Which side: Galatasaray or Fenerbahçe? I was viewed by many of the students the way an evangelist sizes up a potential convert. But I'd be damned if I was going to choose. With the school population split, any decision would alienate half the students. Still people refused to let me remain unattached.

In time, I came to realise this wasn't anything personal. In Turkey everyone must be – or pretend to be – a fan. If they don't personally like football, then they adopt the team of their families or lovers. There is intense jockeying over those whose football affiliations are still up for grabs: the range of baby merchandise sold by teams is vast, driven by a huge market of uncles, brothers and dads (it remains a particularly male phenomenon) buying team franchise to brand and secure a baby's future loyalty. I was once told a story of a newborn child, two days old, whose Galatasaray-loving father and uncles took him out of his crib and painted his penis yellow and red.

Nor was this desire to assign a person to a team limited to football. In Turkey, standing on the threshold seemed a highly difficult, even subversive act. People see less the individual and more the invisible trails of kinship and social connections that gather around them. Familial loyalty and closeness seeps out from the home and colours all of life: strangers address each other as 'brother' and 'sister'; the state is called 'father state'. Groupthink is strong and loyalty to the collective sacrosanct. Criticism of your boss or political party is not reflexive evaluation offered in good faith but grievous treachery, akin to stabbing your father in the back.

But I wasn't to know any of this yet. I just found it irritating that people wouldn't let me refrain from picking a team.

'Which team?'

'I don't really follow Turkish football.'

'OK, well, which colours do you prefer: red and yellow, or blue and yellow?'

'I don't really like any of those, my favourite colour is purple.'

'OK, OK. What is your favourite animal: a lion or a canary?'

'I like dolphins.'

'OK, but you have to choose one! Dolphins aren't an option.'

'OK, I guess . . . a lion.'

'Ah, you're Galatasaray! Why on earth do you like them?'

I began to realise my insistence on remaining aloof was not just irritating people but doing me active harm. Football affiliation seemed arguably even more important for people like me, whose family, occupation and social networks were completely untraceable. Assigning a football team is a way of bringing such misfits into the Turkish schema. Of furnishing them with a group, for everyone is part of a group.

So it was that, when I arrived at the school, the students' first action was to adorn me with a Galatasaray scarf. On the concrete hall of the boy's dormitory, in front of a crowd looking on expectantly, one boy tried to claim me. You're one of us. You belong with our tribe.

Except I didn't accept his attempt. I rejected Galatasaray, and Fenerbahçe too.

*

At the high school there were a few boys who supported a third team whose name was unfamiliar: Beşiktaş.

Beşiktaş were another side from Istanbul, the oldest club in Turkey, the students told me. They played in black and white, had the nickname of the 'Black Eagles' and were less successful than either Fenerbahçe or Galatasaray.

After weeks of being harried for my football allegiance, one evening while sitting on the benches outside the dormitory I finally snapped. 'OK. I am a Beşiktaş fan!' I declared. The boys' excitement that I had finally made a decision was instantly replaced by disappointment, followed by mockery.

My decision was motivated by nothing more than a desire to shut everyone up while not upsetting the Galatasaray–Fenerbahçe balance. And that was the end of the matter. I had never watched Beşiktaş play. I had no idea about the players. When, six months later, it came time for me to leave the school, I headed home and promptly forgot all about them.

That autumn I returned to university to embark on a Master's degree. I threw myself into my new life, trying to learn Middle Eastern languages and having fun, being more successful at the latter than the former. Approaching the end of the first year, the one thing I knew about my future was that I was expected to do research for a thesis. Thinking back to my time in Turkey, one topic crowded out all others: football.

'I hate football,' declared the professor of Turkish studies who I approached about the idea. At that time (the late 2000s) Turkey was topically framed through a few limited perspectives. The most prominent involved exploring the compatibility of Islam with 'modernity', a subject that had assumed new impetus with the emergence in 2002 of the most openly religious ruling party in Turkey's history – the

Justice and Development Party (AKP). Some cried the nation was on its way to becoming an Islamic republic. Others were cautiously optimistic. Alongside matters of such importance, football must have seemed trivial. But it wasn't to me.

During my time in Turkey I had bumped up against some national shibboleths. One night in the dormitory, I asked one of the boys if people ever referred to Turkey's founder, Mustafa Kemal Atatürk, as 'Muzzy'. The question was asked in innocence – growing up as a Leicester City fan, our star midfielder was the half-Turkish, half-British Mustafa Izzet, who everyone called 'Muzzy'. The boy's face became ashen. Unable to make eye contact with me, he lowered his head and muttered quietly, 'No, we don't call him that.' That was how I learnt that people do not joke about Atatürk.

I also picked up on the culture wars taking place. Some women wore headscarves, others didn't. Some people prayed and abstained from alcohol, others downed glass after glass of rakı – the anise-flavoured liquor that is Turkey's national drink – while picking at mezze. I would be frequently irritated by 'secularists' assuming an equal antipathy on my behalf to headscarves or prayers, raising their eyebrows when I told them my school in the UK had both. Teachers at my work would warn me from travelling east of Ankara, which they saw as dangerous and backwards, despite never having set foot in the eastern regions themselves.

This is not to say that I believed football was not inscribed with division and conflict – I had witnessed enough fights between the students to know that much. But because it wasn't political parties but football teams, might perhaps the contours of conflict and unity be able to tell us something new about Turkey? Or at least allow us to look at the country in a different light, escaping from clichéd metaphors of Turkey as a 'bridge' (between East and West, Muslim and Christian, modern and traditional) or a 'land of contradictions' (what nation isn't?).

Back in his study, my professor followed his declaration about his lack of interest in football with a roaring laugh – he was endlessly good-natured – before being suddenly struck by a thought. 'There's this supporters' group for Beşiktaş fans called Çarşı. They're supposed to be politicised and socialist, but I don't know if that's true or not.'

Within a month of the conversation with my tutor, I found myself back on a plane to Turkey. But instead of returning to Ankara, I had a new destination: Istanbul, home of Beşiktaş.

*

It was through Beşiktaş fans that I began to truly love Turkey and its football. More accurately, it was through Özgür. Of a similar age to me, Özgür had a big round belly, a laugh like a hyena, and an extreme distaste for drinking chilled water which, even in temperatures of 30 degrees, he believed would make him sick.

Özgür became my friend and guide – the only person who didn't seem to mind me attaching myself like a limpet, asking endless questions. I ended up spending three months with him and his Beşiktaş gang in Istanbul, being introduced to the fan leaders, going to matches, hanging out.

During games Özgür would grab me round the shoulder and hoist me onto the seats. He would lace his arms through mine, and compel me to jump up and down in time with him and the rest of the stadium. When a goal was scored and the crowd turned to lava, pouring over the rows and causing hundreds to fall over, he would brace himself and hold me up, like someone trying to stop a beach umbrella from being taken off by the wind.

Özgür instructed me in the art of shelling sunflower seeds with the teeth and discarding their carcasses on the terrace, and taught me how to sing some of the Beşiktaş chants. And what chants! My poor Turkish meant I couldn't distinguish the words at first, only feel the force. I would turn, petrified that there was a huge riot taking place, only to see people with smiles on their faces twirling scarves and singing. It was no surprise to learn that Beşiktaş jostles for position among the world's loudest sports crowds (at a match in September 2017 Timo Werner, a player for the German team RB Leipzig, had to be substituted after 32 minutes because the noise was so intense that it made him dizzy).

I learned that there were chants for kick-off and chants for corners. There were songs about love and songs about death. Songs about shafting Galatasaray and Fenerbahçe and songs designed to comfort and console whenever Beşiktaş lost. Every kind of footballing emotion had its place in the chanting repertoire. In that sense, the experience was truly operatic.

I got to understand the fixation in Turkish football with numbers, particularly the year of the club's foundation – 1903. And so 19 March was an important day (19/03), as was the time of three minutes past seven in the evening (19:03). There was also an almost childish obsession with colours. Because Beşiktaş played in black and white, fans would frequently tell me that they just 'hated colours'. I had to retire a green jacket of mine, because whenever I wore it to Beşiktaş matches the others would joke that I was supporting Bursaspor, Beşiktaş's hated rivals who play in green. Once when poised with a bottle of ketchup and about to squirt it on my chips, a fan leant across the table and put their hand on the bottle. 'Be careful. You know what that will mean,' he told me gravely. I looked at him, completely puzzled. 'Ketchup on chips. Red on yellow. Galatasaray!' he said, his eyes lighting up. I squirted it on anyway.

Through Özgür I learnt that everyone was out to get Beşiktaş. Penalties conceded were never the fault of the defender clumsily tripping the attacker – they were because the referee had been bought off by Galatasaray, or the Turkish Football Federation was punishing Beşiktaş supporters. Fans would tie football into a dense, impenetrable knot of references to politicians and political events, their machinations and vendettas, about which I knew nothing. I dismissed such comments as conspiracy-theory nonsense, only for fans to look at me sadly and shake their heads, the way you do at a child who has yet to grasp the harshness of the world.

And just as my professor had promised, there was a political dimension. The fan club to which Özgür belonged, Çarşı, entwined their intense love of Beşiktaş with socio-political causes. Its logo contained the anarchist 'A'. Before games, fans would prepare banners that protested against whatever injustice made the headlines that week: Samuel Eto'o taunted by monkey chants in Spain? *Hepimiz Eto'o* – we are all Eto'o. Government plans for nuclear power stations? *Nükleersiz Türkiye* – a nuclear-free Turkey. 'Labour is holy' Özgür once proclaimed to me in a grave voice once over breakfast. An hour later he was teaching me how to question the referee's parentage in Turkish.

What started as a questionable topic for a university thesis slowly morphed into an obsession. The Master's led to a doctorate in anthropology looking at Beşiktaş supporters, this time among the diaspora in Europe. My Turkish improved to the extent that I could finally understand what was going on, revealing to me vistas of football support that I never knew existed. Turkish football fans, I could see, were political, emotional, obsessed, paranoid – and bitingly sarcastic and funny.

In Turkish the verb used for football support is *tutmak*, which means 'to hold'. When one Turkish speaker wants to find out the loyalties of another, they ask 'which team do you hold?' It is a much closer, more evocative image.

Seeing me all the time with Özgür, people would ask which team I held. I realised that I was no longer a dispassionate observer, that I had grown into the identity that I had arbitrarily picked the summer before. I began to take on its contours, to be welcomed into the fraternity. Beşiktaş held me in its embrace.

*

Over the years, with my trips limited to short visits, I felt increasingly adrift from Turkey and its football.

In 2010, a team I had barely heard of won the top division. It was the first ever league title by Bursaspor, the side from the Western city of Bursa, the first capital of the Ottomans, sat in the shadow of the magnificent mountain of Uludağ. The next season another outsider, Trabzonspor, lost out on goal difference to Fenerbahçe in the championship. It dawned on me that I had been seduced by the logic of the *üç büyükler*, the 'Big Three', as Galatasaray, Fenerbahçe and Beşiktaş are known. I had been charmed by my association, failing to realise that my mind had become limited by its dogma – the vice-like grip on all media coverage and expectation of always winning.

I remember listening to a podcast on a journey to the airport in September 2011, heading home after a month in Istanbul. The presenter and his guest were trying to explain the match-fixing scandal that had engulfed Turkish football that summer. It was complex beyond belief. The same applied to the strange stories I was coming across about a powerful Muslim sect that was supposedly pulling the levers in the police, the judiciary, and even in football.

Each time I visited Turkey, it would seem as though everything had changed. Syria, Turkey's southern neighbour, was plunged into protests and then civil war, causing over three million people to flood into Turkey, changing the landscape of its cities and the language spoken on its streets. In summer 2013, hundreds of thousands of Turkish citizens took to the streets in the largest example of civil unrest since the 1970s. At the centre of the protests was a group of Beşiktaş fans.

The government of Recep Tayyip Erdoğan, which many had hoped would break the cycle of authoritarian intervention in politics, seemed to be engaging in many of the same actions as governments of the past: deploying polarising rhetoric, constraining the opposition and politicising the judiciary. The peace process with Kurdish militants teetered and then collapsed.

I also began to feel frustrated at the image of Turkish football back home. To the average fan in Britain, the game in Turkey seemed to be associated solely with violence. People would ask me about hooliganism, banners declaring 'Welcome to Hell' held up to threaten visiting supporters, and about the night in 2000 when two Leeds United fans were stabbed to death in Istanbul.

My own experiences had been anything but hellish. When I thought about Turkish football, I pictured warm-heartedness, camaraderie and ardour in amounts I had never before witnessed. I thought of Turkish-origin Londoners who would pull on a Fenerbahçe top and fly halfway around Europe to watch their side play. I recalled Beşiktaş's İnönü stadium – a ganglion of excitement with burning flares, rippling banners and elaborate call-and-response chants. In Turkey, I was never made to feel unwelcome. The gap between perceptions and the reality I was encountering was stark.

I decided that I would write a book. I wanted to recount my experiences in order to balance the scales and correct the lopsided image. It was to be a love letter to the Turkish game. Or at least that was the plan.

*

In October 2015 I boarded a plane to Turkey, this time with all the possessions I could fit in a suitcase and my wife – repeated trips to Turkey over the years had managed to convince her of both my own and the country's suitability.

The week we arrived, two bombs tore through a crowd outside

Ankara's main train station. The victims were peace activists, gathered to protest at the resumption of armed conflict between the government and Kurdish militants in the south-east of the country. The bombing was the work of the jihadist group ISIS and left 103 people dead. Three days later in the city of Konya, a minute's silence was held before Turkey played Iceland in a European Championship qualifier. Invited to pause and commemorate the victims of Turkey's worst ever terrorist attack, the crowd booed and whistled.

We didn't yet know it, but we had timed our arrival to coincide perfectly with the most difficult and traumatic period that Turkey had experienced in decades. The nadir would come nine months into our stay, when a violent attempted military coup came close to toppling the government and claimed the lives of 248 people. Against the backdrop of this bloodshed and trauma – and the political divisions that ensued – it would prove impossible for football not to get sucked in.

But it wasn't just the bombings, the conflict and the political upheaval. As I settled into my new life in Turkey, watching events spool out, I was forced to confront a painful truth. For all my supposed knowledge and expertise, I had compartmentalised my experiences. I knew that the place wasn't perfect nor its football fans angels, but those facts hadn't previously seemed important to the story I planned to tell. It began to dawn on me that my previous trips to the country had been like holidays, with all the separation and romance from real life that they entail.

Living in Turkey with no return ticket, my paradigms shifted. Turkey also viewed me differently – now a resident not a visitor; still a foreigner, but no longer a guest. New experiences and perspectives pushed against the old, until they creaked and collapsed.

To write the book I had to expand my frame of reference, beyond the fans whom, over the years, I had grown to love. I criss-crossed the country, speaking to players, referees, managers, club presidents and administrators, each of whom helped to colour in other facets of the Turkish game. And then I went wider still, meeting businessmen, politicians, historians, aid workers and anthropologists in an attempt to understand how football was intertwined in life more broadly. Conversations would quickly veer into dark terrain: bombings, corruption, match fixing, rampant commercialism, government interference, peppered often by the refrain: 'I *used* to like football until . . .'

It is not that my initial instinct was totally wrong. There remains much more to Turkish football than violence. I still encountered endless warmth, hospitality and humour, from dancing barbers and rhapsodising club owners to Trabzonspor fans wearing Leicester City tops. But the more I progressed, I came to appreciate the darkness pushing at the seams.

I had been naive to think I could tell the real story of Turkish football in shades of colour and vim.

SHARP

1

Welcome to Hell

On the night of 5 April 2000, on a small island in the middle of the Bosphorus, Peter Ridsdale had just got up to give a speech of thanks when a mobile phone went off. The Leeds United chairman was being hosted by the directors of Galatasaray, Turkish champions, who were to play Leeds the next day in the semi-final of the UEFA Cup.

The phone belonged to his director of operations, David Spencer. Ridsdale was at first annoyed when Spencer took the call, but irritation was replaced by worry when he caught Spencer's eye. When he had finished talking, Spencer pulled him aside. The call was from the British police liaison officer who had travelled with the fans to Istanbul. There had been fighting between Leeds and Galatasaray supporters in Taksim, the large square at the heart of the city. Some were badly injured and had been taken to hospital, one case was rumoured to be fatal. 'We've been advised to return to the safety of our hotel as soon as possible,' Spencer told Ridsdale.

Ridsdale instead headed straight to the hospital. When he explained who he was, he was ushered inside. The building seemed deserted except for half a dozen Leeds fans stood in a huddle at the end of a corridor. When they spotted Ridsdale, they crowded around him, begging him for information about two supporters who arrived unconscious.

A doctor approached. He took Ridsdale by the arm, leading him along a corridor and down a flight of steps into a basement. They paused before a large steel door like the kind found on a bank vault.

The doctor pulled it open and gestured for Ridsdale to enter. On the inside from floor to ceiling were what looked like giant filing cabinets. The doctor went up to one of the cabinets and pulled it open. Lying on a slab was the body of a bare-chested man covered in stab wounds. He asked Ridsdale to identify the body.

'I can't,' he blurted out in shock. 'I don't know who it is!'

Ridsdale went back upstairs to the group of fans who in turn led him to find Darren Loftus. He was on a ward receiving attention for stab wounds, but got up when he saw Ridsdale.

'Where's Christopher?' Loftus asked, referring to his older brother, a thirty-five-year-old fibre-optics engineer who had also travelled to the game.

'Follow me,' Ridsdale said.

Darren Loftus's injuries meant he had to be pushed in a wheelchair to the top of the stairs. He then limped painfully down each step. In the silence, Ridsdale found himself praying that the man on the slab was not a Leeds fan, that it was all a case of mistaken identity, that the rumours of a fatality were wrong.

The heavy steel door was opened again and the doctor led Darren through. He pulled open the draw of the cabinet. Ridsdale will never forget what happened next.

'The screaming that echoed around that room will live with me for ever.'

The group headed back upstairs to try and locate the second missing fan. They were told it was Kevin Speight, a forty-year-old pub landlord. He was in the operating theatre but needed blood. The hospital had no stocks. They could get some from another hospital but someone would need to pay. Ridsdale handed over a credit card and dispatched his driver to fetch the blood. But it was too late. Not long afterwards, the doctors told the group that Kevin had died from his stab wounds. Ridsdale put his head in his hands. The fans slumped on each other's shoulders and began to cry.

Eighteen years on, that night in April still haunts British perceptions of Turkish football, and of the nation more broadly. For many, Turkey is seen as marred by lawlessness, intimidation, unfairness and violence. In short, hell.

By contrast, I don't think a Turkish fan has ever mentioned it to me unprompted. That whole season has very different associations for people in Turkey. A month after the Leeds game, in May 2000, Galatasaray lifted the UEFA Cup. They became the first Turkish club to win a European trophy, prompting an outpouring of celebration and national pride, the like of which has yet to be repeated. If reminded about the stabbings, most express deep regret about what happened. But from their point of view it was just an unsavoury affair involving English football hooligans.

A clear gap in perception exists between how outsiders and locals view Turkey's footballing culture, a difference that has bred much misunderstanding, distrust and even hatred. This book is an attempt to bridge that gap. But to do that, we must first overcome the stumbling block posed by the events of April 2000.

*

The phrase 'Welcome to Hell' has become synonymous with the Leeds United stabbings, but it does not actually stem from that game. It came into being seven years earlier, in November 1993, when Manchester United played Galatasaray in the Champions League second qualifying round. Two weeks previously in Manchester, the sides had drawn 3–3. Those three away goals handed Galatasaray the upper hand going into the return leg. A draw would most likely send them through.

From the moment the Manchester United team landed in Istanbul, they faced a campaign of intimidation. The United players emerged into the arrivals hall to be confronted by approximately fifty Galatasaray fans screaming 'NO WAY OUT!' in English. While the United players waited on their coach, fans brandished bits of yellow card inscribed with various phrases, most of which displayed a loose grasp of hospitality, and an even looser command of English spelling and grammar:

'Welcome to The Hell'

'Heyy M. United. This is your last 48 hours'

'WELLCOME. Mr Ferguson, Sharpe, Cantona, Hughes, Robson, Erwin [sic] and the others. AFTER THE MATCH: Good bye Mrs Ferguson, Sharpe, Cantona, Hughes, Robson, Erwin . . .'

Years later, Gary Neville described the scene for a documentary. 'To this day it was the most hostile atmosphere that I've ever seen,' he said. 'They were smashing the glass down trying to get to us, it felt like.'

The next day, Galatasaray fans started gathering outside the side's Ali Sami Yen stadium before it was light. When the turnstiles opened at midday, they filled the stands. 'There was no system. I don't remember how exactly I got into the stadium,' recalled Ceyhun Akgül, who bunked off school as a fifteen-year-old to attend the game. Once inside, Ceyhun and his friends stayed rooted to the same spot, petrified of losing their place. By the time that the Manchester United players stepped out onto the pitch that evening, most of the crowd had been in position for over seven hours.

'I'll never forget the singing – each side of the stands to each other,' Steve Bruce, the Manchester United defender, later recalled. 'It was just an unbelievable display of passion from them.' Footage from before the game shows Bruce gesturing amusedly to Ryan Giggs and Nicky Butt, and then at his ears. Giggs laughs, displaying the chewing gum in his mouth, nervous energy dispelled into his teeth, which are working away at a furious rate. Perhaps it was good that the players didn't understand the words:

Manchester faggots, run and hide. No one can handle Cim Bom [the nickname for Galatasaray]

'We were bored,' Ceyhun said. 'When they came out [onto the pitch], we were really excited and we were trying really hard to impress and scare them.' The game itself was a drab affair which finished 0–0. Frustrated at the time-wasting tactics of Galatasaray, Eric Cantona grabbed the ball out of reserve goalkeeper Nezih Ali Boloğlu's hands on the substitute's bench and then knocked him to the ground with an elbow. On the final whistle he was sent off, approaching referee Kurt Röthlisberger and rubbing his thumb and index finger together to suggest he was bought off. In 1997 Röthlisberger was found guilty of bribery and banned from refereeing for life. An ex-official at the Turkish Football Federation (TFF) who was there that night told me that a man in the VIP section bragged to him about how he bribed international referees. The cloud of impropriety has never fully left the game.

It was a cold March day in Istanbul when I talked to Ceyhun, a friend of a friend, about the experience. Now in his thirties and a computer programmer, he relished the chance to reminisce about the match. An important detail came through in his description: in his eyes, the cultivation of the 'Welcome to Hell' image was meant to be tongue in cheek. The throat-slitting gestures and threats were not deployed in seriousness; it was pantomime brutality designed to unnerve their opponents and knock them off their game.

Indeed, if you peer a bit closer at aspects of this 'hellish' welcome, the illusion starts to creak. The signs at the airport looked more like a school arts-and-crafts project than banners of war, the authors incapable of resisting jazzy zigzags and squiggly lines under certain words. The fans, too, were less grizzled hooligans and more like Ceyhun and his friends – teenagers excited by the glamour and attention that accompanies the visit of one of the world's most famous football clubs.

'I didn't see any problem with it at the time,' said Ceyhun. 'Back then I was thinking that it's just a metaphor and it's not a big deal to say it. But when I put myself in the place of a Manchester United fan or, later on, a Leeds United fan, it's really scary.'

When was the joke no longer funny? Perhaps when a policeman punched Eric Cantona in the back on his way to the changing rooms, almost prompting a riot between the Manchester United players and the police. Maybe it ceased to be humorous when the window of the Manchester United coach was shattered as the team were leaving the stadium. Or perhaps it was the night before, when 164 United fans were awoken in their hotel by the police, locked in prison cells for sixteen hours, forced to sign 'confessions' and then deported. There seemed to be a failure on behalf of many Galatasaray fans and police to realise that the behaviour being doled out went way beyond mere tongue-in-cheek intimidation. It was malicious, dangerous and should have had no place in any sporting experience.

'We Turkish people, when it comes to competition, we can really *oppose* the opposition,' Ceyhun said. 'Like wolves or something from wildlife. So it's sort of natural. Although you don't want it, you get hooked and you act like this. But then, when someone from outside of that ecosystem comes in and looks at you . . . for me I realise how stupid it is, this whole confrontation.'

In the British media the intimidation was roundly, and rightly, condemned. But the language and imagery chosen by some writers is noteworthy. Steve Curry in the *Daily Express* compared the Manchester United reception committee to 'the crazed delirium usually witnessed on news bulletins from Islamic rallies in Iraq'. In *United! Despatches From Old Trafford*, Richard Kurt said that 'the lack of what we considered to be proper civilisation in Turkey created such angst in the United team that what followed was scarcely sport as we know it'. In these and other accounts, Galatasaray fans are criticised not for their behaviour as football fans, or the police and security officials as authorities, but for more elemental shortcomings as an 'Islamic' people incapable of exhibiting 'civilisation'.

They add their voices to a frightened fascination with Turkey stretching back over half a millennium. The Palestinian-American academic Edward Said coined the term 'Orientalism' for his critique of the Western world's clichéd, romanticised and racist depictions of 'the East'. He argued that European culture 'gained in strength and identity by setting itself off against the Orient as a sort of surrogate and even underground self'. The Ottoman empire, which for centuries was the dominant political and cultural force in the Near East, played a disproportionate role in this narrative. The tropes of the 'lustful' and 'terrible Turk' vividly symbolised Western fears and confirmed their superiorities.

'You can hardly expect . . . elegance of style from such an utterly barbarous country as Turkey', wrote Ogier de Busbeq, an Austrian diplomat in Constantinople, the old name for Istanbul, in the 1550s.

The works of Shakespeare and Marlowe are sprinkled with warnings of the power of the 'savage' Turk. Victorian and Edwardian cartoons depict Ottomans as lustful, beastly or indolent. One shows John Bull – a personification of the United Kingdom – waving a gun in the face of Sultan Abdülhamid II, hooknosed and cross-legged on his divan, scolding him like a child. The caption reads: 'the Terrible Turk again'.

THE TERRIBLE TURK AGAIN.
J.B.: Look here, I have had enough of your nonsense. I mean it this time.

Nor is the stereotyping confined to print: Alan Parker's 1978 film *Midnight Express*, about an American college dropout locked up in a Turkish prison for smuggling drugs, is an exercise in how many prejudices and fears can be squeezed into one film. Full of sadistic violence, venal officials and racist depictions of Turks, the film was credited with crashing the Turkish tourism industry and poisoning the country's image in the West for a generation (none of which, incredibly, prevented it from winning two Oscars).

The 'Welcome to Hell' experience tapped into this centuries-old reservoir of cultural imagery. It became grist to the mill of larger depictions of Turkey in the world, as a country that falls on the wrong side of many of the divides through which Europe – and Britain

– defines itself: they are Muslim while we are Christian; they are in Asia, we are in Europe (sort of).

It works the other way, too. The actions of Western countries, including Britain, continue to be a source of comparison for people in Turkey. Images of 'the West' are the Orient's mirror image, a powerful metaphor used to examine Turkey's sense of itself. The nation harbours deep anger at what it sees as Western arrogance and meddling in Turkey's affairs, stretching back to its creation out of the ashes of the First World War. At the same time, there is much hand-wringing and embarrassment about Turkey's perceived inferiority in its economic, cultural and political development.

Football does not stand apart from these currents. Indeed, as one of the realms in which England and Turkey 'clash', it frequently becomes the arrow tip. On the footballing field, the sense of injured pride is more unambiguous: it took Turkey ninety-three years to score against England. The teams had played each other only ten times, but in those games Turkey couldn't manage a single goal. It wasn't until 22 May 2016, when Hakan Çağlaoğlu slotted into an empty net in a warm-up game for Euro 2016, that Turkey finally broke the drought. 'We waited 32 years for this photograph' read the headline of sports newspaper *Fanatik*. '10 times we played them, 8 times we lost, 2 times we drew but we had never scored a goal against the English. That is, until yesterday' (Turkey lost the game 2–1).

Talk of Shakespeare and the Orient may seem far removed from holding up a banner in front of Paul Ince and Roy Keane. But packed into that moment was a web of colonial histories and inferiority complexes, of jingoistic pride, racist stereotypes and national team games ending in humiliation. And one final element can be added into the mix. The visit of Manchester United was not long after the return of English fans to European football competition after the ban following the 1985 Heysel disaster, when crowd trouble blamed on Liverpool supporters led to a crush in which thirty-nine people died. In 1993, the English still had a reputation as being murderous hooligans. 'You are barbarians,' read one of the Istanbul airport banners. 'We don't forget Heysel.'

I mention this background not to condone the treatment of the Manchester United players or fans, much of which was, frankly, indefensible. But it is important to be able to assess the events surrounding that match with an eye stripped of hysteria and stereotype. Otherwise it is impossible to understand why Turkish fans might have felt the need to generate a 'hellish' welcome or how, in its own way, English writing and imagery fed into that antagonism.

*

I began my research into the Leeds murders interested in facts. I watched endless videos; I tracked down phone numbers; I procured court documents; I met people in the UK and Turkey who were involved in some way or another. But the more 'facts' I found, the murkier the picture that emerged. When I thought I had confirmed one point or another, something else would come along and undermine that position. So, at the risk of spoiling the ending, I should admit that I find it impossible to say for certain what really happened in Taksim square on that night in 2000.

What is certain is that Leeds fans were drinking in a number of the bars and restaurants that lined the square. The two men who were murdered, Kevin Speight and Christopher Loftus, were part of a larger group of twenty-five or so, watching the Chelsea–Barcelona Champions League match in a bar. When the game was drawing to a close, violence erupted outside between Leeds and Galatasaray supporters in the square. Loftus and Speight's group walked into a confrontation that had already begun. They were set upon by Galatasaray fans holding knives, pieces of scaffolding and broken chairs. In the melee, dozens of Leeds fans were cut and stabbed, two fatally.

Beyond that, facts are lost amid the swirl of claim and counter-claim. Turkish eyewitnesses claimed the Leeds supporters were swearing, harassing passers-by and making obscene gestures, including disrespecting the Turkish flag (some versions say the fans rubbed the flag on their genitals, others say they stamped on it, urinated on it, wore it as a wrap-around dress or pretended to wipe their bottoms with it). From the Leeds side everyone is consistent in their recollections: they were simply having a drink.

In the aftermath, the British journalist Gareth Jenkins managed to arrange an interview with a Galatasaray fan leader who gave his name as 'Murat'. He explained that the fans who carried out the attack came from a group of 250 to 300 people who referred to themselves as *Maç için Sabahlayan* – the Group that Stays Up All Night for Matches.

The group was divided by neighbourhood, each with its own leader, called an *arap* (arab). Kids in their early teens would join up. Initially they would be given a stick and invited along to fights. If they proved themselves, they would then be given a knife.

During the fights there was an unwritten code that assailants wouldn't go for the torso or the head. The key was a knife into the buttock, what Murat called a 'Bursa' – named, for some unknown reason, after the city in western Turkey. If 'honour' was at stake, however, then it was permissible to kill. Demeanours that fell into this category included: insults to a blood relative, informing on someone to the police, and an insult to the country or flag.

This all seemed to explain what happened, through recourse to images of honour and knife culture. Jenkins, the outsider, was not concocting an Oriental trope: Murat himself cast the event in such terms. 'I didn't give the order to kill, but once the Leeds United fans started insulting our women and the flag, the *Araps* knew what to do,' he explained. 'This is Turkey. It was a question of honour. Maybe it is not the same in other countries. But that is how it is here.'

But this version of 1990s fandom is contradicted by Vesyel Giley, who was head of the Galatasaray supporters' club UltrAslan between 2011 and 2014 and a committed fan for the two preceding decades. When I mentioned a group called *Maç için Sabahlayan*, he furrowed his brow in puzzlement. He hadn't heard of them. 'There was a hierarchical system, *abi* and *kardeşler* [older brother and younger brother] which involved showing each other love and respect. But this didn't have a name, it was simply "the terrace".'

I tried to check other details of the account given to Jenkins. Were the *abi*s, the older brothers, called 'araps'?

'No,' Vesyel said, matter-of-factly. 'There was Hussein, his nickname was Prophet Hussein. Who else? Er, there was sleepy . . .' He went on to list a few other nicknames of the *abis*, none of whom was called *arap*.

But people had to prove themselves with sticks or knives?

'No. There wasn't anything like that. It's about the way the person behaves. It's about respect. You don't need to fight to show yourself.'

I was starting to feel silly asking my questions, but I persisted: 'Is it true that being stabbed in the –' I struggled for the right Turkish word – 'buttocks, is called a Bursa?'

Giley misunderstood me at first. Stammering, I rephrased the question. 'A-a guy explained to me, if you stick the knife here –' I gestured – 'it's called a Bursa, no?' His face was a picture of complete incomprehension, like I was speaking Mandarin. After a pause, he replied diplomatically, 'No, I haven't heard that.'

But was he telling the truth? I know from my own experiences that violence is frequently glorified and talked about in fan groups, and stabbings are not uncommon. Still, I had never encountered this formalised code of conduct or witnessed these types of stabbings in the buttocks. Perhaps football fandom in Turkey was very different before my time. Perhaps there could be an airbrushing of fan history. I didn't know what to make of it.

*

It is not just Turkey's football that has a darker side. The scholar Kerem Öktem chose to call his book on the modern history of Turkey *Angry Nation*. Today's Turkey is frequently an angry and violent place. In 2016, 685 people were killed and more than 2,000 wounded in terrorist attacks, on top of the 248 killed in that year's unsuccessful coup attempt. Hate crimes against sexual and ethnic minorities are reported to be on the rise. Domestic violence is far too commonplace. Gun ownership is climbing steadily. Between 2015 and 2017, the Turkish army was drawn into active conflict in the Kurdish-dominated south-east, in Syria and northern Iraq.

Ordinary interactions in Turkey seem continually to drip with latent anger, from the driver who sits aggressively on the tail of my car, beeping his horn and flashing his lights, to the people who jump the queue at the airport. 'In other countries someone pushes into you with their shoulder on the street, says "pardon" or "sorry" and goes away,' a football fan once told me. 'Here you'll turn around saying, "What's it to you if I push you with my shoulder?" And then it doesn't matter whether I insult you or you me, in the end it can go as far as knifing.'

For Öktem, the roots of much anger and violence come from a sinister quirk of Turkish governance: the presence of the *derin devlet* or 'deep state'. The deep state is an amorphous system of shadow government with state policy outsourced to murky alliances of military officers, drug traffickers, paramilitaries and terrorists. Over the years they have carried out killings, engineered riots, organised massacres and supported the removal of democratically elected governments.

The presence of this violent, unaccountable entity poisons the common well in Turkey. It renders elected governments ineffectual (they are only 'half' the workings of power), destroys bonds of trust between civilians and injects a permanent sense of instability into life. The deep state extends into all realms of life – including football – and thousands have died as a result of its machinations.

But the problem for me understanding the Leeds murders was the knowledge that outsiders rarely witness these undercurrents. There is no reason for the casual visitor to encounter the shady world of Turkish politics and history. The guest (*misafir* in Turkish) is afforded the highest social status, as is the case across most predominantly Muslim societies. Extending proper hospitality is a task to be treated with the utmost gravity: a guest's plate should never be left empty and no visitor should be allowed to make even the shortest journey unaccompanied. The word '*misafir*' has magical properties. Utter it, and the bartender will refuse to accept money from your guest and people will move out of the way so that they can move to the front of a queue.

This culture extends to foreigner footballers playing in Turkey. Les Ferdinand recounts how, in his year on loan to Beşiktaş in the late 1980s, he was never allowed to pay for a meal. Another foreign player told me sheepishly how he was once stopped by police when driving home after one too many drinks. The policemen made him step out of the car. He was terrified that he was about to be arrested. Instead, the policeman took his arm and led him to the passenger door, put him into the seat, took the keys from his hand and drove him home. He didn't need to tell them his address – everyone knew where he lived. One British sports journalist told me that he and his colleagues have a joke about coming to Turkey: it's less 'Welcome to Hell' and more 'Killing with Kindness'.

Travelling fans are also often given a warm welcome. In 2013, the Galatasaray fan club UltrAslan hosted 350 fans from Schalke who were in Istanbul to watch their side play the team in the Champions League. They took them to Galatasaray Island, the strange football enclave in the Bosphorus, where they paid for a large dinner and drinks. But the Leeds fans who visited thirteen years earlier were also guests. Why didn't this happen to them?

Well, in part, it did. Gary Edwards, a fanatical Leeds supporter with six books to his name, tells of very different experiences elsewhere in Istanbul that night. 'A big group of our lads who travelled independently were in Fenerbahçe all night,' he told me. The fans of Galatasaray's biggest rival wanted to show the visiting supporters a good time.

Something happened in Taksim square that April evening to short-circuit the *misafir* culture. It seems that stereotypes preceded the arrival of the Leeds fans, with disastrous consequences.

*

Across much of the world, English football is still associated with hooliganism. Millions of people actively *want* the link to exist: they like the history of violence in the 1970s and '80s and the films that glamorise the hooligan lifestyle. They luxuriate in the language – of 'firm', 'casuals' and 'boys' – applying the terms to their own fan clubs and kitting themselves out in the fashions – Fred Perry, Lacoste. For millions of young men (and it is almost exclusively men), hooliganism is as English as afternoon tea and Buckingham Palace.

Turkey is no different. On the day of the Hillsborough disaster, 15 April 1989, Les Ferdinand was in a hotel with his Beşiktaş team-mates, preparing for the game against Sariyer the next day. It transpired later that the crush that killed ninety-six people was due to failures in policing, but in the immediate aftermath people saw it as another instance of English football hooligans causing a disaster. Ferdinand remembered an employee of the hotel with whom he got on well. 'You English,' he said, turning to Ferdinand and narrowing his eyes, 'the hooligans.' Twenty-six years later, the image was still vivid in his mind. 'It just stands out to me because he looked at me with some real disdain, like *I'd* done it!' Ferdinand told me.

There seems to be something about 'English hooliganism' that overrides the *misafir* gene. Once labelled such, outsiders transform from individuals who should receive hospitality to a social group that is reviled.

By all accounts, Kevin Speight and Christopher Loftus were not hooligans. Speight was a loving husband with two small children, Loftus a quiet man, known more for his smile than anything else. Their group in Istanbul deliberately tried to avoid antagonising locals.

'We made sure that we always went inside bars so that there would be less chance of any provocation,' said Steve Wilkinson, who was with Speight and Loftus when they were killed. It is merely a hypothesis, but I wonder if the confrontation in Taksim square was exacerbated by the image of English fans in the minds of their Turkish counterparts. If English fans are ready for 'savage' Turkish supporters, and Turks think that all English fans are violent hooligans, then even a small comment or a scuffle contained the potential to escalate quickly.

That was certainly how most of the Turkish media portrayed the deaths. The headline in the newspaper *Hürriyet* read: 'Once more English hooligans, once more, blood.' The front page of *Star* newspaper was divided into two – on the top half, a Leeds fan on the ground being attacked. 'Like this on the street' it read. The bottom half showed Harry Kewell bent over in frustration. 'And like this on the pitch'.* In big letters along the top it read: *Two size!* 'Two to you!' The noise in Turkish for spitting is 'too', so the headline was a double entendre: we scored two goals past you and we spit on you. Should the play on words not be apparent, the first paragraph of the story made it clear: 'Both on the streets and on the pitch we smashed the hooligans' faces in. We Turks greet our European rivals with flowers and applause. But we send you home SPITTING in your faces'.

The journalist Bağış Erten was outraged by that front page. 'It's a hate crime,' he told me angrily. 'When two people died, they committed a hate crime . . . The problem about that game in Turkish society is that they defend those guys.' The *Star* article makes a key distinction: 'normal' fans from Europe get flowers and applause, (English) hooligans get a beating.

The British consul general in Istanbul at the time, Peter Hunt, had experienced a civil war in Nigeria and an earthquake in Nicaragua that had destroyed his house. Even he was stunned by the horror, and the way that the murders were cast by many in the Turkish press.

* Kewell would go on to play for Galatasaray eight years later. 'My idea was about bringing the clubs together,' he said when faced with the inevitable backlash from Leeds fans. 'What was I supposed to do? I still wanted to play football and that was the only club that really showed interest. As much as I know it hurts them, I hope one day they will [forgive it]. They probably never will. That's football, everybody has their opinions.'

'I was not unaccustomed to the violence of nature or the violence of man. But there was just something shockingly brutal [about the stabbings],' he told me. 'I didn't know the two people murdered but all I heard about them was that they were gentle giants. That they weren't people interested in getting involved in violence. It was just extraordinary the thought that [people believed] they were getting what they deserved. They clearly weren't getting what they deserved.'

The deaths inflamed stereotypes and xenophobia on both sides. 'When you looked at the caged animals foaming at the mouth behind the fencing, you wondered how it was possible to provoke them any more,' wrote Peter Ridsdale after the murders. In the aftermath of the killings, armed police were called to two kebab shops in Leeds city centre after violent threats to staff. Another Turkish shop owner – a self-confessed Leeds United fan who had lived in the city for decades – was attacked and spat at in the street. 'We are living in a situation where groups of friends talk in English so that they cannot be recognised,' said Turkan Turgay, a local shopworker. 'We are genuinely sorry about what happened but it was nothing to do with us.' English and Turkish responses became locked in a race to the bottom, the voices of reason being drowned out.

*

The twenty-four hours following the deaths were a blur of meetings and press conferences. Ridsdale wanted the match postponed, the Galatasaray directors disagreed. The UEFA delegate contacted headquarters and returned with a message: if Leeds didn't complete the fixture, they would forfeit the semi-final.

As the Leeds coach pulled into the ground on the evening of 6 April, the Galatasaray fans banged on its sides, some making throat-slitting gestures. There was no minute's silence. At kick-off the Leeds fans turned their backs on the game, in protest at their treatment. 'I was at that game,' a professor in International Relations at a university where I worked once told me. 'And the [Galatasaray] team just came out as if nothing had happened. I mean, wouldn't you at least have a banner? Something like "Guys, football is above this" or "brotherhood" . . . *Something.* I was really looking for that black armband but nobody said anything.'

Others were frustrated that the football was being overshadowed.

This was the best Galatasaray side of a generation, packed full of exciting talent including Hakan Şükür, one of Turkey's most prolific forwards, the Romanian superstar Gheorghe Hagi, and World Cup-winning goalkeeper Cláudio Taffarel. They had won the league the previous three seasons. They were the first Turkish side ever to reach the semi-final of the competition. But all foreigners wanted to talk about was Turkish brutality and fighting. Leeds United went on to lose 2–0, but the football barely mattered. Fourteen days later, as the rain lashed down at Elland Road, the return fixture ended in a 2–2 draw and Leeds United went out of the UEFA Cup.

*

On the night of the killings the police arrested tens of suspects. In the weeks that followed, five would be charged for murder. In 2002, one Galatasaray fan, Ali Umit Demir, was jailed for seven and a half years for each murder – a total of fifteen years. Four others got just under four months, two were fined and thirteen were acquitted for lack of evidence. But Demir did not even serve that. In 2003, the appeals court quashed Demir's conviction. He was released in 2005 pending a retrial.

To understand what happened, I went to meet Köksal Bayraktar, a high-profile lawyer who represented the family of Kevin Speight. The Bayraktar law firm offices were located near Taksim – less than 500 metres from the stabbings. As he talked, he often gestured in the direction of the square. Throughout the conversation, Köksal picked up documents from the pile on the table in front of him. Those from the first indictment in 2000 were printed on very thin paper, as if they had come out of a machine that issues clothes shop receipts. At one point I was handed one to have a look at. My eye was drawn to the first line, where Christopher's last name was spelt as 'Loffus'. Elsewhere I was shown a section from the original indictment where the Leeds fans were referred to matter-of-factly as 'hooligans'. It did not reassure me.

In the Turkish penal code, unlawful killing carries a sentence of twenty-four years. The invocation of 'provocation', however, instantly halves that judgement. 'In Turkey, rulings on incitement are applied to almost every crime,' said Bayraktar. This is what happened with the Leeds case. In the statements of the defendants and those called as witnesses, incitement was mentioned repeatedly: harsh swear words, aggressive actions and, most heinous of all, disrespect to the flag.

Turkey is a deeply patriotic country, and its blood-red national flag holds a sacred status – you encounter it everywhere you go. It is draped from balconies, etched into the side of hills and is printed on the inside covers of children's textbooks. The side that wins the Turkish Süper Lig gets to print it on the centre of their shirt the following season. In 2008 in Kırşehir – a city in central Anatolia – a group of high-school students painted one out of their own blood.

At international summits, organisers arrange world leaders for the big 'family photo' shot by putting a flag on the floor where each leader is supposed to stand. Most leaders trample on theirs. President Erdoğan always carefully picks his up, folds it and puts it in his pocket. 'When you go to England you can buy panties with your flag on it,' Banu Yelkovan, a sports journalist told me. 'In Turkey it's unthinkable. It's *unthinkable*.' If on that fateful night in April 2000 there was an incident involving the flag, English fans could not have realised how provocative they were being.

Nevertheless, Bayraktar did not believe that the Turkish flag was insulted in the way that was claimed by the defence. He directed my attention to the police reports, which made no mention of a Turkish flag at the crime scene; nor were there any reports of the broken windows that supposedly prompted the backlash from the Galatasaray fans. He said that he managed to bring the judge in the trial round to his point of view. But the suggestion of disrespect for the flag served as a narrative for the defence that the Leeds fans went beyond the limits of normal football supporters.

In June 2007, Demir was convicted for a second time. The conviction involved more fans this time – five in total – but the sentencing was not significantly different: they were all given between five and ten years. 'It wasn't clear who killed the fans, so they reduced the sentencing a little,' explained Ömer Bayraktar, Köksal's son, who sat in on our meeting. 'They reduced it *a lot*,' said his father, clearly unhappy with the decision. The court case raised many questions. No Leeds fans were called to testify. The court rejected a request by the victims' families to hear evidence revealed at the 2004 inquest held in West Yorkshire. Two months later, all defendants were released pending another appeal.

A decade after the murders, the court case was still continuing. Frustrated by the slow pace of proceedings, Andy and Pam Loftus,

Christopher's brother and sister, went to their local MP in Leeds, Fabian Hamilton, to appeal for help. 'They were pretty angry,' the Labour MP told me over a cup of coffee. 'They were incensed. Their view was that, because of the inaction, the Turkish state was saying it's fine to murder British football fans.'

Hamilton pledged to raise the matter with Ünal Çeviköz, the Turkish ambassador to London. Çeviköz agreed to send a cable to Ankara. 'I said, "Look, this is kind of a disgrace for our court system and for our judicial system"', he told me. 'It has been more than ten years and there are two families who have been left in agony here.' He warned that the case was badly damaging Turkey's image in Britain and that action was needed as soon as possible.

The cajoling did the trick. Within weeks, the court process reached a conclusion, with a final judgement and sentencing. Four men were jailed. Though it was undoubtedly a relief for the families of Christopher Loftus and Kevin Speight, it seems more alarming than reassuring that Turkish justice was so susceptible to – or so dependent on – political pressure. Çeviköz relayed the news to Hamilton, telling him that he hoped it would draw a line under the matter and stop it from becoming a 'never-ending issue that is going to harm the relations between the two countries'.

But due to the time they had already served, none of those convicted spent much longer behind bars. By 2017, they were all out of prison.

That year, at a Galatasaray basketball match, I found myself unwittingly face-to-face with one of the four men convicted of the murders. Making light chat, I asked him to name his best ever moment as a Galatasaray fan. He said it was the UEFA Cup win. 'But I didn't see it,' he added.

'Why?' I asked.

'I was in prison.'

'Why?'

'The Leeds United thing.'

'Did you do it?' I found myself blurting out the question before I could help it. Everyone around me burst out laughing.

'No!' said the fan, raising his eyebrows.

'Be careful, there's police over there!' someone else in the group joked.

While I turned around to look, the fan left.

'He's run away!' another fan joked.

It was a shock to realise that I had just met a man convicted for the death of two football fans – and whose actions would leave a huge imprint on Turkish–English footballing relations. His friends could joke about it; I was left with my heart racing.

*

Four months after the Galatasaray game, Peter Ridsdale flew to Geneva to attend the draw for the next season's Champions League. 'The worst thing in the world happened,' he recalled. Leeds United were put in the same group as Beşiktaş. They would be going back to Istanbul.

After the draw, UEFA officials pulled the Beşiktaş management aside and told them they didn't want the game to be played in the city. İbrahim Altınsay, at the time a member of the Beşiktaş management board, pointed out the hypocrisy: 'They played a game there [immediately after the death of the Leeds fans] and then asked us a year later not to play the game in Istanbul!' Beşiktaş ignored the request. Instead, the club president, Serdar Bilgili, contacted Ridsdale. 'I want to prove that we can be perfect hosts,' he told him. 'You will have the best experience of your life.'

This time, the classic Turkish *misafir* treatment was rolled out. 'Having been to the Galatasaray match and literally being scared stiff to go back, Beşiktaş was the most amazing experience,' Ridsdale recalled. 'This whole ethos was to prove that they could out-manage a match versus their famous rivals of Galatasaray. I don't know what they do normally – maybe they're that beautiful and perfect a host at the best of times.'

Turkish security officials took no chances. The Leeds supporters arrived on the day of the game and were transferred immediately to an enforced (alcohol-free) cruise along the Bosphorus. A helicopter kept watch overhead. An hour before kick-off, the boat docked next to the waterside Beşiktaş stadium and the fans were escorted inside. As soon as the game was over, they were transported back to the airport. Despite not being allowed to set foot in the city, the Leeds fans enjoyed it: 'We were met with open arms by Beşiktaş fans,' said Gary Edwards, who watched his side scrap for a 0–0 draw. 'We had a great time.'

Since that game, English sides have been back to Turkey many times without major incident, including Liverpool's 'miracle' European Cup win in 2005, when the side came back from 3–0 down at half time to beat AC Milan on penalties. On that trip, the fans' main issue was with the horrendous traffic on the way to Istanbul's Atatürk Olympic stadium. In 2011, Galatasaray moved from the Ali Sami Yen to a new 50,000 ground on the edge of the city. There are now metro lines, police zones and updated legislation to prevent fan clashes, as Turkish football has found itself following the trajectory of commodification, increased ticket prices (and comfort) that seems to have a corollary of dampening violent confrontation. English fans have also been more measured and cautious in their journeys. 'I don't want to generalise about all Galatasaray or Turkish football fans,' said Dave Johnstone, spokesman for the Chelsea fanzine *cfcuk* before Chelsea played Galatasaray in Istanbul in 2014. 'There will always be the minority of people looking for trouble. My advice to those fans coming out today would be to be on your toes, be wary. Don't go looking for trouble. Be friendly.'

Nevertheless, the deaths cast a long shadow, especially in West Yorkshire. In 2012, Galatasaray were drawn in the same Champions League group as Manchester United. Still serving as Turkish ambassador to the UK, Çeviköz saw it as an opportunity. He called Fabian Hamilton and asked if he would mind co-ordinating a visit of the Galatasaray team to Leeds, to meet the families of the deceased and to pay a visit to their graves.

'I thought that was a *really* good offer,' recalled Hamilton. But when he spoke to Pam, the sister of Chris Loftus, she rejected the proposal. 'I don't want to meet him,' she told the MP. 'That's it. It's over'. It had taken ten years to get a verdict. The Loftus family did not want anything else to do with the affair, with Galatasaray or with Turkey.

'I thought that it was a very human wish,' said Çeviköz, rueing the missed opportunity. 'I can never find a remedy to the trauma that those two families have lived, but at least I could be a part of their agony and to show that, as the highest representative of the republic of Turkey in the United Kingdom, the ambassador of Turkey wants to pay his respect to those families and to visit the graves of the victims. I was sorry that it was not accepted.'

The Loftus family are not alone in wanting nothing more to do with Turkey. 'Somebody had [once] bought a beach towel from the Leeds United supporters' shop,' Gary Edwards told me. 'And they noticed it had been made in Turkey. He kicked up a fuss and there was a big campaign over that. They had to remove them.'

In 2001, Leicester City midfielder Muzzy Izzet was hoping for a transfer to Leeds. Inquiries had been made to his agent, and Leeds were putting together a large bid. And then it went quiet. 'I didn't find out until years later that the reason they went cold wasn't about me, how I played, where they thought I might fit in,' wrote Izzet in his autobiography. '[It was] because I was Turkish and my name was Muzzy Izzet. They didn't think the fans would like that.' Based on the commotion caused by the beach towel, he might have been correct.

Perhaps the most harmful consequence of the murders – with their conflicting narratives and decades of anger – is that it has served to obscure the many ways in which England and Turkey are similar. If we trace a different route through history, right the way back to the sixteenth century, it's possible to discern another, more cordial narrative. Queen Elizabeth built a strong alliance with the Ottomans to contain the growing power of 'Catholic' Europe. These are two nations that bookend Europe, sitting on its eastern and north-western extremities. Two nations that refer to 'Europe' as an outside force, as something they're apart from, while wanting to be included when it comes to trade, travel and sport. Two ex-colonial powers, proud of their distinct history, and obsessed with their football.

Some might find the endeavour of seeking commonalities rage-inducing: too much like condoning behaviour that plumbs the depths of human nature. This is not my intention. Two innocent men were murdered simply for being football fans. The human tragedy of that should never be forgotten. But neither should the deaths be used to pull down attempts at understanding or building bridges.

Indeed, what came through most strongly from all the conversations and research about April 2000 was that the majority of people – English and Turkish – do not want the incident to define how each sees the other. I include myself in that number. What follows, then, is an attempt to look beyond this event, to step out from its shadow in search of the real Turkish football.

N
Galatasaray
New Stadium
to Black Sea
to Atatürk
Olympic Stadium
Galatasaray
Old Stadium
MECIDIYEKÖY
BEŞIKTAŞ
Beşiktaş
Stadium
KAŞIMPAŞA
Taksim
Square
Bosphorus
Golden Horn
Galatasaray
High School
Istanbul
ÜSKÜDAR
SULTANAHMET
Hippodrome
KADIKÖY
Fenerbahçe
Stadium
SEA OF MARMARA
to Princes' Islands

2

Istanbul

In the middle of Sultanahmet, the heart of historic Istanbul, is a large flat area. In summer, young boys in swimming trunks play in the fountains on its edge. Security personnel sit under trees, dragging on cigarettes, looking bored. Clutches of tourists wander across its expanse in waves. You wouldn't know to look at it, but this is the site of Istanbul's first stadium.

Back fifteen centuries, when the city went by its first name of Byzantium, professional sportsmen would gather here in the Hippodrome to take part in chariot racing and gladiatorial combat, watched from the stands by thousands of spectators and the emperor of the eastern Roman empire. The sportsmen were divided into factions, teams distinguished by colour. The crowd, or at least parts of it, was also divided. Partisan supporters' clubs grew up around the factions. Across the former Byzantine empire archaeologists find graffiti, scratched into walls and tablets, declaring allegiances. 'Blues under Justinian'. 'Acclamation to the Greens'.

Hundreds of years later, people in the city still scrawl the names of sports teams on walls. They write 'Galatasaray fucks Fenerbahçe' or 'Beşiktaş is the Greatest'. Now a city of over fifteen million, there are many more walls on which to write.

Turkey is not like Britain, with Manchester and Liverpool as rival power centres to London teams, or like Spain, with its Barcelona–Real Madrid dualism. In Turkish football, three teams dominate:

Fenerbahçe, Galatasaray and Beşiktaş. Each can lay claim to tens of millions of fans. Their histories and rivalries dominate the country; all are older than the nation of Turkey itself. And all of them are from Istanbul.

*

After arriving in Turkey in October 2015, we chose to live in Üsküdar. It was an unfashionable but central neighbourhood on the Asian side of the Bosphorus, the large waterway that runs through the heart of the city. What it lacked in bars it made up for in views of the sea.

From our rooftop, you had to crane your neck to see the historical peninsula with its postcard skyline of Byzantine basilicas and Ottoman mosques. The rest of the view could be enjoyed in a more leisurely fashion: Galata, settled by Italian merchants and financiers in the Middle Ages, its skyline still dominated by a fourteenth-century tower. To its north, a hodge-podge of apartment blocks sandwiched around consulates, crawling up the hill towards Istiklal Street, the centre of the 'European' city.

As the eyes tracked the shoreline, history sped up. First the nineteenth-century marbled palaces of Dolmabahçe and Çırağan, built when the Ottomans craved Western-style opulence. Next, the 1973 suspension bridge, joining the European continent to Asia for the first time. Stood behind it all loomed the skyscrapers of the financial district, their glassy exteriors dazzling in the morning sun.

But the site I used to point out to visitors was one that meant more to me than all of the others. Directly across the water, framed by palace and mosque, stood a round structure like a cake: the Beşiktaş stadium.

The first stadium on the site was built in 1947, a post-war concrete bowl, extended, altered and patched to keep up with every decade. I loved its idiosyncrasies. People were forever sneaking in, pushing two people through the terraces on one ticket, a practice so common in Turkey that it has its own name: *çift turnike* – double turnstile. The players' tunnel was in a terrible location, too close to the die-hards and far too short, meaning the police had to form a long and elaborate shield cordon whenever Fenerbahçe and Galatasaray were visiting. From the top tier of the stand behind the far goal, you had what is surely the best distraction from a poor game: the palace of Dolmabahçe, home to the late sultans, and beyond that the shimmering sea.

My best and worst moment as a football fan have taken place at Beşiktaş's ground. Both within the same game. In 2013, before a match against Fenerbahçe, the last ever derby match at the stadium, there was terrible overcrowding outside – and terrible policing. When the crowd wouldn't budge, helmets and shields were shoved in faces, followed by tear gas. First the coughing and stinging, then the panic of not being able to breathe, like a hand pressing on the lungs. I tried not to fall over in the retreating stampede, all the while dry-retching as the gas took hold. By the time I had filed into the stadium and found my friends, I couldn't give a damn about the football match.

But then came the atmosphere. The stadium was thousands over capacity – all aisles and vestibules crammed. Beşiktaş were trailing, then ahead, then pinned back to 2–2. The game entered injury time. Fenerbahçe were mounting an attack when Beşiktaş won back the ball and shifted it quickly forward. A Fenerbahçe clearance fell to Manuel Fernandes who nudged it to Mamadou Niang. Fenerbahçe had committed too many men forward. Olcay Şahan made a run. Niang found him with the perfect ball. Olcay was through, one-on-one with the keep— *GOAL!!!!!!!!!!!!!!!!!!!!*

The next thing I knew, I was lying on the seats. When I found my bearings I poked the man lying on top of me, a complete stranger who was screaming in ecstasy. I got to my feet and saw one of my friends sat down, weeping into his hands with joy. Next to him another friend was topless, screaming. A primordial scream. A scream from the centre of his belly. His eyes didn't look like his eyes. A chant emerged out of the chaos: *Lalalalalaaaa koyduk mu*? Did we just fuck you?

The Beşiktaş football team takes its name from a district that lies fifteen minutes' walk from the stadium. Beşiktaş is a central, middle-class neighbourhood – one of the most liberal in Istanbul (and Turkey). On matchdays, the centre of town is crammed with thousands meeting friends in front of its many eagle statues (the eagle is the team's mascot). Restaurant tables spill out onto the street, diners nibbling at *meze* and putting away glass after glass of rakı. At the appointed hour, the crowds decamp for the stadium, drifting down the coastal road, past the Ottoman palaces and the mobile meatball vans, laughing and singing as they tread all over the geraniums planted by the side of the road.

*

In 1903, just up the hill from here, in the mansion of a high-ranking Ottoman minister, a group of twenty-two youngsters founded Bereket Gymnastics Club. At that time, football had limited reach. Sultan Abdülhamid II, a paranoid man ruling by fiat, was mistrustful of this Western import. Foreigners playing the game were tolerated, as were non-Muslim minorities, but gatherings of Turks were interpreted as plots to overthrow the sultan and were quickly broken up. The youngsters began training with another local sports club founded by a fencing coach and his wrestler-weightlifter friend. As the participants swelled to around 150 people, the two groups merged under the name Beşiktaş Ottoman Gymnastics Club.

In 1908, the sultan was forced to make a series of concessions after coming under pressure from a group of army officers known as the Young Turks. In 1909, he was deposed. The Young Turks saw football as a way to inculcate the Turkish youth with nationalist values. During this period, restrictions on the game for Muslims were relaxed. Among those to begin playing the sport in the Beşiktaş neighbourhood was a young local man called Ahmed Şeraffettin. He and some friends set up a club devoted solely to football. As its popularity grew, it began to overshadow the activities of the older gymnastics club. Fearful of losing their entire support to this new sport, the gymnasts reluctantly agreed to allow Şeref and his friends into their group.

To this day, the club's crest bears the traces of this history in the form of the initials BJK. The letter J – a letter that today is only used in words of foreign origin – symbolises the 'jimnastik' of the club's early years. Beşiktaş claim 1903 as their foundation year, making them 'the oldest club in Turkey', despite the fact that the club offered no football until 1911. It is best not to point this out to the fan who paid a fortune to include the digits 1903 in his phone number or who inked the date into his arm.

intiba

beko
beko
beko
28

The stadium did not always belong to Beşiktaş. Or at least not exclusively. For most of its history it was a municipal stadium named Mithatpaşa, used at various times by Fenerbahçe, Galatasaray and Beşiktaş while other grounds were under construction or fell out of favour.

During the 1970s and '80s there were no season tickets or allocated seating. The authorities left it to the fans to decide who stood where. Unsurprisingly, on derby days this generated a lot of fighting and jockeying. All fan groups wanted control of the covered terrace (*kapalı tribün*), the stand alongside the pitch that afforded the best view and acoustics for leading the crowd. The most fanatical fans would camp outside the stadium the night before. 'In the morning Galatasaray fans would come and it's fight, fight, fight. Punch, punch, punch,' Kerem, a Fenerbahçe fan once told me. 'Whoever wins the fight goes through that gate.'

These stadium battles coincided with – perhaps even fuelled – the height of the enmity between the fan groups. Beşiktaş, Galatasaray and Fenerbahçe fans were locked in an internecine feud characterised by street battles, kidnappings and stabbings. 'We lived hooliganism, seven days a week' said Ayhan Güner, one of the leaders of the Beşiktaş fan group, Çarşı. 'Nobody went home at night, out of fear that their families would be hurt. Everyone would sleep in the same place. At three or four in the morning, phones would start ringing. There would be news of a fight. Five hundred people would head straight there, some with guns.' A 'truce' in the early 1990s mitigated – but did not eliminate – attacks and violence.

That world had passed long before I arrived in Turkey. By 1998, the stadium was solely for Beşiktaş's use, the name changed to İnönü, named after Turkey's first prime minister.

The stadium experience at İnönü wasn't the most relaxed. In the *kapalı tribün* the terracing was so shallow you frequently couldn't see a thing. Exiting the stand behind the goal was an exercise in how quickly a crowd of thousands can funnel through the eye of a needle. The answer was slowly, and with a dangerous amount of crushing. The place was dirty. There was no space for extra executive boxes, pre-match dining or any of the other recent add-ons that football clubs now use to generate revenue. For years, the club mooted building a new stadium on the site. In 2013, it actually started happening.

Throughout the construction, at any time of the day or night, there would be a small gaggle of people peering into the site from the hill that overlooks it. That spot also had a role in Beşiktaş fandom. Its nickname was *beleştepe* – freebie hill – because from there you could look down onto part of the pitch and watch the game without paying. One hundred or so fans would congregate there without fail on matchdays, with the supporters in the stadium including them in the call and response chants: 'Hands in the air *beleştepe*!'

The site is no longer called *beleştepe*, for you can no longer see the pitch. The new stadium bowl comes up too high. On this site on 10 December 2016, a member of the Kurdistan Freedom Falcons, an offshoot of the Kurdish militant group the PKK, drove a car packed with explosives into a bus of police officers who had just finished their shift at a match between Beşiktaş and Bursaspor – forty-six were killed. It is now officially called 'Martyrs' Hill'.

On a whim when passing one cold winter's day, I asked the bus driver to drop me off at the hill and I joined the gaggle. A man with a grey beard, Harry Potter glasses and a beanie hat was talking excitedly about the stadium to two men.

'And it's 42,000,' he said. 'But that means that 45,000 can fit in, really. And the slope inside is really steep! Soooo steep!'

The man continued to talk – about Barcelona visiting and all the glorious victories Beşiktaş would see in their new home. When he discovered I was a foreigner, he switched into 'Beşiktaş explaining' mode. I didn't stop him, as I always like to hear how people present their team to outsiders.

'We are the most fanatical . . . our fans are from the workers, the working classes. They have a leftist sympathy.'

It doesn't take long around Beşiktaş fans before you're told very sincerely: Galatasaray are the team of the aristocracy, Fenerbahçe of the merchant class and Beşiktaş are the team of the people. It's a cute distinction, but also completely untrue. I've met poverty-stricken Galatasaray fans, and Beşiktaş supporters who live in palaces. From time to time, a survey tries to clarify the percentage of the population that supports Galatasaray, Fenerbahçe and Beşiktaş. The results always hover around the 80 per cent mark nationwide. That's tens of millions for each club, among them Turks, Kurds, religious devotees and atheists, Sunni Muslims and members of religious minorities. There are simply too many fans from every demographic for the maxim to be true.

The old man continued: 'For five years, we won the championship back to back!'

One of the other guys felt he had to chip in at this point: 'Well, four years.'

'Four/five years,' the old guy continued, refusing to be knocked out of his stride.

It was actually three years. He was referring to Beşiktaş's most successful period in living memory, 1990 to 1992, when they won the Süper Lig title three years in a row under the stewardship of Englishman Gordon Milne. The team had arguably the best all-Turkish forward line of all time: Metin Tekin, Ali Gültiken and Feyyaz Uçar, who scored 126 goals between them in three years. The players are never referred to individually but described as a collective of their first three names: Metin-Ali-Feyyaz. This is so ubiquitous that for many years I thought it was one person. I know a fan in Hanover who has their faces tattooed on his inner-arm.

The conversation with the enthusiastic fan reminded me of just how unimportant the truth is when it comes to Turkish football. Clubs are receptacles for longing, hope, pride, despair – whatever people want to pour into them. In this enterprise, an almost-finished stadium is the greatest prop, full of expectancy, and yet to be tarnished by disappointment.

Suddenly the old man ran out of steam, the conversation having run its course. There was a heavy silence. We all knew that most of what he had outlined would never come to pass. That being a Beşiktaş fan – being any football fan – is never simply unmitigated glory. But no one wanted to shatter the dream. Before parting ways, I asked if I could take a photo. The men arranged themselves in front of the stadium, arms aloft, fingers outstretched – the pose of the Eagle's talons that all Beşiktaş fans like to make.

*

Going up the hill from the Beşiktaş stadium, the road climbs steeply, winding past the German consulate and a gaudy upmarket hotel before disgorging into Taksim square. If you hug the left-hand side, going past more hotels and, these days, shops selling overpriced baklava to visitors from the Gulf, you reach the start of Istanbul's most famous street: Istiklal Caddesi. Independence Avenue.

The road is the city's main pedestrian thoroughfare, its 1.5 kilometres lined with shops, cafés, restaurants, art galleries, cinemas and night clubs. The surrounding network of backstreets are home to hundreds more. If you know where to look, you can find unassuming doorways that lead through to lifts to rooftop bars, from where you can watch the sun set over the domes and minarets of the old city. But the neighbourhood on this side of the water was shaped by non-Muslims and foreigners: Greek and Armenian businessmen, French and Russian and British diplomats. There are arcades, churches and tramways that wouldn't look out of place in Paris. Perhaps that's why, until the creation of the Turkish republic in 1923, most people called it the Grande Rue.

Halfway down the street, just before it takes a bend, the buildings fall away to reveal an elaborate, curlicued portico. It is the gate to one of Turkey's most famous schools – and the original home of its most successful club.

The Galatasaray High School was founded in 1481. The legend goes that Ottoman Sultan Beyazit II was out for one of his many walks in the city (disguised, as he liked to be, as an ordinary citizen) when he came across a shabby hut in a large, beautiful garden. Meeting the hut's owner, Father Gül, the sultan wanted to reward him for the care he had shown by building a school in its grounds. It was called Galata Sarayı – the name of the area (Galata) added to the Turkish word for 'palace'.

In the mid-1800s the school was re-established on the French Lycée model, part of the great Tanzimat reformation that strived to close the gap with European powers by modernising state administration, the military and education. Today it is a state school entered by exam. It remains one of the most influential in Turkey, producing graduates who occupy the top crust of Turkish society.

In October 1905, a pupil of the school, Ali Sami Yen, established Galatasaray football team. He began by organising each class at the school into a side, and then eventually formed a single XI to take on the English, Greek and Armenian teams. In order to avoid censure from the palace, Galatasaray were referred to in press reports and conversation by the English expression 'another team'. Ali Sami declared the team's founding principles: 'to have a name, to have our own colours, to play football like the English and beat all the non-Turkish teams' – not yet realising the contradictory nature of playing like the English and winning.

In 1909, Galatasaray became the first Turkish team to win the Istanbul league. The connections between the school and high political office allowed the side to stay at the forefront of football through the following decades. When, in 1952, football in Turkey first became professional, Galatasaray were consistently in the race for championships. They had one of Turkey's most famous footballers, Metin Oktay. Nicknamed the *taçsız kral* – the king without a crown – he scored a goal a game for Galatasaray throughout the 1950s and 1960s.

After a fallow period, the side went on to dominate Turkish football again in the late 1990s, winning four championships back-to-back and then, in 2000, the UEFA Cup and Super Cup – which, as mentioned previously, makes them the only Turkish side to have won a European trophy. The club has been home to some of Turkey's most famous players and managers: Fatih Terim, Hakan Şükür, Ümit Davala, Bülent Korkmaz and Hasan Şaş. Foreign stars to have worn the team's red and gold colours include Didier Drogba, Gheorghe Hagi, Franck Ribéry and Wesley Sneijder.

It is the link to the high school that led rival fans to describe Galatasaray as 'the team of the aristocracy'. It's true that the school and football club are linked. Former pupils are given priority membership. Ebru Köksal, Galatasaray's first female director, told me that she found her education more of an impediment than her gender. 'If there was any discrimination against me, it was more because I was not a graduate of the school rather than because I was a woman,' she said. On the terrace, however, it has the same mix of backgrounds as at any of the Big Three.

The school gates are a favourite meeting point for Istanbullus – the term for people from the city – and have witnessed its many ups and downs. In 2009, while waiting for friends outside the gates, I would survey the masses swarming down Istiklal, before a friend would turn up, grab my arm and pull me into the crowd. We would join groups drinking rakı at tables in the backstreets before diving into tiny bars that stayed open until the sun came up. In 2013, we would follow the same pattern, only this time, while I waited, I would have the company of a battalion of police with riot shields and tear-gas canisters standing watch for signs of burgeoning protests.

By late 2015, the police were replaced by men in camouflage, tear-gas canisters swapped for automatic weapons. The street where they stood was far emptier than the bustling thoroughfare I was used to, with both tourists and locals scared away by a spate of bombings by ISIS and Kurdish militant groups. In March 2016, just 100 metres from the school, a suicide bomber blew himself up next to a group of tourists. Amid the turmoil and flux, behind the gates, the school stood on.

*

While Galatasaray school has always sat in this spot, its football team has led a more peripatetic life. Galatasaray have never really had a neighbourhood identity, as if from their inception they were gunning for nationwide support. By the 1930s Beşiktaş had an agreement to use Şeref Stadium in the garden of the Çirağan Palace, home in the 1870s to Sultan Abdulaziz. Fenerbahçe had obtained the rights to build a stadium on the Asian side of the city. Galatasaray needed to keep up. For their home they settled on Mecidiye köyü – *köy* is the Turkish for village – outside the city limits.

If 'hell' has to have a geographical location in Turkey, I can think of no better place than Mecidiyeköy. Not only was it the site of the Manchester United's infamous 'Welcome to Hell' moment in 1993, but traversing modern-day Mecidiyeköy is truly infernal. The area is a major retail and business hub, and home to one of Istanbul's largest transport intersections. At any time of day, the metro, buses, buildings and shopping malls are disgorging tens of thousands of people into a tangle of roads and concrete. Clustered on either side of the eight-lane highway are huge skyscrapers, their only unifying feature being how unsuitable they look for human habitation. The sound of horns and the fumes of cars constantly fill the air. There is no green space. Passing through the area will remind you that Istanbul is no longer the city of the Ottomans, or even the post-war metropolis. It's now a crowded, fuel-choked mass of more than fifteen million people, infrastructure and quality of life creaking under the load.

In the 1930s, however, the area was still dominated by agriculture. The first site that Galatasaray explored was a mulberry orchard. They eventually settled on a spot next to a liquor factory. Efforts to build and then use a stadium in the area were peppered with setbacks, including transportation problems, strong winds and the Second World War. The famous Ali Sami Yen stadium – named after the team's founder – finally opened in December 1964. One stand promptly collapsed during its opening game, injuring eighty-four.

By the 1990s, as Galatasaray entered the most successful period in their history, the club wanted to expand. But by then it was too late on the current site. The village of Mecidiye was now part of the city centre. In 1973 a raised flyover leading to the Bosphorus bridge was built just behind the northern stand. On my first trips to Istanbul I remember driving along the highway during matches, glimpsing the backs of thousands of bodies crowded onto the terraces.

The club decided on a piece of land further north: a hill by the second ring road. There they built the Turk Telekom Arena, a 50,000 all-seater stadium, which opened in January 2011.

My first Galatasaray match at the new stadium was very different to my İnönü experiences. A friend of a friend, Yörük, had a spare ticket. A match against Konyaspor on a cold Saturday in February was clearly not much of a draw. I stood by the metro stop in Levent until a car pulled up. A man with a soft demeanour, excellent English and a large belly kindly ushered me in.

Together we belted along the six-lane highway towards the huge saucer-shaped bowl looming to our right. Yörük flashed a magic pass, a security guard pointed us into the bowels of a multi-storey car park. We parked, climbed several flights of stairs and then, to my shock and surprise, we emerged straight in front of the stadium. The car park was under the pitch.

As we entered, Yörük went into host mode. 'We have a bakery and a tea place. But the other side is better, they have an open buffet.' He paused and rethought his assessment. 'But here is OK. "The nice side of economy class", you can say.' This being Turkey, where money is discussed with little embarrassment, I felt I could openly ask the cost of his season ticket. The answer was 5,000 lira – around £1,000. That same year, the pre-tax salary of a worker on the minimum wage was 19,740TL (approximately £5,000).

We found our place on the terrace alongside two of Yörük's friends. Yörük gestured to the stand opposite us, saying that they had hoped to move over there but it was hard to find six tickets together. 'It's empty now but it's actually sold out,' he said. I furrowed my brow.

What he meant was that the seats were taken over by season-ticket holders, most of whom had not come to the game. The stadium capacity is 50,000. There were possibly 15,000 in attendance.

The match was truly dire. Konyaspor parked the bus and Galatasaray lacked the creativity or conviction to break them down. At one point Galatasaray's Dutch captain, Wesley Sneijder, lost the ball and howled in anger. His shout reached our ears from 30 metres away.

At half-time, giant heaters hovering 50 metres above us in the roof of the stand began glowing into life. 'It's environmentally unfriendly,' Yörük conceded. 'But if you turn your face up you can feel it on your skin.' I did as he suggested and felt a slight increase in warmth. 'Heating the air,' he added, returning to a more negative stance. 'They mocked me,' he said, gesturing to his friends, 'because I actually wrote to the club to protest about this.'

The second half was little better than the first. The closest Galatasaray came to scoring was a header that smacked the underside of the bar and bounced out, causing everyone to howl in frustration. It had been that kind of night. As we entered injury time, Yörük gestured to the others that we should leave. We headed up and out, rubbing shoulders with others doing the same, grumbling about the chairman on the way. After a short walk back to the car, we were back on the highway and suddenly back at my metro stop.

I was shocked by the speed from which I had gone from pitch back to normal life. It was the opposite of my experiences of games with the Beşiktaş fans, who take part in a drawn-out, protracted build-up and aftermath that lasts all day.

But this is increasingly the nature of attending matches at the big clubs. Season-ticket prices at Fenerbahçe for the 2017–18 season started at 1,400TL. In the main stand at Beşiktaş a live string quartet plays before Europa League matches. Facilities and experiences are increasingly designed to cater to people who want proper food, a parking space and a comfy seat — all part of the 'middle-classification' of football.

*

If you head back down from Mecediyeköy to the water near Beşiktaş, you can swipe through the turnstile at the pier and hop on an old white and yellow ferry. After twenty minutes on the world's best form of public transport – watching oil tankers, fishing boats and pods of dolphins making their way from the Black Sea down towards the Mediterranean – the rubber tyres on the front of the boat bang into the side of the pier. The Asian Side.

The liveliest district of this side of the city is Kadıköy, older than Istanbul itself. The first human settlement in the area – the ancient maritime town of Chalcedon – was built on the curving bay, which today acts as a major transport hub. One of the ferries that clog its port, spewing out black smoke, is the one from Beşiktaş. In many ways, the two ends of the route mirror each other. Both are liberal hubs: fish shops, bars, coffee shops, grocers and delis all compete for space with each other, waiters and shopkeepers shouting their wares at the crowds squeezing through the narrow streets.

Carry on round the corner – past the million-dollar flats with views across the sea – and you come to a harbour filled with expensive yachts, their masts jangling in the wind. From here, the headland obscures the European side of the city and you feel miles away from its clamour and history. The view is instead of endless water. On the inland side of the harbour, near the road heading along the coast, stands the home of the third and final member of the 'Big Three': Fenerbahçe.

When football first came to Istanbul at the end of the nineteenth century, this area was fields. One in particular was called *Papazın çayırı*, the priest's meadow. It was where the European expats used to gather for some Sunday afternoon respite from Constantinople. Many would take a ferry or rowboat and cross the Bosphorus to have picnics and play football.

Students from the elite school Frer Mektebi (Saint Joseph), which sat up on a nearby hill, were among those who used to watch in fascination the game that the British and Greeks would play. In 1907, half a dozen young graduates of the school got together and decided to form a team. They chose the name Fenerbahçe, meaning 'lighthouse garden', because of the lighthouse that stood on the nearby coast. The yellow in the club's yellow-and-navy stripes is apparently a reference to the daisies that used to grow nearby in spring.*

The team became the second Turkish side to take part in the Istanbul league. At first, their presence was welcomed by the fledgling Galatasaray. 'To see Fenerbahçe in my land full of foreign and non-Moslem teams would be like meeting a friend in a foreign land,' said Ali Sami Yen. The first derby between Turkey's two most famous clubs took place on 17 January 1909 and finished 2–0 to Galatasaray. Competition would soon replace courtesy.

Modern Fenerbahçe are a juggernaut. They are self-appointed as the most-supported football team in Turkey: '25 million fans arm in arm!' the fans chant. In the 1990s the club had the slogan 'one day everyone will be a Fenerbahçe fan' (Beşiktaş fans would reply, 'everyone shouldn't be a Beşiktaş fan – let that distinction rest with us'). For the last eighteen years they have been under the control of Aziz Yıldırım, their irascible, partial, combative president. Under his watch the side have signed world-class stars – Roberto Carlos, Nicholas Anelka, Nani, Robin Van Persie, Dirk Kuyt and Ariel Ortega (most, admittedly, at the end of their careers). They have reached the quarter-final of the Champions League, the semi-final of the Europa League, and claimed a host of domestic titles.

Of the Big Three, only Fenerbahçe have their home on the Asian side of Istanbul. Over 90 per cent of Turkey's landmass is to be found in Asia (also called 'Anatolia'), leading to the idea of Fenerbahçe as the most 'Turkish' club, a reputation enhanced by the organisation's early years.

* Some of the Fenerbahçe founders were involved in an ill-fated attempt in 1899 to found a Turkish club team with the English name 'Black Stockings FC'. The team only played one game, in 1901, which ended in a 5-1 defeat. Sultan Abdülhamid II's notorious spies got wind of the match. One of the team's two founders, a diplomat at the ministry of foreign affairs, was sent to serve in Tehran. The other, Fuat Hüsnü, was put on trial. After donning his football kit in court, he persuaded the judge to let him off with a small fine. The premature demise of Black Stockings FC doesn't stop Fenerbahçe from claiming 1899 as their 'true' year of foundation.

After the First World War, when the Allies occupied Istanbul, football games between Turkish sides and Allied servicemen took on added nationalist spice. Fenerbahçe were particularly successful in these matches, and they were invited in June 1923 to represent Turkey in a final match with the occupiers before they left the city. Known as the Harington Cup, after the British general in charge, Fenerbahçe beat a select British army side 2–1, the winning goals scored by their star player Zeki Riza Sporel. A replica of the cup (its name misspelt as 'Harrington') stands in the Fenerbahçe museum. The description proudly exclaims, in shaky English, the glory of Fenerbahçe 'to win this match of Turk's pride'.

A sense of incipient Turkish nationalism was no doubt an important plank in the early activities of these clubs, although the subsequent emergence of a patriotic, independent Turkey has obscured the multi-ethnic mixing of the game's early years. Few of today's fans know that in the picture of the 1909 championship-winning Galatasaray team, the man with a moustache like a brush head sitting with his legs crossed was none other than Englishman Horace Armitage. Also forgotten is that the first Turk to play football – Fuat Hüsnü – went by the nickname of 'Bobby' and competed for the English side 'Cadi-Keuy' (Kadiköy) football club.

*

Today, Fenerbahçe are renowned for their rivalry not with foreign sides but with Galatasaray, their neighbours across town. But how did this famous antagonism begin? Istanbul is not Glasgow, where the sectarianism of the city weighs heavily on the decision of which team to support. Nor is it Buenos Aires, where the historic link of clubs with distinct classes generates equal pressure. Amateur historian Mehmet Yüce believes that the Galatasaray–Fenerbahçe rivalry – one that has destroyed friendships, generated forests of press coverage and even claimed lives – can be traced back to a squabble over a shield. In the 1914–15 season, two-times champions Fenerbahçe reacted badly when their late request to join the league was rejected by the other clubs. Galatasaray won the championship that year. When they did, Fenerbahçe refused to hand over the winner's shield.

Another commonly held belief is that the animosity dates back to Turkey's first serious outbreak of footballing violence. When Galatasaray played Fenerbahçe on 23 February 1934, a bad tackle prompted a mass brawl among the players that quickly engulfed the stands. After the police intervened, things calmed down, only for the Fenerbahçe goalkeeper Hüsametin to run and punch the Galatasaray manager, Englishman Sydney Puddefoot, in the back of the head. The game had to be abandoned. seventeen players were fined, and some were given six-month bans.

But I'm not sure that there was one single trigger. It seems most likely that the rivalry was the product of the irritation and determination that comes from living cheek-by-jowl with a competitor. Galatasaray and Fenerbahçe have been level-pegging for the honour of Turkey's most successful club for a century. Galatasaray have 20 league titles, Fenerbahçe 19; Galatasaray have 17 Turkish cups, Fenerbahçe have 6. Galatasaray have won the UEFA Cup, but Fenerbahçe have most recently come closest, reaching the semi-final in 2013. Beşiktaş didn't become a serious footballing side until the 1930s, by which time the duopoly was established. No side likes to lose to another. But for Fenerbahçe and Galatasaray, losing to Beşiktaş never cuts as deep (the reverse is certainly not true).

As I have already stressed, I do not want to downplay the violence and anger that sometimes mars Turkish football. Like many derbies, Istanbul's big clashes do occasionally spill over into violence. Between 2011 and 2016, visiting team fans were banned from derby matches to avoid incidents. Take a bus into the games as an away fan now, and there's still a chance of a stone coming through the window. After games, as hundreds of thousands tip onto the streets across the country, fights erupt. The competitiveness extends beyond the realm of football: in 2012, Beşiktaş and Galatasaray fans were banned from attending games following a riot at a wheelchair basketball match.

But it pays not to accept as gospel the hyped words of bravado given to outsiders. This is not (only) some fixed, eternal clash of hatred. For me, the defining characteristic of Turkish football is not fighting or enmity but mad, silly, excessive enthusiasm. And in this regard, the Big Three are much alike.

*

Once, when waiting to depart for a Fenerbahçe match in the headquarters of a supporters' group, the middle-aged president suddenly got to his feet and shushed the crowd. He opened his mouth and tumbling out came a song full of such longing that it almost made me cry:

Yellows and blues, believe I'd sacrifice myself for you
Bro, my eyes are blind to any other colour
I only love you, if they say I love any others it's a lie

It reminded me of a Beşiktaş song that is forever being sung at games:

We came to add strength to your strength
We came to be the sweat on your shirt
Beşiktaş, we came to die for you

Galatasaray fans, too, have songs in this vein:

Rather than be without you
I choose to die
I swear, my Cim Bom,
You are my life, my everything.

Love, sacrifice, death – the emotion contained within Turkish football chants elevates the terrace experience to a different plane. At matches I felt these words before I understood them, my ribcage resonating with the vibrations. It was only later, when my ear had caught up, that I realised the comparative oddness. Seeing them translated and written down pulls them yet further from their true context. Here, the imagery of death seems melodramatic to the point of ridiculousness.

Its presence is no doubt related to the wider importance placed on sacrifice in Turkey – the school textbooks declaring that there is no action more honourable than martyrdom for the nation, the privileging of the collective, the pooled consciousness that I register among friends and which leaves me both sad and slightly relieved that I can never fully be part of it. But the transfer of a wider social concept to football clubs is, I feel, only one dimension. Of the 40,000 people belting out the songs, I suspect very few would literally want to die for Beşiktaş. Deliberately excessive, rude or scandalous statements are a way for fans to push against a strong current of rationalism in modern life that frequently downplays the experience of going to games. It shows an intuitive knowledge of the power of the crowd to reconfigure life, to conjure a new lodestar to follow and adore, if only for ninety minutes.

The same goes for how fans express love for their team. Love is not intended as a synonym for 'like'. Supporters speak and sing about the team in the same way they would an unrequited lover or passionate affair:

You, the sadness of my every night, the tears in my eyes, the smoke from my cigarette
You, the blood in my veins, my destiny, my glorious Beşiktaş
Right in the middle of my heart is a big fire, all in flames
Beşiktaş, I swear to you, your love will never die, not even in my grave

The idea of lovesickness is particularly acute on the Beşiktaş terrace. Because the side is less successful, lagging behind Galatasaray and Fenerbahçe in terms of trophies, fandom cannot be constructed around continual success. Instead supporters often glorify melancholy. They claim beauty in understanding that, even when things are going well, Beşiktaş will find a way of messing it all up.

Chanting has its ally in the relentless physicality of the terraces – the touching, the holding, the pushing. Both hasten the disappearance of one into many. Although stadiums are all-seater, no one apart from the rich, disabled or young really sit; although fans could choose not to take part in the songs, no one takes up this option. Fans seem to know instinctively that in order for the experience to be transformative it needs proximity, tactility and the participation of all.

Humour is important, too. Not the piss-take, self-deprecation of the British terraces, but something more vaudeville, almost slapstick. Beşiktaş and Galatasaray fans sing a song entitled 'Opera to Fener'. To the tune of 'Those Were the Days', it outlines what model fans they are, before descending into an enthusiastic chorus: 'But suck my dick, Fener!' Matches are punctuated by silly call and response chants and mass callisthenics. Fans bend down, stand up, cross arms, wave scarves – even take off and wave shoes – all in perfect synchronisation for about ten seconds, before stopping to watch the next stand echo the performance, howling with laughter.

The communality and over-the-topness of the terraces make sense in a country where emotions are normally externalised and shared. Loosening the reins on individual agency lends a bonhomie and *carpe diem* to life in Turkey that instantly attracted me. It causes people to view rules as suggestions, to drive without wearing seat-belts, smoke like chimneys and, when you mention what will happen when the large earthquake hits, shrug before pouring another glass of rakı.

A product of British health-and-safety culture, I found much of this absolutely terrifying at first, and occasionally still do. But within the framework constructed in Turkey, I never struggle to feel life is being *lived*. Nerves and sinews being stretched and released, humans are being exposed to a proper range of moods rather than encased within an iron cage of stiff upper lips and terse handshakes. 'I secretly like the chaos,' confessed Jessica O'Rourke, an American who plays centre-back for Beşiktaş's women's team. Another foreigner bitten by the Turkey bug.

*

As well as having similar chants and rituals, the clubs themselves are structured in the same way. Rather than being owned by a rich businessman, the Big Three are owned by a *dernek*, a foundation run by its members. This is the structure for nearly all teams in Turkey. Fans feel proud they are not the purview of foreign capital or investment, although to get round strict laws governing foundation investment and debt, the Big Three have opened publicly traded companies which run the *dernek* like any private business. This mitigates somewhat the image of a 'people's side'.

The set-up does have its problems. Club chairmen are elected by members, encouraging unwise spending in pursuit of short-term success. Presidents eschew sound financial management safe in the knowledge that presidential terms will be remembered not for the amount of debt accrued but the number of championships won. In 2017 UEFA warned that Turkish teams were the most indebted in Europe. 'European clubs improved substantially overall while aggregated losses of Turkish clubs quintupled,' said Andrea Traverso, the head of financial fair play.

The dominance of the Big Three makes it very difficult for smaller regional sides to attract fans or hold on to their best players. I have climbed aboard shared taxis in Van, a city geographically closer to Tehran than Istanbul, to see them adorned in Galatasaray stickers. On the border with Bulgaria and Greece, the Edirne municipality enshrines star players from the Big Three on its municipal pavements.

Sponsorship and media revenues perpetuate the Istanbul hegemony. Like the banks systemic to the financial system, so the Big Three in Turkey are 'too big to fail'. Galatasaray were banned in 2016 from European football for breaching financial fair play rules. In 2017 they had to sell off land to balance the books. But no president of the football federation – or of the country – is willing to let one of the big clubs go to the wall on his watch. When Fenerbahçe were accused of match-fixing in 2011, the TFF balked at relegating them to the second division.

Even as a Beşiktaş fan, I find nauseating the sense of entitlement shared by the Big Three. Woe betide they are forced to play in the afternoon (rather than evening) or on a weeknight. They nurture victimhood complexes and complain about conspiracies against them while hoovering up trophies. When three teams gobble up 80 per cent of the country's fans, they feel they *are* Turkish football. They warp the game so utterly, I have sympathy with the few people who, disgusted, turn their backs on it all.

And yet, and yet. Submit to one of them, faults and all, and you are hot-wired into life in Turkey. You have a horse in the race, not simply on the pitch but in wider life – an instant common bond with millions of others across the country.

The clubs are social organisations as much as football teams. 'UltraAslan is not simply a group on the terraces singing and supporting the team,' Veysel Giley, the ex-president of UltrAslan, the Galatasaray supporters group told me. 'We show people the way. It should be people who understand what we can do when united, when together.' Groups donate blood and fundraise for disadvantaged children. A capillary system – co-ordinated by fans in the eighty-one regions of Turkey – feeds requests to the centre, funnels donations and distributes support. 'Our aim is to use our name, our existence not just on the terraces but for the benefit of humanity, our country, our motherland,' said Alen Markaryan, a leader of the Beşiktaş fan club Çarşı. The group raised so much money after a forest fire in Antalya that the woodland was renamed the Beşiktaş forest.

And what of politics? None of the Big Three fan clubs are political with a capital 'P'. Even at Çarşı, the Beşiktaş fan club with the socialist reputation, the views expressed are not those of a political platform but rather a diffuse sense of ethics and morals infused with a strong streak of contrariness. And all of this comes a distinct second to supporting the team.

But of course you can't deny a connection. Football in Turkey is political because any decision about how and when thousands can amass is intrinsically political, especially given recent clampdowns on public gatherings. It is political in that these fan leaders are in charge of the rare, raw, uncontrollable power of the crowd. It is political in so much as the authorities recognise this and act accordingly: with police, with laws, with discouragement. The lack of accountability in many areas of life in Turkey renders citizens frustrated. In the face of powerlessness elsewhere, football can make people feel influential. Football contains the illusion that the 22 people on the pitch have assembled for you. At the end of the game you shout: 'Come over here Beşiktaş!' and they do it.

Sometimes this overlaps with organised politics. Fans stand shoulder to shoulder with a group demonstrating about trees being torn down in a park, or those protesting at the murder of an Armenian journalist for being Armenian. For a moment – seconds, hours, weeks – contact is made. Resources are pooled, that latent energy of the crowd transfers, leaping across the gap. But it is putting the cart before the horse to believe that this is the primary purpose of such groups: 'At the end of the day, we are football fans,' said Ayhan, one of Beşiktaş Çarşı's leaders.

The clubs, their fans, the geography and history all combine to make Istanbul one of the world's great football cities. The impact of the Big Three is glaringly obvious when a match is taking place, as supporters descend en masse to the footballing districts and crowd around TVs everywhere else.

But even on a regular weekday, Galatasaray, Fenerbahçe and Beşiktaş structure so much of life in the city. The stadiums and the networks of businesses that grow around them have shaped the geography of neighbourhoods. The teams' bright colours lighten up the winter commute, providing splashes of red, yellow, blue and white on scarves and hats. And the sound of their names pepper the air, as the latest successes or failures are thrashed out over canteen lunches, the conversation interrupted by recorded chants set as ringtones on mobile phones.

And for all the talk of fearsome rivalry, the enmity is tempered by traditions and cultures that long pre-date the game's arrival. Just as football has changed Istanbul, so the city has itself taken the game and moulded it in its likeness.

*

When Beşiktaş won the league in 2016 it prompted an explosion of Beşiktaş support in public – not simply in the team's neighbourhood but across all of Istanbul. Everywhere I went I spotted banners in black and white. They were in the fish market, strung between trees on leafy streets, hung from apartment buildings on not-so-leafy ones and billowing from wires suspended high over Istiklal Avenue. Many questions arose: Who arranges these flags? Is it the local council?

Residents? Do they have three flags, one for each of the big teams, which they cycle through each year?

One morning, when passing one such flag near my home – a large Beşiktaş eagle on a black and white striped background – curiosity got the better of me, and I popped my head in an estate agent's shop located right below it. I was greeted by two men: Hakan, who worked there, and his friend Yunus, who was keeping him company.

'Oh, you want to speak to Kenan Bey [Mr Kenan],' said Hakan when I asked who was responsible for the flag. He got out of his seat, walked to the door of the estate agents and shouted across the road, 'Hey, Kenan Bey!'

I could hear snatches of the conversation. 'What do I want with an English guy?!' It didn't sound too hopeful. But after a few minutes, a man in his fifties, with wispy, thinning hair, appeared in the doorway, a sheen of sweat on his forehead.

He sat down, nodding his assent when I asked if I could interview him.

'We collect money from the whole area,' Kenan Bey explained. 'Normally it's 600 lira [£150]. We collect the money – 10 from him, 5 from him, 20 from him.'

Hakan piped up: 'It's not only from Beşiktaş fans. All fans contribute. Next year who will be champions – Fener? He's Galatasaray, but he will give 10 lira, he will also. Everyone.'

I must have looked sceptical. 'Yes, Galatasaray and Fenerbahçe fans,' said Kenan Bey, looking deadly serious. Hakan chipped in again: 'Mate, this is *mahalle* culture. You won't find it everywhere, but you do here.'

Mahalle is the Turkish word for neighbourhood. Historically, Istanbul was less one city and more hundreds of distinct, self-contained *mahalles*. Each had its own local economy and culture, its known figures: the shopkeepers, the religious men, the *kabadayı* gangsters, who claimed to keep the residents safe, and the grandmas who fed the street cats. In other words, a clear community, in which neighbours would help each other out, and live life in the plural.

I still couldn't quite believe what I was hearing. 'So, for example, say Galatasaray are champions next year—'

'We will do it for them too,' Kenan Bey replied.

'You will organise it?'

'Yes, I'll do it.'

'But you're a Beşiktaş fan?'

He shrugged. *Olsun* – it doesn't matter.

At that point, Yunus, the other guy in the shop found his voice. 'Football is brotherhood,' he said. 'We've been hanging them up for 20 years.'

For the rest of the summer, wherever I went I photographed the flags. There were flags with eagles and flags with crests. Flags suspended from flats, slung across roads and attached to lampposts. Some were so large their bottom had to be tied in a knot, lest they get entangled in a passing lorry. Others were more modest – to look up at them was to glimpse more sky than flag. Some had holes cut into them to allow the wind through, others had been caught by the same force, twirled around the line until they resembled a rag to be squeezed. Written on some were the names of their patrons:

'Flower-seller Hakan,' or 'Hairdresser Erol congratulates champions Beşiktaş'. Others hung demurely, an anonymous homage to the team.

Remembering my conversation, I thought of all the people behind them. Groups across Turkey collecting donations and poring over designs. People hiring ladders, teetering on top of them and then climbing down to admire the finished product. And I felt comforted. Despite the arguments, the passion – even violence – whoever won next year, they would do it all again.

BJK
1903
BEŞİKTAŞ
ESNAFI
KARTALL
KUAFÖR EROL
BJK
1903
ÇİÇEKÇİ
HAKAN
ŞAMPİYON
BEŞİKTAŞ

BJK
1903
BJK
1903
BEŞİKTAŞ
ŞAMPİYON
1903
BJK
BJK
1903
ŞAMPİYON
BEŞİKTAŞ
KARTAL BAKIŞI
www.kartalbakisi.co

3

Reis

The Big Three teams of Istanbul dominate Turkey's sporting landscape. But perhaps the most important footballer that the city has ever produced played for none of them.

The man they call *Reis* – the chief – is best known to the world as Turkey's mercurial, irascible president, the man who has dominated his nation's politics since 2002. But Recep Tayyip Erdoğan started life as a semi-professional footballer in some of the rougher neighbourhoods of Istanbul.

Erdoğan's sporting career has become part of his personal mythology – it is used to reinforce his image as a salt-of-the-earth, masculine leader in tune with the masses. Like much about Turkey's most contentious public figure, his love of football has intermingled with his politics in ways which will reverberate in Turkey for decades to come.

Erdoğan was born in 1954 in Kasımpaşa, a working-class district on the shores of the Golden Horn. The family were poor. After school, the young Erdoğan would work selling stale *simit*, the hoop-shaped sesame bread that is Turkey's most popular snack. But what he really wanted to do with his free time was kick a ball around. 'I loved football. It was my passion. It entered my dreams at night,' Erdoğan said years later. 'But my father never gave permission for me to play.'

According to the officially sanctioned narrative, Ahmet Erdoğan – nicknamed 'captain' because of his work on the Istanbul ferries – was fiercely against his son's obsession. 'Football won't feed the belly,' he used to growl. The young Recep Tayyip defied his father, sneaking out to play, hiding his football boots in the coal bunker upon his return.

Aged eleven, Erdoğan won a place at an Imam Hatip college, one of Turkey's religious high schools founded to train imams for the nation's mosques. He was not particularly hard working but excelled in religious studies and sport. While still at school, he began playing for the amateur side Camialtıspor. In 1974, a year after graduating from high school, he moved to a team linked to the Istanbul transport authority, İETT, on the recommendation of the team's captain, who was one of Erdoğan's neighbours in Kasımpaşa.

Erdoğan played for İETT for seven seasons. 'At first I played up front, then in midfield, then later I moved into the back four and played sweeper,' Erdoğan recalled in 2016. 'Apart from goalkeeper, you can say I played everywhere!' The president has a scar on his chin that he describes jokingly as 'my footballing memento'. During his first season at İETT in a match against Çapa, he received an elbow from Hayri Ülgen who would later go on to play for the national team. 'This spot filled with blood. They gave me stitches,' Erdoğan said. 'The scar is still visible. Every time I look in the mirror I remember my time as a footballer.'

In 1994, when he was on the verge of being elected Mayor of Istanbul, Erdoğan gave an interview about his footballing career to the newspaper *Milliyet*. He went to great lengths to weave a strong thread of religiosity into his years as a footballer, explaining that, when he played for İETT, he used to lay out his prayer rug and pray in the changing rooms. His team-mates already jokingly called him *hoca*, religious teacher. Erdoğan explained how, before matches, he and the coach would take the side to the Eyüp Sultan Mosque, where Erdoğan apparently led them in prayer. 'We won all our matches in Eyüp,' he states as proof of its effectiveness. 'Belief is 50 per cent of success. Even Maradona used to kiss a cross when heading out onto the pitch.'

The same interview also sees Erdoğan discuss the most fiercely disputed claim about his footballing career: that he was almost signed by Fenerbahçe. He reports that he was on Fenerbahçe's transfer list in 1977 but that his hopes evaporated with the departure of the team's manager, the Serbian Tomislav Kaloperović. Erdoğan is a Fenerbahçe fan, and some writers believe there is some burnishing of the historical record. But the claim that he could have played for the Canaries would be repeated again and again throughout the course of his political career.

Erdoğan's supporters line up to trumpet his footballing experience. A book called *Please Don't Let My Father See* was published in 2005 by Haci Hasdemir, a journalist from *Zaman*, at that time a pro-government newspaper. It begins with an introduction from Hayri Beşer, a fellow *Zaman* writer, which sets the tone for what follows: 'When reading, some might arrive at the conclusion that it is "the anatomy of an angel",' warns Beşer. 'Because in Tayyip Erdoğan's 15 year footballing adventure, there's barely a blemish.' A 2017 biopic of the president shows him as a child coming on to score the winner in the closing minutes of a 9–9 game with a stunning overhead kick.

A series of sceptics have lined up to cast doubt on some or all of the central assertions of Erdoğan's footballing career, part of a wider mistrust of his story that also includes a disputed university degree. Mustafa Hoş, a journalist, who mockingly describes the Hasdemir account as 'the Holy Book', compares Erdoğan's footballing days to trying to uncover evidence about events that took place almost 100 years ago. 'Everything is ambiguous and contradictory.' Soner Yalçın, a journalist who has written a 400-page take down of Erdoğan, makes no effort to conceal his contempt. He believes that the entire Fenerbahçe story is fabricated: 'Erdoğan's official historians all write different years for when he got his transfer proposal . . . according to some, he was spotted playing in an amateur league match in Eskişehir. Others say it was in Kasımpaşa . . . the manager at Fenerbahçe who liked him also changes, some say Waldyr Pereira Didi, others Tomislav Kaloperović.' Yalçın also claims Erdoğan spent his first two years at Camıaltıspor as assistant to the kitman, and maintains that he only got on the pitch because of 'Kasımpaşa pressure' exerted on the coach by a neighbourhood friend.

It is testament to the polarised nature of Turkey today that even questions of the president's footballing ability become sucked into the vortex of division. Depending on what you read, he is either a total charlatan or Kasımpaşa's answer to Pelé.

At the age of twenty-seven when most footballers are hitting their stride, Erdoğan left İETT. He carried on playing football for Erokspor, a neighbourhood team, but by this time other aspects of his life were starting to take precedent. From an early age Erdoğan had been involved in politics. He was part of the shifting landscape of religious-inspired parties that had their roots in Imam Hatip schools and conservative neighbourhoods like Erdoğan's Kasımpasa. In 1976, aged twenty two, he had become chairman of the local youth branch of the Islamist Millî Selâmet Partisi (National Salvation Party). It was shut down after a military coup in 1980, but in 1985 he became the chair of the Istanbul district (and member of the executive committee) of its successor, the Welfare Party.

When Turkey was founded as an independent nation in 1923, its leader, Mustafa Kemal Atatürk, established a secular state similar to the model in France. A directorate of religious affairs was established and imams were brought under government control. Islam was deemed a private matter, not a public identity. Civil servants could not grow a beard and girls in headscarves could not sit university exams without removing their veils. These policies highlighted two distinct groupings: an urban, secular elite in charge of the levers of the state and a larger, poorer mass of 'religious' citizens.

A common misconception is that this fault line is solely about religion. It isn't. Among secular elites, religion was a shorthand way of signifying a distaste of provincialism and perceived cultural backwardness of the rural working class. From the 1920s, these people were cut out of the state-building process, spoken to rather than engaged. For politicians or organisations that could cast their appeal in language that resonated with them, there was a growing constituency to be tapped.

Erdoğan is a politician who grasped this intuitively. 'Your brother Tayyip is a black Turk,' he declared, casting himself as a member of an oppressed underclass in opposition to the old 'white Turk' elite. In 1994, he won the Istanbul mayor's office for the Welfare Party – part of a wave of victories across the country that marked a watershed moment for Islamist politics in Turkey. Seven years later, after a spell in prison on political charges, he led a breakaway movement and founded a new party: the Justice and Development Party, known by its Turkish initials as the AKP. Erdoğan had learnt from previous battles. He and his party downplayed the importance of religion, including unveiled women in its election posters and emphasising an economic platform built around deregulation and free trade. It worked.

In the general election of November 2002, the party won two-thirds of the seats in parliament, sweeping away the status quo. In March 2003, Erdoğan became prime minister. A year after his ascension to the top job, Fenerbahçe had a home match against Akçaabat Sebatspor, a team from Trabzon. In the home end, a banner was draped across the advertising hoarding: 'A manly man: Recep Tayyip Erdoğan'. The footballer from Kasımpaşa had become the most powerful man in the land.

*

I have never known a Turkey without Recep Tayyip Erdoğan. When I first arrived in 2008, the AKP project was already six years old. A major part of the party's success was built on its social and political empowerment of those who had been sidelined by the old elites. Many benefited from reforms to education, healthcare and social security, and a relaxation of Turkey's strict secularism that placed restrictions on women who wore headscarves. The party presided over a period of strong GDP growth, fuelled by booming construction. Rising wealth and a surge in spending on the back of consumer lending meant millions were buying their first car and home. The spending spree was being fuelled by foreign capital that flooded into Turkish markets, attracted by the high returns.

Football rode the wave of these economic developments. The game in Turkey has many of the corporate bells and whistles that are familiar to a modern-day British fan: the electronic advertising boards, the stadiums named after corporations and the club merchandise that ranges from beer holders to baby-grows. But Turkish football also has additional features that even the hyper-commercialised English Premier League has yet to implement. On team shirts, the players' names are relegated to below the squad numbers. The more visible spot across the shoulder blades is given over to adverts. I am certain that my player recognition is much lower in Turkey because any close-ups give the appearance that they are all called 'Halley' (a chocolate brand), 'Garenta' (a car rental company) or 'Beko' (a manufacturer of home appliances).* When watching a game on television, the screen

* This might not be apparent if your only experience of Turkish football is in European competition, as UEFA requires the player's name to be displayed above the number.

suddenly shrinks to allow a banner advertising a petrol brand to flash across the bottom. Such commercialism has contributed to the Turkish Super League becoming the seventh wealthiest football league in Europe by revenue. Many people are grateful to Erdoğan personally for these developments. 'In the last fifteen years we've started to gather the fruits of your leadership. Our football has started to rise', Yildirim Demirören, the president of the TFF said in 2017.

Erdoğan is of course not solely responsible for all of this. From economic performance to the reforms leading to the commencement of EU accession talks, he and his party often implemented or continued processes set in motion earlier. Perceptions matter, however. And it is salient that across Turkey many people view the transformation of the country as not simply presided over by Erdoğan but stemming directly from his words and actions.

Such personification of government speaks to what the anthropologist Jenny White calls the 'Big Man' conception of politics. The Big Man is 'both a father figure and a hero', sat at the top of a strict hierarchy, where relations are cast in terms of personal patronage in exchange for political support: you do something for me, I do something for you. The Big Man does not inherit his position of leadership but acquires it through securing and protecting his flock, be that positions in the cabinet for close confidants, or new roads and health insurance schemes for supporters at the grassroots.

'Despite the trappings of elections and the appearance of a stable, modern state,' writes White, Turkey's political culture has long been characterised by the idea of the 'Big Man'. The trope stretches back at least to Turkey's founder Mustafa Kemal, the archetypal hero and father figure whose presence suffuses all of Turkey: from pictures and statues in government buildings to aphorisms printed inside textbooks. All the same, Turkey did not have a Big Man of comparative stature until the former footballer from Kasımpaşa rose to prominence.

Though I did not know Turkey in its pre-AKP era, I have witnessed change in the party itself. Back in 2008, when Erdoğan was prime minister, he was one among a small cadre of powerful figures in the AKP. After maxing out his party's three-term limit as prime minister, in 2014 he ran as the country's first directly elected president. In the years that followed, he gradually forced out all rivals and dissenters. By 2016 he stood above all. Today television channels devote hours of coverage to his speeches, his every move dissected in minute detail by supporters and opponents alike. After a failed military coup in July 2016, one poster seemed to imbue him with deity-like powers. 'No matter what they do, there is a decree that comes from the heavens,' it proclaimed, next to a large portrait of the president.

Erdoğan is notoriously thin-skinned. In eighteen months to March 2016, charges were brought against 1,845 people for insulting the president. They included a man who compared Erdoğan to Gollum from *Lord of the Rings* and a tea boy who said that if the president came into his canteen, he would refuse to serve him a drink. In 2017, while love for the AKP had begun to sour after fifteen years in charge, Erdoğan's approval ratings remained high. Songs have been composed in his honour, including a 2014 hit with the lyrics: 'The man of the people, the lover of justice / He is the light of hope for millions / The confidant of the oppressed, the companion of the abject / Recep Tayyip Er-doğ-an!' The song was purportedly stolen from Arslanbek Sultanbekov, a folk musician born in Karachay–Cherkessia, an autonomous oblast of the Soviet Union. The singer who was accused of 'borrowing' it, Uğur Işılak, claimed it was an anonymous melody from Central Asia. Işılak was later rewarded with a seat in parliament where, in his first session, he was pictured falling asleep.

Football remains a central part of Erdoğan's Big Man persona. In a country where the game is entwined with notions of virile masculinity and hero-worship, it is the ideal tool with which to bolster a reputation.* He was still taking part in games well into his sixties; at a charity match in 2014, he scored a hat-trick with some surprisingly decent finishing. Erdoğan's displays of sporting prowess are reminisicent of those of Russian President Vladimir Putin – also in his sixties – who regularly takes part in ice hockey matches in which he scores upwards of eight goals. Erdoğan frequently descends to the dressing room after matches to congratulate players. In August 2017 he joked with Martin Skrtel who missed a good chance to score: 'If you curled the ball a bit more, it would have gone in. Clearly you haven't seen my goals when I played for the Istanbul municipality.' Erdoğan is forever taking penalties at the opening of new stadiums

* Erdoğan's political hero, former Prime Minister Adnan Menderes, is widely reported to have also been a star footballer, playing as a goalkeeper and forward for the Izmir teams Altay and Karşıyaka in the 1920s and '30s. Historian Günver Güneş, however, has cast doubt on this claim: 'as someone who's gone through the period's press with a fine-tooth comb, I'm curious where [people] get this from', he wrote in 2005.

or football conferences, which are always widely documented. 'The first goal from Erdoğan', *Fotomaç* reported at the opening of the new Trabzonspor stadium in December 2016. Next to the picture, the newspaper placed a star that read 'a master stroke'.

*

'When I was a youth, in all of Istanbul you could count the number of acceptable pitches on the fingers of one hand,' said Erdoğan in March 2017. 'In the entire history of the republic up until 2002, the number of sports facilities stood at 1,575. In just fourteen years we added another 1,924.'

Perhaps the largest change to sports in Turkey under the AKP has been the surge in sports construction. From neighbourhood AstroTurf pitches to world-class stadiums, every level of the sports pyramid has seen huge investment in infrastructure. Many thousands now have affordable and accessible sports amenities close to their homes and schools.

New sports facilities are part of a wider construction boom that has swept across the cities of Turkey. It is impossible to escape the sound of jackhammers and drills as buildings are pulled down and thrown up at dizzying speed. The restless movement is not a consequence but a cause – in a country where construction and its affiliated industries make up about 20 per cent of the economy, permanent building keeps the economy afloat. To achieve this end, there has been deregulation of state entities, changes to planning laws and the loosening of credit. The boom has helped power the country to greater wealth and prosperity, but it has also had a darker side, with environmental damage, poor workers' safety and allegations of corruption and cronyism.

Pride of place in the building spree has been given to Erdoğan's beloved mega-projects. They include a third bridge across the Bosphorus and a road tunnel and metro line under it. In 2015 construction began on a third airport, due to be the world's busiest with six runways. Football stadiums, too, are an important example of the policy in action.

Turkey has become UEFA's leading builder of new stadiums. Between 2007 and 2015, eighteen new grounds were built. The rate of development eclipsed even Russia, which was preparing for the 2018 World Cup. The cities of Bursa, Eskişehir, Trabzon, Diyarbakır, Gaziantep, Samsun, Antalya, İzmit, Adana, Adapazarı, Antakya and

Konya all have – or in 2017 were soon to get – a new stadium. Nearly all follow the same pattern: an old stadium, built in the 1940s or '50s, is knocked down. It will have been part of the republican project, located in a central area alongside a park or some other recreational space and named either after Atatürk himself (Bursa, Eskişehir, Konya, Sakarya, Antalya) or key dates from the Turkish war of independence (Ankara, Samsun).

By contrast, the new stadiums are named after sponsors (the Türk Telekom Stadium, the Medical Park Stadium) or the municipality. They often stand on the outskirts of the city, accessible only by car or laborious journeys on public transport. Most Turkish stadiums are owned by the government and leased to the clubs. Consequently, the old city-centre plots can be sold off by TOKI, the government housing agency, to developers for a lucrative price. 'Let the stadiums be a thousand witnesses,' Erdoğan said on the campaign trail in March 2017. 'Most were in a dilapidated state. We brought – we are bringing – new stadiums that are the envy of most cities in the world.'

Many fans are happy with the changes. Old stadiums had disgusting toilets and nowhere to eat; many didn't even have roofs – fine on a Mediterranean summer's evening but less appealing in January on the Anatolian steppe. The new stadiums are more comfortable and safer than their predecessors.

In many ways Turkey is going through a process that the UK underwent in the 1990s, when the governance and infrastructure of the game was rapidly overhauled. In England the process was prompted by the Hillsborough disaster. Turkey, thankfully, has never experienced a stadium disaster on that scale, although it has suffered major tragedies. In August 1967, forty died at a match between Sivas and Kayseri when rock throwing between the fans prompted a stampede. On the frequent occasions when I have been caught in crushes, violently pushed through turnstiles by police shields or herded onto rickety terracing erected on scaffolding, images of Hillsborough have flashed through my mind.

But safety and comfort were not the only motivations. Stadiums are seen as a vital source of revenue for heavily indebted clubs. Ceyhun Kazancı, who was in charge of selling boxes and VIP seats for the new Galatasaray stadium, explained the flaws with the old ground. 'The capacity was 25,000 and there were no boxes. But there are a lot of rich and important people at Galatasaray . . . and they want to show off.' According to Kazancı, the sale of boxes at the new stadium, plus 2,500 VIP seats on a three-year contract, earned the club $80 million.

Some go as far as to say that the stadium's existence is solely due to the opportunity to award a construction project and enrich friends, a process captured in Turkish by the wonderfully onomatopoeic word '*rant*'. Turkey isn't Russia. There is no culture of everyday mini-bribes to traffic police or civil servants. But business is riddled with conflicts of interest and corruption. For example, in Turkey many construction companies are part of a wider portfolio of business interests. It has been alleged that in return for contracts, they may be asked to acquire newspapers and TV channels and ensure that they turn out obsequious coverage. In February 2013, the $66 million contract to build the stadium for the Istanbul club Başakşehir was given to a conglomerate called Kalyon Group. Later the same year, Kalyon was part of a consortium that won the $29 billion tender to construct Istanbul's huge new airport.

It was later alleged, based on leaked recordings of conversations between Turkish construction magnates, that Kalyon was pressured into acquiring a pro-government media group from Çalık Holding, another AKP-friendly business that was eager to dispose of the TV channels and newspapers that were running up big losses. The companies refused to comment on the alleged quid pro quo.

Local politicians jostle to have the 'best' projects built in their patch as a way of showing their power and influence. Stadiums are constructed as money makers and status symbols rather than community facilities. 'In Konya the capacity is nearly 42,000. Do you know the reason?' a sports administrator once told me. 'The code of Konya on the car plate is 42.' Konya does not have a sporting culture that can fill a 42,000-seater, but it matters little. Bestowing a new stadium on a town is one of the rewards that the Big Man can dole out in exchange for support. 'He persuades the president to build the *biggest* one in our city.'

These days, Erdoğan is selective about which matches he attends in person. He was subjected to his first ever large-scale public booing at the opening of the new Galatasaray ground in January 2011. The team's fans are convinced that this act has had repercussions. I have heard many insist that the horrendous traffic bottlenecks that precede and follow every match are caused because a second access road was denied planning permission – supposedly an act of punishment for the fans' behaviour.

*

On a cold March day in 2016, I decided on a whim to go and inspect the site of the old Galatasaray stadium, the Ali Sami Yen – scene of the original 'Welcome to Hell'. The fate of the team's former home ties together the threads of Big Man politics, construction, contracts and commercialism.

The last time I had been there was a hot day in September 2011, waiting for a bus of Beşiktaş fans to pick me up en route to an away match. Returning almost five years later, I was in for a shock. Half a dozen crenellated skyscrapers were rising up out of the site like a giant Lego creation. I walked around, trying to avoid the muddy puddles and the construction vehicles reversing out of the site without looking. I came across a security guard. When I inquired about the old stadium, he shrugged and said he was new to Istanbul. I asked him what the site would become. It would be luxury homes, he said, costing four hundred thousand dollars. 'That's the lowest,' he said, before adding: 'It's not for normal people.' He was probably earning a couple of dollars an hour.

The Ali Sami Yen was one of TOKI's most lucrative projects. Like the site of the old stadiums in Diyarbakır, Adapazarı and other cities, there had been talk of developing the land for the public good. But the plan changed, and in 2010 a construction firm paid 461.5 million lira for the rights to develop the plot. Later that same year, it entered into a joint agreement with Torunlar Construction, a shopping-mall developer whose owner, Aziz Torun, attended the same Imam Hatip college as Erdoğan (he once claimed that they used to catch the ferry to school together). The firm drew up a 1 billion lira plan to turn it into luxury offices, shops and flats called the Torun Center.

The project was hit by a series of squabbles between the parties, which slowed down development. Then, in 2014, the site was struck by two tragedies less than six months apart. In April, a nineteen-year-old worker from the eastern city of Van, who was working on the site to save up for further studies, died after falling from the fifteenth floor. In September of the same year, a lift plunged to the ground from the thirty-second floor, killing ten workers.

Turkey has a notoriously poor record on workplace safety. According to the Council for Workers' Health and Work Safety (İşçi Sağlığı ve İş Güvenliği Meclisi), 1,970 people were killed in industrial accidents in 2016 (in the 12 months to March 2017, the figure in the UK was 137). The country is still haunted by a mining disaster in the town of Soma in 2014, which left 301 people dead. Erdoğan had to hide from protesters in a shop when visiting the town. The enduring image of the tragedy for many is not the weeping families but of an Erdoğan adviser taking a swinging kick at a protester who had been wrestled to the ground by police.

After the Torun Center deaths, the site manager and the technical director of the lift company were among a group of people arrested and put on trial on charges of causing death by negligence. Prosecutors sought penalties of up to twenty-two and a half years in prison. In 2017 the case was still ongoing. Meanwhile, Western investors were worried: what about their returns? A 2016 HSBC research note on the firm behind the project struck a reassuring tone. 'This project had a series of unfortunate events,' it conceded. 'However, with construction nearly complete and rental agreements speeding up, we expect sales of the remaining 340 units to intensify.'

*

The changing physical landscape of Turkish football has been accompanied by a parallel development: a remodelling of the profile of those who watch the game. On 14 April 2011, the Turkish parliament passed the 'Law to Prevent Violence and Disorder in Sport', better known in Turkey by its numerical code in the Turkish statute: 6222. The 6222 law was aimed at stamping out problems at sports events (read: football matches) by establishing a brand-new framework of regulations.

Taking inspiration from similar legislation in Europe – chief among them the 1990 Taylor Report that followed the Hillsborough disaster – the law involved almost fifty lawyers and took five and a half years to design. It gave wider powers to authorities policing stadiums and their vicinities, required the federation and police to gather and hold greater information on fans, and increased the punishments for misbehaviour.

There seems a disparity between the law's stated aim and its actual effects. On the surface it is about combating violence in sport. 'There was a need to devise something against the unruliness and hooliganism in stadiums,' said Yunus Egemenoğlu, a lawyer and former board member at the TFF. 'It was clear that there were no administrative measures being taken and that club administrators always walked away without reprimands.'

Yet the way officials talked about the law suggested it was introduced with wider objectives in mind. 'As stadiums modernise, as they get more luxurious and as ticket systems change, the *çapulcu* [looter, vandal] won't be able to afford going to matches,' one official told the academic Yağmur Nuhrat in 2011. The law seemed to be less about keeping fans safe and more about transforming football fan culture from an occupation of the poor and working class into a more bourgeois pursuit.

In a way, the law was an assault on the culture of the terrace leader, a position that emerged in Turkish football in the 1980s and '90s. 'Terrace leaders started leading groups, young people, a hundred men or so, and the leader gave out free tickets,' the academic and writer Tanıl Bora once told me. 'He got the tickets from the club management. Or not only tickets – maybe hashish, a little money – and in return he organised the crowd for the club . . . and this also resulted in power for him and it grew.'

The language used by the government was very telling. The word *çapulcu* re-emerged in 2013 when Erdoğan used the term to refer to anti-government protesters. 'We won't do what a handful of çapulcus have done,' said Erdoğan to his supporters. 'They destroy the shops of civilians. They destroy the cars of civilians . . . They are low enough to insult the prime minister of this country.' The real import of his speech, however, came in the next sentence: 'As long as you walk with us, the Justice and Development Party administration will stand strong. As long as there is life in my body, your prime minister . . . will not be deterred by anything.' His language was designed to drive a wedge between protesters and AKP supporters. They, he was telling them, are not like you.

The labelling of opposition as undesirables and hooligans has grown in frequency as the splits in the nation increase. Speaking in March 2017, Erdoğan accused the opposition of behaving like 'hooligans in football' and deploying 'hooligan politics'. He said: 'God willing we will get rid of them. They have the nerve to still be match-fixing and cheating.' Not content with leaving the metaphor there, Erdoğan then shifted to comparing the opposition CHP to over-the-hill footballers: 'It's long past the time for their testimonial but still they resist. All the matches that they go out to play they lose . . . Hopefully this time they'll get the message.'

The comment seemed like one of those moments where the metaphor revealed more perhaps than the speaker intended. To cast one's political victories in football match terminology is not simply cute but reveals a lot about your view of politics, namely a 'winner takes all' conception of democracy. Over the years, Erdoğan has deployed increasingly harsh language against his opponents, casting them as terrorist supporters and traitors to the nation.

*

In Turkey in 2017, it is no longer possible to buy an old-fashioned ticket to a football match, at least in the top two leagues. Every person in the stadium must have what is known as a Passolig card. This holds the fan's name and surname, their ID number and a photo. Tickets for games are purchased online and 'added' to the card.

The Passolig system is the element of the 6222 law that has most affected the ordinary Turkish football fan. The card is only the tracker chip in a much larger system of monitoring. The 6222 law required stadiums to install high-tech security camera systems capable of distinguishing an individual face in the crowd, and large screens above the turnstiles to allow officials to match each person entering the ground with the picture on their Passolig card. 'If 40,000 people go to a game, the government wants to know every single person,' explained Kazancı, Passolig general manager, in an interview from his Istanbul office. 'They want to know who came to that game. They want 40,000 separate ID numbers.'

Ostensibly, the government wants to know in order to stop people from causing violence and disorder. The new cameras theoretically allow individual troublemakers to be pinpointed and punished. In practice, the TFF applies blanket bans to entire blocks of the stadium that they see as being culpable for any wrongdoing. This sometimes results in comic situations. In January 2017, a large group of fans of

Sivasspor, in the first division, were blocked en masse as punishment for 'bad and ugly chants'. Among those banned was Ilhan Biçer, who was watching the match with his fifteen-year-old son. Biçer is both deaf and mute. Kazancı told me that he himself was once given a one-match ban on account of swearing at a match that he attended. 'Our system is capable enough to personalise and find every single person who did this,' he lamented. 'Fifteen thousand people were in the stadium. Only forty or fifty said these things and I did nothing. I watched the game and I'm banned!'

The government decided to outsource the task of implementing the system. The contract was put out for tender and awarded to a small investment bank called Aktif Bank. The bank owns a technology company called e-Kent, which produces the e-payment systems for transport networks in many cities across Turkey. This is purportedly why Aktif Bank won – making them well placed for the almost 50 million dollars' worth of investment needed to install technologies in stadiums. According to Kazancı, the firm put in a 'hugely detailed tender'. Others were less sure. 'Aktif is a corporate investment bank, not a retail bank, and has no experience in credit cards, so it's difficult to see how this fits with their business model,' an unnamed Istanbul banking analyst told the *Financial Times* in 2014.

Kazancı also conceded there could be other driving forces behind the changes. 'Security could be a reason behind this,' he said. 'But marketing tools could also be a reason. Because when you know the people who enter the stadium, you can create lots of products for them. If you know all the details about them, then it's easier to market to these guys.'

That marketing is perhaps of higher importance is also suggested by the card itself. In its bottom-right corner is a Mastercard logo. The bank sells the tickets. But the card on which you buy them can also be used as a credit card. Kazancı explained the thinking. Since fans were obliged to take out cards, they would make three different versions. 'One is a credit card, another one is a debit card and the final one is a prepaid card. So if a client chooses a credit card or a debit card, they will become the bank's clients. So thanks to this Passolig system they are able to sell credit cards.'

Critics suggested there was another reason why Aktif Bank was chosen. The bank is a subsidiary of Çalık Holding, a large conglomerate owned by Ahmet Çalık, a billionaire businessman who is close to President Erdoğan. It was Çalık whom Erdoğan helped out by forcing Kalyon, the builders of the aforementioned Başakşehir stadium, to buy his ailing media group. Between 2007 and 2013, the company's chief executive was a young businessman called Berat Albayrak. But he wasn't just any businessman. In 2004, he had married Esra Erdoğan, the president's eldest daughter. Throughout the ceremony, attended by 7,000 guests, Çalık stood right by the prime minister's side. Now Erdoğan's son-in-law, Albayrak left Çalık Holding in November 2013 after fourteen years at the firm. His departure came just before the Passolig tender was awarded to Aktif Bank. But he was succeeded in his role as CEO at Çalık Holding by the founder. Two years later, Albayrak joined the cabinet as energy minister and became one of his father-in-law's closest political confidants. The episode highlights the close intertwining of business, politics and football in modern-day Turkey.

Aside from the political murkiness, the system is also just plain annoying. Each Passolig card is associated with a club, and entitles the holder to priority tickets for that team. This makes it difficult to be a roving football fan. I have four Passolig cards: a Beşiktaş card (so I can buy advance tickets for Beşiktaş games); a card with a season ticket for the Ankara club Gençlerbirliği (I can't upload this ticket to any other card); a neutral card not affiliated to any club (which I took out before realising it bestowed no advantages); and a Fenerbahçe card (so that I can buy tickets for Fenerbahçe games in advance). You have to pay an annual fee to 'renew' your card. The amount varies from club to club. At the Big Three it's 33 lira (£8). If your card is lost or damaged and you want a replacement, well, tough. You need to make a new application.

This is all very irritating, but perhaps the saddest consequence of Passolig is its suppression of spontaneous match-going. Match attendance in Turkey has always been highly variable. Fans are more often swayed by the performance of the team, filling grounds when they are doing well and staying away if the football is poor. But you can no longer simply turn up on a whim and get a ticket. Going to a ticket booth now involves stepping around fans on their phones, quickly applying online for a card so they can attend the game (once registered electronically, the club can issue a single entry card to enter). If it's sold out, instead of touts swapping paper tickets for banknotes, people stand on street corners whispering bank account and ID card numbers.

Most fans were deeply unhappy about the new system. Progressive fan clubs boycotted games. Attendances plummeted. Stadiums were half empty. Yıldız Holding, a confectionery giant whose brands include McVities and Godiva, pulled its sponsorship out of Turkish football. It looked unsustainable.

But these glitches turned out to be growing pains. While I've not met anyone who celebrates needing a card to go to matches, most people got used to it. Some fans were broadly sympathetic to the law's wider efforts to overhaul decrepit stadiums and reduce the threat of violence. The clubs also like the new system. For each Passolig card sold, 47 per cent of the revenue goes to the club. Aktif Bank takes the rest. Galatasaray made 4 million lira, almost a million pounds, in 2015 through Passolig card sales. They also like the fact that it reduces their sometimes difficult relationship with fan groups. In the past, the most hardcore would get free tickets from the club. Some of them they would give away for free to members of the group, others they would sell as a way of making money. Now the clubs can be much more standoffish towards fans while claiming that their hands are tied.

The law has had an effect on terrace culture beyond numbers. 'Stadiums in Turkey are a place where suppressed emotions erupt. You spend ten hours at work every day, getting bottled up, then you come here and release it,' explained Murat, an Adanaspor fan. 'But this Passolig system. There are 120 cameras in the stadium. If I swear, they can see it on the cameras. They'll block my card. I'll get a three- or six-match ban.' At Champions League and Europa League games the level of profanity has increased since the same regulations do not hold.

In 2017 the TFF president, Yildirim Demirören, declared mission accomplished: 'The fans that we don't want aren't coming to the stadium. The number of spectators has dropped by 10 per cent but now more quality fans come to the game. It dropped 10 per cent but it will rise by 50 per cent. The profile is quickly changing.'

But despite the new cards, the increased monitoring and harsh punishments, misbehaviour at games has not abated. Every week in the margins of the sport press another story is told: a team forced to play without fans for one match due to their offensive chants; or a fan banned for hurling a mobile phone at a goalkeeper. In the Turkish Super Cup final in August 2017, a fan threw a flick knife that landed metres from Beşiktaş attacker Ricardo Quaresma. But this should perhaps not be surprising, as stopping violence seemed to be secondary to turning fans into consumers.

There is much grumbling and nostalgia for the old days. '[We used to have] that beauty, that continuous, magnificent atmosphere – 20,000 to 25,000 football lovers on the terraces at Galatasaray, everyone chanting as one,' Veysel Giley, a former leader of the Galatasaray fan group UltrAslan, told me. 'That society has gone. Now it's the ones with money in their pocket, cigars in their mouths, a glass of booze in their hands, sipping alcohol who watch the matches – I mean, that's commercialised football. It's their product now.'

*

On 10 April 2016, Erdoğan stepped out onto the turf of the Vodafone Arena – the brand new Beşitkaş stadium. Lessons had been learnt from the opening ceremony from the Galatasaray game five years earlier. This time, the stands were empty.

Beşiktaş president Fikret Orman made a speech in which he addressed Erdoğan as 'dear president', 'venerable president' or 'the people's president' no fewer than thirteen times, angering many Beşiktaş fans with his obeisance. But Orman knows his football club had to exist in Erdoğan's Turkey. The head of the Turkish Football Federation, Yildirim Demirören, publicly backed Erdoğan in a 2017 referendum. In a political landscape divided starkly into friends and enemies, many influential companies and organisations know on which side they want to be.

Erdoğan's reach into the Big Three football clubs, however, is perhaps more limited than anywhere else. With their enormous cultural weight and vast numbers of fans, they are difficult to conquer. The AKP has thrown its weight behind efforts to create new teams, such as Istanbul's Başakşehir and Osmanlıspor in Ankara. On the pitch, Başakşehir have been giving the more established sides a run for their money – they finished second in 2016–17 and narrowly missed out on qualifying for the Champions League. But the club is a long way from rivalling the social clout and broad appeal of Fenerbahçe, Galatasaray and Beşiktaş. When I went to watch them play in the 2017

Turkish Cup final, they couldn't even sell out their 15,000 ticket allocation. And for Erdoğan, stepping out onto the pitch in front of the rowdy, unpredictable fans of the Big Three teams remains politically risky.

*

The real opening of the Vodafone Arena came the day after the president's carefully stage-managed appearance, when Beşiktaş played their first game in the new ground against Bursaspor. The game was a sell-out. I did not get a ticket. Still, I decided to go along on the off-chance. In the worst-case scenario, I would soak up some atmosphere and watch the game in one of the Beşiktaş bars.

By flashing my passport I managed to get into the cordon sanitaire set up by the police around the ground. It was here that I had my first doubts about how 'finished' the stadium really was. On a floor still covered in builder's dust, a huge pile of aluminium struts lay in the middle of the path. A man led his small daughter gingerly around it. Broken tiles, cardboard and wiring lay scattered everywhere. By one turnstile a chunk of the marbling was missing from a column. A bit further on I encountered a brand new turnstile, with its expensive system of cameras, alongside a 15-foot gap in the side of the stand that looked straight into the stadium concourse. Standing in the hole were three security officials, holding a piece of chipboard. The board only came to their waists.

There is a saying in Turkish: *Türk gibi başla, İngiliz gibi bitir* – start like a Turk, finish like an Englishman. It reflects the idea that Turks have enthusiasm in spades, but lack the methodical approach needed to see a job through (in news to me, this is apparently an English trait). As I inched around yet another pile of building waste, trying not to trip down temporary steps made out of plywood, for some reason the phrase came to mind.

Following the path I reached a large concourse with an open door at one end. After knocking and receiving no answer, I tentatively walked in and found myself in a corridor. Following it to the left led to a store room with more building materials. Retracing my steps, I spotted another door, standing ajar. I pushed it open and suddenly was hit by bright light. Glass walls on my right looked out onto the pitch. On my left was a buffet and bar. And, in my near vision, sat on plush red sofas, were three men eyeing me oddly.

It slowly dawned on me where I was. On the most anticipated day of the season, at a time when the terrorism threat was high, in the newest and most high-profile stadium in the country, I had just wandered into the VIP section.

No one expressed anger at my presence, more bemusement. I looked on at the well-dressed clientele. People were being given wristbands as they arrived and collecting free cups of tea and champagne. I wasn't allowed to stay. One security guard fetched another, who fetched another who led me to a door. He opened it and gestured for me to walk through. Behind me, I heard the clunk as it closed.

I was in a large, cavernous space under a stand. Hundreds of fans were milling around, the air abuzz with excitement. I looked to my right and saw fans slowly entering through a turnstile. The guard hadn't led me out of the stadium. He had simply taken me into the main fan section. Exactly where I wanted to be.

As kick-off approached, the terrace slowly took on that familiar feel: bodies packed together, arms round shoulders, vodka on breath. Finally, it was time. After three years of playing home games in the Olympic stadium on the other side of town, the inflated ticket prices, the glossy adverts and hype, here we were. Back.

The action almost didn't feel up to it. It was as if the actual football was too fragile and basic a thing to bear the weight of the emotion loaded onto it. The players and the crowd slowly eased into the match, as if tentatively testing the first planks of a rope bridge.

In the 22nd minute, Beşiktaş striker Mario Gomez rounded the keeper and . . . GOAL! In the next day's papers, there would be headlines declaring him 'the MAN who wrote HIS name into history'. It was rather bathetic that it fell to a foreigner who, two months later, would leave Beşiktaş for a club in Germany.

Bursa equalised. Half-time came. As the players ambled off, I realised the purpose of the giant screens at either end of the stadium: to turn the live experience into the television experience. The crowd in the stadium used to be the lucky 40,000 who escaped the adverts. No longer. Commercials flickered across the screen and boomed on the sound system. People seemed to respond to the cue and behaved as they would to adverts on TV at home. A man in front of me took out an iPad and started playing a Tetris-type game.

The second half began, and Beşiktaş started attacking the goal in front of me. Early into the half they scored. Fans fell over themselves, hugging strangers. I got a tap on the back. I turned to see the guy gesturing with his phone: 'There's wi-fi!' I looked confused. 'Free wi-fi!' A gap of a few seconds. 'Use it!' he insisted so forcefully that I felt I could not say no. He watched as I went onto the network. 'Thank you,' I said, not really thankful at all.

Another goal for Beşiktaş was followed by one by Bursa. In the 90th minute the score stood at 3–2 to the home side. The onslaught of whistling stung in my ears, like a thousand kettles coming to the boil.

Then there was an incident on the pitch. Beşiktaş winger Ricardo Quaresma was cynically fouled. He overreacted, getting up and pushing the defender in the face. A mass riot appeared to be on the cards as all the players waded in. I was waiting for the referee to deal with it all but then the Bursa players and staff started trooping off the pitch.

'The game's over,' said the man next to me. At some point the final whistle had been blown. It was hardly a fairy-tale victory, but Beşiktaş had won their first game in their new home.

Outside, the atmosphere was anarchic. The crowd from the stadium combined with the larger ticketless mass, just desperate to be there. Boys on motorbikes were gunning their engines and honking their horns while their friends on the back waved black and white Beşiktaş flags. I passed four young men crawling along in a caterpillar formation, shouting and singing as they made their way down the middle of the street on their hands and knees. This was one of the busiest roads in central Istanbul, now surrendered to the fans.

Walking through the chaos, I couldn't help but reflect on the disparity. The Big Man has exerted a tighter and tighter grip. A year later, Erdoğan would arbitrarily outlaw the use of the word 'arena'. 'You know what they used to do in arenas in the past?' he would say. 'They chopped people to bits in them . . . there's no word "arena" in our language'. Clubs would scramble to change the name of their grounds. Having been open barely a year, the 'Vodafone Arena' would suddenly become the 'Vodafone Park'.

But here was a wild, untameable mass of people doing whatever they liked. I reached central Beşiktaş. The square was filled with 500 or so people chanting at the tops of their voices. The ground was completely covered in beer bottles, cigarette packets and a mush of wet cardboard. There was a constant background tinkle of breaking glass, as drunken fans got up from nearby tables and staggered giddily into the nearby streets.

You can keep tightening people but there's natural energy to a crowd that can spurt up in unexpected ways. In modern-day Turkey, where people cannot congregate in large groups or speak their minds without fear of arrest, for many people football is the last realm in which they can breathe. Passolig tries to limit it but it still comes through.

I think this lack of control is why the government doesn't like football fans as a grouping. But this is why I love football: this unpredictability, that giddy, heady excitement of surrendering autonomy to a crowd. It happens at matches in England too, of course. But in Turkey it just feels more loaded with potential, both positive and frightening. That is why it remains one of the most interesting domains in which to test the temperature of the nation.

'I speak of a game that gives hope,' Erdoğan said in 2017. 'From the deserts of Africa to the Brazilian slums, everywhere in the world it gives hope to kids who life has shoved to the side.' He was talking about players, but football also gives hope to the fans. For those who are angry or worried about the direction of their country, the game is a chance to melt into a mass of people – to forget what is going on elsewhere, or to find the inspiration and solidarity to try and change it.

4

Izmir

The fire broke out in the Armenian quarter at lunchtime on a Wednesday. By late afternoon, fanned by a strong wind, it had reached Smyrna's waterfront. Flames licked at the stone buildings, the custom houses, consulates, hotels and theatres. By the next day, the entire city was ablaze. Half a million people were trapped on the quayside between the inferno and the sea.

On board the British battleship the *Iron Duke*, moored hundreds of metres away in the bay, the officers dressed for dinner. To mask the screams from the distant shore, the ship's band were ordered to play. When that didn't work, they switched to sea shanties.

By Friday, the fire had largely run its course, but the stench of burning flesh caught in the lungs. The water was littered with corpses. Three-quarters of the city was no longer standing. 'Smyrna Wiped Out' ran the headline of the *New York Times*.

The events of September 1922 were a humanitarian disaster. The city of Smyrna, one of the Ottoman empire's most wealthy and cosmopolitan, was reduced to rubble, its diverse community of Greeks, Turks, Europeans and others dispersed – many perishing amid the confusion and brutality of the final hours of the Turkish war for independence. The American consul George Horton captured the universally sombre mood. 'One of the keenest impressions which I brought away from Smyrna was a feeling of shame that I belonged to the human race.'

The fire brought to an end one city, its multi-ethnic and multi-religious history stretching back centuries, and began another, Turkish, chapter. The name 'Smyrna' departed with most of its non-Turkish inhabitants: henceforth the new city would be known by its Turkish title of Izmir.*

Walking down the grand boulevards lined with towering palm trees, a visitor to twenty-first-century Izmir might never realise this history. Today it is a buzzing city of nearly three million, smeared around the shores of a large gulf on the Aegean Sea. Located halfway down Turkey's western coast, from April to October it is sweltering. It has a reputation as liberal and laid back. The downtown pedestrian zone is crammed full of bars. In summer, people sit out in the balmy night air, drinking and smoking until the early hours, watching the lights sparkle on the far side of the gulf.

Yet amid the apartment blocks and the amusement parks, if you know where to look, old Smyrna can still be glimpsed. Nearly a century on from the fire, traces of the city's former identity remain, in the form of a tiny community and the sport that, many years ago, they helped bring to Anatolia.

*

Izmir is heralded as the site of the first ever football match on Turkish soil. But trying to discern when the first game of football was played in Turkey – and by whom – is a bit like trying to work out which grain of sand was the first on the beach. Across the Ottoman empire were groups of Europeans – merchants, sailors, consular staff – most of whom knew the game from home and enjoyed a kickabout.

One of the earliest recorded matches took place on Saturday 27 November, 1880 among members of the Kadiköy Constantinople Football Club in Istanbul, an association of Englishmen who would choose often humorous names for sides in their scrimmages. 'We saw the most enjoyable match between two teams, formed of the Uglies and the Handsomes,' a newspaper report of the game states. Among the Uglies was a certain Cumberbatch, almost definitely one of the

* The name Izmir in Turkish actually derives from the Greek for *eis teen Smyrna*, 'into Smyrna', in the same way that Istanbul is derived from *eis teen polis*, 'into the city'.

sons of Robert William Cumberbatch. He is great-great grandfather of *Sherlock* actor Benedict Cumberbatch and served as consul general of Smyrna between 1864 and 1876.

While Izmir perhaps cannot claim to have hosted the first match, it was unquestionably the most dynamic site of early football in Turkey. In 1883, Bornova Football Club was founded, followed quickly by a slew of other local sides. These teams were the brainchild not of Turks, but of a group with a special role in the life of the Ottoman empire – the Levantines.

The term 'Levantine' refers to Europeans who settled in the Eastern Mediterranean. The word comes from the French *levere*, which literally means 'rising', but also refers to the land where the sun rises – that is the lands of the Eastern Mediterranean, today's modern states of Greece, Turkey, Syria, Lebanon, Israel and Egypt. While Europeans had been settling in the region from the eleventh century, the modern meaning of the term Levant refers to the period from the sixteenth century onwards, when the Ottomans granted concessions to the French and other Western European powers. The concessions, or 'capitulations' as they were known,* led to the arrival and settling of Europeans who pioneered the growth of international trade between the Ottoman empire and Europe.

No place was as heavily settled as Smyrna. Constantinople might have been the capital of the Empire, but Smyrna was the main Ottoman port, and merchants flocked to it from across Europe. They joined existing communities of minorities already living in the city, foremost Greek Orthodox, but also Jews and Armenians. By 1900, 55 per cent of all Ottoman exports were passing through Smyrna, with the Levantines and minorities handling the bulk of the trade. The large fortunes amassed helped change the fabric of the city. Smryna's waterfront became lined with clubs, theatres and hotels serving the Levantines. Large mansions dotted its suburbs. Churches and synagogues went up in similar numbers to mosques. So diverse had Smyrna become that, at the start of the twentieth century, the Turkish population of the city stood at barely 33 per cent, a situation that prompted the Grand Vizier Ali Pasha to petition the sultan. The

* Named so because they were written in chapters, or *capitulae*, although the idea of acquiescence is quite apt.

Christians, he complained, had formed 'an effective and fatal superiority over Your Majesty's Muslim subjects'.

It was the Levantines of Izmir who played the first matches in the city. A picture exists – probably from the 1890s – of the first of these sides, Bornova Football Club, in hooped black and red jerseys. Their 'manager' was Herbert Octavius Whittall, part of the famous Whittall family that were at the heart of Smyrna's Levantine life (amongst the players are three Whithalls). He stands at the back in a jacket and bowler hat. The number of players in the picture – fifteen – is a reminder that early football clubs were playing the Rugby Union version of the game as frequently as Association rules.

*

Izmir's football culture was a microcosm of the city's cosmopolitanism. But its football teams also hinted at the rising tide of destructive nationalism that was to come. Following the example of the English Levantines, sides were largely founded along ethnic lines. In the 1890s, the Greek Orthodox community established the sports clubs Pelops, Apollon and Panionios, all of which had football teams. The Armenian community founded the team Vartanyan. The students and staff at various non-Turkish institutions started teams, including the American college and Evangelidis high school. Turkish involvement, at first, was limited to spectating.

Sides would play each other on the fields of Bornova, the small cluster of European mansions and villas located five miles from the centre, or at the sports complex by Alsancak railway station, acquired in 1911 by Panionios and converted into a football pitch. The Izmir football league is believed to have been set up in the late 1890s, before leagues in Istanbul, although the 1922 fire means we do not have the documents to confirm this definitively. In 1906, a team consisting of Levantines and Armenians from Izmir represented the Ottomans in football at the Olympic Games in Athens.

The Levantine community of Izmir still exists. Or, more accurately, several communities do, for Levantines were never a single entity, divided as they were by language (French, Italian, English), schism (Catholic, Anglican, Orthodox) and social class (there were as many railway workers and sailors as there were merchants and consuls). From a maximum of maybe 15,000 in 1900, today no more than 1,000 people in Izmir claim Levantine heritage.

These few remaining Izmir inhabitants are a fascinating and curious bunch. Many descend from industrial magnates and world travellers. Some can trace their family heritage in Izmir back 200 years. Some are married to Turks, others to Europeans. All are multilingual, speaking a mixture of English, French, Italian and Turkish. Most importantly, from my point of view, today's Levantines are still involved in football.

*

Andrew Simes is a sixth-generation Levantine – and football obsessive. We chatted on a Friday evening in Izmir's top pastry shop while around us upper-class Izmiris had their post-dinner cup of tea and slice of cake.

Andrew is, by his own description, an Englishman. But if you were to bump into him in the street you might consider him American, his accent the product of the American military school in Izmir. If you were to overhear him making certain phone calls, you might think him Turkish, a language he speaks fluently.

Like many men in their mid-thirties in Turkey, he is consumed by football. Unlike most, he is also obsessed with history. For Simes, history is not abstract or vicarious – its weight presses down keenly, reminding him of his responsibilities. His grandfather played for Izmir club Altay, his father played in teams against the British Navy. It was this history that, in 2008, drove Simes and some friends to establish Levant United FC, a Levantine football club for the twenty-first century. 'I felt like I'd be letting a lot of people down if we didn't,' he told me.

The club is a poster for Izmir's diverse past. 'We have eight Levantines, eight Jews and eight Turks in our team,' related Simes. They play against other local teams but also the odd match against sides from the nearby Greek island of Chios. Levant United has generated much pride among the small Levantine community, and many others in Izmir have welcomed its development. The mayor of Bornova invited Levant United to play the council team. In 2011, in the same neighbourhood where some of Anatolia's earliest football matches played out, Simes's side battled to a 3–3 draw.

I spoke to Simes about what it means to be a modern-day Levantine and found his answers compelling, argumentative and often a complete contradiction. 'I don't believe in assimilation,' he told me flatly. 'We've been here six generations and I'm not assimilated.' But then most of our time was spent discussing his love for Beşiktaş. He has a season ticket and flies to Istanbul every fortnight to attend. We watched a video of him and a friend celebrating the team's comeback to beat Napoli in the Champions League a few days previously. When I pointed out that his goal celebration was more Turkish than English, falling over his friend, grappling him to the floor in delight, he looked proud. 'Very aggressive!' he agreed.

'I'm Levantine and I'm English,' is how he sees it. 'If it's a national game, it's England always . . . On a club level, it's 51 per cent Beşiktaş.' (He's also an Arsenal fan.) Simes began to get up a head of steam, eyes shining. 'Here's the thing: being a Beşiktaş supporter is akin to being a Levantine . . . Being a Levantine, it's a minority. And so is being a Beşiktaş supporter.' His answer revealed the malleability of football clubs – how we meld and stretch their associations to fit the story of belonging we most want to hear.

In some ways, Simes experiences a more extreme example of what all minorities face – in Turkey or any other country – namely, a constant battle to fit in. He explained how he responds when people compliment him on speaking good Turkish.

'My answer is: "So do you!" And they say, "What do you mean?" I say, "Where are your parents, or your grandparents from?" Usually the common answer is Crete or Salonica, and I say, "Well, when your grandparents came here, we were already here for three, four generations. So I've been here longer than you have."'

But away from football Simes has found it difficult to continue the legacy of his forebears. He has been forced to quit the tobacco industry which sustained his family for three generations, and he's turned his hand to English tutoring. When he told me he would be busy from eight o'clock, I assumed it was a dinner engagement but when we parted he explained that he was returning to his teaching – another four hours from 8 p.m. till midnight. Another challenge is love: 'When I was twenty-two or twenty-three I was very curious and I looked at all the [Levantine] girls in my age group. And I tried to calculate which one I was not related to, because we all inter-married in the last two generations. There were about two girls that I could date.'

'Levantine' is a self-selecting label. There are probably far more Izmiris who are descendants of Europeans but who don't realise, don't care, or simply don't like the associations that come with emphasising this link. Those, like Andrew, who want to accentuate the 'Levantine' part of their heritage are shrinking in number – dying out, inter-marrying, moving away. By placing a hoop marked 'Levantine' around activities such as work, marriage and football, Simes is helping preserve the cultures and traditions of these unique communities. But the unfortunate corollary seems to be confining himself to a smaller and smaller frame of movement, like a fish in a rapidly evaporating pond.

'I think this is the last breath of our footballing community. Most of our youth are leaving for Istanbul, if not abroad,' he said. 'And then of course the way the country is going as well . . . not only Levantines but many Turks are leaving . . . So, you know, the future's not looking too good,' he concluded. 'But we'll continue as long as we can.'

*

The 1908 Young Turk revolution affected Izmir football much as it did the game in Constantinople. In contrast to Sultan Abdülhamid II, the Young Turks viewed Britain as a great example and inspiration. In sporting matters, they readily imbibed the Victorian edicts of gentlemanliness and moral self-improvement. Football went from being a game monitored for sedition to an arena in which Turks could learn educational discipline, and become physically strong and mentally tough. Turkish players – including those at incipient clubs Galatasaray, Fenerbahçe and Beşiktaş – no longer had to mask their involvement.

In Izmir, the culture changed first in schools, where sports were encouraged for the first time. A particularly forceful Armenian sports teacher and pool champion – named in records only as 'Melikyan *efendi*' (the esteemed Mr Melikyan) – was behind a lot of the activities, establishing teams at his school and arranging for them to play against the Greek side Pelops. Other school football teams were founded, and they began to play against each other.

Not long after, the first Turkish football clubs were established in Izmir – Karşıyaka in 1912, and Altay in 1914. This period coincided with the Balkan wars, when the Ottoman empire lost all of its European territory. The geopolitical events were a key factor fuelling the nationalism that was to consume the region a decade later.

Just like in Istanbul, early games of football in Izmir have subsequently found themselves heavily racialised, pulled into the retrospective weaving of the nationalist narrative: that Turkey and the Turks were the strongest, that they suffered great injustice and were always inevitably going to be eventual victors – both on the pitch and in the larger war for independence. And, like in Istanbul, the reality was more complicated. The team Altay – its name, inspired by a Turkic tribe in central Asia, an explicit reference to ethnic Turkishness – counted the Clark brothers, Edwin and Joe, among its players in the 1940s. Centre-forward Edwin was given the nickname '*bombacı Klark*', bomber Clark, for his rocket-like shots on goal. But judging from the local press, nationalism was frequently the preferred lens. After beating the English Levantine team Paxer 4–3 on 9 November 1914, a local newspaper described how the game 'swelled feelings of Turkish power'. It went on to lecture its readers to 'take serious pride in Altay Club, formed of young Turks who beat the English in the game of their own invention.'

Even so, a cosmopolitanism survived through the 1910s. Those Turks who were in Smyrna were often less conservative than their Anatolian counterparts. Many would drink, and copy the European styles of dining. 'The manners and customs of the city were as effective in changing mentalities as government decrees,' writes Philip Mansel, a historian of the Levant. One man who shares this idea is Brian Giraud, who hails from another prominent Levantine family. 'I think the Turks who come to Izmir from the east have been assimilated by Izmir, rather than the other way round', he told me on the veranda of his mother's home in Bornova. 'You find a special culture here, which is more enlightened, more tolerant, less religious than anywhere else in Turkey.'

The Girauds were at the centre of Levantine sport. Brian's forebear, Edwin Giraud, was a founding member of Bornova FC. Two Girauds played in the 1906 Olympic football team. Brian, however, is not into football. He chuckled at the memory of the time that Fatih Terim, the giant of Turkish football management, rented his mother's home for a family wedding. He had no idea who he was.

From 1812, Brian's family were part-owners of Oriental Carpet Manufacturers, a huge enterprise which not only dominated carpet exports to Europe but was the largest business in the Ottoman empire – a reminder of the economic power and influence held by some Levantines. It was on Brian's watch that the story of the company finally reached its end. 'The Pakistanis and Indians started getting in on the act, exporting, and we gradually started shrinking. And by 2005 we decided to close the whole thing.' He is now retired, spending his time looking after the garden, maintaining a nearby Anglican church and speaking to the stream of researchers who turn up at his mother's door.

At my request, Brian took me to the English cemetery in Bornova. We left the car on a road which looked too busy to park on, and headed to a metal door in a six-foot high wall. Large palm trees loomed over. A rattle on the door sent loud angry barks floating over from the other side.

Brian knocked on the door of a small rickety bungalow, built out of cast-off bits of wood and breezeblocks. A sleepy boy in his late teens emerged and Brian sent him into the cemetery to tie up the dogs. A few minutes later he popped his head out to give the all clear, and we stepped through the door into a small cemetery, housing perhaps seventy graves.

'Dry as a bone,' said Brian, a little embarrassed at the parched, dusty soil that lay between them.

'My father's there. My grandmother's there. My father's nurse – his nanny – is there. Anywhere I look: it's full!' But it was not one of Brian's relatives that I was looking for.

I scanned the graves. Eventually I found it. A sparse concrete plinth with a simple three-foot cross on top. 'In loving memory of James La Fontaine,' said the inscription. 'Faithful until death.'

'If there's football in Turkey, it's because of James La Fontaine.' The words of the cigar-smoking amateur historian Mehmet Yüce came floating back to me. The author of *Ottoman Angels*, an exhaustive account of football's origins in Turkey, had once regaled me with some of its best tales over coffee in Istanbul.

James La Fontaine was a key component in football's early organisation in Turkey. Growing up in Izmir, he was a founding member of Bornova Football Club and the force behind the organisation of a Greek and Armenian league in the city. In 1899 he moved to Istanbul and in 1902 founded the 'Constantinople Association Football League', the city's first officially organised league, along with his good friend Henry Pears. The goal was to set up a competition like in England, and La Fontaine ordered a shield from Britain to be awarded to the champions.

'They were a bit stuck up, these green-eyed, pink-cheeked English,' Mehmet told me with a grin. He related La Fontaine's behaviour at matches. 'James wore golf trousers and had a baton in his hands . . . The spectators were standing behind him but sometimes in the excitement they'd cross the touchline and he would say, "Back to the line! Back to the line!" Waving his stick he would push them back.'

After a trial season in 1904–05, James and Henry's team, Cadi-Keuy [Kadiköy] Football Club, won the first full year of the league in 1906. A photograph of the victorious side, posing with the winner's shield, features La Fontaine at the back, dressed in a suit with an unusually high, stiff collar. The second season saw the addition of a newly formed team called Galatasaray. In 1909, Fenerbahçe joined. This Constantinople Football League is the hinge around which the sport pivoted – from a Levantine-dominated pastime to the game of Turkish Ottomans. Within a decade of its

foundation, the number of Turkish teams in the league outnumbered the English ones, and the management of the league passed out of the hands of James and Henry to these new Turkish sides. The game, however, remained an upper-class pursuit, played by an Ottoman elite who shared its code of sportsmanship and amateurism. It wasn't until the 1930s, when the government assumed organisational responsibility, that football in Turkey began to develop mass appeal.

The declaration in 1923 of an independent Turkey, and subsequent decades of ethno-religious nationalism has led to a diminution of communities like the Levantines, people who are neither Muslim nor Turkish. The wars of the early twentieth century – when Britain and France battled the Ottoman empire and occupied Istanbul – live long in the Turkish memory. Today's Turkey is one of the world's top 20 economies, a country with a population of 80 million and NATO's second biggest army. Still, many carry a paranoiac belief that external powers have their eyes on invading. Persistently viewed as fifth columnists, many Levantines no longer felt welcome and departed. Those who stay find themselves minimising their public visibility. There I was, in front of the grave of the founder of football in Turkey, in a cemetery that has to be locked and guarded by dogs, lest it be vandalised.

*

Izmir football today is in the doldrums. Despite being Turkey's third largest city, for many years Izmir didn't have a side in the Süper Lig. In 2017 Göztepe returned to the top tier, but its other professional sides – Altınordu, Altay and Karşıyaka – remain in the second and third divisions. There wasn't even a proper stadium for the sides to play in.

Izmir had one of Turkey's most historic and atmospheric stadiums, the Alsancak arena, squeezed into a plot of land big enough for stands on only two sides. Football had been played on the site since 1910; the stadium that was in use dated back to 1929. It hosted the first game in Turkey's first professional league in 1959, and was the home to all four Izmir football sides.

In 2014, at the government's behest, it was declared unsafe. The stadium had apparently been built without foundations. As such, it was in danger of collapse in the event of an earthquake. The site was evacuated immediately. A year later, in August 2015, the bulldozers moved in. To rub salt into the wound, the TFF fined all four teams for not having a stadium for their games.

Locals are convinced the fiasco was politically motivated. Izmir is one of the few provinces in Turkey to return a majority for the CHP, the opposition Republican People's Party established by Atatürk. While smaller cities in AKP-voting regions have received brand new stadiums, Izmir remains without a permanent location for its teams.* They have instead been scattered to temporary homes – Altay and Karşıyaka are in the 55,000 concrete bowl of the Atatürk Olympic stadium, built for the 1971 Mediterranean Games; Göztepe and Altınordu play in a 5,000-capacity municipal arena in Bornova built for local amateur sides. The Alsancak site has been left empty. Locals were worried it was going to be turned into a shopping mall or assigned some other non-footballing use.

The original owners of the Alsancak land were a Greek team, Panionios. After the Izmir fire in 1922, Panionios relocated to Athens, along with the hundreds of thousands of members of the Greek Orthodox community who supplied its players and support. After their departure, Turkish teams moved in and took over the space. It's hard not to view the 2015 demolition as another example of a land grab.

When I visited in July 2016, it was like stepping into the set of a zombie film. The bulldozers had left the pitch intact, complete with goals and floodlights. Circling it was a ring of rubble and scree where the stands used to be. In old pictures of Panionios playing on the ground, large cypresses stick up from behind a picket fence. Today's trees are probably new but their dimensions are almost exactly the same as a hundred years previously.

At the time of writing, people's worst fears did not look like they would be realised. In June 2017, tenders were assigned for the building of three new stadiums in Izmir. Two grounds, in Karşıyaka and Göztepe, would be constructed by an arm of Rönesans Holding, the firm that built Erdoğan's giant new presidential palace. The contract for the Alsancak site went to a firm called Metro Inşaat, owned by the chairman of a small club in Isparta. Although it looked like the city would not be left without homes for its football teams, the

* Football is not the only sport affected by Izmir's anti-AKP reputation. An ex-official at the Turkish Basketball Federation told me the 2016 All Star game was originally scheduled to take place in Izmir until a call from 'up high' required the match to be moved to Ankara.

tendency towards knocking down and building from scratch, rather than restoring, is symptomatic of a certain mindset among many decision-makers in Turkey: an impatience with remembrance. A desire simply to move on. Accumulate. Grow.

*

A sleek car pulled up outside my hotel. I gathered my belongings thinking that it must be him. Sure enough, a call on my phone confirmed that it was Giuliano. I got into the front seat and received a shock: I was sitting next to a younger version of Roberto Mancini, all long hair and smiley boyish face.

Giuliano received another phone call and took it in flawless Turkish. An Altay crest dangled from the rear-view mirror. When he was done, he switched into English. 'I'm third-generation Levantine,' Giuliano told me, the accent pitched somewhere between Italian and Turkish. 'My grandparents were born here.'

Giuliano is the captain of the second of Izmir's two Levantine football teams, Azzurri. Established in 1994, twenty of the team's twenty-five players were Levantine. 'Now unfortunately we have Levantines but not a lot,' Giuliano said. 'Out of thirty people in our team we have just –' he paused to count – 'five or six Levantines. We have two or three Jewish players, and all the others are Turkish.'

Azzurri are different to Simes's Levant United in a few ways. Their origin was in the Italian Levantine community, as suggested by their name, which is the nickname of the Italian national side. Secondly they take part in the 'senior' league for players over forty. The new season kicked off the following weekend, and Giuliano was driving me to their final training session. But first we were to pick up his son.

He parallel-parked and disappeared into an apartment block where his mother lived and he was born. Ten minutes later I heard some rattling and a small boy climbed into the back seat wearing a Juventus kit and chattering in Italian. This was Dario. We picked up another player, a Turkish man called Birol who was equally chatty, before driving out of the city, up into the hills that encircle it. Dario kept asking Giuliano to change the music, which was playing Italian songs.

'Papa, numero cinque!'

'What's that tongue you're speaking? What are you saying? Bad things probably!' quipped Birol. It was a joke, but a telling one.

By this stage we were well outside the city, passing through scrubby countryside, parched from months of summer sun. We climbed higher still, entering a village. At its top was a brand-new, full-size artificial pitch. Below in the haze was the sea, shining, ringed by the urban conurbation, skyscrapers glinting like razor blades.

More men arrived. Soon there were almost thirty, laughing, joking and waiting to start. The training was disciplined: an intense warm-up followed by strict passing drills which, in their complexity, confused more than a few. Everyone seemed grateful when, after half an hour or so, the session switched into a game.

At some point I had a sudden revelation. Nothing felt unusual about the scene. The banter and style of play was exactly as I'd seen across the country. Turkish was the only language spoken. I wouldn't know who was 'Turkish' and who wasn't unless it was pointed out to me. After the match Giuliano and his son took a shower. When Dario came out he covered his crotch in shyness. 'Don't be shy, let it all hang out!' said one of the other players. He obliged, revealing that he was circumcised. My mind flicked back to Andrew and his comment about some Levantines 'assimilating' or becoming like locals. The current environment seemed to be what he was acknowledging.

But what else are you meant to do? Giuliano seemed at ease in his milieu. He had a family, a job in construction – a pretty good job, judging by his car – and a position at the centre of an active football team. It's a nice illustration of the challenges facing those who see themselves as different. My mind flashed back to the joke in the car. 'What's that tongue you're speaking?' But it's not like the UK is so different. I think of the second- and third-generation Turks I know in London, the intolerance that they sometimes come up against, and the sense that they never truly fit in.

In the second half Giuliano gave up refereeing and came on to play. Dario chattered to a few other small children who were watching their fathers from the bench.

'My dad used to play for Juventus.'

'What? No. You lie!'

'He did but aged twelve or thirteen.'

Just then Giuliano broke through and rifled one low past the keeper. Five minutes later he scored a second – a cute lob. Perhaps it wasn't a lie.

After almost two hours, the session came to an end, sweaty men traipsed off the pitch, got changed and headed home. Giuliano and his son were the last to leave. When they came out of the shower, they displayed the Turkish distaste for walking barefoot on the floor, using an elaborate combination of football boots and islands of dirty kit to move across the room.

*

Most people in Turkey aren't quite sure how to deal with people like Andrew, Brian and Giuliano. They speak fluent Turkish, have roots in the area that far outstrip those of many 'Turks', but who never fully act or view themselves as solely Turkish.

The more paranoid and xenophobic still see them as Trojan horses working for outside powers that are trying to destabilise Turkey. Simes told me of a rumour that the Levantines were behind the 15 July 2016 attempted military coup. 'Of course, five hundred people in Izmir are going to try and take over the country! I mean, we can't even put together a football team sometimes, but we're trying to take over the country . . .'

Their Christianity upsets some people, tapping into a deep-seated fear of the missionary in Turkish culture. Even innocent activities are seen as a front for more nefarious attempts at conversion. 'We've had the police come and ask us what we're trying to do,' Simes said. 'They came to one of our trainings and I as captain had a little chat with them. Nothing serious, I wasn't taken away or anything. But they got hold of a rumour'.

For many Turks the presence of Levantines reminds them of a period in history when they were on the back foot. 'We were not the owners of the country. It was the foreigners,' wrote the Young Turk newspaper *Tanin* in 1922. The advantages bestowed on them were certainly egregious. They were subject to their own laws rather than those of the Ottomans. They leveraged their status, owning the biggest businesses, the nicest coastline and the largest houses. It is understandable that this is a past that some in Turkey want to forget, and others want to emphasise.

But there is clearly nothing in this diminishing community that should make their present-day compatriots feel threatened. And it is hard to see the harm in making space in histories of the past for memories of intermingling and diffusion. Football can be the leading edge for such tales. Many people in Turkey can tell you Galatasaray were the first Turkish champions of the Istanbul league. Fewer can name their starting eleven: Ahmet Robinson, Milo Bakiz, Hasan, Horace Armitage, Fuad Hüsnu, İdris, Kiril Steryo, Celal İbrahim, Highton, Emin Bülent and Bekir, the side a mix of Levantines, Greeks, Armenians and Turks. A rounded history would recognise football's role in both sharpening and attenuating ethnic and religious divisions. Any story that concentrates on only one of these elements is like a jigsaw missing key pieces.

When he set up Levant United, Andrew Simes chose the logo of a phoenix, with very deliberate symbolism. To him, the black bird rising from the licking orange flames was well-suited to his efforts to resurrect a part of the community's culture from the devastation of the 1922 fire.

But what he did not expect was to receive the support of those who are not Levantines. Simes has been happy to find Turkish players willing to bolster the side. They now make up around 60 per cent of the team, and have become its biggest cheerleaders. 'They're actually very keen on preserving this heritage,' he said. 'Because it's different. It's not just another football team in Turkey and they're very proud of playing for it.'

The participation of Turks in Levant United is a reminder that this history belongs not only to shrinking groups who like to call themselves 'Levantine'. It belongs to anyone in Turkey who has ever picked up a ball, gathered together friends and headed off to play a game of football.

5

Ankara

It's one of those questions that often appears in pub quizzes: 'What's the capital of Turkey?'

Most people sense the trickery. 'It can't be Istanbul, that's too obvious.' But what *is* it? Brains are racked, brows furrowed. At least Brazil's attempt at a new capital sounds the same as the name of the nation – Brasilia. But Turkey . . .

The answer is, of course, Ankara. In 1923, this city of 30,000 inhabitants was chosen to be the centre of the newly founded republic. The Ottoman empire had Constantinople as its capital: one of the world's largest cities, the centre of three empires over two millennia. The new Turkish republic would be governed out of a small town in the centre of the Anatolian plain, famous for the angora wool from its rabbits.

Today, Ankara is Turkey's second largest city with a population of more than five million. It is a place of angular government buildings and wide concrete boulevards that crawl and sprawl up hills as far as the eye can see. Tourists never come to Ankara. Many Turks also try to avoid it. But this neglect is a shame, for modern Turkey is impossible to understand without knowing Ankara and its role as a place of blank slates and new starts.

'Ankara has always existed on Turkey's football stage, but never cast in the lead role,' wrote Tanıl Bora, football academic, publisher and denizen of Ankara. Just as the city is marginalised culturally by Istanbul, so its football teams are shunted into the background.

Trabzonspor have won the league six times, Bursaspor once, but no Ankara side has ever won the top division title in the professional era.* The city of Samsun – with one football team and a population of half a million – has a gleaming new 35,000-seater arena. Citizens of Ankara, with three major football teams, make do with the crumbling 19 May stadium, built in 1930.

I have been as guilty as many others in overlooking Ankara football. When I was working at the Ankara science high school in 2008, I was so desperate to wrap my head around Turkish football's most obvious elements – its big clubs, games in Europe, the national team – that I neglected what was on my doorstep. In six months living in the city, I never attended a live match.

Then, in 2016, I was offered a job in Ankara. It involved uprooting from Istanbul, with all the annoyance that entailed. But it provided a chance to make amends.

*

'To be a Gençler fan . . . I think it's related to the feeling of adapting to the city.' Başar Yarımoğlu, a mechanical engineer fond of craft beer and cycling trips, explained to me why he supports Gençlerbirliği. The club (pronounced 'Gench-lair-beer-lee') was founded in 1923 by a group of high-school students. According to the story, the pupils objected to the teacher's selections for the school team, so they rebelled and set up their own. This insurrection is immortalised in the side's name, which translates as 'Youth Union' or 'Youth United'.

Yarımoğlu is in many ways a typical Gençler fan. First, he's not from Ankara. Born in Western Anatolia, it was only in the 1990s, when he moved to the city for university, that he started to support the side. Second, he is middle class. In a city where nearly everyone is a migrant from somewhere else, Gençlerbirliği seem to attract mostly the white-collar newcomers.

The impression of Gençlerbirliği as a club for the educated has been around since its inception. When the side lost the 1929 Ankara cup

* Local professional leagues were formally established in 1952 and a national equivalent in 1959. Before then, many Ankara sides won the 'Turkish Football Championship', a knockout competition between the winners of the top amateur regional leagues.

final to the working-class *Imalat-ı Harbiye*, a Gençler board member exlaimed in disgust: 'Will the . . . cup, which Atatürk founded, be given to a team of workers with dirty hands?' One of the side's players from the 1960s, Tugay Özçeri, went on to become Turkey's permanent representative to NATO. Today, with the team a staple of the Süper Lig, it still carries this image of the educated elite, although thankfully with less condescension. Its terrace is small – a few thousand at most – but unlike any other in Turkey, it is dominated by students and professors, civil servants, members of left-wing political parties and trade unionists.

More than anything, however, what characterises Gençlerbirliği fandom is defections from the Big Three Istanbul clubs. 'I was a Beşiktaş fan,' confessed Yarımoğlu. 'But after a while . . . I found Istanbul teams and their fans a bit arrogant.' Attending Gençler games for fun lapsed into actively supporting the side. 'I was new here. I wanted to be part of a community,' he said. Every Gençler fan has a similar story of why they switched.

Fans can get very passionate about their new side, and often feel both embarrassed and angry about their former identities. 'We don't call them the Big Three teams, we call them the three Istanbul teams,' Kemal Ulusoy, lawyer and Gençler fan told me. 'As far as we are concerned, they are small.' Another fan refused to name the side he used to support, simply saying, 'One of those . . .' When I playfully pushed him, he exploded: 'Why? Why would I? It's irrelevant!'

In rejecting Istanbul football, Gençler fans are echoing a central part of the republican project's break with the Ottoman past; in order to form modern Turkey, the founders of the nation turned their back on Istanbul.

At first this was literal. In May 1919, Mustafa Kemal had to leave Istanbul for Samsun – a town on the Black Sea coast to the north east of Ankara – in order to co-ordinate Turkish resistance. Istanbul was occupied by Allied powers, the sultan and government forced to bend to their will.

Mustafa Kemal didn't choose Ankara so much as it chose him. The city was the furthest point west that he and his supporters could safely stay while fighting the War of Independence against the Allies and Greeks. Central Anatolia was the only salvation of the Turks – too wild, vast and unappealing for their enemies to occupy fully.

In this small market town, with Kemal at their head, the nationalists organised. They founded a parliament. They marshalled an army. And they started to push back the varying powers that had occupied the rest of Turkey: the Russians in the east, the French and Italians in the south, the Greeks in the west.

Kemal achieved a stunning victory, forcing the Allies to agree to a peace treaty, signed in 1923 which formed the basis of the borders of Turkey today. Though the Turks had won, the new nation of Turkey was exhausted, bankrupt and lying in ruins. It seemed better to keep the capital where it was – in the centre of the country, safe from the threat of foreign invasion.

From a stone house on the capital's southern slopes, Mustafa Kemal set about generating a nation. He was determined to drag Turkey out of what he saw as poverty, superstition and ignorance, and into the light of Western rationalism. In 1918, he revealed his hopes to a friend: 'After spending so many years acquiring higher education, enquiring into civilized social life . . . why should I descend to the level of the common people? Rather, I should raise them to my level.' He now had his chance.

Mustafa Kemal abolished the sultanate and declared a republic. As well as his drastic curtailment of religion in public life, Atatürk also changed the day of rest from Friday to Sunday. The alphabet was changed from Arabic to Latin script. Women were given the vote, and traditional hats – an ever-present reminder of one's rank and profession in Ottoman society – were banned. Reforms were made to education, the legal system and the economy. This doctrine later became known as 'Kemalism', after its eponymous founder. It stressed Turkish cultural unity and a westernised, secular society held together by a firm, authoritarian hand.

Ankara was to be what Istanbul was not: a self-reliant capital to replace the vestigial reminder of dynastic empire. In Istanbul you cannot move for reminders of the Ottoman past. Ankara was a blank canvas. The new city was built to conform with Mustafa Kemal's wider vision, with a series of German, Austrian and Swiss architects invited to design tree-lined boulevards, public squares filled with statues and government buildings with sharp modernist lines.

The clean break with Istanbul was more a figment of the imagination than iron-clad reality. Senior civil servants and reformers of the new republic were forever slipping off to Istanbul for the fun and comforts of the metropolis. The War of Independence was not fought solely for the Turkish nation, but in the name of a patchwork of Anatolia's diverse Muslim groups: Kurds, Laz, Circassian. Still, the dialectic stuck fast and underscores a strange paradox: the Turkish state shifting geographically eastwards in order to propel its cultural outlook to the West.

Gençlerbirliği was founded the same year as the new Turkish republic. Its name captured the youthful self-sufficiency of the fledgling nation. The new Turkey was going to be entirely different from the old empire from which it emerged. A modern nation state, maintained and developed by an elite who saw their mission as following in Mustafa Kemal's footsteps, taking their compatriots and 'raising them to their level'. And Gençlerbirliği were their football team.

*

I don't think I had met a proper communist before coming to Ankara. I had encountered members of the Socialist Workers Party faithfully manning their stall on a drizzly university concourse. Or sixth-formers who had newly-imbibed the *Communist Manifesto* and, flush with its message, declared themselves ardent believers. But someone who truly believed the revolution was coming? Never. Then I met a man I shall call Mehmet.

'I don't really want to be a teacher,' Mehmet confessed to me over a beer. 'I'm a football coach. Friends of mine, people who graduated at the same time as me, they work at Konyaspor with Aykut Kocaman. They're making good money. But the door's barred to me, because I'm a leftist'.

Gençlerbirliği fandom centres on bars and cafés run by leftists in the back streets of central Ankara, frequented by civil servants, embassy staff, professors and students. Think black paint, stickers on toilet doors and Led Zeppelin cover bands on a Friday night. As the generations who pioneered the republican project started to die off, the Gençlerbirliği crowd became campaigners for a different kind of change, one coloured by more recent campaigns of the left.

'But I'm happy,' continued Mehmet. 'Because in Turkey you never know – there's the possibility of revolution. In England, there's no chance.' He sat with a look of contentment on his face.

On the whole, Turkey is a country marked by strong deference and respect. But there is also a streak of defiance, a vein of resistance flecked with the doctrines of the left, which stretches back to the republic's earliest days.

The height of the leftist struggle in Turkey was the 1960s and '70s. In those decades political violence rose sharply as left-wing organisations were fighting a violent war, with both the state and right-wing groups, to bring about a socialist republic. Parts of Turkey's leftist scene were ultramilitant. Even today, there is a radical fringe that carries out armed attacks. In March 2015, a group called the Revolutionary People's Liberation Party-Front (DHKP-C) shot dead a prosecutor in an Istanbul courthouse.

The poster child in the late 1960s and early '70s was Deniz Gezmiş, a Marxist student leader and political activist. Ideologically incoherent, prone to what Christopher de Bellaigue calls 'xenophobic internationalism' and handsome in a parka jacket, Gezmiş and friends terrorised Ankara from 1970 to '71, opening fire on policemen, holding up banks and kidnapping American servicemen. Days after the last incident, the army intervened for the second time in just over a decade, forcing the government from power. Gezmiş was arrested and, on 5 May 1972, he and two friends were hanged. To this day he remains a hero of the left. 'If revolution in Turkey is indeed the longest marathon,' wrote the poet Can Yücel, 'he ran the most beautiful hundred metres.'

The 1971 coup did little to halt the violence. Leftists and rightists continued to pick each other off in ever-increasing numbers. Neighbourhoods were barricaded and university campuses divided. Ankara – with its many universities – was one of the bloodiest sites in the country. American academic Jenny White talks of coming home on the Hacettepe university bus one day and seeing a student smacked on the head with a sledgehammer. His body was thrown from the moving vehicle. He had got on the wrong bus.

The street violence came to an end on 12 September 1980 with another military coup. But the repression continued; 178,565 were arrested, most of them leftists, and many tortured. All political parties, associations and trade unions were banned.

Election after election seems to show Turkey as a fundamentally conservative country. To be a committed leftist is to swap stories of police beatings and spells in prison. But the sentiment, albeit a minority one, has stayed alive. On any given day, if you go down to the pedestrianised side street called Yüksel Caddesi not far from the central Kızılay crossroads, you will find trade unionists handing out flyers and being eyed warily by riot police. Try and buy a Coke at one of Turkey's many Nazim Hikmet Cultural Centres (named after another leftist, an imprisoned and exiled poet) and the waiter will give you a withering look – American drinks, like American politics, are off the menu.

In the 1990s, this leftist culture began to infuse the Gençlerbirliği terrace. It began with Karakızıl, a fan group whose name means black and red – the team colours, but also an invocation of the colours of communism and anarchism. Karakızıl was founded by Yarımoğlu and some friends. 'To be honest, at first we weren't trying to establish a fan group,' he confessed. 'It was just a couple of friends attending the matches and . . . we wanted to put a name on it, on our movement or what we do. In those years we were mostly related with the punk culture and things like that. We were producing fanzines and the do-it-yourself stuff.'

The reference to punk is apt. Joe Strummer – singer of the Clash – was born in Ankara, son of a high-level diplomat working at the British embassy. 'Ankara is one of the things that formed my identity, developed my musical style and always provides inspiration,' he recalled years later in an interview with *Rolling Stone*. This little-known fact is a badge of pride for the city's leftists, rebels and Anglophiles. The Alerta pub – another Gençlerbirliği haunt – has Strummer's picture on its door.

In the 2000s Karakızıl became more popular. 'It attracted people, especially young people, because we started to prepare for the matches, bringing the flags, things like that. It was quite new for Gençler fans,' Yarımoğlu told me. Gençlerbirliği fans see their terraces as more egalitarian and less corrupt than those of rival teams. 'We've never been banned because of swearing or bad behaviour,' Yarımoğlu said proudly.

Gençlerbirliği play their games at the 20,000 capacity 19 May Stadium. Built in the first decade of the republic, it feels like it's barely been updated since. Rust runs down the wall with the consistency and colour of blood. You have to pace the speed at which you pee to make sure the urinal doesn't overflow. The seat numbers are in spray paint at the back of the stand on the floor – unreadable to anyone but people in the back row. But it doesn't matter, because there are so few fans you can have five seats to yourself.

Not all Gençlerbirliği fans are political, of course. Indeed, there are frequently disputes, factions breaking away, the formation of new groups, as fans jostle and disagree about which comes first: the football or the politics. But for the most part, the matchday experience is peppered with behaviour that suggests sympathy with left-wing movements. When Gençlerbirliği score, the crowd celebrate with a chant with strong leftist overtones. *Bu daha başlangıç mücadeleye devam!* This is only the start, continue the struggle! In 2017 at the end of games the fans would chant for the manager to resign, regardless of the result. They objected not to his coaching but his occasional racist remarks.

The high-water mark of Gençlerbirliği fandom came after the Gezi Park protests in June 2013. Named after the park in Istanbul's Taksim Square where they started, the demonstrations mushroomed into nationwide unrest. Most of the media attention was devoted to Istanbul, which increasingly came to resemble a music festival. In Ankara, meanwhile, the protesters were on the receiving end of violence, with daily gatherings being dispersed with tear gas, water cannon, riot shields and truncheons.

'After Gezi happened, many left-wing people were extremely interested in the Gençler stands,' another fan, Orcan Yiğit, told me. 'Because they knew that even prior to Gezi, these people were standing strong about their political views and not allowing any right-wing shit to go on within the stands.' Gençlerbirliği were attracting attendances of 10,000, the stadium shaking to chants of 'everywhere is Taksim, everywhere is resistance'. But it was not to last.

After the introduction of the Passolig football ID card, Gençler fans were at the forefront of a boycott of live attendance. Overnight, numbers dropped to barely 1,000. Three years on, a small rump of fans were still refusing to go, choosing instead to watch home games at bars and cafés in the centre of town.

Gençler fans are also at the forefront of fan activism. Yarımoğl

and Ulusoy are founding members of TarafDer – a supporters' rights association. 'We established TarafDer because we thought we cannot save ourselves alone,' said Yarımoğlu. 'We have to unite across football against the 6222 law.' The association has links to left-wing fan clubs across Turkey. Together they have organised boycotts and filed court proceedings to repeal the Passolig system.

One case continued for three years. It went to the highest court in Turkey, which agreed the fans had a legitimate argument on consumer-rights grounds. But when they sent it back, the consumer-rights court threw the case out. TarafDer believe the decision was politically motivated – a product of Turkey's increasingly compromised judiciary.

The issue of protesting against the Passolig system gradually took a back seat as wider political problems in Turkey became more pressing. 'The fans don't care about Passolig any more,' said Yarımoğlu, somewhat glumly. From his office in central Ankara, Ulusoy captured the reasons: 'While there's so much lawlessness in Turkey, when there's so much repression, when the economy is going badly, unemployment is increasing, things like fans' rights don't seem very important to people'. His eyes met mine. 'Including to us, actually. We're all in the same boat.'

*

'As a terrace, we're ugly!' said the fan, smiling. 'Look, we have the ugliest fans. Perhaps only one in a hundred is beautiful!' He scrolled through Facebook for a picture. He eventually found one of a man who – it has to be said – was not the prettiest. 'See!'

The fan – I shall call Bilal – was cheekier than I expected, with an almost-permanent grin plastered on his face. I had gone to meet with the fans of Ankaragücü (pronounced 'goo joo'), the second of Ankara's professional clubs.

I had joined Bilal after brunch at Ankara's most chi-chi art gallery. After a short walk to the stadium, I was transported from a lavish open buffet being enjoyed by diplomats and upper-class art lovers to people shoving *simits* in each other's faces and shouting in incomprehensible Turkish.

With Bilal were two younger fans who looked to be in their late teens. One had a beard, camouflage jacket and cap that had a picture of a rooster on it; 'COCK', it announced in capital letters beneath the image. The other had longer hair, a bit of a leer, and brown boots that were flawlessly clean.

The leery guy disappeared into the scrum around the ticket booth to buy our tickets. Five years ago Ankaragücü were in the Süper Lig. In 2017 they were in the third tier, having dropped down as a result of mismanagement and bankruptcy. But there was one good thing about being in the third tier: match tickets cost 10 lira, around £2.50, and were not subject to Passolig.

My previous visits to the stadium were to watch Gençlerbirliği, who share the venue and whose fans barely make up one block of one stand. I was shocked, therefore, to see the stadium three-quarters full.

The crowd was decidedly more working class in feel, signalled by fashion styles, accents, haircuts and even dental standards – I spotted quite a few mouths destroyed by a Turkish vice: the continual drinking of sugary tea. The atmosphere was noisier and more boisterous than a Gençler match, despite being lunchtime on a Sunday. Fans jumped up and down with their scarves, hats and, at one point, their shoes, waving them in the air whilst they sang.

I was made to feel at home. The leering guy repeated some of the chants again for me, more slowly, so I could understand the swearing. COCK boy filled me in on which teams Ankaragücü like and don't like:

'Konya: enemy. Beşiktaş: enemy.'

'Anyone else?' I asked.

'Göztepe: enemy. Adana Demirspor: enemy.' He then paused to consider. 'Everyone's our enemy.'

The game itself was pretty poor. Ankaragücü had the lion's share of possession but did not create many chances. Close to half-time, the left-back broke from the wing into the box and slotted a shot into the near corner. Behind me a group of guys pushed each other to the floor. One of them, who remained standing, began kicking his mate – supposedly playfully but with quite a lot of force. It was not until the ninetieth minute that Ankaragücü got a second. And then in injury time a third. It was a win that took them top of the league in the first week of February. There was a crackle of excitement among the crowd. Maybe their side could go up this year.

*

If Ankara's first decades as a capital were characterised by the republican project, during the second half of the twentieth century it became associated with another trend: rural-to-urban migration. The city was to become a blank slate for other sections of Turkish society, a change that would transform the geography, culture and politics of Turkey for ever.

In 1950, Turkey was a rural country. Less than a fifth of its citizens lived in cities. Ankara's population stood at 286,000. Prime Minister Adnan Menderes was determined to end Turkey's subsistence, peasant-driven economy. He built new highways, delivered 40,000 tractors to rural communities and industrialised agriculture. Turkey experienced a benign synthesis of declining need for agricultural labourers at the same time as demand for workers to man the growing urban industries. Millions left for the cities.

When they arrived there were insufficient homes. Those houses that were available were completely unaffordable. Migrants would settle illegally, building their own dwellings on the edges of cities – on public or unclaimed private land. These dwellings became known as *gecekondu*, which means 'put up at night'. Ankara had more of these settlements than any other Turkish city – by the late 1960s, 59 per cent of the population lived in informal housing which crawled up the sides of its steep hills.

This mass migration had huge impacts. It fuelled the vast increase in wealth that saw Turkey leap up the list of national GDP. Politically, it generated a new class of voters as the 'old' city and its elites were swallowed up and outnumbered. Musically, it gave birth to the *arabesk* genre, a mix of Turkish folk music and pop, its references to death, suffering and hopelessness capturing the difficulties of life in the new squatter neighbourhoods. And this migration had made its mark on the city's football.

On a bright spring day, I went to see Ali Imdat, head of Ankaragücü's main fan club, Gecekondu. Before meeting him, I thought the name was a romantic imagining of the working class, migrant life that sprang up in the cities. What I didn't realise was that their headquarters would literally be in one of Ankara's few remaining pockets of *gecekondu* housing.

The building is easy to spot from the outside. It is painted in Ankaragücü blue and yellow, a splash of colour among the grey plaster, breezeblocks and tumbledown housing of the area.

Imdat grew up in this house with his six siblings. 'We spent many days here without electricity or water. But we're proud of it,' he told me from behind his desk. Imdat is far from alone: 'On the Ankaragücü terraces almost everyone grew up in *gecekondu* neighbourhoods so Ankaragücü adopted this name,' he said. For many years the stand behind the goal at Ankaragücü matches was nicknamed the *gecekondu* end. In 1993, Ali and his friends appropriated the label and turned it into a group that would become famous throughout Turkey.

Ali is not originally from Ankara. He was born in the Black Sea town of Rize, where President Erdoğan also traces his roots. He attended his first Ankaragücü match aged nineteen. The crowd at games is mostly like him, working-class migrants from Anatolian cities: Yozgat, Kayseri, Çankır, Kırıkkale, Sivas. They are the taxi drivers, small traders, soup makers and street sweepers who keep Ankara ticking over.

Like Gençlerbirliği fans, many Ankaragücü supporters have come to the side having initially held an allegiance to an Istanbul club. 'We have many among us who are like that,' Ali told me. He added seriously: 'This is nothing to be ashamed of. We haven't sold out our country or been traitors. We continue loving Ankaragücü.'

What characterises the Gecekondu spirit? 'There's a lot of sharing here,' said Ali. 'We make sure not to forget people. We like helping people in difficulties. But we've also been through difficult days. We see that as fate too'.

Another fan who was present provided a more detailed explanation: 'In the old times of *gecekondus* . . . in winter everyone would stay in the same room, because there was a heater. You needed it to warm yourself. Everyone slept in the same place. What did that ensure? Sharing increased a lot. When sharing increased, your togetherness increased. When togetherness increases, what happens? You become more respectful, loving and you look after one another more.' The communality of *gecekondu* culture translated easily into solidarity on the terrace.

What Gençlerbirliği came to represent for the middle classes, Ankaragücü did for the working man. 'Ankaragücü played a role in helping migrants consolidate their relations with the city and be called "Angorians",' wrote Bora, using the nickname given to Ankara – pronounced in the local dialect, the 'k' becomes a 'g'. 'Standing together behind the goal on a weekend afternoon provided a route into the life of the city. And the club itself became coloured by these peoples, its terraces developing a more . . . "redneck" identity.'

French sociologist Gabriel Tarde talks about crowds needing a magnetiser – a person in whom the mass recognise themselves, who rides their energy and triggers their potential responses. Without question, Ali is the Ankaragücü magnetiser. The fans love him. 'Ali Abi [Brother Ali] has become a star and a brand,' one of them told me. 'We need that kind of person. We need a leader. That's actually the biggest contribution Ali Abi has made to this tribune. He has taken on the *abi* role, the leadership.'

The next Ankaragücü home game I went to, I made sure to watch Ali. He stood directly at the centre of the Gecekondu tribune, perched precariously on the wall above the entrance onto the terrace. He twirled his arm, shouting, gesticulating and encouraging the crowd with an energy that belied his age. After the game, I was escorted with the inner circle into the toilets, where Ali *abi* was surrounded by four people. He proceeded to take off his top layers – first the outer coat, then the yellow Ankaragücü one, then a jumper. He took off a T-shirt, handing it to a fan, who began rubbing down his back. Steam rose off his hot skin into the cold air – Ankara is at an elevation of 900 metres and bone-chillingly cold in winter. He stood and shivered while the fan got to work, diligently mopping the sweat like trainers preparing a boxer in his corner. Then someone else handed Ali a fresh vest, which he slipped over his head, followed by a new T-shirt and then the rest of his clothes.

Be sure to whisper it when around fans such as Ali, but Ankaragücü was first an Istanbul club. It can trace its roots back to 1910 when workers from the İmalat-ı Harbiye munitions factory founded two teams. It wasn't until the 1920s, when the factory reopened in the new capital, that the sides merged to form a single Ankara club.

One of the things a visitor to Turkey – particularly Ankara – quickly notices is the centrality of the military to everyday life: men guarding buildings in khaki, areas closed off with high fences, angry red signs hanging from them, warning about the consequences of taking photographs. 'We are a military nation. From ages seven to seventy, women and men alike, we have been created as soldiers,' wrote Mustafa Kemal in a letter to his adopted daughter Sabhia

Gökçen, who went on to become Turkey's first female fighter pilot.

The militarisation of society was central to the republican project. Under the tutelage of Mustafa Kemal – himself an officer who made his name at the battle of Gallipoli – the idea of military service was elevated above simply war and fighting, and was instead presented as an essential element of the Turkish race. In 1927, military service was made compulsory. Ninety years later, it still is compulsory for every man. 'Every Turk is born a soldier' became a leading aphorism, printed in school textbooks and uttered by men on military service from Erdine, near Bulgaria, to Hakkari on the border with Iran.

The privileged position of the military is one trend at the heart of Turkey's difficulties with democracy. It has allowed the generals to play a tutelary role over Kemal's republican project, seeing themselves as guardians of his legacy. The years 1960, 1971, 1980 and 1997 all mark points in time when the military has brought down an elected government.

Football is an arena in which the militaristic underbelly of Turkish society is often evident. The national anthem is played before every league match, a result of the commemoration of soldiers killed in fights with Kurdish militants. Terraces frequently ring out with militaristic chanting: 'We are all Mustafa Kemal's soldiers!' 'Martyrs never die, the nation is indivisible!' When in December 2016, fourteen commandos were killed in a bomb attack in Kayseri, an entire page in *Fotomaç* – a sports newspaper – was devoted to the words to their 'commando anthem'.

Ankaragücü's entire history has been associated with soldiers and the military, as perhaps befits a club whose name translates as 'Ankara Power'. During the Turkish War of Independence, the factory was closed by the British. Its workers formed an underground resistance movement, stealing and smuggling weapons and ammunition from occupied Istanbul to Mustafa Kemal's insurgency in Anatolia. Until the 1950s, football in Ankara was dominated by military teams like Ankaragücü, their rough style and connections to the top offices of state frequently irritating the civilian sides. After the 1980 coup, General Kenan Evren manipulated the rules of the football league to ensure the team were promoted to the first league, on the grounds that the capital of Turkey needed a side in the top division. The connection to the repressive Evren regime, which put hundreds of thousands in jail, means that many other fans in Turkey dislike Ankaragücü. Today, the side's link to the military still lingers. Its full name is MKE Ankaragücü – the initials stand for Mechanical and Chemical Industry Corporation, a weapons manufacturer based in Ankara and the nearby town Kırıkkale.

When I finished talking with Ali, he led me outside the Gecekondu HQ and pointed to some graffiti on an adjacent wall. Blue spray paint on cracked, rough plaster, it was a reworking of a line from the Turkish national anthem. Composed initially as a military march during the Turkish War of Independence, the original reads: 'View not the soil you tread on as mere earth – recognise it! / Think – there are thousands without coffins lying nobly beneath you.'

Here, the words had been requisitioned, used not to turn Ottomans into Turks but newcomers into Angorans. In a neat, thin blue, the graffiti addresses passers-by: 'Hey stranger, View not the soil you tread on as mere earth – recognise it! / Get to know the place / This is Ankaragücü's home'.

*

Ankara also has a third football club. Indeed, in the mid-2010s, they were the city's most successful side, reaching the final 32 of the Europa League. If you go to their stadium, come rain or shine, there will be a hardy group of a few thousand fans. They will be chanting, singing, and wearing the purple and gold of the side. But all of this is actually a mirage, of sorts. For Ankara's most successful team is a made-up football club.

Osmanlıspor were founded in 2014. They play in a 10,000-capacity stadium outside Ankara in an exurb called Yenikent, a windswept new town in the middle of the Anatolian Steppe. There's one road in and one road out, clogged with traffic before and after games. Their name – Ottoman Sport – gives a clue to their politics. The team was the pet project of the AKP mayor of Ankara.

Arriving at the stadium one cold January evening, the snow piled up knee-high by the side of the road, I ordered a tea from one of the vendors outside the ground. It gave me a chance to get chatting to the two men next to me, both in their late twenties.

'Do you go to every match?' I asked.

'Yes,' they replied.

'Home and away?'

'Yes.'

'Wow, you're big fans!'

One of them looked at the other a bit hesitatingly before continuing. 'This should stay between us . . . we're forced to attend.'

It is an open secret, but the crowd at Osmanlıspor matches is manufactured, made up of employees of ANFA, a large private security firm that fulfil contracts for the municipality. The workers are required to attend as part of their professional duties, and fear of being sacked if they don't show up.

Armed with this knowledge, elements of the Osmanlı matchday experience begin to make more sense: the free municipal buses to and from the game, the atmosphere on them – no singing or alcohol – more akin to a commute to work than a bus ride to a football match. It's why many members of the crowd appeared so chummy with the security guards, hugging them or stopping for a chat – because they were work colleagues. Finally, it explained the lists: match-goers were checked off to confirm their attendance. The whole experience felt like an elaborate play – a cross between the *Truman Show* and a North Korean song-and-dance display. You were either working in security at the game or, if it was your night off, you were there in your yellow fleece, scarf and hat, cheering on a team that you don't necessarily support.

The man responsible for all of this, Ankara mayor Melih Gökçek, took charge of the city in 1994. He developed a reputation for what might be termed maverick behaviour. He became famous for his tweets, which were plentiful and always written in block capitals. One of his favourite topics was accusing the US of experimenting with a machine that causes earthquakes in the Istanbul region.

Gökçek had unique tastes in design and urban planning. In 2014, he spent 25 million lira – £5.5 million – constructing five gaudy ceremonial 'gates' over the main road entrances into Ankara. He spent around £1.5 million installing fifty small clock towers at Ankara's various road junctions. Large statues dot the city, including a Tyrannosaurus rex, a diplodocus, a robot and, my favourite, a 30-foot diving goalkeeper that greets you on the road from the airport.

The Ankara mayor also brought his distinctive aesthetic to Osmanlıspor. Outside the ground stands a replica of the Gate of Salutation from the sultan's palace at Topkapı in Istanbul. No one apart from the sultan was allowed to pass through the gate on horseback. At Osmanlıspor it's the entrance to the VIP section. Before and after games, fans are pushed aside to let sleek black cars with flashing lights go through. Standing either side of the gate are golden 20-foot high statues of Janissaries, the sultan's private troops. The back of the stand is sculpted to look like the crenellations of a battlement. Going to a game is a bit like visiting an Ottoman theme park.

Osmanlıspor began life in 1978 as Ankaraspor, a football team run by the local municipality. It is common in Turkey for local authorities to run clubs as a service for the city, especially in sports with limited commercial potential. As mayor of Ankara, Melih Gökçek was the honorary chairman of Ankaraspor. Under his watch, money was poured into the club with the aim of generating a successful Ankara football franchise.

But there is a problem with municipal football teams: they have few fans. Ankaraspor played in the top division but to empty stadiums. The only team in Ankara with a sizeable fanbase was Ankaragücü. Gökçek eyed it covetously.

In 2009 he made his play. His eldest son, Ahmet, was elected president of Ankaragücü. Ankaraspor was handed over to friends of the mayor as the Gökçeks planned to turn Ankaragücü into a title-winning side. The TFF, however, were not happy at this, seeing it as a breach of the rule that one person cannot be in charge of more than one club in the same league. Ankaraspor were kicked out of the top division in punishment.

Gökçek held onto Ankaragücü but the team's supporters turned against him. They had been promised trophies and high-profile signings. They got mid-table finishes and Darius Vassell, who made a brief cameo for the side in the 2009–10 season. In 2010, Ahmet Gökçek was forced to stand down as chairman and became embroiled in a long and tangled legal battle about his management of the club.

Under his watch, the club's debt ballooned from 22 million to 95 million lira, forcing its new owners to sell off all its players (including Vassell) and consigning it to relegation from the top flight. The following season, 2011–12, it sank again into Turkey's third tier. Unsurprisingly, the Gökçek name is still like ditchwater to most Ankaragüçü fans.

But a football-loving mayor can sit on the sidelines for only so long.

In 2014, Melih Gökçek turned his attention back to Ankaraspor, now competing in the second tier. The side was renamed Osmanlıspor – reflecting the AKP's nostalgia towards the Ottoman Empire, but with the added advantage of being the name of Gökçek's younger son, Osman.

The team performed well. In their first season Osmanlıspor lost out on promotion to the Süper Lig in the play-offs. In their second (2014–15) they finished in second place and were promoted. In their first season in the top tier they finished fifth, qualifying for the Europa League.

When he was elected in the early 1990s, Melih Gökçek was the first 'Islamist' mayor of the nation's foremost Kemalist city. He is from Keçiören, a conservative residential area. In many ways, he represents the success of *gecekondu* politics on the national stage. Those people cut out of the state-building process and subject to attempts to refashion them into 'modern' citizens now had their voice. Under his watch, the city changed in appearance. A large mosque was completed in Ulus – the historical centre and the heart of Atatürk's republican revolution. The old Ankara logo of a sun disk, a symbol of the Hittite civilisation seen by Atatürk as the forefathers of the Turkish people, was replaced by an image of a mosque.

This pattern applies to the country as a whole. Erdoğan's official title is 'President of the Republic', but he shows little love for Ankara and its republican symbolism. He refused to live in the presidential mansion, originally the home of Atatürk and occupied by the ten men who followed him. Instead he had his own, 1,000-room palace built on another of Ankara's hills.

Drip by drip, the Kemalist model of statehood has been eroded as the AKP has brought more religion into the public sphere. It has pivoted back to what it sees as an Ottoman worldview, with Erdoğan casting himself as leader of the global Muslim community. The process to loosen the tighter strictures of Kemalism began decades before, starting with the election of populist Prime Minister Adnan Menderes in 1950. But that does not make the actions of the AKP any less controversial among the staunchest defenders of Atatürk's legacy.

From today's vantage point, it seems that Ankara will never

overtake Istanbul, which has remained the country's hub for business, culture and tourism. Many of the capital's republican buildings stand, unloved, next to busy roads, dwarfed in size and shininess by new skyscrapers and shopping malls. While the AKP works to turn Istanbul into a global air hub, in Ankara you can fly to just twelve international destinations. Per week.

It's also true that, on the football pitch, the Ankara teams are further away than ever from countering the dominance of the Istanbul elite. As the commercialisation of football became more cemented, so the imbalance between Istanbul and Ankara was further entrenched. In this light, Osmanlıspor seems in some ways to be a literal embodiment of efforts to erase the last nine decades of history. A municipal team for a city generated by the republic now being named after the empire that it replaced and tried to ignore. A huge 'fuck you' to the idea of Ankara, its symbols and self-image.

But I don't think it is right to cast Ankara as a complete failure. 'Ankara suffers inevitably from comparison with Istanbul, but the new capital has its own beauty – a beauty made of sun, pale earth and almost limitless space,' wrote the journalist David Hotham in 1972. And, almost fifty years on, I think I agree. I find Ankara a far easier place to live than Istanbul; it is cheaper, more relaxed, friendlier. Among the sprawl and shopping malls, a culture of universities, monuments, art galleries and museums makes for an under-appreciated dynamism.

In October 2017, President Erdoğan managed to succeed where the opposition had failed and finally forced Melih Gökçek to step aside. With eyes on the 2019 local elections, the president decided that Gökçek was unlikely to win for the sixth time in a row (accusations of voter fraud – denied by Gökçek – haunted his fifth victory in 2014). After twenty-three unbroken years, Ankara's Gökçek era came to an end.

It remained to be seen what this would mean for Osmanlıspor, but the signs did not look good. At the time of Gökçek's resignation they were rooted to the bottom of the Süper Lig. Fan attendance seemed not to have grown beyond those compelled to attend. Perhaps the Osmanlıspor venture is closer to the project of Turkey's founding father than either side would acknowledge. The club's main import is not the shining success story of a new team, so much as a cautionary tale of masterplans imposed from the top. It is early days, but Osmanlıspor seem to prove that, although you can create a football club out of thin air, it is much harder to generate loyal fans.

*

Ankara's pride in its local teams is special in a nation where football is so dominated by the Big Three. I admire the size and passion of the Ankaragücü terrace, the obstinacy of the Gençler fans who drop their old footballing loyalties and embrace their new city. But much as I have come to love Ankara football, this new arrival will not be switching.

Beşiktaş have sunk their claws too far in. They were the first side I saw play live, my lens onto Turkish football. After being so close to the centre, a seat on the outer periphery feels too cold and lonely.

Simon Kuper and Stefan Szymanksi write about how capitals have less to prove than provincial cities. 'They have bigger sources of pride than their football teams'. But Ankara isn't an ordinary capital. It's not like London, Rome or Paris, where the size, the history, the grandness of the buildings seem to act as a brake to true change or real innovative thought. There's no chance of suffocating under history in Ankara – here it seems you can just change it, the way you can transform a football club from Ankaraspor to Osmanlıspor.

Maybe for that reason, Ankara football feels both more important and less satisfying. Like a frozen lake in spring, you can't put your full weight on it comfortably for fear of falling through. One year Gençlerbirliği get 10,000 fans and the next they're gone. Those who invest everything in their club take a risk; tomorrow it might be made bankrupt or moved to the other side of the city. An eccentric mayor might take it over and change its name.

So perhaps the instability in Ankara, in Turkey as a whole, is another factor driving fans to the Big Three. People have so much uncertainty in other aspects of their lives – their jobs, the environment, personal security – that the permanence of these institutions offers respite and calm. Governments come and go, but there's always Beşiktaş, Galatasaray and Fenerbahçe. There is a certain comfort generated by everyone supporting one of the Big Three. Even those who reject the logic are defined by it. Like it or not, we're all oriented towards the same lodestar. In football terms, at least, Ankara cannot eclipse Istanbul.

ARDA
7
unice

6

Arda

I knew I wouldn't be able to speak to Arda Turan, Turkey's most successful current player. So I did the next best thing and visited the street named after him.

Arda Turan grew up in Bayrampaşa, a working-class suburb on the European side of Istanbul just outside the historic city walls. A boy wonder, he was picked up by his favourite club, Galatasaray, where his performances in midfield led to a transfer to Atlético Madrid. In July 2015 he moved to Barcelona in a €34 million deal, making him the most expensive Turkish footballer in history. He also offers an insight into that little-known and under-explored phenomenon: the Turkish style of play.

When his Barça move was announced, the local mayor of Bayrampaşa was excited. 'That a child of Bayrampaşa should go and join the world's greatest football team makes us happy. We will change the name of the street on which Arda himself was born and grew up.'

Before Arda Turan had even pulled on the famous jersey, Ordu Caddesi, Army Road, in the Altıntepsi neighbourhood of Bayrampaşa had become Arda Turan Street.

'How should I describe it? It's Bayrampaşa's most *hareketli* district,' Birol Çalışkan explained to me. With slicked-back white hair and a small white mustache, neatly clipped, Çalışkan is the local official in charge of urban planning The word he uses means restless, animated, abuzz.

'Not many healthy kids are raised there. Alcohol . . . other things – it's a little troubled as a neighbourhood.'

Çalışkan's desk at the town hall overflows with maps and plans. I had gone to him for help in finding Arda Turan Street. Although the Bayrampaşa parliament passed the change and the Istanbul city authority confirmed it, no one had told Google Maps. As Çalışkan clicked through various architectural plans on the hunt for the Turan family home, we sat and chatted.

Turan's family originally came to Turkey from the Balkans. So too did the family of Çalışkan. 'Seventy per cent of Bayrampaşa are migrants from Yugoslavia, or the families of migrants,' he explained. Çalışkan has a theory that this is why the area has produced so many sportsmen (basketball players Semih Erden and Hidayet Türkoğlu also come from Bayrampaşa, as does Beşiktaş midfielder Necip Uysal). 'In the past – really really in the past – they played more ballgames in places like Bosnia, Yugoslavia, Macedonia, Kosovo.'

While the theories about Balkan sporting prowess are questionable, Turkey's rich historical link to the region is undisputed. Seen through Western eyes as the epitome of the Muslim Middle-East, the Ottoman empire actually controlled sizeable territory on the continent of Europe. The Balkans were a key part, but defeat in wars in 1912 and 1913 saw its hold on the region collapse. As if pulling out the wrong block on a Jenga tower, Albania, Macedonia and Bulgaria all quickly fell from their hands. It was, in the words of the historian Caroline Finkel, a 'body-blow' to the Ottoman Empire. Bloodshed, ethnic violence and devastation ensued, pushing hundreds of thousands of Muslims eastwards to modern-day Turkey, among them the families of Birol Çalışkan and Arda Turan. Many settled in the countryside outside the western walls of Istanbul.

Çalışkan told me that the location of Turan's street used to be a farm called Ferhatpaşa. Stand-out features today include the Istanbul bus station, the eight-lane raised highway, a cemetery and IKEA. 'In the old days people came here from other neighbourhoods to spend a day in the countryside, in the greenery . . . now it's finished,' said Çalışkan, with a strangely cheerful tone. 'There's nothing like that any more.'

Eventually, Çalışkan found what he was looking for. With a click of his mouse, he tapped a plot on the map to open up an image of an apartment block. 'This is the building,' he said.

'The top floor. And the one below.'

As we parted ways, he made me recite back his very detailed instructions for finding the place. They turned out to be absolutely, completely perfect.

*

The discovery was a little anticlimactic. The street itself was just like thousands of others in the poorer, far-flung districts of Istanbul. A public high school sat on one side; on the other stood apartment buildings, their street-level units given over to retail. The rolling roar of the motorway was ever-present, obscured by the buildings but barely 50 metres away. I wandered down the street until I reached the corner and my destination.

The apartment block stood quiet. Its yellow and brown tiles gave it a dated feel, reinforced by the Swiss cheese plant sat on the first-floor windowsill. A few Turkish flags fluttered from balconies. But there it was, the characteristic Istanbul red street sign. It confirmed that I was, indeed, on Arda Turan Street.

'My professional game reflects my background playing street football,' said Turan in 2013. Turan frequently talks about how kickabouts with friends in this area became integral to his style – skilful close control, based around jealously guarding possession.

Turan's game, for me, is redolent of Turkish football more broadly. Turkey has not exported a particular football style to the world. It is not Holland with its flowing total football, Italy with its defensive *catenaccio*, or England, famed for its 'passion', all heat and no product. Even its neighbour across the Black Sea, Ukraine, during the era of Valeri Lobanovskyi's Dynamo Kiev, gifted the globe a particular way to play.

But there is a Turkish style. I affectionately think of it as 'blinkered skilfulness'. Playing in Turkey, I am frequently amazed by the ability levels. Even those who elect to play in defence have a good touch, close control and an instinctive knowledge of when to carry the ball. But this skill is too often paired with a lack of awareness of the wider game. People do not play with their heads up. The eye is focused on the ball. Play revolves around a charge, an attempt to beat a man. Only when this attempt succeeds or, more often, comes grinding to a halt, will someone possibly pass. But not if they are within shooting distance of the goal. 'Shooting distance' is defined liberally – often it begins as soon as you cross the halfway line.

I find parallels with wider life. People do not make eye-contact on the street. They continually walk out of doors into me, or change lanes on the road without so much as a backward glance. It is as if in Turkey you are not taught to be aware of your immediate vicinity. On the street it results in bumps, on the pitch it means there's often minimal link-up play. I sometimes ponder this trend. Is it to do with a wider distrustfulness of society? Turkey regularly comes out near the bottom of global surveys on inter-personal trust. Perhaps there is little belief in collective division of labour because you cannot trust those outside of your kith and kin. Few seem to derive pleasure from things that would be considered courteous in the UK – holding a door open for a stranger or setting up a goal with a weighted pass. Better to put your head down and just dribble.

Turan is renowned for his dribbling but would no doubt reject the characterisation of being blinkered. 'Rather than score I love to set up goals, that's more in keeping with my character,' he said in one interview. His game is very much about assists. But former Galatasaray manager Michael Skibbe revealed that it wasn't always that way. 'He was an unbelievably good dribbler but after dribbling he had no idea what to do next,' recounts Skibbe. 'He was obsessed with dribbling. I said to Arda: "Arda, you can dribble but you have to have an end goal. When you get to the end, either pass or cross." He said: "OK, coach, I'll do it." And he understood. He improved so much that now he's a global star'.

Even today, I think it would be a mistake to deem him selfless. Turan needs to be *seen* to be setting up the play, with a dribble, some skill, a through ball. His contribution must be recognised and admired.

Turan says that his style stems directly from his informal games in confined spaces in Bayrampaşa. 'There was a goal on one side of the district. It wasn't possible to cross from the right-hand side so we could only do it from the left. Sometimes I would cross with my left foot from there but normally I'd cut inside and hit it with my right. The famous thing that I do in matches — that cross-pass shape — it comes from that.'

He was talking about the street around the corner from the flat, a quiet bend on a hill where Turan and his friends would play. It was quiet when I visited. Opposite the apartment was a small bread station, against which was propped a sign-board, exhorting people to save their leftovers with reference to Islam. On the next street, small children were crawling around on a carpet someone had pulled out of their house and laid on the pavement.

It was an afternoon in the summer holidays, but no one was playing football.

I walked down the street, taking a left and then a right, and emerged in front of what looked like a café. A signpost in the window declared that it was the headquarters of the neighbourhood football team, Altıntepsi, whose name means 'golden tray'.

Arda Turan's father is the president of Altıntepsi and can be found most days sitting outside the café among the men on stools.

'You just missed him!' I was told cheerfully by a portly man in a blue apron. 'He's gone to the bank I think.'

The man led me outside and introduced me instead to the coach of the Altıntepsi team. He was surrounded by six young men, who were themselves surrounded by piles of orange Nike shoeboxes stacked on the table and floor, glowing like oversized Lego blocks.

'Who has bought all these?'

'No one,' replied one of the young men.

'They come for free. From Arda's sponsorship deal with Nike,' said another. He then returned to rifling through the boxes, extracting brand-new pairs of football boots and cooing over them with the others.

Suddenly a large, black SUV pulled into the street, barely able to squeeze down the narrow lane.

'Ooh, the boss has come.'

The car stopped in front of us, and out of the passenger's side climbed Adnan Turan, who promptly dropped his phone on the floor.

'Goddammit. Mother—' the curses slipped out.

Turan's father was not what I had expected: he was more friendly, sardonic and potty-mouthed. The resemblance with Arda was striking – the same small, stocky build, cheeky smile and thick beard, although Adnan's had been bleached grey with age.

Bales of sports equipment tied up like laundry were carried out of the building and loaded into the car. 'We're heading off to training,' I was told by the coach. Expecting an invitation to join, I instead received a handshake and a 'nice to meet you'. But Adnan Turan kindly stayed behind to chat.

'There's no football in Turkey worth mentioning!' he replied mischievously when I told him about my book.

Altintepsi was Turan's first club. He started playing for them aged ten, before he was spotted by Galatasaray. In Arda's telling, the story of his discovery takes on a romantic hue. He had hurt himself in a match and went over to the touchline to get some ice. A man approached asking what was the matter. He then asked: 'What's your dream?'

'I'm a Galatasaray fan. I want to play at Galatasaray,' young Turan replied.

'In which case take this card and go to Galatasaray training.'

Turan attended a trial, was selected and never looked back.

The Turkish sports magazine *Socrates* presented a less varnished version. The magazine tracked down the man in question, İlker Akbaş, who had a slightly different take: 'I went to watch a match of

Altıntepsi. They were 7–0 ahead. Arda had scored four of the goals, I think. When the manager took him off he got angry. "'Why are you taking me off?" he started shouting. I called him over: "What an ego you have boy! Leave it off, let one of your friends play," I said. "But I love football" was his response.' Akbaş asked Turan which team he supported. 'Galatasaray' was his reply. So Akbaş took a scrap of paper from a Coke bottle label, wrote on it the name of the Galatasaray youth team manager and gave it to the young Turan.

Akbaş told *Socrates* magazine that he later asked his friend at Galatasaray about the outcome of his trial. His reply?

'My God, İlker, that one's straight from the devil!'

Turan struggled at first at Galatasaray. He was small and slight for his age. Today he still stands at a smallish 5ft 9in, although he has filled out. But his ability shone through. In 2005, the team's Romanian manager, club legend Gheorghe Hagi, gave him his debut in the senior team at the age of just seventeen, a skinny teenager on the wing. Before the age of twenty-one he was a regular. At twenty-two he was handed the captain's armband. During his captaincy, Galatasaray won the league and Charity Shield equivalent. 'It was a pleasure to watch him grow after Hagi,' said Sarp Tiryakioğlu, a Galatasaray fan. 'To see that kind of performance by a Turkish player when the majority of the time these talents are imported, there's a sense of pride.'

His time at Galatasaray also had blips. The 2010–11 season saw Galatasaray finish in eighth spot and Turan was frequently out of the side with injury problems. Questions were raised about his commitment, and he was accused of becoming lazy. Nevertheless, it was clear his talent would naturally lead to a move abroad. In August 2011, Atlético Madrid came calling with an offer of €12 million.

'I said: "Go son, go. If they give you five pennies, then go,"' Turan Senior told me. But others around Arda found it hard. In a documentary produced by Barcelona, his friend Egemen Türk tells how he and Turan's brother Okan cried when he left. 'Truthfully, it was difficult,' Turan said in the same film. 'A lot of people were crying when I went. I also cried. I had the opportunity to be a Galatasaray legend but I had other objectives, other dreams. I wasn't able to stay.'

*

Turkish football is a bit like its British counterpart, in that few players naturally gravitate overseas. The relative weaknesses of the Turkish league, however, means that for those who seek to reach the highest levels there is no real alternative.

In the post-war era, Turkey's best footballers have frequently made the move to more storied European clubs. In the 1950s a clutch of players, including Lefter Küçükandiyonadis and Can Bartu, went to Italy. Later came Metin Oktay, Galatasaray's most beloved forward. In the 1990s, Hakan Şükür spent a spell in Italy at Torino, Inter Milan and Parma. In recent years, Emre Belezoğlu, Alpay Özalan and Tuncay Şanlı have all spent time abroad, at clubs from Inter Milan to Middlesborough.

But frequently they flop. None of the aforementioned players managed to last more than a season or two at a side. There are no Turkish all-time greats on the Continent in the mould of other players from nations with weak domestic leagues – no Puskás, Cruyff or Shevchenko. There remain a few exceptions, most noticeably Tugay Keremoğlu, who became a club legend at Blackburn Rovers in the 2000s. But Turkish players seem to share the characteristic of English footballers in that they don't travel well. It's not me but Adnan that makes the connection: 'Michael Owen, he was at Real Madrid. You have one or two who left and became world stars. We don't even have one or two – there's Arda and that's it.'

Galatasaray fan Tiryakioğlu thinks that it's to do with the conservative nature of Turkish society. 'Not in a religious and political way but in the way people do things,' he clarified for me. 'I'm saying conservative even when it comes to food. People take pride in the way they do things and they're not willing to change. But at an international level you *have* to open up, you *have* to be collaborative.'

It wasn't initially clear if Turan would break the mould. But his transfer to Atlético was followed four months later by a far more significant arrival at the club, in the form of Diego Simeone as manager. Under Simeone's stewardship Turan blossomed as a player – becoming more hungry and hardworking.

The story of Turan's ability is not found in statistics. His time at Atlético consists of an average-looking 177 games, 22 goals and 32 assists. Turan is neither a winger, nor a creative number 10, nor a battling defensive midfielder, but somehow all three, all at once. He is a shape-shifter, a sticker-togetherer, capable of the moment of brilliance that turns games. For Simeone he was an integral component of his midfield, and part of the side that won the Copa del Rey in 2013, La Liga in 2014 and reached the Champions League final. 'Turan provides the *pausa*, speeding the game up and slowing it down, playing on his own time and his own terms,' wrote the sports journalist Sid Lowe in the *Guardian*. 'He has tremendous calm,' his team-mate Tiago Mendes said. Perhaps the most concise appraisal comes from his biggest fan. Simeone simply said: 'We need him.'

Outside of the webs and tendrils of family and background, Turan seems to have reinvented himself in Spain. Since the move to Barcelona, he has tried to drop a little Spanish and English into his media appearances, and with his big beard and sunglasses he has developed the reputation as a bit of a dude. Juan Rodríguez Garrido wrote a biography of him before he had turned twenty-seven, coining the term 'ArdaTuranizmo' to describe what he sees as his essence. Journalist for *AS* magazine, Iñako Diaz Guerra, calls him 'a hipster's Jesus Christ'. Writer Fran Guillén likens him to Lou Reed. 'He's different, special . . . you have to understand him the way he is,' wrote author and Atlético journalist Picu Díaz.

This is all news that will have many in Turkey scratching their heads. For back home, the image of Turan could not be more different.

*

In Turkey, most people do not view Turan as an enlightened hipster. Rather, he is seen as a boorish, egotistical bully, a symbol of all that is increasingly wrong with the 'Turkish attitude'. Even Galatasaray fans, who should be proud of him, frequently make the same complaint.

As the captain of Turkey at Euro 2016, Turan was at the centre of a dispute with the team's management over unpaid bonuses. The players apparently refused to train until they received payments promised for qualifying for the tournament – half a million euros each, more than the Portuguese squad would receive a month later when they won the entire thing. The press and fans were heavily critical. They booed Turan mercilessly after a 4–0 loss to Spain. As he walked off the pitch, visibly upset, he was comforted by his Barcelona team-mate Andres Iniesta.

Like all public figures in Turkey, Turan has found himself dragged into the political sphere. In this he is not blameless. Recep Tayyip Erdoğan was invited to his wedding in 2013 (later called off when he broke up with his fiancée). In March 2017, Turan publicly backed Erdoğan in a highly divisive referendum. Turkish actor Erdal Beşikcioğlu lamented how Turan had been positioned in the debate. He criticised him ('You are a national treasure. It's meaningless for you to take sides') but saved most of his ire for the wider public sphere which pushes people into camps: 'I've chatted with Arda, and he seems like a great guy. . . are we going to separate people into "yes" and "no"?' One fan complained to me that Turan was in 'the perfect position to distance himself' from the politics. 'He resides in another country, he plays for a non-Turkish club.' Instead he waded into the fray.

Fuelled by his celebrity, his behaviour has frequently crossed a line. In June 2017, after a goalless draw in a friendly match in Macedonia, the Turkey national team was boarding a plane to Slovenia. Turan was sitting in the same row as Bilal Meşe, a member of the sports press corps with forty-four years' experience. According to news reports, while settling into his seat for the flight Turan grabbed Meşe by the throat and said: 'Fuck your mother, your wife, your girls . . .'

He continued cursing Meşe until he was restrained by two team-mates.

That evening he posted a long, rambling 'explanation' on social media. Turan had been stewing over the abuse he received during Euro 2016 and proudly stated his refusal to tolerate insults to his family or his characteristics, neither of which Meşe had done.

TFF president Yildirim Demirören tried to get him to apologise, arranging a press conference for that purpose. Turan attended and promptly announced that he had quit the national team. 'I left the national team. I'm as light as a bird,' he said.

The comment drew near universal condemnation. 'The national jersey is not something you leave,' wrote the journalist Arif Kızılyalın for opposition paper *Cumhuriyet*. 'Don't forget, that jersey is entrusted to us from . . . the soldiers. When they died they were buried in white shrouds with stars and crescents on them. It is holy cloth left to us as a legacy from battle.'

Arda was hardly contrite. 'Mine was an honourable mistake – they were the dishonourable ones. They told me, "Go out and apologise. We'll sort it." Rather than behave like that, I've decided to quit.' His response was straight out of the refuse-to-apologise school of masculinity often associated with Fatih Terim, the giant of Turkish football coaching. Turan then promptly flew to Saudi Arabia to perform the Umrah pilgrimage.

In summer 2017, the newly appointed Turkey manager, Romanian Mircea Lucescu, travelled to Spain and persuaded Turan to rejoin the side. His return drew a lukewarm response. Old referee and football commentator Ahmet Çakar said angrily: 'He's a great footballer but after his disgraceful actions no manager should be running after him to Spain.'

If being generous, we can remember that Turan's tale is, in part, an example of the extraordinary upward mobility that football engenders. Turan has gone through a double dislocation, first socially upwards and then abroad. It has allowed for complete reinvention, but it must also cause difficulty trying to reconcile the different personas, all the while dealing with the enormous pressure of being at 'the World's Biggest Club'.

Cracks started to appear in the wall separating his Spanish and Turkish lives. Barcelona fans and the Spanish press reacted negatively to his support for President Erdoğan. Some see the egotistical outbursts and incidents as a defence mechanism, cries of frustration from a player who knows that he's not performing at the level he is capable of and is expected to reach.

By the start of the 2017–18 season, Turan's career appeared to have hit a buffer. His performances at Barcelona under Luis Enrique were mixed – a hat-trick in 17 minutes in the Champions League but also many games on the bench. In the summer of 2017, Enrique was replaced by Ernesto Valverde as Barcelona manager. Valverde made it clear Turan was not part of his plans. Galatasaray were keen to re-sign their young star. Aged thirty, after six years abroad, it looked like Turkey's most famous export might soon be coming home.

*

'Does Arda visit often?' I asked his dad.

'Hah,' he replied. 'Arda comes, but only for half an hour. Because everyone wants something'. I had clearly touched a sore spot. 'As soon as he comes he's given letters. They come one after the other from all sides, they are like beggars!'

Turan does support the community where he grew up. Apparently, he pays the utility bills for struggling neighbours, and I had witnessed first hand the fruits of his support at the Altıntepsi football team. 'Thanks to Arda, some pennies are coming in,' Adnan Turan told me. 'Nike are sponsoring us. Otherwise the door would be locked, and we would have to give the key to the local council.' He wishes there was more interest from the authorities in grassroots sport. 'No one gives any help. There's no interest.'

Nearly all Turan's off-the-pitch incidents have occurred when on duty for the national team. It's almost as if those who know him best see through the foreign languages and fashionable baubles. Turan falls back in with the old crowd he's outgrown. It is possible that he is frustrated with the Turkish style of management, like the precocious student returned home from university for Christmas, only to find his old friends hopelessly parochial and unsophisticated.

His ambition appears to extend far beyond playing. He has said in the past that he would like to become president of the Turkish Football Federation. His father suggested the same thing. 'Arda will either become Galatasaray president or join the management at Galatasaray,' he said. 'Or TFF president or UEFA president. His targets are big.' Maybe that helps to explain the clumsy interventions in politics.

But for now he is still playing. And many fans in Turkey are frustrated that, when Turan is mentioned, people no longer talk about the football. 'Am I happy with all the news flicking around? No, not really . . . [but] am I still a fan? Yes, at present,' Tiryakioğlu told me. 'He's a special player . . . when you have that talent and creativity, it's a delight to watch.'

*

The evening of my trip to visit Arda Turan Street, I took part in my new five-a-side game. Two weeks previously it had gone well – I scored two goals and we won 3–2. But this time, my side got a thrashing.

No one passed to me. I spent the hour watching unsuccessful dribbles, passing balls I never got back, standing in empty space.

Afterwards in the dressing room, I paid my fee to my friend who had arranged the game. 'You're welcome any time!' he said cheerfully. Incapable of containing my frustration, but keen not to offend, I blurted out: 'I don't think I'm used to the Turkish style yet.' Everyone broke out in giggles.

'Dribble dribble!' said another player in the dressing room. He then paused, eyes shining: 'Everybody wants to be Arda.'

7

Ordinaryüs

The ferry was full of warm autumn light. Istanbul's European side slowly receded as we moved out into the sea. With the commotion of boarding over, the rhythmic thud of the engine soothed the passengers into silence. Dust motes played in the shafts of light.

Suddenly, a school of dolphins arrived alongside. Day-trippers rushed to the windows, cameras flashing, trying to capture them. But they retreated as quickly as they appeared, fading into distant humps and plops in the sea.

The ferry called in turn at four islands, small outcrops that grew in size the further you moved away from the city. In English they are known as the Princes' Islands. In Turkish they are just 'the Islands'. The people who have called them home for hundreds of years have other names for them – Proti, Antigoni, Chalki, Prinkipo – exotic consonants that catch and stick in a Turkish-speaking mouth. By the time the boat pulled into its fourth and final stop at Büyükada, The Great Island, the crowd had dwindled to a rump.

The staff moved like clockwork, tossing the thick ropes around the bollards on the quay. The captain put the ship into reverse and the ropes started to tense and creak, guiding the boat softly and carefully to the side.

Stepping ashore and unsure quite who to speak to, I approached the sleepy tourist-information booth and asked for the priest whose name I had been given.

I was led silently across the way to a small bookshop occupying a corner of the ferry terminal. A man in his sixties with a bushy moustache and a flat-cap introduced himself as Mikael. I repeated my question. Mikael's son sidled up, pulled out his phone and called the priest.

'*Kalimera*,' he said, using the Greek for 'good morning', before continuing in Turkish. He handed the phone to me. On the other end I heard the voice I had spoken to earlier in the week, fluent in Turkish but with an accent.

'The cemetery is open,' he said. 'You can go whenever.'

*

I propped my rented bike against the wall and surveyed the scene. The graveyard sat on a slope, perhaps 50 metres above the sea. It lay in the bend of the two main routes around the island. Every five minutes, a horse and cart trundled past with the sound of jingling bells and clattering hooves. No cars are allowed on the islands. The only motorised vehicles I saw were a police car and a rubbish truck.

I pushed open the gate and walked in. A movement metres away in the bush caught my eye – a man was doing some pruning. As I progressed a bit further he noticed me. He offered a loud *buyurun* – 'at your service!' The tone twisted the word from entreaty to scrutiny.

As he approached I saw it was the gardener. Hanging at his waist was a large knife in a scabbard. After coming closer, his demeanour softened. 'Ah yes, I've been expecting you,' he said, and introduced himself as Yusuf.

We walked down the main path and round the side of the hill. Graves littered the slope above and below. Yusuf talked continuously.

'We get lots of people. Tourists,' he said. 'But we don't let them in. They come in, they tamper with things, stomp about, leave litter . . .' He was warming to the role of grumpy groundkeeper as we picked our way through the headstones. '. . . and they don't show the right respect. Anyway, here we are.'

We came to a stop at a grave in grey speckled marble. Sharp edges and a shiny surface suggested it has not been here long. I studied the inscription but could not understand the lettering. I moved round to the back. Here, set into the stone, was a blue plaque which I could make out: 'Fenerbahçe's "Ordinariyus" Lefter Küçükandonyadis'.

Lefter, as he is universally known, is Fenerbahçe's most famous player. A striker, he played for the club from the late 1940s to the 1960s. Though he stood at just 5ft 7in, he was possessed of exceptional strength, skill and sense of positioning. He scored hundreds of goals, almost single-handedly powering the team to cup and league success. Lefter played for the national team more than 50 times, and was one of the first Turkish citizens to earn a transfer to play abroad. He is not only a legend of Fenerbahçe, but one of the greatest to have ever played in Turkey, adored by football lovers across the country. And the interesting thing: Lefter was not considered fully, or exactly, Turkish. Lefter was a Rum.

Lefter was born 'Eleftherios' in 1924, the son of a Büyükada fisherman called Christofis and a tailor called Argyro. His family was part of Turkey's Greek-speaking Orthodox community, a minority that called themselves Romans – *Rumlar* – and could trace their lineage in the city back 2,700 years.

Around the time Lefter was born, there was a sizeable number of Greek speakers in Istanbul – more than 200,000 people, or approximately a fifth of the city's population. They played a prominent role in its day-to-day life – 1,169 of the city's 1,413 restaurants were owned by Rums. The Greek patriarch – the spiritual leader of Greek Orthodox believers across the world – was based at a cathedral in Fener, a waterside district on the Bosphorus inlet known as the Golden Horn. The main district at the heart of Istanbul, engulfing Istiklal Caddesi, is still known as Pera, its Greek name, reflecting the vivid presence of the Rum community who lived there.

In the years before Lefter's birth, over 1.2 million Rum Orthodox Christians in Anatolia were compulsorily removed and 'returned' to Greece, while 400,000 Muslims from Greece came the other way. The justification for the 'exchange' was to protect minorities from reprisals – a final wave of ethnic and religious separation following the genocide, tension and nationalism unleashed by the First World War. Yet the law was written as if it was simple and straightforward to distinguish between Greek Christians and Muslims. Many had never visited nor spoke the language of the 'homeland' to which they were 'returning'. Although Istanbul and the Princes' Islands were exempt from this process, some Istanbul Rums moved voluntarily to Greece, fearing reprisals in the new nation state of Turkey. But Lefter's family stayed put. They were poor – by the age of twelve he was working full-time. Perhaps they could not afford to leave.

Lefter showed footballing promise from an early age, obsessively playing with a ball made by his mother out of old socks. He was such a talented footballer that his first club, Taksim, altered his ID card to make him seem two years older in order to get him a professional footballer's licence. He found the adjustment to adult football difficult at first. 'I spent the first fifteen minutes just watching as the ball whizzed to my left and right,' he later recalled, looking back to one of his early games. 'There was a terrifying difference from the football that we played in the neighbourhood.' With encouragement from the coach, however, he began to get the hang of the rough-and-tumble style at a time when the game was dominated by big and burly players. He scored four goals in his first season with Taksim, five in his second.

But it was at Fenerbahçe that he made his name. Between 1947 and 1964, Lefter made 615 appearances for the club, the second-highest total of any Fenerbahçe player. His career bridged two eras in Turkish football, as the game shifted from amateur to professional. In his eleven years at the club, he scored 423 goals, helping them to become champions – first of Istanbul and then, when the national league was established in 1959, of all of Turkey.

Those who played with him describe an extraordinary talent. 'Lefter had a style of play that meant that you couldn't take your eyes off him,' said his Fenerbahçe team-mate Yüksel Gündüz. 'He was incredibly competitive and technical. He was great at free kicks . . . He had an extremely athletic frame. He almost never got injured. He was a man with the spirit of a boy.'

Lefter was frequently compared to dribbling winger Stanley Matthews, one of Britain's greatest footballers. 'Even if it was possible to fit the ball in the palm of my hand, he'd find a way of nicking it and dribbling on,' wrote Vittorio Pozzo, World Cup-winning football manager for Italy, who watched Lefter in the 1950s. His supreme ability led to his nickname 'Ordinaryüs', which looks similar to the English 'ordinary', but is actually the old Turkish term – by way of German – for 'professor'.

Lefter inspired the Turkish national team to one of its greatest successes: a 3–1 victory at Mithatpaşa stadium over Hungary on 19 February 1956. This was the Hungary side dubbed the 'Magnificent Magyars' – the team that thumped England 6–3 at Wembley in 1953 and narrowly lost to West Germany in the 1954 World Cup final.

They were generally considered the best side in the world, with the world's best player in Ferenc Puskás. But they were 2–0 down after 42 minutes after two goals from Lefter: a shot from the edge of the area and a penalty after he was tripped up.

Following the Second World War and the resumption of football on the Continent, Lefter was one of the first footballers in Turkey to play abroad. He went first to Fiorentina (1951–52) and then Nice (1952–53). There is black-and-white footage from his time in Italy, with the commentator referring to Lefter as 'il Turco', seemingly unaware of his true heritage.

Lefter's skill and his fame were so great that he became a cultural icon well beyond the realms of football. His name featured widely in Turkey's blossoming domestic film industry, known as Yeşilçam cinema, in the 1950s and '60s. And he was the subject of chants and poems, such as the one penned in 1960 by Bedri Rahmi Eyüboğlu:

When you say 'Istanbul' what comes to mind
Is the stadium
I feel my blood warmly mingle
With the people of my country
I want to move closer to them
And I'll join them in shouting
Until my voice gives out
While my breast swells
'Pass the ball to Lefter and it's a done deal!'

*

'We're not a museum, we're a cemetery.'

Yusuf was still talking.

'We get people all the time who come to look at his grave. Some weeks one, some weeks ten. On holidays, we have more than ten.'

'So you let them in, the Fenerbahçe fans?'

'Yes, we do.'

'But you said you only allow in people who have relatives here?'

'We let them in, but they have to be respectful. They want to take pictures, say some prayers and then they— oh, what have they done! See, they mess with it!' He suddenly interrupted himself to pick up a lantern sitting on top of a grave that was lying on its side.

'It could be animals?' I tentatively suggested squirrels.

'We don't have squirrels here,' he said, furrowing his brow as he puzzled over who has knocked it down.

The cemetery was almost silent except for the distant chug of a boat. The weather was beautiful: not a cloud in the sky, the late autumn sun slanting through the cluster of pine and cypress trees. On the horizon was the sprawl of Istanbul. Twenty metres below us, a horse and cart went past on the road. I heard the driver shout his tourist spiel to the passengers.

'See the flag, that's Lefter's grave'.

I missed the passenger's response but heard the driver again. 'That flagpole – yes, right there!' Next to the grave stands an eight-foot flagpole with a blue-and-yellow Fenerbahçe flag, hanging limp in the still air.

I slowly made my way back to Yusuf, who had retired to a bench on the path. As we walked back towards the gate, I asked him if anyone else famous was buried here.

'There's another footballer, last name was Kasapoğlu. He played for Istanbulspor.'

'Did he and Lefter know each other?'

Bilemiyorum ki! 'How can I know!' Yusuf replied. Yusuf answered a lot of questions '*bilemiyorum*'. Turkish is a very particular language, in that people frequently make a distinction between 'I don't know' and 'I can't know'. The latter expresses an inability of the person in question to have access to the information. When we moved onto matters theological, it became Yusuf's favourite word.

He led me to a lump of overturned earth – it looked like scree from a building site.

'Ah, the picture's going,' he said, as he picked up a framed image of a silver-haired man in an Istanbulspor T-shirt, waving with a big smile from what looked like a hospital bed. The top quarter had peeled away, probably a result of weather damage. His face was still visible, precariously close to the rotting edge.

'The family didn't come, we just did this,' he said, gesturing at the freshly dug mound.

'I don't even know his first name,' Yusuf confessed. 'And there's no plaque to say. Just this,' he said, picking up a band inscribed with the words 'Istanbulspor club legend', equally weather damaged. 'Most graves have at least a cross,' said Yusuf, lamenting the lack of presentation. 'But that's not our responsibility,' he added defensively.

'Two footballers, one whose career was at the top, one whose was at a lower level,' sighed Yusuf.

But for all his goals and creative flourishes, at times it was not Lefter's skill that people saw.

*

On the night of 6–7 September 1955, an anti-Greek pogrom erupted in Istanbul. At first it appeared to be a spontaneous protest triggered by a bomb attack on the Turkish consulate in Thessaloniki (located next to the house that was the birthplace of Atatürk). Later it emerged that it had been planned by the government and executed by elements of the shadowy Turkish 'deep state' in order to distract attention from the government's political problems. Mobs looted shops, burned houses, vandalised churches and attacked members of Istanbul's non-Muslim communities.

The rampage extended to Büyükada. Looters arrived at Lefter's house while he was in the process of putting his children to bed. They hurled stones. They shouted: 'Hit the *gavur*!' – a derogatory term for a non-Muslim. Lefter waited inside clutching a weapon, hoping they would move on. They eventually did.

Over the course of two days of rioting, at least a dozen Greeks and Armenians were killed, an estimated 200 women were raped and hundreds of others were wounded. The events of September 1955 shook Istanbul's Greek Orthodox community to the core.

When the Fenerbahçe goalkeeper Şükrü Ersoy heard what had happened to Lefter, he gathered teammates and boarded a boat to the island. A group of Fenerbahçe fans also made the journey independently.

'Who did this? Give the order, Lefter brother, and we'll put them in their place,' they demanded of him. Lefter was captain of Fenerbahçe and a key member of the national team. His treatment at the hands of the mob was an embarrassment. Club officials and government ministers pushed Lefter for the names. Lefter knew exactly who the perpetrators were but he refused to give them up. He would remain reluctant to talk about it for the rest of his life.

'Only one or two people did this,' he explained years later in a rare exception. 'The whole nation shouldn't be tarred with the same brush.'

Less than ten years after the pogrom, the Istanbul Rum community was hit with another blow. Without warning, in 1964 the Turkish government cancelled the residence permits of Greek nationals living in Turkey. Around 12,000 people who had never acquired Turkish citizenship were given two weeks to leave. They were told that they could only take 22 dollars and 20 kilos of belongings with them. Their remaining property was seized. As Turkish citizens, Lefter and his family were spared.

But that was not the end of it. In May 1974, at a time of heightened tension with Greece over the island of Cyprus, the Turkish government passed a law that forbade non-Turks from owning property. Four months later, Lefter was called to the police station on Büyükada in relation to a disagreement between him and another man over the sale of a flat.

According to newspaper reports, his adversary, his lawyer and a police team were present. They swore at Lefter and manhandled him. One of the police invoked the 1919 Greek defeat in the Turkish War of Independence. 'Look, buddy,' he reportedly said. 'We plucked you out of Anatolia and dumped you in the sea at Izmir. So we'll chuck you out from here.' After replying that he was a Turkish citizen, Lefter – by this time forty-nine years old – was given two slaps.

Lefter's mistreatment was universally condemned. Even the prime minister, Bülent Ecevit, waded in: 'If the incident is because of his Greekness and Lefter was hit then this man will immediately be fired.' But it is worth noting the reasoning behind some of the criticism of Lefter's mistreatment. The incident was condemned not because it was racist, but because Lefter was 'one of us'. 'Lefter's not a *gavur*,' said columnist Tahsiz Öztin, a statement that is technically wrong, given his Christian faith.

'Lefter gave his two daughters to Turks,' ran the headline of a story a few weeks later, showing how, for many, Lefter was foremost a non-Turk. 'Has Lefter not given everything for this country?' asked the author rhetorically. 'Now his two girls who he loves from his heart, he gives to two Turkish youths.'

Like spectacles that could not be taken off, many people seemed incapable of viewing Lefter outside the frame of ethnicity. When in 1948 Turkey played Greece in Athens, one of the opposition full-backs, Andreas Mouratis, ran up to Lefter after the game, shouted 'Turkish sperm' and attempted to beat him. The incident stands as a reminder that Lefter was no more at home in Greece than he was in Turkey.

Lefter was unquestionably loved by many millions. But people had difficulty when it came to accepting his differences as a Rum. He had to be Turkified.

Lefter himself seems to have been acutely aware of this need. In a 2012 documentary about his life made by Nebil Özgentürk he is shown jokingly chastising a friend he bumps into on Büyükada for talking to him in Greek. 'Speak Turkish!' he says. In the same documentary he is filmed kissing a bust of Atatürk in his hallway. 'Every day I kiss the bust of Atatürk before I leave the house,' he explained. This is the same Atatürk who led the Turkish army to victory against the Greek army in 1919, a success that led to the expulsion of the majority of Rums from Anatolia. Atatürk then pioneered reconciliation with Greece, but it was in his name that harsh anti-minority politics were introduced. Lefter's homage is a reminder of how minorities are always required to go above and beyond to prove their loyalty.

When Lefter died in January 2012, his coffin was set up at Fenerbahçe for fans to pay tribute. It was a splendid display. Tens of thousands came to the stadium to see him off. Recep Tayyip Erdoğan – a Fenerbahçe fan who counts Lefter among his all-time favourite players – looked on as Lefter's coffin was carried out by contemporary Fenerbahçe stars, including Emre Belözoğlu and Volkan Demirel.

But even in death, there was a final twist of the knife. Until 2015, the Fenerbahçe ground used to be called the Şükrü Saracoğlu stadium, named after a former club president and one-time prime minister of Turkey.* When Saracoğlu was in power in the early 1940s,

* It changed its name in 2015 to the Ülker Stadium, part of a $90 million sponsorship deal with confectionery firm Yıldız Holding, who own the Ülker brand. No Fenerbahçe fans I know refer to it by its new title.

his government introduced a wealth tax. In theory it was introduced to counter speculators who had grown rich during the upheaval of independence. But Saracoğlu was explicit about its real purpose: it was to 'get rid of the foreigners who dominate our markets and give the Turkish market back to the Turks.'

Although the tax was in theory payable by all Turkish citizens, Christians and Jews were charged 10 times or more the rate paid by Muslims. So great were the sums demanded that many went bankrupt and their property was seized. It served to transfer many valuable assets from minorities into the hands of Muslim Turks and destroyed much of what was left of the non-Muslim merchant class in Turkey, which had been heavily concentrated in Istanbul. Today, the Rum community of Istanbul has dwindled to fewer than 2,000 people.

Lefter was seventeen at the time the tax was announced. After his death, it emerged that, while filming his documentary, Özgentürk had asked Lefter, then in his eighties, about the tax. 'Turn the camera off,' Lefter is said to have replied. After checking that it really had stopped rolling, the former star leaned into the film-maker's ear and said: 'They made my father suffer so much. Because of his poverty he was saved from going into exile, but all of my relatives had to leave Turkey.'

'He said he was scared,' Özgentürk said later. 'He was a living legend, but he made me turn off the camera.'

And so Lefter Küçükandonyadis, the most famous member of Turkey's once-thriving Rum community, bid farewell to Istanbul from a stadium named after a man he was frightened to talk about, even in old age. Saracoğlu and his successors helped ensure that future generations of fans would never see a great Greek-Turkish footballer.

*

'I see all sorts here. I try and learn from everyone that comes past. For instance, just earlier some girl made a guy have sex.'

'Sorry?' I had been jolted from my reverie by this bizarre interruption from Yusuf.

'On the benches over there.' He gestured to the other side of the cemetery wall. 'They came on bikes. When there weren't any horse and carts or anything, she jumped on him. "No! No!" he said.'

'What, and they had sex? For how long?'

'Oh not, long. Five minutes.'

All the way through our conversation, there had been silences, looks, shrugs, smiles. Yusuf told odd stories like this one, and asked a lot of questions – I felt like he was continually playing with me. It emboldened me to chance my next one: 'Are you Christian yourself?'

A pause. 'What are you?' he asked mischievously.

I hesitated. 'I was baptised a Christian and brought up—'

'Catholic?' he asked

'Well, yes as a matter of fact, but my dad wasn't religious and—'

'Ah, so you don't believe in anything!'

'No, no, I do!' I replied, racking my brains for the Turkish for 'agnostic'. There is nothing worse than being an atheist in Turkey. This sort of topic is where my Turkish grinds to a halt, crunching noisily and spectacularly on the rocks of nuance.

I felt bad for having brought it up. But at the same time, it blew away the niceties. Yusuf's next comment arrived from an altogether different place: 'We Muslims, our religion is fiercely divisive. It's there for war, for Jihad, for saying everyone else is wrong.'

This was a pretty controversial comment. I decided to stay silent.

'We want to say "Christians are wrong, we are right." But who knows that? Who knows the real truth?'

He held out his hand.

'See, in my philosophy there are Muslim, Christian, Alevi, other things,' he said, pointing at each finger. 'All of them are their own routes –' he continued with his finger, tracing it up his arm – 'all different routes, to here.' He tapped his temple. 'Whatever you call him, there is a God for everyone. In the end, you'll be united with God. I mean, it all finishes here.' He paused and smiled, before adding: 'Unless you're an atheist. In my eyes that's insufficient.'

I felt like I was in a film. The Muslim groundskeeper in a Greek Orthodox cemetery, offering gnomic nuggets of tolerance with a smile, the sun coming through the trees. It was a comforting counterpoint to the prejudice and intolerance that Lefter sometimes encountered; a reminder that, for every person wanting to sharpen distinctions, there are many more willing to let them dissolve.

I said goodbye to Yusuf, shook his hand and stepped through the gate.

When I left, cycling away down the hill, I made sure to look out for Lefter's flag. I scanned the hillside where it should be, but couldn't see anything. I knew it to be there, though. A scrap of blue and yellow among a forest of green.

8

Yabanja

Not a lot of people know this, but the game of football was invented by Turks. At least that is the claim made by Fahrettin Süldür in his 1977 book *Turkish Football*.

'Eight thousand years ago, in the period when Turks in Central Asia began the Iron Age, among the many sports they played was a game that involved the feet,' Süldür wrote. This ancient ball game was called *tepük*, from the Turkish verb for 'kick' or 'hoof', and involved kicking around an inflated sphere made of sheepskin. *Tepük* soon passed to China and India, where the English encountered the game when they conquered the subcontinent. The English took it back home, adapted it and came up with their own version – the association rules that gave birth to the football we play today. 'Instead of "football", we Turks should call it "*tepük*" and beatify the souls of our Central Asian ancestors,' Süldür suggested.

Sadly, this story is untrue. There is no archaeological evidence before 2000 BCE of a sphere fashioned by humans that could be kicked. Across the world, people have played games with their feet for millennia, including, most probably, a version in Central Asia. But no Central Asian game was the master copy from which all football flowed.

The desire to indigenise football as Turkish speaks to one of the central tensions in modern Turkey: its love-hate relationship with foreign influences, especially from the west. 'Admiration of the foreign and xenophobia [are] forced to live side by side in a single soul, a sense of inadequacy and grandiosity, victimhood and defiance,' wrote the academic Nurden Gürbelik of the Turkish condition. This paradox generates odd behaviours: from wallowing in despair at outside superiority, to claiming Turks to be the original inventors of everything – a project that goes far behind football, positing Turkish as the first ever language and the Turkish race as the first human civilisation.*

Outsiders normally talk about Turkey as a 'bridge between east and west', but it ill-suits the metaphor. Turkey is better conceptualised as having many orientations. For sixty-seven years it shared a border with the USSR and today has important connections with Russia. Ankara has a close relationship with the Turkic-speaking republics of central Asia, those '-stans' that stretch as far as the Uighurs, a Muslim Turkic-speaking minority in Western China. Half a millennium of rule over the Arabic-speaking lands that fan out from its southern edge has also left its mark. It is quite wrong to cram these histories, traditions and influences onto a see-saw between 'Occident' and 'Orient'.

When it comes to football, however, the picture is far less ambiguous: Turkey is European. The country has been a member of UEFA since 1962. Turks pay no attention whatsoever to the football abilities of its neighbours on its southern and eastern borders.

But there is a problem. Turkey always loses to sides from Western Europe. Galatasaray won the UEFA Cup in 2000, but since then no club has won a European trophy. The national team finished third at the 2002 World Cup but failed even to qualify for Euro 2004. (Turkey didn't play a single European nation at the 2002 tournament, leading some to view their route to the semi-finals as fortuitous). No Turkish player has ever captured the imagination of the Continent and been transferred for world record sums, their name emblazoned on replica shirts.

* The idea of Turks as the first 'civilized' human race became state policy in the early years of the Republic. Known as the 'Turkish history thesis', it was the dominant theory, written in textbooks and taught in schools for many decades. It had its corollary in the 'Sun Language Theory', whereby Turkish was the first tongue from which all other languages derived.

This lack of recognition consistently jars with a central tenet of Turkish nationalism, that Turkey is a powerful and important nation. Turkey's population is almost 80 million, larger than the combined total of the ten Eastern European countries that joined the EU in 2004. It is the world's seventeenth largest economy. Its strategic position means it's at the heart of discussions on the Syrian conflict. 'The world is bigger than five,' says Recep Tayyip Erdoğan frequently, a reference to the five permanent members of the UN Security Council, where he believes Turkey should be.

On the football pitch, the results of this contradiction manifest themselves in a wild merry-go-round with Europe. When Turkish sides do well, their triumphs become loaded with historical and cultural significance, clothed in the imagery of Ottoman invasions of Europe, warriors, war and sexual conquest. When Turkish teams lose – or are thrust into the international news by unsavoury episodes – it generates existential despair. One bad night for an inexperienced official becomes 'a dark night for Turkish refereeing' more generally. Crowd violence at a match in Turkey will cause people to wring their hands about their 'uncivilised' nation, never mind that hooliganism still occurs in England and other Western European countries.

It is safe to say, then, that Turkish football has an inconsistent, enigmatic relationship with Europe. Nowhere is this better encapsulated then in the experiences of foreign players and managers who have, over the years, graced its game.

*

'In the early days I thought, well I'm not going to survive here. This is not going to last.' Gordon Milne, former Liverpool player, and manager of Coventry City and Leicester City, arrived in Turkey in 1986 and took the reins at Beşiktaş.

The club finished second in his first year, and then second again the following season – a failure for a side expected to win the league. Fans were getting impatient. 'I can remember going out at İnönü one day and there were some people there with a big placard,' recalled Milne. 'It said, "Please go to your home Gordon."'

And then it happened. With Milne's lead-by-example style of coaching and a clutch of talented players, Beşiktaş started to click.

They won the league in 1990. The next season they repeated the trick. And then the one after that – a third championship in as many years. They went the entire season without losing a league game – only the second side to have done so in the professional era.*

Success on the field was important, but what truly endeared Milne to the locals was that he flung himself into life in Istanbul. He used the Turkish assistants the club provided for him, rather than bringing in his own staff. He would shop at the local grocer's and eat at the workaday fish restaurants. Even today, when relating tales from his Leicestershire garden, his conversation is peppered with Turkish words: *başkan* (president), *çay* (tea), *balık* (fish). 'I was on my own among all the Turks,' he told me. 'I was the only foreigner. I gained a little bit of respect in a way for that.'

A little effort goes a long way in Turkey. Over the years, Milne has become Beşiktaş's most-lauded manager. He is treated like royalty whenever he travels back. A constant stream of Turkish football journalists beat a path to the Milnes' bungalow. 'I liked the people,' he said. 'You know, you look at 'em and you think they're gonna cut your throat when you first go there, don't you? But it's the opposite.' Milne paused and a playful smile broke across his face. 'Maybe if the football goes wrong they'd do that sometimes . . .'

The word for foreigner in Turkish is *yabancı*, pronounced 'yabanja'. It comes from the word for 'wild' or 'savage'. Built into the term, then, is a sense of the foreigner as a stranger from lands more uncivilised and uncouth. When that person is Roberto Carlos, who arrived at Fenerbahçe in 2007 with World Cup and Champions League winner's medals in his pocket, the image doesn't quite fit.

The *yabancı* is the saviour from lands where the game is played better and more efficiently organised. The foreigner can come, sprinkle his stardust and drive a team on to greater success. But the *yabancı* is also the mercenary, come only to burnish his pay packet. He pulls on the hallowed jersey and serves to debase it in a show of past-it mediocrity. The presence of the *yabancı* can be a reminder

* The first was Galatasaray in the 1985–86 season, although in that year Cim Bom finished in second place.

of how 'behind' Turkish football is. But the *yabancı* is also a guest, someone who has chosen to come and play in Turkey, and should be welcomed accordingly.

The success of football in modern-day Spain, Italy or Brazil means those nations can look back fondly on the period when foreigners brought them the game. The idea of having had to learn from outsiders – especially the English – is a pleasant anachronism when your club sides win everything Europe has to offer, or your national team sticks four goals past the Three Lions. In Turkey, however, the continuing importance of the foreigner in a strongly nationalistic nation is one of football's great tensions.

Generations of Turkish coaches have stood firmly in the shadow of the *yabancı*. Men like Metin Türel, whom I arranged to meet on an August morning at the betting shop near his home. 'Football in this country is behind,' he told me. 'In Europe they started professional coaching courses in 1945. Here it was 1966.'

Now in his eighties, Türel has had a management career that spans five decades at over a dozen teams in Turkey, including the national side. But his most significant impact on Turkish football is educational. Türel was largely responsible for introducing 'European'-style professional training for coaches in Turkey.

When he started his work in the early 1970s, the nation was accustomed to failure in European football. The idea of the 'dignified defeat' and 'honourable draw' were very much in vogue, at a time when Turkey would routinely be on the receiving end of a shellacking, such as two 8–0 losses to England in the 1980s. These games are seared into the football fan's consciousness in Turkey. When I first came to Turkey, people would be amazed that I didn't know them, especially as it involved my own nation. That they weren't legendary victories in England was a further slap in the face. Little did they know that England had its own self-flagellating to worry about in regards to losing to Germany.

Türel was determined to improve standards. In the late 1970s, while coach of the national team, he went to England, spending a week each at Chelsea, West Ham United, Spurs, Arsenal and Charlton Athletic to learn their techniques. In 1990 Türel wrote an 800-page book on coaching, based on hours of VHS cassettes of European and South American teams training. 'All those who did the course at that time read it and liked it,' he said. 'Now those who would read it would be relegated straight away!' He laughed at how quickly ideas are superseded.

The 1980s were a key milestone in Turkish history. At the start of the decade, the nation was under martial law following a military coup. The economy was heavily protectionist. Imported products were banned. You could only buy two types of car and one type of milk. By its close, the country was courting foreign capital. McDonald's opened its first restaurant in Turkey in 1986.

Football went through a similar transition. Expertise was imported from abroad: managers like Gordon Milne and the German coach Jupp Derwall, who was in charge of Galatasaray from 1983 to 1987. Milne remembered Derwall fondly. 'He said to me –' Milne adopted a firm, expressionless face as he prepared to mimic Derwall: 'I told Galatasaray: "No grass, no championship . . . Just tell them: no grass, no championship!"' Derwall is credited in Turkey with 'modernising' the coaching and management – beginning with forcing Galatasaray to make their training pitch full grass.

The injection of cash, capital and ideas began to have an effect. In his first year, the side that Milne and Beşiktaş lost out to was Galatasaray, managed by the young Turkish coach Mustafa Denizli. Soon Denizli would be followed in his success by Fatih Terim, Şenol Günes, Aykut Kocaman and Abdullah Avcı – all graduates of Türel's training courses.

A look at the Süper Lig table at the end of the 2016–17 season suggested Turkish football management was in rude health. The league table read: Beşiktaş, Başakşehir, Fenerbahçe. The managers of those clubs were all Turkish: Şenol Güneş, Abdullah Avcı and Aykut Kocaman respectively (Kocaman joined Fenerbahçe in June 2017). And they are all former assistants to Metin Türel. In other words, Türel has influenced the cream of the current generation of Turkish managers. But this is often not what the managers themselves think.

'There is no football culture in Turkey,' Mustafa Denizli told me flatly. Denizli is one of Turkey's most successful managers, the only person to have won the title with Beşiktaş, Galatasaray and Fenerbahçe.

We spoke in an electronics store in a shopping mall. The conversation took a post-modern turn at one point when he broke off the conversation to turn up a TV so as to listen to an interview with himself. '[Turkey] is behind in terms of culture, experiences and education,' said Denizli. 'In Turkey we never applaud a team that does wonderful things but cannot win the match.' Türel is equally negative about Turkish football – at both the club and national level. 'They have continuity in Europe . . . We show improvement from time to time but we have no consistency . . . Turkish football doesn't have self-confidence.'

This negativity sometimes becomes racialised. Football in many people's eyes reflects the supposed Turkish characteristic of starting well but then not being able to follow through. Tanil Bora captured the familiar lament: 'Our children are technically skilful – maybe even more skilful than those in Europe but they're weak in playing collectively and don't understand tactics. We can't play them in a system'.

A false paradigm is frequently set up by managers, commentators and fans: Europe is lauded and Turkey is denigrated beyond all measure, often to the point of parody. 'In Britain, in Germany and in Spain, when the match ends it's not important if you've won or lost,' Denizli told me. 'They [the players] go to the fans in the stands, who thank them.' I often push back – 'you clearly weren't at Filbert Street when we lost to Derby!' – but it doesn't seem to have any impact. In these conversations I am a visitor from the World of Superior Football, my presence a reminder of backwardness, another stick with which people can beat themselves. Fans take a masochistic delight in soliciting the views of outsiders, to wallow in a sense of grief ('we're so terrible!') or alternatively rouse them to a state of anger ('how dare he say that about our country!').

But it is not only in the realm of managers where the *yabancı* is looked up to. The more common objects of attention, love and interest are the people who make it happen: the players.

*

One of the set rituals of Turkish football fans, frequently adduced as a sign of their 'crazy fanaticism', is the 'Airport Greet'. Fans gather at the airport to welcome a new signing, arranging themselves so that, when the player emerges out of the baggage hall, blinking, he is met with hundreds of chanting supporters, lighting flares and competing with each other to hang a team scarf round his neck. In Turkish the Airport Greet is simply called a 'show' or sometimes 'fan show', which seems a strangely muted form of description for what is a riotous, chaotic event – holding aloft the hero and bringing him into the city.

Airport Greets are reserved almost exclusively for foreign transfers. As such, they tap into the deep well of hospitality that Turks feel towards foreign guests. They are showing the players they are welcome; although the amount of excitement, smoke, noise and jostling might lead some new arrivals to question the effectiveness of the approach.

These reception committees are a stock event in the summer transfer window. In 2015 Robin Van Persie and Luis Nani received textbook Airport Greets, thousands thronging the airport arrivals lounge and clogging the approach roads. 'I must have looked like a rabbit in headlights,' wrote former England striker Darius Vassell about his own Airport Greet when he arrived to play for Ankaragücü in 2009. 'People were bouncing up and down chanting 'Dar-ee-us Varr-sell!, Dar-ee-us Varr-sell, Ole, ole, ole! . . . There were thousands of supporters there to greet me, with flags, shirts and they made such a noise'.

In July 2016, Slovakian defender Martin Škrtel was on his way to Istanbul to sign for Fenerbahçe. I had never witnessed an Airport Greet first hand, and so I vowed to be present at his triumphant welcoming. I spent the afternoon ahead of his arrival sending messages to various fan groups on Facebook. None replied. They were obviously too busy preparing the flares and banners and rehearsing the chants.

It took me an hour to reach the airport. Ten days earlier, three suicide bombers had attacked the building, blowing themselves up and killing over forty people, one of the most deadly in a long line of bombings that were becoming the backdrop to daily life. There were, therefore, masses of police, gendarmes and army, all brandishing quite serious-looking guns. Half the terminal windows were covered in chipboard. A gantry stood in arrivals where they were still repairing the roof. It was not the most enjoyable place to hang around.

As I passed through the strict security and headed into the arrivals section of the terminal, I scanned the building for clusters of people in blue and yellow. I couldn't see any. At that exact moment my phone suddenly beeped. A message from one of the fan groups! Underneath my finely crafted question about Škrtel's Airport Greet there was a short answer in English.

'No'.

Slowly the message grew, the fan adding details line by line in broken English.

Van Persie and Luis Nani striker

Skrtel defense

Important striker for Turkish fans

I wondered if he was just talking about his fan group. Surely there must be some people here, I mean, it was Martin Škrtel! With over 242 appearances and 16 goals for Liverpool! The centre-back who looks like he spends his free time wearing bovver boots, listening to the Clash and kicking the crap out of people who annoy him! I walked in and out of the terminal twice – no mean feat, when it took ten minutes and the emptying of every pocket to get through security. I made a sweep of the entire airport in case the welcoming committee was having a coffee somewhere. But the fan had summed it up: no.

Heading back into the city, I chatted on Facebook with the fan, who turned out to be a student called Ozan. My Turkish was better than Ozan's English, but he stubbornly clung to it. It was a bit like having a conversation with a teleprinter that thought it was William Carlos Williams:

2011–2012

Sukru Saracoğlu stadium

Full

50,000 people
2012–13
20,000 people stadium

Ozan told me the fans hated the Fenerbahçe president, Aziz Yildirim. Many wanted him to go – they felt he had been there too long and the team had grown stale. They were protesting by refusing to go to games.

There's one thing you have to write in your book
Fenerbahçe fans 25 million.
If it's necessary we'll set the world on fire

I was struck yet again by the passion. It can be so intense. But it is also contradictory. This huge passion, this sense of willing to do anything for the team . . . but then nobody can be bothered to turn up to greet the latest signing just because he is a defender. And the stadium is half-full. Passion is expended only in certain directions and at certain times. Rather than the rolling, consistent plod of the British fan – going to games, never overly happy, never despondent to the point of quitting – you have huge peaks and troughs: every waking moment devoted to the team when they're doing well, followed by abandonment when they're not.

The Airport Greet illuminates another important pillar in the foundation of life in Turkey: many people are desperate to be liked and valued by foreigners.

The question I am asked by strangers, more than any other, is 'How is Turkey viewed in your country?' A significant chunk of the country's media content is stories about Turkey from Western news outlets, translated into Turkish and then extolled or denounced on social media.

*

The airport greet is a chance to show the *yabancı* they will be welcome in Turkey. And there are two ways the *yabancı* can respond to this fanatic welcome. The first is for the *yabancı* to show the kind of passion and support for Turkish fans as they have done for him.

One of the most loved foreigners in Turkey is the Frenchman Pascal Nouma. Nouma played for Beşiktaş for only two seasons in the early 2000s, but he played like a *fan*. He would jump into tackles.

He got suspended for seven months for thrusting his hands down his shorts after scoring against Fenerbahçe. And he was utterly, completely adored by the Beşiktaş faithful. Since retiring, he has become a celebrity in Turkey, advertising ice tea on television and starring in crap feature-length comedy films. In effect, a bit like Eric Cantona in England. Nouma still avidly follows Beşiktaş. When I attended an away match in Kiev in 2011, I emerged onto the terrace to see him, dressed in the thickest puffer jacket I had ever seen, posing for photos and leading the 500-strong crowd in chants.

Another *yabancı* who is loved is the Scottish player and manager Graeme Souness. In April 1996 when he was manager of Galatasaray, Souness provided one of Turkish football's most legendary moments. His side were playing Fenerbahçe away in the second leg of the Turkish Cup final. A Dean Saunders goal in extra time saw Galatasaray win a close-fought match in Fenerbahçe's backyard. The players were celebrating in front of the travelling fans when a large red and yellow flag was handed over the fence. Each player took his turn waving it before it was handed to the manager.

Souness had endured a difficult season. It was his first at Galatasaray. The side were out of the championship race by February. He had come in for barracking by some, including the vice-president of Fenerbahçe who, when Souness was hired, publicly stated, 'What are Galatasaray doing hiring a cripple?'. Souness had gone through open-heart surgery a few years before he arrived. The comment stung.

'I started to jog up to the halfway line with this great big flag,' Souness recalled in a BBC podcast. 'And I'm looking into the emptying stands. And I can see in the director's box, I can see this chap who – nine months previous[ly] – had said some pretty unkind things. I thought – in a moment of madness – "I'll show you who's a cripple."' He took the flag, raised it above his head and then drove it into the kick-off spot.

To the Fenerbahçe supporters watching on, the act was red-rag to a bull. They started throwing objects and trying to get onto the pitch. Realising it perhaps wasn't the greatest of moves, Souness ran for the changing rooms.

'I got into the tunnel and thought I'd got away with it,' Souness remembered. 'And just as I thought that, I got a clump on the side of the head – a supporter had got into the tunnel. So I ended up having a bit of a tussle with him. But I managed to get back to the safety of the dressing rooms.'

When the directors came down to the changing rooms to greet the team, Souness thought he was going to be sacked. But it was the exact opposite. 'When they came in, some of them had tears in their eyes,' he said in wonder. 'I've never been hugged and kissed by so many men in such a short time.'

The image of the flag planter resonates historically. A central myth of the conquering of Constantinople in 1453 is the story of Ulubatlı Hasan. Apparently one of the first Ottomans to scale the city's walls, he planted the Ottoman flag before being slain by the Byzantines. Souness found himself nicknamed 'Ulubatlı' Souness. 'I'm not sure quite if I'm on that level', he said when told about the nickname. 'But I'm extremely pleased and proud that people remember me for doing this'.

The 'Ulubatlı Souness' nickname reveals an important element in the process of accepting foreigners. They are Turkified. There's a verb for it in Turkish. Occasionally when I say or do something considered uniquely Turkish, people will laugh and say 'ah *Türkleştin*' – you've become Turkish.

The sports newspapers ran a picture of Trabzonspor's Nigerian player Ogenyi Onazi making the Turkish breakfast dish of menemen: 'Looks like he's quickly getting used to life in Turkey', said one headline. When Wesley Sneijder posted a video of him pretending to play the Saz – a traditional Turkish stringed instrument – it went viral. The academics Tanıl Bora and Necmi Erdoğan write about two German players who played for Galatasary in the early 1990s. Before the side played Eintracht Frankfurt, they won plaudits for saying, 'On that day I will forget that I'm German'.

There's an element of this everywhere – this need to absorb someone into the schema of the country. But in Turkey you cannot do something that Turkish people do without *being* Turkish. As Bora and Erdoğan summarise: 'Football has no nationality – but even so, it's good if foreigner footballers in our teams are like Turks!'

*

If Nouma, Milne and Souness are seen in Turkey as good *yabancıs*, then on the other side stands Guus Hiddink.

The Dutchman has a reputation as one of football's cosmopolitan globetrotters, a peripatetic fixer who can be dropped into any scenario and get results. But Hiddink has never got on well in Turkey.

He first worked in the country in 1990, taking over the reins at Fenerbahçe while Milne was across town at Beşiktaş. Milne relates an encounter between them as they watched a reserve-team game. Hiddink grabbed Milne's arm and started gesturing angrily at various events on the pitch, exclaiming, '"They've got to change. If they don't change—' Milne interrupted: 'In my opinion Gus, *you've* got to change,' he said. Recalling the episode he told me: 'He didn't like it.'

Milne expanded on his thinking: 'What I meant by that is that some of the characteristics and things they do can be annoying, right? . . . You could get upset with lots of things, but . . . that's their characteristics. They're *Turkish*, they're not bloody Dutch . . .' Hiddink left Fenerbahçe midway through that season. Milne went on to win his third championship in a row.

Two decades passed before Hiddink returned to Turkey, this time to manage the Turkish national side. The experience was no more successful, coming to an end after fifteen months when Turkey lost to Croatia in the play-offs for Euro 2012. An official at the Turkish Football Federation at the time was damning about Hiddink's modus operandi. 'For everybody else . . . Hiddink is a very well-educated Western manager. For me, Hiddink is a son-of-a-bitch – he is the most ego-centred man. I think he can speak four, five languages. In every language the first word he would learn would be "money",' he alleged. 'His world was built upon money. Nothing else. NOTHING ELSE.'

The Turkish press grumbled at his contract, reported to be €4.5 million a year, all of his expenses paid, and housed in a hotel costing €3,500 a night. Writing in his 2006 autobiography about his time at Fenerbahçe, Hiddink frequently brings up the subject of money. 'When we were at the point of signing, I still hadn't seen any [money]. Not cash, but also not with the bank in Istanbul. "Just sign," they said. "It'll come" . . . I said "No, show me *now* that it's in the bank" . . . Everyone went their way and an hour later the Turkish newspapers were folded open and you saw the German marks being handed across the table. Piles of notes of twenty, fifty, a hundred'. He also wrote about the endless meetings that would end in fighting and management interference in the team selection. 'Before the discussion began they were at each other's throats. That culture of whispering. The behaviours to please and flatter. "You can trust me, but with him and him you've got to be careful."'

According to the Turkish official, Hiddink didn't recognise any of the players in his side, never watched any league games in Turkey and spurned the suggestions of his Turkish assistants. 'He hates football. For him this is only a drama he's making money out of,' he claimed.

Although he has had considerable success elsewhere, Hiddink is seen in Turkey as an extreme example of another of its footballing trends: the overpaid foreign journeymen. In 2015 57 per cent of the players in the Turkish Süper Lig were foreigners, significantly higher than Germany, Spain, France and the Netherlands (but still short of the top league, England, with 66 per cent). Another statistic reveals a bit more about who these foreigners are. At twenty-seven, Turkey has the oldest average player age in Europe, jointly held with Russia. Many of the foreigners are at the tail-end of their careers, attracted by the opportunity of playing in front of fanatical crowds and one last pay-day.

Turkish clubs – in co-operation with the state – offer foreign footballers an appealing package. The tax rate on foreign players in the Süper Lig is 15 per cent, and 10 per cent in the second division. Many teams pay the tax on the players' behalf. The clubs often arrange villas with Bosphorus views, cars, chefs – a level of comfort and service that is not possible in other nations. So when a foreign star fails to shine, fans and pundits alike feel cheated.

In any normal week, you'll find at least one opinion piece in the sports newspapers bemoaning the number and quality of foreigners in Turkey. 'I'm not against quality foreign players but our clubs are full of foreign players who are past it,' wrote columnist Sinan Vardar in March 2017. 'It should be like Barcelona, who every year take 70 talented 12- to 15-year-old footballers who will contribute to the squad'. In August 2017, when Robin Van Persie was ruled out with yet another injury, the columnist Erman Toroğlu moaned that 'Top-notch players don't choose Turkey unless they're injured!' Another columnist, Hakkı Yalçın devised an imagined conversation in his article between Van Persie and a small child in a Fenerbahçe top selling *simits*.

'I have honour in selling *simits*,' the boy tells him, 'something people like you, who make 5.7 million euros while sleeping, wouldn't know about.'

'I think you don't recognise me,' Van Persie says.

'No, I recognise you very well,' replies the boy.

'Do you know my value?'

The kid grabs the badge of his kit and kisses it.

'Cheap love like yours comes with a cost.'

*

Turkish players are referred to by their first name: Arda, Emre, Volkan. These are printed on their shirts and used in conversation. It is something that Turkey has in common with Brazil, a place with a very different footballing history but which shares the desire to hold its native sons closer than an impersonal surname allows.

Foreigners, however, retain their last names. During the game, commentators switch between first and last name in a dextrous show of demarcation, continually drawing attention to who is and isn't Turkish, who does and doesn't belong. If the same principle was applied to reading out the 2017 Leicester City line-up, it would be as follows: Schmeichel; Danny, Wes, Harry, Fuchs; Ndidi, Matty, Mahrez, Mark; Okazaki and Jamie.

It's perhaps no coincidence that one of Turkey's most loved foreigners was Brazilian and could be slotted into this naming system. Alexsandro de Souza – known simply as 'Alex' – was Fenerbahçe's most successful number 10 in the 2000s. In a team not short on foreign talent (Roberto Carlos, Nicolas Anelka and Pierre van Hooijdonk featured during his spell), Alex excelled. In eight seasons he won three championships, scored 171 goals and made 136 assists. He quickly became a fan favourite – a statue was cast in his honour – and he even spawned a saying: *Bi' Alex değil* (not quite an Alex) is used to describe something good but not exceptional.

But then it all went wrong. In 2012 Alex fell out with the coach and chairman and had his contract cancelled. He went from good *yabancı* to bad in the blink of an eye. 'Before we liked him lots but now he's always talking,' a Fenerbhaçe fan called Barış told me. 'After he went [back] to Brazil he talked too much against Fenerbahçe. He earned more than 20 million euros from Fenerbahçe . . .'

Distinctions over names reveal an issue that confronts all *yabancıs*, be they professional footballers or middling writers. Namely, the big difference drawn between visiting Turkey and staying. Foreigners are welcome as guests, but if people want to stay for longer and make Turkey their home, then their foreignness needs to be downplayed or ignored.

One easy way to do so is for a player to become naturalised and take a Turkish name. Although not a requirement, a clutch of foreign players who have stayed have taken Turkish names: Colin Kazim-Richards became 'Kazim Kazim'. Brazilian Marco Aurélio became 'Mehmet' and played over thirty times for the Turkish national team. Nigerian Uche Okechukwu was transformed into Deniz Uygar. My personal favourite is Wederson Luiz da Silva Medeiros, who became Gökçek Vederson. His unusual first name was a dedication to the mayor of Ankara, Melih Gökçek, who brought him to Ankaraspor and 'treated him with the compassion of a father'.

There are some for whom no name change is enough to signify belonging in Turkey. Shortly after Aurélio's 2006 call-up to the national team, Galatasaray fans unfurled a banner: 'You can't become "Mehmet", you're born "Mehmet".' Casting citizens as *yabancı* does not only affect naturalised footballers. Turkish passport holders with non-Muslim heritage – members of the small Armenian and Jewish communities, or Greek-speakers like Lefter Küçükandonyadis – have suffered a century of denial of their claims to belonging, caused by interpreting citizenship as stemming from 'Turkish' ethnicity and blood.

I don't think it's a coincidence that, aside from Kazim-Richards, the other players are not European. That is, they come from a country that Turkey sees as 'like' itself: historically the victim of European colonisation attempts and outside the small coterie of states making the world's decisions. The Europe–Turkey relationship seems to have just too much geopolitical baggage for Europeans to be accepted in the same way. In the case of the many Brazilians who have become citizens, it also helps that breaking into the Turkish national team is a bit less difficult than the Brazilian one.

*

The separation of foreigner and local is one of the many lines of division that score the surface of the nation. Turkey is divided in on itself, an increasingly polarised and fractured country. Currently, the biggest fault line is pro- versus anti-government, which splits the country roughly in two. The relationship with Europe is very much refracted through this internal, ever-revolving hall of mirrors. Being pro-European in the 2000s aligned you (willingly or not) with the AKP government, Erdoğan and the push for EU membership. Nowadays, it normally marks you as being on the opposite side.

Although Turkey has been in UEFA for over half a century, EU membership has proved elusive. When the AKP came to power in 2002, it began a large push for EU entry. A raft of legislation was passed to bring Turkey more in line with its European counterparts (following a framework laid down by the previous government). Over the course of a few years, the judiciary was reformed, trade barriers reduced, torture was prohibited (though did not totally disappear), the death penalty was abolished and ministers promised to improve minority rights. It had its desired reward: in January 2005, Turkey was formally admitted as a 'candidate' country for EU accession. When Erdoğan returned to Ankara after the negotiations, despite the sub-zero temperature, the streets from the airport to the prime ministry were lined with jubilant supporters.

Twelve years later, and the EU membership bid was in deep freeze. Brussels accused Turkey of sliding ever deeper into an authoritarianism that is incompatible with EU membership. The Turkish government charged Europe with acting in bad faith, of going through the motions of allowing Turkey to join without ever really meaning it.

The reaction of ordinary Turks to this debate depends entirely on their own political compass. Erdoğan's opponents, though not always exactly pro-EU themselves, tend to believe that the president has got what he deserves from Brussels for dismantling the judiciary, locking up journalists and cracking down on human rights groups. His supporters, by contrast, see their president as the victim of double standards and Turkophobia from a perfidious Europe. 'See,' they say, 'they never really wanted us anyway.'

Foreigners are pulled into the domestic culture wars, their pronouncements and perceptions used as ammunition in the battle over the direction of the country. At the height of a diplomatic spat in March 2017 between Turkey and the Netherlands, the Dutch Galatasaray captain Wesley Sneijder was criticised by the press in Holland for shaking hands with Erdoğan at a charity match. By contrast, the Turkish press applauded him: 'He gave a lesson to Holland's press who want to escalate the crisis,' one headline crowed. Erdoğan even used the player in an election campaign: 'Look at Galatasaray's Sneijder. He doesn't think like a Dutchman.' It has reached the point where attacking – and being attacked by – Europe is politically beneficial for the president.

Amid mounting tensions with Europe and a growing number of terror attacks, some foreign players decided to leave. On the day that Martin Škrtel flew into the country to sign for Fenerbahçe, José Sosa, a Portuguese winger for Beşiktaş, posted a poorly-written letter on social media to explain his reasons for going the other way.

'I ask for my transfer to [from] Beşiktaş club, and I need this because I have some personal problems with my family. The point is that my wife is afraid to live in Istanbul, Turkey, and I have fear for my daughters too. The last attack at the airport was very closely to us, because my Agents were there two hours before. After this, my family and I have taken the decision to leave Istanbul.'

He was not the only one. In the same transfer window, Mario Gomez at Beşiktaş and Lucas Podolski at Galatasaray also claimed the 'security' situation as the reason behind their wanting away.

Those unhappy with the government seize on scared foreign players as a sign that the country is going down the wrong path. People continually express amazement that I like living in Turkey. Once, stuck in horrendous traffic in central Ankara, my taxi driver let out a long sigh. 'Look at this traffic. Cunting traffic,' he grumbled. 'Fuck this country!' he added. The first swear seeming to loosen up his tongue. 'I mean, do you like it here? Really?' I replied that I did. He scoffed in a friendly fashion. 'You've just moved here and we're all trying to move away!'

Others who are more patriotic, however, react angrily. The excuse of terrorism doesn't wash with the majority, who are living the same reality, along with their families and loved ones. Many people refused to take Sosa at his word, believing his real intention was simply to move away, and that he was using the terrorism as a pretext. That made him not simply a bad foreigner but also a devious one.

Much of this debate is hyped up by the media, which over the course of the Erdoğan era has become dominated by pro-government press and TV. Throughout 2016, when the terror threat was at its peak, pro-government *Fotomaç* would have an interview every other week with a foreigner explaining how safe Turkey was and how they loved being here. 'Turkey is no more dangerous than France or Germany. But every [foreign] player has this idea. In my opinion those who leave use it as an excuse. I'm here,' said Samuel Eto'o, still doing the business at the age of thirty-six, banging in the goals for Antalyaspor. 'Nice to be back in Turkey! What is Europe? Not as good as us [sic] Turkish,' wrote Nicolas Anelka while on holiday in Istanbul in summer 2016. His pro-Turkey comment was lapped up by *Fotomaç*: 'You're the man, Anelka!' it said. 'While there continues to be hostile black propaganda about Turkey in many European countries, old Fenerbahçe star Nicolas Anelka teaches everyone a lesson'.

Internal division was not always so pronounced, at least on the football pitch. In the 1990s, Turks would unite in support when their club teams played abroad: 'Europe, Europe, hear our voices!' was the chant of the period, as Fenerbahçe and Beşiktaş fans cheered on Galatasaray in their European adventures. Nowadays, large swathes of the population don't even support the national team, believing as they do that any success will be leveraged by Erdoğan for maximum political gain.

But at times, all parties can snap into position and it becomes Turks against outsiders again. There is nothing like a common enemy to bring people together.

*

December 2016. A sub-zero night in Kiev. After a see-saw of a campaign, a point for Beşiktaş against Dynamo Kiev would have taken them through to the last-16 of the Champions League for the first time in their history. The match did not start well – Beşiktaş fell behind to a cheap goal in the ninth minute. Not long after, Dynamo Kiev played a ball behind the Beşiktaş line. Beşiktaş defender Andreas Beck and a Kiev forward ran after it. On the edge of the area the Kiev forward gave Beck a nudge in the back. He fell over. As he did so, the attacker fell over him. Beşiktaş keeper Fabri collected the ball and was about to launch a counter-attack when he realised the Scottish referee, Craig Thomson, had blown his whistle. He had given a penalty. As the last man, Beck also had to go. Kiev converted the penalty, Beşiktaş went to pieces and the night ended in a 6–0 thrashing.

The next day, Turkish media picked up on the terrible decision. What was interesting was not that there was criticism – it was a bad call – but the tone. 'The enemy of the Turks, Scottish referee murdered Beşiktaş in Kiev,' said the headline in *Fotomaç*. Mehmet Demirkol wrote in *Fanatik*, a sports paper from another stable: 'I'm not actually someone who believes in conspiracy theories like "the whole world is against us". But now we can say comfortably that we have a serious deficiency in lobbying.' Drawing attention to the fact that a Turk, Şenes Erzik, is vice president at UEFA, Demirköl argued that 'this shouldn't be happening over and over again . . . From now on we must work to be an equal and strong member at UEFA once more.' The commentator Turgay Demir wrote: 'The Scottish referee turned the Champions League into vinegar . . . If this is Europe, let's not be European!' Even the UK ambassador to Turkey, Richard Moore, a well-known Beşiktaş fan, had a grumble on Twitter: 'Generally I don't complain about referees, but tonight . . . and a citizen of ours!'

I used to dismiss such mutterings as sour grapes. But living in Turkey, these thought processes start to get to you. The notion of a direct conspiracy is easy enough to discard. But what about indirect partiality? Could a general anti-Turkish mood in Europe have fed into the decision?

Frequently Europe has been unfair to Turkey. Before EU accession talks even began, some European nations expressed explicit opposition to Turkey ever becoming a member. The French parliament passed legislation requiring a referendum on the final decision of Turkey's entry. For many, Turkey's size, geography and its mainly Muslim population has proven psychologically too large a hurdle. With the rise of far-right parties in Europe, the gap seems to be growing. Criticism of Turkey has become louder, often shading into blatant Islamophobia. Even Boris Johnson – the great-grandson of an Ottoman government minister – decided to use Turkey-bashing as a tool in his campaign for Brexit. Johnson's Turkish cousin, Sinan Kuneralp, scolded him for his 'ridiculous' and 'irresponsible' slurs.

In football matters, double standards are often at play. In November 2003, Istanbul saw four truck bombs (over two different days) kill fifty-seven. The Beşiktaş–Chelsea Champions League match was moved by UEFA to a neutral venue in Germany. Twelve years later, 130 civilians were killed in a series of terror attacks in Paris, including a bombing outside a France–Germany match. The 2016 European Championship still took place in France. After the ISIS bombing of Atatürk airport, UEFA refused a minute's silence in the Euro 2016 competition, only to relent in the face of criticism.

Can we blame Turkey for thinking there's a deeper reason behind such decisions? Turkey looks at Bulgaria, a nation riddled with corruption and with an economy fifteen times smaller than its own, or Hungary, where rule of law has been steadily eroded, and wonders why these countries were allowed in but it was not. The recent turn towards authoritarianism in Turkey of course makes the EU dream increasingly unlikely. But Europe must also shoulder some of the blame. Who knows where Turkey would be now if the accession process had moved forward instead of stalling?

So perhaps some of this does percolate into the minds of referees, in a process that can be seen as the reverse of 'Fergie time' at Manchester United. Just as Man United under Sir Alex Ferguson more often than not seemed to get the benefit of the doubt from referees at key times, so perhaps the image of Turkey means it disproportionately comes out on the wrong side of decisions, both political and footballing. It's hard to muscle into Europe when no one likes your government. Turkish football may be struggling to climb out from under the shadow of its politics. After the Kiev match, on the mailing list of Beşiktaş fans that I am part of, someone wrote: 'The fruits of our foreign policy came home to roost.'

In the days following the Kiev fiasco, *Fotomaç* tried many theories for size. The first was that UEFA didn't want Turkey to pass Belgium in the country coefficient table, the complex formula used to allocate places in European competitions. Next was the theory that UEFA punished Turkey for giving its vote for the body's president to Slovenian Aleksander Ceferin over the eventual winner Giani Infantino. A series of ever-more elaborate theories followed before the article concluded: 'In the moment that the EU is closing the door on us, are the incidents in such a match coincidence or deliberate?'

The comments reveal a defence mechanism buried deep inside the national psyche: the lack of success in Europe is not Turkey's responsibility. Rather it is a result of forces lined up to prevent the nation's success. UEFA, the referee, the FIFA mafia. It is a neat displacement of accountability that has its roots in a larger narrative – dating back to the early republic – of the threat of 'enemies within and without'.

Such was the outcry over the game that *Fotomaç*, with the help of the Scottish newspaper the *Daily Record*, tracked down Craig Thomson. 'On the pitch I blow the whistle according to what I see and give decisions,' he said. 'I don't believe I made a mistake.' He then added that he really liked 'Turks and kebabs' and said: 'I know that Turkey is a beautiful country. The people are very warm.'

The episode reminds me of some other press campaigns against referees. When England went out of Euro 2004, the *Sun* newspaper launched an attack against Swiss official Urs Meier, who was seen as responsible when he disallowed a Sol Campbell header. The paper printed where Meier lived and worked, prompting him to go into hiding with twenty-four-hour police protection. A year later, in 2005, Swedish referee Anders Frisk quit football after receiving hate mail and death threats from Chelsea fans following their Champions League semi-final exit.

That is not the only echo. I have been talking about a country with a love-hate attitude towards foreigners. A country concerned that the number of imported players is killing the game for locals. A country that has an uneasy relationship with Europe – seeing itself as both a part of and apart from the Continent. There is one other nation I can think of to which all these points apply. When it comes to football, England and Turkey are not always so far apart.

9

The Emperor

Fatih Terim is Turkey's most famous footballing figure. A Galatasaray legend, he bossed the defence for eleven years as a player. As the team's manager, he oversaw six championships and is the only coach to have won a European trophy at a Turkish club. As head of the Turkish national side, he guided Turkey to the brink of the Euro 2008 final.

For many people – both inside and outside Turkey – Terim also personifies the stereotypical Turkish man: proud, combative, exuding a coarse virility and power, whether screaming and gesticulating on the touchline or smiling and charming his way through a press conference. It is a persona captured in his nickname of *İmparator*, the Emperor.

He has come far: from a poor family to the largest figure in football in Turkey. His story is a microcosm of many of the changes the country has been through: of astonishing social mobility and growth in wealth; of migration to the cities of the West; of Turkish skills and power competing on the world stage.

From all the people I spoke to for this book – fans, players, agents, managers – no question elicited as strong a reaction as asking, 'What do you think of Fatih Terim?' He divides opinion. In the eyes of some, his motivational techniques and success make him deserving of a seat in the pantheon of the world's greatest coaches. For others, he is a charlatan, an egotistical tyrant, bringing shame on Turkey, its football and the image of its men.

Terim is from Adana, Turkey's fifth largest city, located in the south of the country. It is a riot of concrete, hustle and bustle. In summer, the temperature is often over 40 degrees. Like their most famous son, Adana people carry the reputation of being fiery and hotheaded, of reacting first and asking questions later.

The city is large enough to have two professional football teams: Adana Demirspor and Adanaspor. Adanaspor are one of Turkey's few solely 'commercial' clubs, owned by a businessman rather than a fan association. They play in orange, and their nickname is 'the Tigers'. Demirspor are the club with vintage. Their name literally means 'Iron sport' and reveals the side's origins, founded in 1940 by employees of the Turkish railways. It was Fatih Terim's first club.

In March 2016, the two teams were due to play each other in the Adana derby. Adanaspor were top of the second league, their rivals in fifth place; both had the chance of promotion to the Süper Lig. It seemed the ideal moment to visit Terim's home town to try and learn more about the man. At the airport I texted a friend who has family in Adana. I asked him what image came to mind when people mention Adana football. His reply was simple: 'fight', followed by emojis of a fist and a bicep curl.

*

My first port of call was the Demirspor training complex. Located next to the river that runs through the centre of town, it was unmissable, every surface painted in the team's light-and-dark-blue colours. I was greeted by Ali, the general manager.

Ali was born and raised in the Netherlands, which explained his excellent English. He took me to the cafeteria which, confusingly, was accessed through the gym. As we ate a late lunch – the leftovers from the players' meal – I asked what brought him to Adana.

'The mayor, actually. When he became mayor he called me up and invited me back to Adana. He knows I'm one of the best sports managers and he wanted me to work with Demirspor'.

Ali has known the mayor for twenty years through being part of the same political party – the MHP, the Nationalist Movement Party. Right-wing and ultranationalist, the MHP was founded by ex-colonel Alparslan Türkeş, its identity built around the idea of the primacy of the Turkish race.

Given Ali's political leanings, his explanation of the club's story came as a bit of a surprise: 'The club was founded by people involved in the railway,' he says. 'We have sympathy with Livorno and with Beşiktaş' – both clubs with left-wing, socialist traditions.

A young man came in, smaller in stature and younger in age. He was introduced as Halil and stood next to where I was sitting. Ali dictated orders to him, a display of hierarchy for my benefit. Halil was to become my personal chauffeur and tour guide. A schedule was made of people I should visit and places I should go. I knew the futility of trying to avoid this facet of Turkish hospitality.

When he was done with the tour, Halil gave me a lift into town to the place where I was staying.

'It's a conservative hotel,' he said.

'What makes you say that?'

'They don't let unmarried couples stay. They need to show a wedding certificate.' Perhaps conscious that he was giving a bad impression, he then added, 'But it's mostly to stop prostitutes using it.'

*

'When I say tumultuous, I mean very rough', said Ahmet Yaşar – known as *tombik* Ahmet, fatty Ahmet – a childhood friend of Fatih Terim. He told me what the footballing legend was like when he was young: 'Very courageous, tough, brave. He wouldn't bat an eye, you know? He would plunge in head-first. If a friend needed someone to fight with him, he would be there ... That's the essence of Adana.'

We were sitting in the office of the Demirspor youth set-up, located a stone's throw from the railway that gave the team its name. It was a weekday morning and the facility was deserted, aside from a clutch of retired footballers, like Ahmet, who spend their days here.

Fatty Ahmet and Fatih Terim's football careers started in parallel. In the late 1960s they played together in the Demirspor youth team, and then in 1970 moved into the first team. Ahmet was a barrel-chested winger, while Terim was the defensive midfielder.

'He was a very lively footballer. And intelligent. He could use the ball well – look, note this down,' he said getting more excited. 'In 1973 the side won the second division title. That year, he scored eleven goals. It was magnificent. You normally talk about a defensive midfielder chipping in with three or four goals but Fatih Terim scored eleven goals!'

Someone rummaged around in a cupboard and produced a team photo from the 1972–73 championship-winning season.

'See, can you see his hair?' says Ahmet, pointing at a man standing in the back row, cradling a ball. Without the guidance I would never have guessed which one was Terim. The photo showed him sporting a shock of frizzy hair, like a guitarist in Led Zeppelin, a far cry from his current look.

Ahmet seemed to be warming to his task: 'He liked to take care of himself. In those days, he would do things no one else would. His hair, for instance. . . He would have his hair curled in a women's hairdresser before a match.' He then added for emphasis, 'A women's hairdresser – a *coiffeuse*!'

The revelation seemed to jar with the image more commonly associated with Turkish football's premier alpha male. But then again, definitions of macho behaviour in Turkey are very different to those back home. Men link arms, they unabashedly sing chants about love and heartbreak, they cry in public. That does not change the fact that Turkish society remains deeply patriarchal.

In Demirspor's first season in the top division, Terim's performances began to draw attention. While covering as sweeper for an injured team-mate, Demirspor played an away match against Galatasaray, beating them 1–0. The Istanbul club liked what they saw. Before the season was out, they had put in a bid for the twenty-one-year-old. Fatih Terim was ready for the first transformation: from local to national fame.

*

During my week in Adana, I spent my afternoons at the Demirspor club, hanging out with Halil. He occupied much of the time trying to persuade me to be photographed making the hand gesture of the Grey Wolves, a hardcore wing of the MHP. The aim is to repeat the look of the wolf's head. Given their reputation for racism and violence, I was not exactly keen to comply.

One day after work, Halil needed a haircut so drove me to his barber's. There was no one inside, save the barber, Mehmet, and his teenage assistant. Mehmet was wiry, with short hair and a permanent grin like a hyena. Perhaps in order to balance this out, the assistant was podgy and sleepy. He didn't speak; the barber never shut up.

'Mexicano!!!!' screamed Mehmet and gave me a high five. I wasn't sure what it was for. Every sentence he uttered dissolved into laughter. He offered cigarettes round.

'Good man!' he said, when I politely declined.

'In Adana this –' (mimed smoking).

'This –' (mimed drinking).

'This –' (mimed fighting). 'HAHAHAHAHHAHAAHAHAHAHAHAHAHAHAHAHAHAH.'

Halil grinned and looked at me. His glance conveyed mixed emotions: wanting confirmation that this was funny while also proffering an apology for having introduced me to this man.

After a short while, the barber's friend came in, wearing a puffy gilet and flash trainers. He sat behind the till, messing about with something on a tablet. 'Do you like music? I will play you an English song,' he said. A minute later, blaring out of the sound system came Kurdish pop.

'HAHAHAHAHAHAHHAHAHAHHAHAHHAHHA,' laughed the barber and his mate.

'Kurmanci! Kurmanci!' I was told, just in case I missed the joke.

Instead of an English song, it was actually a Kurdish one.

The barber paused in his cutting. He stood away from the chair and started tapping his feet and shaking his head.

'I'm not Kurdish,' he said. 'I'm Turkmen. But my friend here, he's fully Kurdish. He does all the dance!' He then grabbed one of the towels lying about and started leaping around the shop, one hand behind his back, the other twirling the towel, to the soundtrack of booming Kurdish music and the laughter of the others.

Halil had spent the last few hours extolling the virtues of the MHP, a party whose supporters are not known for their love of Kurdish culture. But here he was laughing along with this guy. The ultra-nationalist who chooses a barber fond of Kurdish folk dancing; the macho football manager who has his hair done in a women's hair-dresser – these are reminders that things are never straightforward in Turkey.

'He's very lively, isn't he?' Halil said as we walked back to his car. 'He's especially like that with new people.'

*

Terim's first season at Galatasaray was a mixed bag, but by the time the second started he had begun to grow into his new role as sweeper. It was ideal, allowing him to read the game, anticipate play and – most importantly – boss about his team-mates. That same year, 1976, he was made captain at the age of twenty-three. For others it might have been overwhelming, but Terim seemed to be inspired by the challenge.

He stayed at Galatasaray for the next eleven years, making 505 appearances in league and cup competition. His style was no-nonsense, characterised by good reflexes and a reputation of always being in the right place at the right time. 'He would pluck the ball out of the goal like in a magic trick,' one middle-aged fan from Istanbul told me. 'For example, in a national match the ball came, the keeper missed it. He was running back. On the line, he pulled out an overhead kick to clear it.' This ability led to his first nickname, Samantha, after the sorceress who starred in the TV series *Bewitched*, which had started airing in Turkey in the 1970s.

Some suggest a headstrong personality, combined with the fame, started to inflate Terim's ego. Despite being a defender, he had the biggest contract of all the players at Galatasaray. Stories abound of his life in Istanbul's coffee houses and drinking dens – difficult to verify, but all very believeable. 'There was this café in Beyoğlu where the artists would hang out,' the director of the Galatasaray museum once told me. 'Men would go there. They'd sit at the table and play Okey [a game played with tiles]. When Fatih was at Galatasaray, he'd come in, his shirt unbuttoned down to here, wearing Cuban heels. Because he was from Adana. A real *kabadayı*. He'd be there playing Okey from morning until night.'

Literally, 'rough uncle', the term *kabadayı* emerged in the nineteenth century to describe local strongmen who would 'protect' an area. Violence was intrinsic to the role. Today *kabadayı* is synonymous with a particular type of man in Turkey – one who is fiercely loyal to friends, aggressive towards enemies, quick to anger, excessively benevolent and deeply concerned with the importance of 'honour'.

So, was Fatih Terim a *kabadayı*? On the pitch his behaviour was frequently violent. In 1980 he was arrested, accused of punching an official during the half-time break of a Fenerbahçe–Galatasaray match. Terim, however, takes umbrage at this characterisation: 'I don't wear my jacket like a cape and I don't shove my feet in my shoes, but people see me as if I'm that kind of person,' he says, referring to two of the stock images of the *Kabadayı*.

The common narrative is that this all changed when Terim met his wife. Fulya Aksu was a girl from a wealthy background who had studied in Switzerland and Italy and lived in Nişantaşı, one of Istanbul's most glamorous neighbourhoods. They fell in love and married in 1982. Friends like to say that the rich girl tamed the wild Adana boy.

But the facts don't really back up the romantic story. Terim's behaviour on the pitch was still often highly aggressive. He head-butted the captain of his old team, Adana Demirspor, in a match in 1983. The following year he was banned for two matches after slapping Fenerbahçe's Suad Karalić. In 1985, in a match against Antalyaspor, he spat at the referee. 'I'm very sorry,' he said after the match. 'But if this incident hadn't happened today, it was going to happen at some point.' It was not exactly an unqualified apology.

Terim was stripped of the captaincy and was looking at a heavy punishment. Instead, he decided then and there to finish his playing career at the age of thirty-two. Everyone was surprised, not least his manager at the time, the German coach Jupp Derwall.

It wasn't immediately apparent that Terim would be a successful coach. He spent two modestly good years at Ankaragücü. Terim then dropped down one division to take on the management of promotion hopefuls Göztepe, one of Izmir's top sides.

While in Izmir, Terim tried to address his greatest barrier to progressing as an internationally renowned coach: his lack of a foreign language. He tried English courses, but he couldn't adapt. Instead he opted for private lessons. But the lack of linguistic flair would haunt him throughout his career. A video of a press conference from the early 2000s, in which Terim mumbles in heavily accented English, is famous in Turkey. He is ridiculed for lines such as 'what can I do sometimes?' and 'look at the tabela,' using the Turkish word for 'league table'. Once, in the toilet of a pub in Bursa, I came across an advert for a travel agency that had a laugh at his expense. 'Is your English as bad as Fatih Terim's? Don't say "What can I do sometimes?" Come to London with Pons Travel . . .'

Terim had barely settled at Göztepe when he received a call from the president of the Turkish Football Federation, Şenes Erzik. Erzik had just landed Sepp Piontek as the national coach, the German reputed to have invented the 3-5-2 formation. Erzik asked if Terim would be his assistant. For a man as ambitious as Terim, it was an easy decision.

Terim eagerly consumed all Piontek taught. Results with the national team, however, were a mixed bag. The Under-21s, for whom Terim had sole responsibility, fared much better. When Turkey failed to win a single point in the qualification campaign for Euro 1992, Piontek left and Terim took over control of the main team. He successfully oversaw the transplantation of the Under-21s to the main national side. Turkey qualified for Euro 96, their first major tournament since 1954 (though their results at the tournament make for less-impressive reading: played 3, lost 3. Goals for: 0, goals against: 5). 'Our biggest success was making the national team the people's team,' said Terim after the competition.

By July 1996, Terim had enhanced his reputation. He had learnt from the world's best coaches. He had experience on the world's highest stage. It was time to return to Galatasaray.

*

'The meeting is this way, is it?'

A bunch of youths nodded imperceptibly and pointed down a dead end. I was in the backstreets of central Adana trying to find the Demirspor fan headquarters. I walked down the road and into the building, a draughty structure with its breeze blocks exposed. I eventually found my way to the meeting room. A few fans were putting out chairs, enough to seat eighty or so.

I sat. Slowly the room filled. A few people eyed me strangely. The group president, Telat, emerged. The chatting stopped. Telat set out the plans for Sunday's game.

'We'll meet here early. At 1.30. We'll be getting into the stadium *early.* No one should drink alcohol. We'll be a small terrace on Sunday, just 2,200 people . . . we can't afford issues when we're such a small crowd. So just don't bloody drink!'

Once the plans for Sunday were finished, Telat worked through other business. The vibe was 'village meeting': Telat led but others chipped in at points, both older and younger. Everyone who spoke was listened to.

He talked about an order of Demirspor bomber jackets which he'd had to cancel due to poor manufacturing. 'This is Adana. It's hot, the colour will run.' People tittered.

There was an extended talk on behaviour at away matches.

'You shouldn't get drunk, you shouldn't be antagonising the police, you shouldn't be nicking stuff from places. You shouldn't be attacking the coach driver, or swearing at him –' At this last one, there were more laughs from the back. Telat's mood instantly switched.

'Don't laugh! Who laughed? I want the name of the person who laughed.' A deathly silence.

In front of me, a man with a baseball cap and huge beard turned around: 'On one trip, a guy stole eighty watches.' A young guy in a leather jacket to my left chides him: 'You shouldn't be saying this to him!'

'Please, don't write that,' the bearded man added.

Telat eventually said, 'Look, to cut a long story short, any *namussuz* person will be chucked out. We will simply just leave them.' *Namussuz.* Here it's just a swear word, thrown out to insult, but the literal meaning is 'without honour'. Its sudden appearance shows again how the words of Adana men – their vocabularies, postures and acts – bear the impressions of a deeply ingrained machismo.

And then the meeting was over. Later on, when the clubhouse was empty and quiet, Telat sat down with me and told me more about the fan group and the city. He spent much of his time relating how the Demirspor fans were social democrats. He used to travel to Istanbul in the 1980s to hang out with the Beşiktaş fan club Çarşı – they learnt to marry football fanaticism and activism from them.

But, I pointed out, the chairman of the club was a supporter of the MHP – the right-wing nationalist party. How does that work? The arrangement was born of financial necessity, Telat explained. The club ran up 7 million lira of debt so they allowed local officials to take on a management role.

'Our spectators are poor, and they can't support that economic burden,' Telat said. 'If we had continued to say politicians shouldn't run Demirspor, then we'd have killed Demirspor and we would have been closed down. You need to be a realist.'

There was a silence as we ruminated on the conflict between hopes and pragmatism. As we got up to leave, Telat added: 'Turkey's a young nation, and it can't be realistic. It always acts on emotion.' He looked me square in the eye before adding, 'If you act on your emotions, you'll be roasted, you'll die and you'll be gone.'

*

At the end of Terim's first season at Galatasaray, the team won the championship. They repeated the feat again and again. From 1996 to 2000, the team topped the league four consecutive times, an astonishing record that has yet to be beaten. Which prompts the question: what is the secret to his success? It was in this period that Terim began to be labelled as a 'motivational genius', able to inspire his players to unbelievable performances. These motivational abilities were pretty unique.

Videos from inside the dressing room at Galatasaray show him to be the prototypical Big Man – casting himself as a father-figure, overflowing with love but also vengeful and brutal if crossed. In one of the videos, before a domestic cup final, Terim gathers his players into a huddle.

'Listen to me carefully: we didn't come here to put on a show', he says. 'The fans are doing the show. You are here to win this cup for Galatasaray and yourselves. WHAT IS WRONG WITH YOU! YOU ARE PLAYING IN THE CUP FINAL!'

Terim's aggression is extremely focused, highly intense pinpricks of anger, rather than a rolling boil of rage. His words fly out, lightning fast, battering everyone for a second, with pauses between each volley.

'Did you get this far with this attitude?!'

'You came all the way to the final by maintaining your seriousness.'

'Pull yourselves together.'

'Add another title to your achievements. That is what big players do.'

'Now let me see my team!'

A huge roar goes up.

'MAY GOD BE WITH YOU!' screams Terim. He then positions himself by the door out of the changing room, clasping hands and hugging each player as they leave for the pitch.

Mehmet Şenol, a former editor of the Galatasaray club magazine, believes that Terim's formula works because it is based unashamedly around him. The record shows that he was ill-suited to 'schooling' in the traditional sense. His is a style built around sheer force of ego, a sense of self-esteem strong enough to make him believe without reserve in his way of doing things. 'Why shouldn't there be a Turkish school of football?' he once asked rhetorically. 'Is it impossible to create a playing style particular to us?' Terim has a tendency to speak in the first-person plural. Consequently, the 'us' is also a 'me' – Turkey becomes Terim and Terim Turkey.

Given Turkey's acute sensitivities about its image overseas, success on the European stage is the ultimate test for a star player or manager. As Galatasaray were steamrollering all opposition domestically, eyes inevitably turned towards the one field in which Terim – and Turkey – had yet to prove themselves: Europe.

*

The day before the Adana derby, the Demirspor fans gathered to cheer the team off. Like monks embarking on a retreat, they were going into pre-game isolation in the sparse and taxing surrounds of the Sheraton Grand Hotel.

The fans gathered at their headquarters. One young supporter came in and said something to me. I had no idea what he meant. He repeated it. I remained confused.

'Oh, you're not Kurdish?' the guy said in Turkish.

'No'.

'I am from Zazaistan!' he annouced proudly.

The others cracked up. An older guy mimed throwing something at him and said, 'Where the hell is that?!'

'Zazaistan!' The boy continued with a straight face. 'It's in the east. You go to Elaziğ, and Batman . . .'

'What's the flag then?' asked the older guy, playing along.

'It's this,' said the younger one, unzipping his hoody to reveal a Demirspor top underneath, then kissing the crest.

He quickly changed tack. 'Na, I'm only joking. I'm Turkish. Turkish. But also Zaza, do you know Zaza?' The Zaza are a people from eastern Anatolia. There is much ethnic overlap between Zaza and Kurds, although the Zaza tongue is an independent language in its own right. The incident is a reminder of how Adana – like all cities in the south and west – has received many migrants from eastern Turkey.

We walked to the training ground, passing first through a park and across a footbridge over the river. A fan near the back started to sing the name of the Turkish president: 'Re-cep Tayy-ip Erd-oğ-an!' At first I thought it was a piss-take, but then he turned to me. 'You know Erdoğan? They're mostly communists,' he said, waving at all the fans in front of me, 'but I like him.'

When we reached the Demirspor training facility, three-hundred or so fans were already gathered outside. The gates opened up and the fans poured into the complex, congregating around the fence looking onto the nearest pitch. A few adventurous ones shimmied up and perched on top. In the crowd, I spotted Telat. He was with a few other fans who were handing out boxes of flares. Not single flares. Boxes.

The sun had set and it was beginning to get dark. The floodlights of the training facility were switched on. By now, the number of fans sitting on top of the fence had swelled to seventy or so. I expected a sudden cheer when proceedings started, but it was more chaotic. Blue puffs of smoke started to billow up all along the fence, from smoke bombs held by the fans. I went up on tiptoes and craned my neck and was surprised to see the team already a good distance across the

pitch, walking over towards the fans. Then a red flare was lit. Shouts of 'Don't light it yet! Don't light it!' floated across from some places. But the first flare was followed by all the others. Then everyone began singing at the tops of their voices.

Believe kids, believe!
We'll see good days, sunny days
The blue engines will continue
We'll sing the championship song!

The words are adapted from a poem by Turkey's most famous poet, Nazim Hikmet, who spent much of his life in exile in the Soviet Union for his leftist views. It seemed a perfect meeting of message and purpose, and utterly at odds with the game in England. It's hard to imagine the crowd at Stoke City suddenly belting out a W. H. Auden poem.

*

It became impossible to see anything apart from red and smoke. Flares were being held up everywhere. I felt bits of ash falling all over me.

'Believe, kids, believe!' Surrounded by the noise and colour, it would be hard to do anything else. With this much energy, this much passion, of course they were going to win the league! There was that feeling you get when members of a crowd are all on the same wavelength – the resonance was almost debilitating in its power.

And then, all of a sudden, it was gone. The flares finished and the chant petered out, leaving in their wake the background babble of conversation. The manager addressed the fans, before turning and walking back across the grass with the players. Supporters turned and then left. Most streamed out on foot. Others fired up motorbikes. They jumped on them, revving the engines loudly, before letting out the clutch and driving away.

*

The name 'Fatih' does not travel well. Pronounced correctly – *Fah-tee* – it sounds, unfortunately, like the British slang for someone suffering from flatulence. But in Turkish it means 'Conquerer'.

The most famous Fatih is Fatih Sultan Mehmet, known abroad as the Ottoman sultan Mehmet the Conquerer who, in 1453, captured Constantinople from the Byzantines. Fast-forward to the year 2000, and the language of Turks against Europeans was used again, this time to describe events on the football pitch. Even the name of the chief protagonist was the same.

In the 1999–2000 season, Galatasaray reached the final of the UEFA Cup, the first Turkish side ever to do so. All that stood between them and glory was Arsène Wenger's Arsenal.

The sociologist Cem Emrence has chronicled how the cup run became a matter of national pride. The Turkish Football Federation built the fixture schedule around the team, moving games to ensure Galatasaray extra rest days after European fixtures. For the final, a third of all members of the Turkish parliament travelled to Copenhagen to watch.

We know exactly how Terim and the team prepared for the match, thanks to an extraordinary documentary made by Galatasaray TV. In the dressing room, Fatih Terim is stood in front of a tactics board, on which he scribbles furiously: 'We start off strong. There is no offside trap and when we press forward, we move altogether – bam, bam, bam – towards the ball. And we are going to play. With God's help, play like a lion!' he shouts. Then some advice for his midfielders – 'Watch out for that Petit, he likes to throw an elbow' – before he gathers his players into a huddle.

'Today we are playing our seventeenth European match,' he told them. 'This time it's the final. You will win. You will fight to win. But no matter the result, you've always won in my heart, you are always champions. WITH GOD'S HELP!'

The final itself was a scoreless epic. After plenty of argy-bargy in extra time – including a red card for Galatasaray's Gheorghe Hagi – it went to a penalty shoot-out. Galatasaray went first. Penbe hooked it into the corner above a diving David Seaman. Arsenal's first taker, Davor Suker, had a long run-up and saw his shot bounce back off the inside of the post.

'We're 1–0 in front!' screamed the commentator on Turkish television.

It soon became 2-0 when Hakan Şükür sidefooted into the top corner. Ray Parlour scored Arsenal's second, but the two-goal advantage was restored by Umit Davala: 3–1 to Galatasaray. Patrick Viera walked up. He hit the ball hard and high. It bounced back off the inside of the bar.

'My God! My God! The post hasn't allowed two of their shots now!'

The miss left George Popescu with the chance to seal it.

'Come on my son, come on son, come on son,' implored the commentator nervously, as Popescu placed the ball and took his run up. He smashed it in the bottom corner.

'Gooaall! Gooaall!! Gooaall!!! The cup is ours! The cup is ours!'

Terim had done it: he had finally lived up to his nickname. *Avrupa'nın Fethi*. The Conquerer of Europe.

In victory, Terim was humble. 'We can't succeed with the players alone. I thank our harmonious management board, wonderful spectators and, of course, the writers and visual media gathered here. When such a group comes together, there's no success that cannot be reached'.

*

Derby day dawned bright and sunny. A perfect early spring sky, with not a cloud to be seen. Three hours before kick-off, I began walking towards the stadium. When I got to within a block or two, the atmosphere changed. There was a crackle in the air. I got to one street and found it completely cordoned off by the police. They pointed for me to double back on myself.

As I did so, hundreds of Adanaspor fans rounded the corner directly in front of me. They were clutching glass bottles with scarves pulled over their faces, most looking no older than sixteen. 'You're all sons of bitches!' they chanted as they ran up the road towards the police. It was like something out of *Lord of the Flies*. Later on I found out that there'd been a fair bit of skirmishing between fans pre-game. Two Adanaspor fans had been stabbed, one seriously enough to require a trip to hospital.

Demirspor had arranged for my name to be added to the entry list for the VIP section. But when I approached the turnstile my Passolig card didn't work. After much checking of lists and trying of various solutions, the security official eventually gave up and waved me through.

The VIP section felt very much like the city's society event. All around, people were greeting friends, hugging and carrying cups of tea back to their seats. A man in jeans and a jacket got to the top of the stairs and paused in front of my chair, scanning the crowd. My eyes were level with his behind. Sticking out below his belt was the barrel of a pistol.

The Adanaspor players came out to warm up. The crowd stirred. 'The kings of the universe are coming!' echoed round three-quarters of the ground. From the Demirspor fans, a shrill whistle. Five minutes later the Demirspor players emerged and the crowd reversed roles. Four Adanaspor players crossed the halfway line and embraced a couple of the Demirspor players, making a mockery of the terrace partisanship.

The match itself was dull. Nothing happened until the 14th minute, when a weak Adanaspor header took a deflection and looped over the goalkeeper into the net. Demirspor couldn't seem to rouse themselves to fight back. The game was very unlike a derby, lacking both bite and edge. At the final whistle the Adanaspor players fell to the ground. It was a significant victory, not only to beat their local rivals but also to cement their position at the top with only half a dozen games to go. The crowd stayed behind to cheer their team, who paraded and danced on the pitch.

Outside on the streets, the atmosphere was wild. Youths were swaggering around, pulling up their Adanaspor scarves to cover their faces. Motorbikes were revved loudly, cars drove past with people leaning out of the windows waving flags and honking horns. There was a burst of sirens and two ambulances rushed past. I arrived back at the Demirspor fan headquarters to find everyone stood around on the street. I spotted one of the fans I had hung out with earlier in the week.

'A fight broke out,' he said, and he mimed someone being stabbed.

Another fan interrupted us to pat down his shirt, checking for blood stains. He didn't find any. My mind whirred: did *this guy* do it?

'Did the Adanaspor guy get stabbed or was he doing the stabbing?' I asked.

He looked mortally offended by the question.

'No, he got stabbed of course!' He couldn't help a smile.

That would explain the ambulances then. Three stabbings in a day.

*

Fresh from his European success, in July 2000 Terim was appointed manager of the Italian side Fiorentina. He was the first Turkish manager to work in Italy. The fans loved his attacking style – the side were the highest-scoring in the first half of Serie A. But the club's president Cecchi Gori was less of an admirer. News of a serious personality clash began to leak out. Results started to slide. By the end of February 2001 the situation was untenable and Terim resigned. AC Milan swooped, but he only managed nine games there before he was dismissed.

Terim's time in Italy lasted just twenty-nine matches. It was the first significant setback of his career. There are suggestions that at both Fiorentina and Milan Terim was the victim of internal politics and squabbling, but his belligerent attitude can't have made it any easier. 'A really strange fellow who seemed allergic to rules,' wrote Milan midfielder Andrea Pirlo of Terim. 'He'd arrive late for lunch, turn up for official engagements without a tie, run off . . . just so he could watch *Big Brother*'. His failure in Italy seemed to reveal the limits of his persona and motivational strategies. While the *kabadayı* image seemed to resonate with a particular masculine, working-class culture in Turkey, when transposed to Italy it led to ridicule.

In 2002, Terim returned to his beloved Galatasaray, embarking on a second management spell. It didn't go well, and ended with his resignation in March 2004. In 2005 he returned to the national team, tasked with guiding them to qualification for the upcoming 2006 World Cup. He took Turkey to second in their qualifying group, good enough for a two-leg play-off tie to decide who went to the tournament. Turkey's opponents would be Switzerland. What was to follow has now gone down in footballing infamy.

The first leg finished 2–0 to Switzerland. Turkish players and staff complained of insults while in Berne, including the whistling during the Turkish national anthem. Terim raised the temperature with comments to the media. 'Playing dirty suits them,' he said. 'We didn't come here to be sworn at. We came here to play football.' TFF representative Davut Dişli went further still. 'The things they did [in Berne] created an atmosphere of terror. But let's not forget – we can do this in Istanbul too . . . We're going to give the Swiss a day they won't forget'.

The result was an epic 4–2 victory for Turkey but, due to their clean sheet in the first leg, Switzerland scraped through on away goals. The game, however, is remembered for what happened when the referee blew the whistle for full time.

The Swiss players raced from the field. Terim is captured on video footage, waving for his players to run after them. The cameras show Swiss player Benjamin Huggel kicking at Mehmet Özdelik, Turkey's assistant coach, as he runs off. Then Turkish defender Alpay Özalan wades in and shoves Huggel and Marco Streller. Off camera, a huge melee erupted in the tunnel. Alpay kicked the Swiss midfielder Stephane Grichthing so hard, he spent the night in hospital with a perforated urethra. 'We expected an electric atmosphere and for things to be hot, but not like that,' Swiss midfielder Johann Lonfat said later. 'They went well beyond the limits of intimidation. I was told, "We're going to slit your throat."'

FIFA decided to ban Turkey from hosting the next six home internationals – the entire qualifying campaign for Euro 2008, in addition to bans for individual Turkish players, coaching staff and a Swiss player. The punishment elicited a furious response. Sports minister Mehmet Ali Şahin accused FIFA president Sepp Blatter – a Swiss citizen – of speaking as a fan rather than an official.

'Terim's a schizophenic guy,' said Galatasaray fan Ceyhun Akgül, who was at the Switzerland match. 'He doesn't know what to do. From time to time he wants to pose himself as the father of Turkish football, in a very wise way . . . but I saw Fatih Terim ordering his bench to chase after the Swiss players when the final whistle was blown. So there's a lot of hypocrisy.'

The debacle was very damaging. 'After the events at the Switzerland match, the image of the combative, belligerent Turk became dominant in Europe,' wrote journalist Alp Ulugay. Three years later, when Turkey was about to compete in the Euro 2008 championship, the president of the Turkish Football Federation, Hasan Doğan, realised that action was needed. He put in a call to a friend.

It was Yiğiter Uluğ, a former journalist and sports writer. Hasan Doğan wanted him to rein in the irascible Terim, especially in his dealings with the European media. Uluğ did not want to do it. 'I said: "This is an impossible task!"' he recalls. But backed into a corner, he agreed.

At the tournament, Uluğ coached Terim on how to respond to the media. 'Our meetings were like a [self-help] class,' he says. 'I would say: "Calm down. Be grandiose. We are bigger than them. We will beat them. And after beating them we will not look back. They are losers. They are pathetic. And we are going to conquer the world. So just laugh at them."'

In the first game, Turkey lost 2–0 to Portugal. The pressure was on. They needed to win the second game to keep qualification hopes alive. But there was a problem. The match would be against the Swiss. In Switzerland. With the memories of that night in Kadiköy all too fresh. Uluğ remembers seeing a grotesque caricature on the front page of a bestselling Swiss paper on matchday. It showed Murat Yakın, a Swiss citizen of Turkish origin, as a döner kebab chef, ready to slice up Fatih Terim, super-imposed onto the rotating döner meat. The headline read: 'One way or another, today we're having kebab.'

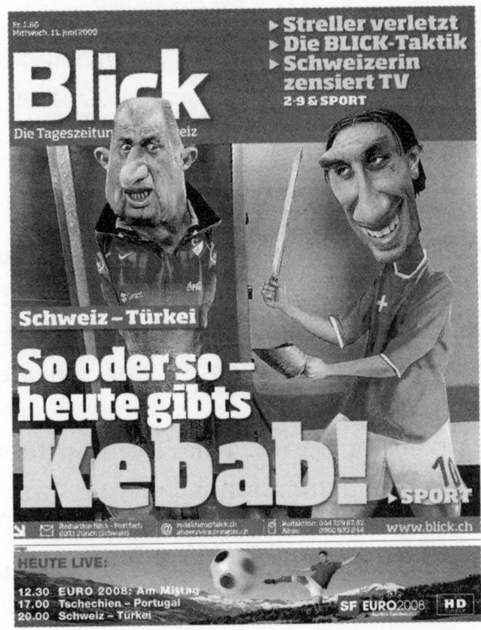

Fr. 1.60
Mittwoch, 11. Juni 2008

Blick
Die Tageszeitun[...]eiz

▸ Streller verletzt
▸ Die BLICK-Taktik
▸ Schweizerin zensiert TV
2-9 & SPORT

Schweiz – Türkei

So oder so – heute gibts Kebab!

▸ SPORT

www.blick.ch

HEUTE LIVE:
12.30 EURO 2008: Am Mittag
17.00 Tschechien – Portugal
20.00 Schweiz – Türkei

SF EURO2008 HD

The game took place in monsoon conditions — the ball continually held up in puddles, or slipping out from the goalkeeper's grasp. The Swiss scored first, with a tap-in from Hakan Yakın, another Swiss-Turk. In the second half Semih Şenturk equalised with a header, before Arda Turan grabbed the winner in the second minute of stoppage time.

Just after the game, Terim was giving the customary flash interview when a Turkish journalist popped up brandishing the Swiss front page. Uluğ was on tenterhooks. 'For the old-fashioned Fatih, that was the perfect stage to kill the Swiss. They tried to humiliate him but they lost the game. He's Caesar in Rome! . . . It was the moment of truth.'

Terim laughed at the reporter. 'These things happen. We are very happy right now. I don't care what they say.' At this point in the story, Uluğ leant back with a contented smile: 'That was my sweetest victory in the whole tournament.'

Turkey went on to reach the semi-finals where they lost 3–2 to Germany. But the performances and the character shown by the side again breathed hope into Turkish football.

Uluğ summed it up: 'It was a brilliant campaign. An incredible ride. But also I believe, according to international media, Terim was one of the stars of that tournament. He erased that arrogant, son-of-a-bitch look. He erased that. Because he wanted to.' Because he could.

*

I had gone to Adana with the aim of debunking notions of the 'feisty Mediterranean' and Orientalist assumptions of 'honour' and 'shame'. In the UK, masculinity is not all stiff upper lips and downing twenty pints; so in Turkey there are many ways to be a man. I longed to give oxygen to some of the less-stereotypical, to show that it is not all hyper-masculine posturing. The anarchy and violence following the derby, however, made this hard to do.

The same was true for Terim. I had wanted to give him a fair hearing, to consider that there might be more to him than his coarse public image. I went to see him at his Istanbul office and, during my brief audience with him, he was unfailingly charming and polite. Three months later, he messed it all up again.

In July 2017, he got into a fight with a restaurant owner and became embroiled in a saga that the British media quickly dubbed the 'Kebab Wars'. His adversary was Selahattin Aydoğdu, a former president of Adana Demirspor. Aydoğdu opened a restaurant next door to one owned by Terim's son-in-law in Alaçatı, an expensive resort town on the Aegean coast. Newspapers reported a dispute over the positioning of an oven and partition wall.

On 14 July, after an angry phone exchange with Aydoğdu, Terim got in a car with his sons-in-law and drove the 500 kilometres from Bodrum to Alaçatı. Security camera footage showed a brawl, with chairs and punches thrown, before Terim and his entourage climbed back into their vehicle and left.

Like two Silverbacks clashing, the incident quickly became an argument over 'true manliness'. Aydoğdu gave a statement to the police and press in which he questioned Terim's virility. 'Does a real man run away? I've done what no one has dared to do for years [stand up to Terim]. Now he's leaning on a neutral friend to make me withdraw my complaint . . . but I won't.'

On 19 July, Terim organised a press conference to give his side of the story. For him, the real issue was that the sister of his son-in-law had been 'insulted, threatened and abused' by Aydoğdu. 'I spoke to this guy on the phone and I got a nasty response,' said Terim. 'I hung up the phone, put on my trousers and got in the car.' Terim's *kabadayı* streak rose to the surface in the press conference. 'My rage couldn't be cooled. No one talks to me like that,' said Terim. 'I accepted the invitation [from Aydoğdu]. After that point it's very difficult for someone to get me to turn back.'

Terim's justifications were straight out of the alpha male playbook, revolving around his responsibilities as a man of honour, father and head of a patriarchal household. His press conference was also noticeable for lacking in apology or remorse. 'They say that Turkey's football manager shouldn't do this. But I see this incident as a father protecting his family . . . Be sure, I will always do everything for my family, always. As a father if this happened again, I'd react the same [way].'

There are some in Turkey for whom this explanation makes his actions admissible. Adana residents, in particular, seem unembarrassed by these crude outbursts and his violent behaviour; in fact, the opposite. He is the man who has proven their value and success on the national and international stage. 'A tough, hot-blooded son of Adana who always sticks to his principles,' stated one local newspaper breathlessly. 'There's only one word to define him: the pride of Adana and Adana people.'

But for many others there is much to dislike. He frequently refers to himself with the royal we, seemingly never defers to experts or says he's sorry and keeps questionable company (he is said to be close to Mehmet Ağar, a former interior minister with ties to 'deep state' groups blamed for the extrajudicial killings and disappearances that marred the 1990s). 'Many people – especially the more educated middle and upper classes – really hate Terim,' says Emre Delivelli, a die-hard Beşiktaş fan who lost his job at a Turkish paper for being too critical about the government. 'He symbolises everything that people who are not happy in this country are not happy about.'

Comparisons are made with Turkey's biggest Big Man of all, President Erdoğan, and the conclusion drawn that the wrong style of male behaviour is being encouraged. Many feel unable to support the national side when they are so upset at the direction in which the country is heading. 'Any sporting glory is used by Erdoğan, which really pisses people off. So many people are saying: "OK, if he's going to use it, then we should have no glory at all!"' said Delivelli. In Euro

2016, he found himself cheering for Turkey's opponents.

The restaurant brawl, however, was the straw that broke the camel's back. Press and public reaction turned against Terim. The Turkish Football Federation was compelled to act, its president calling an emergency meeting. 'Some non-football issues are wearing out our football director Fatih Terim and the TFF management,' they said in a statement twelve days after the incident. 'We have agreed that it would be healthier for the both parties to part ways.' But Terim couldn't accept going quietly. 'I did not resign,' he posted to social media. 'Let me be more clear: I was sacked by Turkish Football Federation.'

The emperor had been dethroned.

10

Amazons

A guilty pleasure of mine is my daily copy of *Fotomaç*. The owner of the corner shop across from my house has learnt the drill. Every morning when he sees me approaching, he pulls the paper out of the rack before folding it and handing it over, in exchange for the 1 lira coin in my hand (around 25 pence).

The newspaper is strictly devoted to sports – like Italy's *Gazzetta Dello Sport* or Spain's *Marca*. There the similarity ends, because *Fotomaç* don't really do stories so much as paragraphs accompanying pictures. It's Turkey's fifth most-read newspaper: highly nationalistic, pro-government, and my slice of normal life – the gossip column when I'm craving opinion from outside my bubble.

When I bought my copy on 8 March 2017 I was greeted by a pink headline: 'Today's *Fotomaç* was prepared by women!' Next to the title was an illustration of a mouth with pouty lips and a Marilyn Monroe-style beauty spot. My eyes were drawn to a poem below the headline, seemingly penned by the paper's editor. It was titled: 'Every beautiful thing has the trace of women':

> Woman; in the War of Independence with a baby on their back
> and torn shoes on their feet moved cannonballs to the front
> Women: are the face of the sun
> Women: are treasure, are diamonds
> Women: are a flower garden

Women: are mothers, are lovers
We thank the successful women on the screens of our sports world who prepared today's special *Fotomaç* for 8 March World Women's Day.
They signed off a first in history for the Turkish press . . .
They, when given the chance, show that they can topple even mountains . . .
To all women, happy World Women's Day . . .

International women's day is an event that largely passed me by in the UK, but is a big deal in Turkey. I flipped through the paper and saw that all the comment and opinion sections were written by female sport TV presenters. Their contributions were framed in pink, lest the women's thoughts were mistaken for the normal football stories.

Accompanying each writer's section was a table where they chose the 'Süper Lig's best'. The list contained the usual: best foreign footballer, Turkish footballer, manager, referee. The question given top billing, however, and the only one to feature a photo, was the question readers of *Fotomaç* clearly ponder most of all:

'Who is the most handsome footballer?'

A week later I was sitting in the office of Necla Güngör, a director of coaching at the Turkish Football Federation. In her mid-thirties, chatty, with a directness that is instantly disarming, Güngör told me her CV: a decade as assistant coach in the Süper Lig (at Gençlerbirliği, Ankaragücü and Manisaspor), eight years working in women's football, currently in charge of the Under-17 women's national team and adviser on women's football strategy.

I showed her the *Fotomaç* front page and she let out a long groan.

'It's really bad,' she confirmed. 'Because you're not seeing [a woman's] worth. You're only seeing her gender. "Women" is the meta-thing going on.'

Turkey is little different in this regard to most countries around the world. It is men who play, watch and write about football. Women make up less than 20 per cent of the crowd. When they play, it is seen as an irrelevant sideshow or transgressive danger. And as commentators, women get the chance to express their opinions in print on 'their' day, once a year.

'Unfortunately society looks at women like this: mother; cook; nice-smelling; capable of being a ballet dancer, gymnast or volleyball player.' Güngör listed for me the stereotypes, ticking them off on her fingers: 'Women wear pink, women wear skirts; they're obliged to wear make-up, they need to look beautiful.'

What stands out for me in Turkey isn't the stereotypes themselves – many of which I was familiar with from home – but their fixity and the frequency with which they were pointed out. Back in Britain, there seems to be increasing awareness of the fluidity of gender and a growing clamour for chipping away at its more extreme manifestations – the London Underground removing 'Ladies and Gentlemen' from its announcements, or the rise of gender-neutral toilets. In Turkey, however, gender seems often interpreted as a binary strait-jacket assigned at birth – another group to which loyalty is required and criticism discouraged.

'Society says, "You're obliged to fit this pattern,"' Güngör reiterated. 'When you don't fit the pattern then they say, "no – you can't be one of us." When you leave the herd, the wolf will grab you – tak! – And what will happen to you? You'll be excluded.' She uses the metaphor I hear again and again: *Sürüden ayrılmak*, 'To separate from the herd'. To stand out, be an individual. It is always a negative, always to be discouraged.

It leaves very little room for manoeuvre for the women – and men – trying to improve the profile and reach of women in football.

*

Once, when I was on a bus in the southern resort town of Antalya, a German man in his fifties got on, confused as to where he was going. After helping him out, we got talking. It was his first time in Turkey, and he was loving it. I listened as he rattled through the expectations that had been confounded. Suddenly one jarred. 'And there are lots of women who are not wearing the headscarf!'

'Er . . . yeah?' I thought to myself, surveying the bus. When Europeans picture Turkey, the image of women in headscarves appears to be a dominant theme. One of the most outwardly manifest symbols of Islam, around the world it seems to hold a vice-like grip on the public imagination whenever they think about Islam, modernity and piety.

According to official statistics, Turkey is more than 98 per cent Muslim.* It's almost impossible to escape hearing the call to prayer broadcast on mosque soundsystems in the early hours. And yet, far from being mandatory, as many outsiders often assume, it used to be illegal in many contexts to wear the headscarf.

The prohibition stemmed in part from the reforms of Mustafa Kemal Atatürk. Turkey's first president never banned the headscarf, but he did discourage women from covering their heads as part of what he considered a drive to 'modernise' Turkey. The more recent ban dated back to the 1980 coup d'état and applied to public institutions such as schools, universities and military establishments. In 1997, after the military forced the resignation of the Islamist ruling party through a 'memorandum', it became harshly enforced. For a while it added an extra element to the morning commute for some pious women – the need to stop in a mosque or public bathroom and don a wig before entering the university campus in order to avoid revealing their hair. Some went abroad to study. Others missed out on university altogether.

When Recep Tayyip Erdoğan's AKP swept to power in 2002, it tiptoed around the issue of headcovering, even though it was close to the hearts of the party's core voters. By 2007, however, the issue had reached crisis point. The AKP wanted to nominate Abdullah Gül for the presidency. His wife Hayrünnisa wore the headscarf, which would make her Turkey's first 'covered' First Lady. The army and many secularists were fiercely opposed. Pro-secularist demonstrations were held, attended by hundreds of thousands. The military threatened to 'openly display its reaction', no idle warning from an institution that had intervened in politics in the form of four coups in as many decades.

The AKP, however, stood its ground. Parliamentary elections were brought forward, which in effect turned the vote into a plebiscite on

* The official number most probably does not reflect the true religious make-up of society. Until a reform in 2016, identity cards contained a field marked 'religion' that invited citizens to choose either Christianity, Islam or Judaism, or to leave the space blank. Members of other faiths, atheists and converts from Islam faced the choice of leaving an empty box and facing possible discrimination, or misrepresenting their faith.

the controversy. Secularist newspaper *Cumhuriyet* ran a front page with a picture of two eyes under a dark veil with the heading 'Do you see the danger lurking in the ballot box?' But it didn't work – the AKP won a landslide. On 28 August 2007, Gül was elected president. In the years following the election, laws were passed to remove the ban on headscarves in public life.

In Turkey today, women who wear the headscarf can join the police force, be elected to parliament and enter the university classroom. Coming from a country with liberal attitudes towards personal dress and public displays of religious belief, it can be hard to understand why anyone would object to this.

Those in Turkey who are opposed to the headscarf feel that, during the AKP era, there has been a creeping shift in the status quo towards covering. They say they are made to feel uncomfortable in certain places, or turned down for certain jobs – the same complaints that covered women used to harbour. They fear a time may come when they are deprived of their right *not* to wear a headscarf. That would, of course, be wrong. But the opening of public spaces to covered women is, in my eyes, a positive step. And that includes the football terraces.

*

The image abroad of Turkish football is that it is very male. But in Turkey I have come across far more women who are explicitly fans of football than in the UK. Given the country's obsession with the game – its blanket coverage in the media and domination in conversation – this is completely unsurprising.

But many of these women who I have encountered have felt highly constrained in how they can express themselves as fans. Like in many countries, football fandom is tied up in patriarchal, macho images of what it means to be a man, given weight by the behaviour of public figures such as Fatih Terim.

Banu Yelkovan, a journalist and Galatasaray fan, used to go to matches in the 1980s. 'We [women] were very rare,' she recalled. There weren't even toilets for them. 'Every time my sister or I wanted to go, there was a policeman who took all the men out and would wait so we could go in.'

Today there are women's toilets, but every aspect of the experience of going to a match is codified as masculine. From the importance of holding onto strangers in the fan chants (something seen as socially unacceptable for women to do) to the words of the chants themselves. A popular Beşiktaş song begins: '*Our district is the boys' district! . . . Let no one be left out of the shadow of the flag!*' It is belted out by thousands, with no hint of irony that this invocation of the 'boys' district' excludes half the population.

In order to take part fully in the fan experience, women are forced into the position of behaving like classic 'male' fans. They can gain respect by downing large quantities of alcohol, or singing songs replete with the language of sexual violence. Itir Erhart, a university professor and football fan, described the moment she deconstructed her singing of *yarağımı ye fener*, 'suck my dick Fenerbahçe', a popular taunt. 'I had been passionately singing about actions I cannot perform as a woman and had completely adopted the hegemonic male discourse to fit in with the men in the family, to fit in with the football stadium environment.'

Some men readily accept women participating in such a manner, viewing fandom as more important than gender. Others titter at it. More still see it as completely wrong. Male fans frequently grumble about the presence of a woman, which they often feel constrains how they can act. Attending one away match, a fan who had earlier acted hysterically – shouting, screaming, annoying passers-by – suddenly became deathly quiet when our group met up with another group that included a female fan. I asked him what happened. 'Around her I can't behave like that,' he replied glumly, lower lip stuck out like a pouting toddler.

Many male fans believe that women should not come to games – especially away matches – not because of the threat of violence from the other team, but because of the profanity of their own supporters.

Swearing in Turkey is a far more serious transgression than in the UK. Fans are banned from stadiums for such mild collective swearing as calling the opposition 'dogs'. This of course doesn't stop profanity. People feel it is not only their right but their duty to swear at games, the majority of expletives involving the language of sexual violence – 'shafting' the opposition, who are frequently referred to as fags (*ibne*) and arseholes (*göt*).

These words reveal how in Turkey – as in many places – being gay is still seen as shameful. But the definition of homosexuality may surprise some. Men who penetrate are seen as powerful and virile. Only those who 'receive' are perceived as weak and effeminate. As a result, male fans can talk and gesture about fucking a rival male fan without worrying about the connotations. The vocabulary is one of sexual dominance and power. Only those who 'are fucked' are seen as gay and therefore fundamentally unmasculine.

Yet swearing in Turkey is not simply a form of (homophobic) abuse. It is also a way of generating closeness among friends or bringing the pretentious down a peg or two. The anthropologist Yağmur Nuhrat has even argued that, whether aimed at a referee who has given a poor decision or an opposition player who has dived, cursing the transgressor is about fairness. It is, she says, less a comment on a man's sexual orientation and more an insult on his manliness. The logic is about ensuring the wrongdoer receives the condemnation he deserves.

But there's a problem for women: swearing is highly gendered, something men can do but never in front of a woman. Banu Yelkovan recalled the effect she and her sister had on the crowd at Galatasaray matches. 'No matter where we stood, there was a circle around us – people who stopped swearing, people who stopped throwing things on the pitch . . . they were like, "Shh – there are girls!"'

The notion of 'gentlemanliness' (*efendilik*) in the presence of women pervades many notions of the game. A common punishment for fan misbehaviour at matches is an order from the TFF for the next game to be played in an empty stadium. In 2011, Fenerbahçe embarked on an experiment. Faced with one of these bans, they asked the Turkish Football Federation if they could instead make the game female-only. Women, so the argument went, could be relied upon not to swear or otherwise behave badly.

On 20 September 2011, the first 'all-female' crowd at a professional match in Turkey was comprised of 40,000 women and children. They watched Fenerbahçe struggle their way to an uninspiring 1–1 draw with Manisaspor. It was the first of what would be fifty-eight matches over three years that were played in front of women and children.

The coverage of these matches revealed much about how women's relationship to football is conceived. The TFF still referred to the games as 'spectatorless', despite the attendance of tens of thousands of women. The fact that women were given tickets for free makes it clear that they were not considered to be real fans. Secondly, the lumping of women together with children under twelve reinforced the patriarchal notion of a woman's first role as mother. Add to these the assumption that women wouldn't swear – wouldn't use that vocabulary dripping in sexualised imagery – and the entire event deprived women of a sexual character. They were child-rearing, polite-talking, non-fans.

Just like in the stadium, in order for women to participate in the life of the nation their sexuality needs to be played down. A key image in the early years of the republic was a woman civil servant going to work, androgynous in her suit jacket. In the 1960s and '70s, a trope in vogue among Marxists was that of the *bacı*, sister, the female comrade who was sexually unavailable. When I was learning Turkish, I was told that 'woman' was *kadın*. I would go around saying the word in all circumstances, not really noticing the responses I was getting. Then one day, someone told me the word was rude. A *kadın* is taken to mean a sexually active woman. Unbeknown to me, many people found the image squeamish. They suggested I instead use the word *bayan*, a more ambiguous term that could be Miss, Ms or Mrs.

Men, of course, do not go through the same process. On the contrary, men's role in public life is often sexualised – their virility not hidden but loudly celebrated. The dominant ideology of honour and competition is inescapably wound, culturally and psychologically, with phallic penetration. This goes doubly for football crowds. Once when attending a Beşiktaş away match at Fenerbahçe, I noticed a fan opening a Japanese flag to riotous cheers from the Beşiktaş section. Confused, I asked my friend what was going on.

'It's not a Japanese flag,' he responded. 'It's a . . . sheet.'

What I had taken to be a flag was actually a representation of a bloody bedsheet. My friend hesitated, but then decided to give the full explanation. 'In 2001 Fenerbahçe had gone twenty-four games unbeaten. If they went twenty-five, it would have been a record. Their twenty-fifth match was against Beşiktaş, and Beşiktaş beat them.' Traditionally in Turkey on the wedding night, the couple would show a blood-stained bedsheet to prove the marriage had been consummated – and that the bride had been a virgin. Its appearance here was suggesting that Fenerbahçe were virgins until Beşiktaş fucked them in the game. As the match unfolded, fans in the Beşiktaş end would display more 'Japanese' flags, mocking their 'shafting' of Fenerbahçe fifteen years previously.

Such sexist behaviour would, of course, never happen at an all-women's game. Imagine yourself a Fenerbahçe fan at one of these 'spectatorless' matches. You are attending with your friends or family, soaking up the atmosphere, settling into that exhilarating environment that makes it OK to loosen the belt of individuality a few notches and submit to the consciousness of the crowd. The players flicker by, the floodlights casting shadows. Your side has just taken the lead against Galatasaray. The stadium reverberates to the sound of 40,000 people cheering when suddenly, out of the roiling cheer a chant emerges. You find yourself following instinctively, like a twig swept along in the current:

'Cimbom [Galatasaray], what's going on? Your ass and head keep moving, shaking your hips like a belly dancer.'

Against the expectations of the authorities, women at the games did swear. Loudly. And often.

I might show you something that spreads from my groin to my knees . . . I stepped up on the ledge and opened my legs. Suck my balls Fener as you pass beneath

The belief that women in Turkey would not – indeed, could not – swear was so strong, that the reaction of the Minister of Youth and Sport, Suat Kılıç, was to suggest that men had clearly infiltrated the stands. 'It can't be women's doing,' he said on television. 'Turkish women do not sing ugly chants.' But the swearing continued. At one match, a Beşiktaş–Fenerbahçe derby in May 2012, chanting of the homophobic phrase 'Fenerbahçe faggots, you can't be champions' was so loud that the TFF was eventually forced to recognise what was going on and fined the club 60,000 lira (£12,500).

In 2014, perhaps in response to their unexpected behaviour, the Federation reverted to the previous rule. 'Spectatorless' games returned to being truly spectatorless. The era of female-only matches lasted three years.

*

Were you feeling curious about women's football in Turkey, you might type www.galatasaray.org into your web browser. A horizontal menu offers you many options. You hover over 'football' but the next level of links all refer to the men's team. Undeterred, you move on, over the tabs marked 'basketball' and 'volleyball', to rest on 'other sports'. Your eyes scan the list: swimming; water polo; rowing; sailing; athletics; judo; horse riding; bridge; E-sports – E-sports! You pause to chuckle over the inclusion of team computer-game playing. You then continue: tennis; chess. Hold on. You've reached the end. You read the list again. You then read it for a third time, just in case you got the Turkish wrong. You click on all the other links, even the one for the club shop, but you were not mistaken. Galatasaray, a club known for over a century for its football, does not have a women's football team.*

Fenerbahçe also has no women's football team. Erdan Or, responsible

* Galatasaray had female football sides for four years, from 2012 to 2016, but never an adult side, only at youth level. The club closed their female youth teams in October 2016, citing a lack of money. The same season Galatasaray spent over €20 million on transfers for the men's side.

for overseeing women's football development at the TFF, told me about a 2009 visit to Fenerbahçe when he had just started his job. Buoyed with the enthusiasm of a new role, he met with the co-ordinator of the club's youth system. Erdan started to make his presentation about bringing more women into the game when the man flagged him to a halt: 'Ey ey ey! Stop stop stop!' He related what he was then told: 'It's not necessary [to go on]. Our club managers don't believe in the youth system and they don't want to spend money for the men's football youth structure, therefore we don't care about women's football and we don't want to do anything on women's football.'

'That's . . .' Sat opposite me, Erdan found himself lost for words. He instead simply held out his arms, a gesture of bemused exasperation.

Of the Big Three clubs that dominate Turkish men's football, only Beşiktaş has a women's football team. They are seriously underfunded. A club insider once told me that, despite finishing second in the top division in 2016–17, the Beşiktaş women's side was denied the budget and support of even the male youth teams. Once, when the side was flying to an away game in Antalya – 700 kilometres away – people at the club grumbled at the cost, wishing they had taken a bus instead.

Across Europe, wherever professional football clubs have men and women's operations the women receive less money. Rare is the case like Olympique Lyonnais in France, where the club president finds it easier to secure sponsorship for the women's team than the men's. In Turkey, the situation is not helped by the institutional structure of the game. There are no professional women's leagues and women's football is classified by the federation as a 'developing league', falling under the same organisational umbrella as futsal and beach football.

'That is the typical structure of all national associations,' Erdan Or told me when I raised the issue. 'It's not necessary to establish a specific department for women's football because they are in the process of development.'

Erdan is not a TFF stooge. He is unafraid to point out where his organisation or UEFA could be doing more, although the rings round his eyes and occasional sighs generate the impression that he struggles to have his voice heard. 'You can either use a carrot or a stick,' he tells me. When it comes to dealing with clubs in Turkey, Erdan favours the stick. He asked UEFA to pass regulations requiring all professional clubs to establish women's teams. 'The mentality of UEFA, however, is to give some carrots, they don't want to make it mandatory.'

He suggested that improving women's involvement requires change in how women are perceived in public life, a task well beyond his remit. The irony is not lost on him that it is him – a man – who is charged with this. 'I'm one of the UEFA consultants of women's football and I am the only man in that group [across Europe]. They are *all* women. It should be a woman.'

So what are some of the wider issues to which Erdan alludes? Distrust of women playing football is tied to fundamental notions about what social roles women should fulfil in Turkey, most obviously manifested in policing the look of women's bodies and the clothes they wear.

Across the world, the female body is seen as a legitimate subject for public commentary and judgement. Like Iran, with its compulsory headscarves in public, or France, the Netherlands, Bulgaria and Belgium, which restrict full-face veils, Turkey is among a group of nations where policing women's clothing has become a state practice.

The journalist and author Ece Temulkuran notes how a central tenet of the project of westernisation in Turkey was the exhibiting of women, dressing and undressing them like mannequins. Mevhibe İnönü, wife of Turkey's first prime minister Ismet, apparently felt 'tremendously uncomfortable' in Western fashion but nevertheless submitted to wearing dresses and hats to set an example for the new Turkey. The anthropologist Ayşe Parla has written about the more extreme example of state intrusion in the form of virginity examinations, demanded by prosecutors in cases of rape, prostitution or adultery but also deployed by families eager to prove their daughter's chastity. Although virginity testing was banned in 2002, the 'routinised intrusion into women's bodies' continues through dint of women undergoing them 'voluntarily'.

This concern with sex and virginity in turn comes from a wider fear – of a woman not fulfilling her primary role as a mother. Some sports are seen as posing a fundamental threat to this role. It does not apply to all games: gymnastics and volleyball are viewed as suitably 'feminine'. The women's volleyball league is televised and its top players have professional contracts. Football, however, is seen as male. Consequently, there is the perception that it will change a woman's body in undesirable 'male' ways.

'Parents ask us: "If I send my daughter to play football, will she grow hairs on her chin?"' Mutlu Can Zavotçu, coach of the Beşiktaş women's team told me. Necla Güngör related the conversations she had with the mothers of girls, anxious about allowing their daughters to play. 'I give the example of a girl in the A team – does it look like her appearance has changed at all? No . . . Are our legs distorted? No. There's a perception generally that a girl who plays football, her physical appearance, her legs will change and her appearance becomes less attractive. No! Nothing like that will happen.'

Tied closely to this fear of women developing masculine characteristics is the suggestion that they will exhibit other socially unacceptable traits, such as homosexuality. Many conversations I had with those involved in the women's game – men and women – would venture onto this terrain, with often bizarre results. I was told by one coach about the two different types of homosexuality – the natural kind linked to hormones, but also 'unnatural' lesbians, the latter being people who supposedly pretend to be homosexual in order to 'gain social status'. They continued: 'It's totally about curiosity, excitement – disobedience and insubordination in the face of their parents and society.'

Some within women's football see it as their role to 'stamp out' this sort of behaviour. How? Again it comes back to physical appearance. Lesbianism is figured solely as the stereotypical image of a gay woman, perceived as someone who has short hair and who exhibits 'unfeminine' behaviour.

A coach at a first-division side told me he requires his girls 'to look like a woman' and gave examples. 'We generally try to get the girls to look after their looks and keep their hair long. When they go out for a match they are neat and tidy. They do a little make-up. They can put blusher on. Of course, not big lipstick or nail polish, but they present themselves as that kind of woman, like actresses going out on stage.'

Many involved in the women's game believe that the only way to overcome the prejudice around female footballers is for them to look like the stereotype of an attractive woman. 'As long as you look like that, you're an example, and you increase interest . . . If they see you with your hair like a man's they'll say, "Yes, football is a man's sport,"' one administrator told me.

Although women worldwide face challenges when they attempt to break free from the constraints of being defined solely as mothers, in Turkey the orthodoxy has a special twist. As mentioned previously, Turkey is a highly nationalistic, militaristic nation. School children are taught that Turkey is on a constant war footing – and that martyrdom in defence of the nation is prized above all else.

Women cannot serve on the front line, but their role has been clearly defined in this narrative – to give birth to and rear the soldiers who will fight for the nation.

Motherhood, then, is not a private choice but a national topic. It is this perception that allows President Erdoğan to liken birth control to treason and lecture the nation on how many children to have. No one is spared. When Beşiktaş full-back Gökhan Tore got married in October 2017, the president, acting as witness, addressed the couple: 'I expect three or four children from you both.'

One of the things I love about Turkey is how utterly crazy everyone is about children. After growing up in the UK, with its culture of caution around other people's kids, it was a revelation to see people pick up and kiss strangers' children. When going through the airport scanners, parents hand their babies to security guards who instantly forget about their jobs, so thrilled are they to coo over a baby. This love crosses generations and sexes; indeed, men are often much worse in the fawning and cooing.

But the downside is a vilification of anyone who, for whatever reason, does not have children. Because childbearing has become so entwined with notions of soldiers, defence of the country and continuation of the nation, there isn't the 'live and let live' shrug when confronted by a woman who decides not to bear children. Her refusal to become a mother threatens the very notion of the nation itself.

*

Özge Özel always enjoys the reaction of strangers when she tells them she is a footballer. 'First of all they're surprised. Maybe their facial expression changes.

'Then you explain that there's a lot of women's football in Turkey – a first league, second league, third league. You invite them to our matches. When they watch our matches, they're surprised. But the more they watch, the more the idea that women can play football dawns on them . . . when they see that we can play, the ideas in their heads change.'

Until 2016, Özge was a player for Konak Belediyespor, Turkey's top women's side. Founded in Izmir in 2006, the team has won the Turkish championship for the last five years back to back. The club is the most important and successful product of a determined effort underway across Turkey to build up the women's game.

The team is nicknamed The Amazons, a name derived from the ancient female warriors, long assumed to be a fictitious entity of Greek myth. Recent archaeological evidence, however, suggests that the story is broadly true: there really were Amazons, horsewomen who fought alongside men on the steppes of Eurasia. Some accounts locate their territory in part of today's Turkey. They were heavily tattooed, pot-smoking warriors who fired bows and arrows on horseback. Their skeletons show head wounds from battle axes. But they have been given a hard time by chroniclers throughout the ages, who characterised them as man-hating, one-breasted lesbians who castrated, killed or abandoned their own sons.

Growing up as girls who liked football, the women of Konak Belediyespor have had their own problems to contend with: fights with parents opposed to their playing, or patronising PE teachers who want to make every decision on their behalf. When playing against boys and men, Özge said, their adversaries were often deliberately rough. 'They get very voracious, because they're like, "They're girls, how can they beat us?" They start fouling. They shoulder barge. They trip you up.'

The Konak team are backed by the local district council, which provides their funding – another example of a municipally supported team. Although it is quite common throughout Turkey, I still find myself frequently wondering: if the team manager goes on a spending spree does the bin collection suffer?

Until a few years ago, Konak relied heavily on foreign football talent. Women footballers from around the world were offered generous contracts to come and play in Izmir. When Şema Pekdaş was elected mayor of Konak in 2014, she shifted the focus, getting rid of expensive foreigners in favour of a focus on the youth structure.

The municipality is proud of this work. 'We have 300 footballing girls,' explained Zeki Günen, an adviser to the mayor. 'We are the pioneer in Turkey. There's no other team . . . that puts as much emphasis on its youth training. Ours has become a women's football factory. We are always trying to develop them.' One of Konak's coaches, Ali Alanç, says that there is a real hunger for women's football. 'The children really want it. The girls in the neighbourhood look at the boys when they're playing and want [the coaching] too.'

I first encountered Konak women's team when a contact took me to watch one of their training sessions. The team's home is an AstroTurf pitch in the shadow of the Atatürk Olympic stadium in central Izmir. On a Saturday afternoon in October, the stadium echoed to the sounds of a few thousand people watching third-tier men's football. Local side Karşiyaka were labouring to a 2-1 victory over Kastamonuspor. As the crowds from the game started to drift away, their red and green tops cut into slices by the fencing, the women from Konak Belediyespor ran through complicated set-piece routines: goal kicks passing out from the back; corner kicks. For the final fifteen minutes of training they played a game on a third of the pitch, full of outrageous skills, pot-shots and audacious lobs.

I returned a few months later to watch Konak play Beşiktaş in the women's league. It was second place against first. This time you could hear the game before you could see it. Half of the small stand running along the pitch had been colonised by Beşiktaş fans making a racket as they worked through their chants.

Fans of the Big Three in Turkish football frequently talk about *arma aşkı*, love of the crest. One Beşiktaş fan explained the concept to me: 'The occasion isn't football for us, it's Beşiktaş. We've been to training camps, handball matches, basketball matches . . . if there's a table tennis match we'll go– the important thing is the crest. Behind the crest, we go everywhere.' The Beşiktaş women's team benefits from this devotion. A coachload of fans had come from Istanbul. Local Beşiktaş supporters had also turned up, bringing the total number of fans for the away team to more than a hundred. The supporters of Konak, by contrast, were limited to players of their youth teams and some of the mayor's retinue. Konak suffered the fate that befalls many sides in the men's Süper Lig; they were outshouted and outplayed by their storied rival. The game finished 4–0 to Beşiktaş.

*

In 2008 there were only thirteen women's football teams in Turkey. The league even stopped for a few seasons due to organisational difficulties. By 2017 the story was much better. In the 2016–17 season there were 120 women's football teams, organised into three divisions.

The TFF, in conjunction with the government, has a whole raft of innovations to encourage female involvement in football. University sports departments often have spots specifically for national team players, and the exam threshold for entry is also lower. Crucially, anyone who plays ten games for the national team has the right to skip the fiercely competitive civil service exam and be appointed to a government job, such as a PE teacher or sports specialist in government, complete with all the perks that come with it, such as a special passport and good pension.

Necla Güngör explained to me how these benefits are key ammunition for her in battles with parents. 'I tell them: "Can you go get a passport and take your child to England? Can you show them Italy?" Ninety to ninety-five per cent come from lower classes . . . When they see this advantage they say, "Yes, play! We give permission and support our girl."'

The fight to improve women's football is being waged at all levels of the game. One July afternoon, I went to see a training session for Dudulluspor, miles away from the Bosphorus on the Asian side of Istanbul. The Dudulluspor women's operation is managed and run by Erdem Göktürk, who got involved by accident after looking for a site to take photographs nearby to the Dudulluspor pitch. The club had just started a women's football programme. With Erdem's help, in 2014 they devised a weekend soccer school for girls aged between eleven and thirteen. It has since expanded to encompass a senior team and Under-13, Under-15 and Under-17 sides. Around 110 girls take part.

He sees girls' football largely as a civic endeavour. 'It is about creating social benefits to the girls and the surrounding area more than it is competing in the higher leagues,' he told me. He ran through their 'four pillars': recruiting talented girls from the local area (a new, mostly poor suburb); keeping them in school; providing them the chance to study at university; and, finally, developing a competitive team to act as a draw for girls.

While we talked, every once in a while we looked up at the action on the pitch. Erdem knew all the girls by name, and frequently passed comment on their performances. The quality of the football was high, especially the touch and footwork. The players were taking on and beating each other, doing back-heels and flicks. The Turkish ability to be much better at close control and dribbling compared to British players – it seems it has translated into the Turkish women's game, too.

Erdem is sceptical about the picture presented by the TFF of women's football being on the up. He sees the growth as quantity over quality and believes much of the impetus comes from UEFA, which he described in terms that made it sound like a foreign multinational eyeing up a local business: 'UEFA sees women's football as a big opportunity to increase the consumer base. They see Turkey as a big opportunity because of the young and growing population. So they would like Turkey to grow. Because of that there were funds coming into the Turkish federation to establish and maintain women's football.'

Back at the TFF, Erdan Or confirmed that he has received money from UEFA. Such funds have allowed the TFF to cover the travel and accommodation expenses for all the 120 women's teams – the remuneration process proving a logistical nightmare. He fears, however, that some clubs game the system, opening women's branches just to get the money, which they then use for their men's sides.

Across all levels of the game there is also a bottleneck in terms of age. None of the players I saw looked older than their early twenties. Turkish women's football seemed limited to girls who are pre-marriage and pre-work. Erdem doesn't have access to the statistics but he thinks the average age of 'senior' football teams in all but the top division – perhaps even that one too – is eighteen to nineteen years old. It seems the lingering expectations placed on women are at work even here. Football seems to echo the high drop-out rates from the labour force among mothers in Turkey. The country has the lowest maternal employment rate in the OECD, a group of thirty-five of the world's most developed economies. When asked why they were not in work, 55 per cent of economically inactive women gave their reason as 'being a housewife'.

The women's game is a long way from being professional. At Konak – the champions of the women's game – players receive less than £350 a month. As a result, the players all do plenty outside of playing football: many are at university; one owns a gym; Özge Özel, the player mentioned earlier, is studying for her civil service exams, after which she hopes to be a school PE teacher.

There is only so much that clubs can do on their own. Günen, the director at Konak, wants to see women's football televised and for people to be allowed to bet on the outcomes. 'Women's football survives on the opportunities provided by their own directors . . . we're already doing what needs to be done,' Günen told me. 'But this is something that essentially needs to be done by the federation. The federation needs to make our leagues professional. It needs to find funding'.

*

Given the obsession with the headscarf in wider society, I was struck by the way that it appeared to be a non-issue in Turkish women's football. After reading in the press about Rabia Ataca, who made headlines in February 2016 as Turkey's first covered player, I called her up to talk about it. Her story made me think about the fact that, over my travels, I hadn't seen any women players wearing a headscarf, even though teams like Dudullu are in socially conservative areas and the players are not all members of the elite. Could it be that women's football is a Kemalist stronghold?

Ataca said that her experience of deciding to play while covered has been very positive. Apart from one former school teacher, everyone was supportive. Although happy to have broken the taboo, Ataca – now playing at 7 Eylül Gençlikspor in Aydın – seems reluctant to focus on the headscarf issue. She sees a bigger battle at hand. 'Women's football in Turkey is a sport that is only very newly developing . . . and has shown quite slow development,' she told me. 'If we add the headscarf issue we'll be divided and won't be able to help it develop.' There's a broader message that Turkish society needs to understand, she said, 'We women can do this work. As women, we can both do this work uncovered or covered. That is, our external appearance and physical condition is never an obstacle'.

Rabia's comments reminded me of what Necla Güngör had told me was her dream for women's football: 'I want girls who play football to be as well known as men who play football . . . I want those girls when they put on the national kit to play in front of full stands. I want to hear applause and comments such as "Come on Didem! Come on Aslı! Come on Ece!" That's my biggest dream.'

There are some great efforts being made by people who are very devoted to the cause. But for all the hard work and local effort, it's clear to see that Turkish women's football needs a boost from above – an injection of exposure and cash to help it become as widespread as the men's game.

When I met Güngor and Or, they were both coy but hinted that something like this was in the pipeline. A few months later when reading *Fanatik* – the more 'high-brow' cousin of *Fotomaç* – I saw what they were referring to. After years of development and a round of negotiations, the Turkish Football Federation had secured a sponsor for the women's national team.

The company? Ariel washing powder. The road ahead is long and hard.

ÇARŞI

11

Manchester

On a cold night in November 2009, I found myself in the away end at Old Trafford, watching Beşiktaş cling onto a slender 1–0 lead. The crowd was its usual broiling mass of excitement. Fans stood on the seats, clasping each other at the shoulder to prevent themselves from falling. The chants were loud and in time to a drum being banged somewhere to my left. As full time approached, and it looked as if Beşiktaş might actually hang on, the cursing increased each time the team lost possession. *Orospu-çocuğu-amına-koyayım-siktir-lan.* Son-of-a-bitch-cunt-fucker.

Suddenly United broke. The ball came to Park Ji-sung, who played a one-two that brought him into the box. He got to the by-line and floated a cross to United forward Federico Macheda, who was unmarked six yards out. Out of the mouth of the Beşiktaş fan next to me tumbled a new word. '*Scheiße*!' he screamed – the German for 'shit'. But Beşiktaş's veteran goalie, Rüştü Reçber, extended dramatically and managed to tip the header over the bar. The away section collectively exhaled.

Here's a secret: whenever Turkish teams play in Europe, few of the away supporters will have actually travelled from Turkey. The pictures of packed terraces and fanatical 'Turkish' fans setting off flares are provided not by Istanbul regulars but by people like the fan next to me, whose linguistic slip inadvertently revealed how he had been raised: as a European with Turkish heritage.

Five minutes later, the referee blew for full time. Beşiktaş had only gone and bloody won. The fans went loopy, jumping on each other, hugging and shouting. They waved frantically and chanted 'bye bye!' mockingly in English as the United fans filed out. The stewards then began to shepherd them away and conversation resumed. A babel of languages rose out of the murmur: I could hear snippets of Turkish, German, English and Dutch. These fans would return to their hotels and take off the black and white of Beşiktaş. The next day they would journey to Manchester airport, exchange pounds for euros and show German and French passports bearing Turkish names to UK border guards. A few hours later they would arrive home; not in Istanbul but in Munich, Paris, Brussels, Berlin.

*

It is more than sixty years since people from Turkey began arriving in Western Europe in significant numbers. After the Second World War, an economic boom combined with labour shortages generated a need for workers. Millions answered the call. They came from southern Europe – Greece, Italy and Spain – from Yugoslavia and North Africa. From town and village, filling factories and warehouses. Most went to West Germany, where at first they were called *gastarbeiter* – guest workers – the term reflecting a period when these people were viewed as temporary, shifted across borders in response to shortage and surplus. Neither the workers nor locals thought they would stay.

Most of all they came from Turkey – at that time a predominantly rural country with increasing pressure on the land. Many migrants were people who had never seen their local town, let alone a big city. 'They have gone in one terrific step from an Anatolian village to Vienna, Paris, Brussels, Dusseldorf or Munich,' wrote the journalist David Hotham in 1972.

In the late 1970s, when the policy of importing labour ceased, the number of Turkish speakers in the European Community (the precursor to the EU) was close to two million. Over the years, their numbers swelled as relatives came to join them or they had families of their own. New waves arrived to claim political asylum, most of them Kurds or leftists fleeing repression but also, recently, members of the Gülen movement accused of plotting the July 2016 coup. Today, there are approximately five million Turkish speakers living across Western Europe. The vast majority – three to four million – live in Germany, but there are sizeable communities in the Netherlands, Switzerland, Austria, France, Denmark and the UK. Turkish speakers represent one of the largest diaspora groupings in Europe. And they are just as obsessed with football as their relations in Turkey.

In the early days it was difficult for fans to keep up with their sides back home. 'Turkish airliners used to bring some newspapers but when it reached us, it was three days old,' I was told by Zafer, a journalist who arrived in London in 1980. The emergence of VHS allowed diaspora fans to watch games for the first time. Someone would record the game in Turkey and send it to Europe, where fans would take it in turn to borrow the tape for a day or two. Satellite TV in the 1990s meant football could be watched live for the first time. New spaces such as coffee shops and members' clubs sprang up to allow fans to follow matches together.

In the internet age, the phenomenon of Turkish diaspora fandom has exploded. Today there are bars, clubs, online messageboards and Facebook groups across Europe devoted to overseas fans. There are European-wide groups, hundreds-strong, tightly corralled into regional branches. Whenever Beşiktaş, Fenerbahçe, Galatasaray – sometimes even the Anatolian clubs – play in Europe, they can mobilise thousands, descend on the city and produce a display like the one I saw in Manchester.

When talking about diaspora fandom I try to avoid the term 'Turk'. Many of these people are not, in fact, Turks. They are German or British citizens. They or their families are ethnically Kurdish, Circassian, Azerbaijani or Cypriot. Because the common point for all is speaking Turkish, I normally settle on 'Turkish speaker', but that term is clunky and some 'Turkish speakers' don't actually speak the language. So here I also use the term 'Euro-Turks', despite it sounding like the name of a bad TV series.

All of my tiptoeing is steamrollered by the vocabulary of host populations – in their eyes everyone is simply a Turk. In Turkey they are often referred to as *gurbetçi*, migrants, but only the very recent are migrants. Many were born and raised in Europe. Often their parents were, too. The difficulties over terminology is a glimpse into the complex politics of diasporas – of putting a hoop around so many people of such disparate backgrounds. Labelling someone as a Beşiktaş, Galatasaray or Fenerbahçe fan is often the safest bet.

In transforming themselves and their family's life chances through migration, these Euro-Turks have altered the way that both Turkey and Europe think of themselves, not least when it comes to football. They have had a disproportionate effect on Turkey's favourite game. The search for the heart of Turkish football, then, is broadening ever-outwards. For the story of the game today – its aspirations, realities and difficulties – unfolds on the terraces in Manchester and the football fields in Eindhoven as much as it does in Istanbul and Ankara.

*

Cars pulled up. Small children seemed to be pouring out from everywhere, clutching the hands of parents, running around, chatting excitedly. We headed into a corridor in the clubhouse to peer at a sheet of paper with the changing-room allocation on it.

It was a Saturday morning in a small town in the Netherlands. The Under-8 league was about to play its next round of fixtures. I was with Utku Kaya, a Beşiktaş friend who I had known for six years, and his son, who was about to play.

Utku began talking me through the Dutch amateur football set-up, which seemed to be regulated to within an inch of its life: age-groups labelled F to A, categorised from age 6 to 18. Ability levels ranked 1–6. Shiny 4G AstroTurf pitches and clubhouses costing a million euros each.

Utku is a football agent, a part-time scout and an overworked father. Born in Turkey, raised in London and now living in Holland, his experience is emblematic of the mobility, hospitality and hustle of Turkish speakers in Europe.

After locating the pitch, his son raced away to warm up with his friends.

'In our town we're the only Turks,' said Utku with a grin, gesturing at his son's team-mates, who all sport bouncy bobs of blond hair. A father and son from another town walked past and greeted Utku in Turkish. Both were wearing matching Fenerbahçe kits. 'I used to play football with him on a Thursday,' Utku said when the pair were out of earshot. 'I stopped playing with them because they're all AKP supporters and it does my head in.'

The game got going. It was fabulously one-sided – by half-time his son's side were 5–0 up. The action saw boys swarming around the ball, kicking lumps out of it and each other. By full time, everyone had lost count of the score but neither parents nor players seemed particularly bothered. After the game, we went to the clubhouse, where the players of all the teams were given free squash and crisps. The building was packed full of parents and children from all walks of life, a riot of modern-day Holland at its most diverse.

It is teams and facilities like these, along with the coaching they provide, that have produced legions of Turkish-speaking footballers, many of whom have gone on to great success. Utku's son has dreams of being the next European-Turkish superstar. And it's people like Utku who have a big hand in spotting and nurturing the talent.

*

Turkish speakers in Europe have reached most realms of public life, especially in Germany. One of the country's most successful film directors, Fatih Akin, was born in Hamburg to Turkish parents. Cem Özdemir, the joint-leader of Germany's Green Party, is the son of Turkish immigrants, as is Aydan Özoğuz, one of the chairs of the Social Democratic Party. In the UK, no members of the Turkish diaspora have entered the political mainstream (I don't count Boris Johnson), but they have made waves in the cultural world. The father of the artist Tracey Emin was Turkish Cypriot. Electro DJ Erol Alkan was born in London to a Turkish-Cypriot father and a Turkish mother. The fashion designer Erdem Moralıoğlu, whose creations are worn by Cate Blanchett and the Duchess of Cambridge, grew up in Canada to a British father and a Turkish mother. That is not to mention the less famous but no less successful doctors, lawyers, businessmen and plumbers who can trace their recent ancestry back to Turkey.

But it is on the football field that European Turks have had the most impact. European-Turkish players play at some of the world's largest clubs – people such as Emre Can at Liverpool, Ilkay Gündoğan at Manchester City, Nuri Şahin at Borussia Dortmund and Mesut Özil at Arsenal.

Born in the town of Gelsenkirchen in North Rhine-Westphalia, Özil was eligible to play for both Turkey and Germany. He chose his country of birth. 'My family and I will always be Turkish, but I was born and I live in Germany,' he said in 2009, picking his words carefully. 'I feel more comfortable in a Germany shirt.' In Germany, Özil has become a poster-boy of the multicultural, largely tolerant nation that has arisen out of unification. But it's interesting to compare his treatment with other mixed-heritage players. Lucas Podolski and Miroslav Klose were both born in Poland yet both have faced far fewer questions about their 'allegiance' to Germany. Özil, by contrast, finds his behaviour scrutinised, receiving criticism for perceived disloyalty, such as the revelation that he prays in Turkish during the German national anthem. The differing treatment doled out to Özil is an important window into the barriers and prejudices Turkish speakers in Germany have to contend with. They are seen as a group less willing – or able – to be integrated, a stance no doubt sharpened by suspicion or hostility to Islam.

In Berlin in 2010, Germany played Turkey in a European Championship qualifying match, the stadium so full of Turkey supporters you'd be mistaken for thinking Germany was the away team. *Die Mannschaft* ran out comfortable 3–0 victors. And who popped up to score the second goal? None other than Mesut Özil, head bowed, a sheepish look on his face. In the Turkish bar in the Berlin suburb of Kreuzberg where I was watching, a few people swore at the screen but then one man stood up and clapped, shouting 'bravo!', followed by others. Members of the diaspora sometimes enjoy calling him a 'traitor' but, if pushed, many will confess to taking pride in his success, and no one really begrudges him his choice. With his World Cup winner's medal, I doubt Mesut thinks he made a mistake either.

Özil, Can, Gündoğan and Şahin are the most high-profile Euro-Turks because they have stayed to play football in Western Europe. But even more numerous are the dozens who have ended up going to play in the 'homeland'. And this is where Utku comes in.

Utku works voluntarily as a scout for his beloved Beşiktaş. Back at his house later in the day, he went to a file and pulled out a sheet of paper. At the top was the Beşiktaş logo and 'Volunteer scout player recommendation form'. The rest of the sheet consisted of different boxes for comments and numerical scores. Utku had filled it all out in meticulous detail.

'See that name, who is he playing for now?' he asked me, pointing at the sheet of paper. Written at the top was 'Sinan Gümüş'.

'Galatasaray?' I responded hesitantly. I was not as good at this as I should have been.

'At that time, who was he playing for?' asked Utku rhetorically, pointing at the space on the form where the team name was written.

'Stuttgart', I parroted back.

'Exactly' he said. His voice was a mixture of pride at spotting Gümüş, mixed with annoyance that Beşiktaş ignored his report.

Utku is a capillary in a vast network of contacts, links and connections, all tracing their way back to the heart of Turkish football: the Big Three Istanbul clubs. As in Turkey, the Turkish diaspora is dominated by support for Beşiktaş, Fenerbahçe and Galatasaray. These clubs leverage the love and loyalty of overseas fans to expand their reach and status around the globe. There are hundreds of men like Utku who devote hours to watching obscure games and writing reports with no remuneration.

But for Utku it was not turning out very well. His plan had been to show his worth, with the aim of landing a proper job within the club's scouting department. But despite being complimented for the meticulousness of his reports, the club never acted on them.

'I said: "'Here's Michael Hector for you – 500k, maximum 800k. You're looking for a central defender, there you are.'" He was referring to a Reading player he had wanted Beşiktaş to sign.

'What happens? Two months later, Chelsea pay £5 million on the last day of the transfer window!' Recently, Utku has started doing the same work for Crystal Palace, hoping they will take him more seriously.

Their Turkish surnames mean Euro-Turks are not always easy to spot in the Turkish league. But speak to anyone involved in football in Turkey and you realise that the entire apparatus of the game – from its clubs to the national team – is based on the piping in of European talent.

Take for instance the Beşiktaş side that won the league in 2016. On the surface, the side was a balance of Turkish and overseas stars. Foreigners like Ricardo Quaresma (Portuguese), Atiba Hutchinson (Canadian) and Mario Gomez (German) took their place in a starting XI containing Turkish players such as Olcay Şahan, Gökhan Tore, Cenk Tosun and Oğuzhan Özyakup.

Except none of those 'local' players was born in Turkey. Most grew up in Germany (Şahan in Düsseldorf, Tore in Cologne and Tosun in Wetzler). Özyakup was born in Zaandam in the Netherlands. Two further members of the Beşiktaş squad, Veli Kavlak and Kerim Frei, are from Austria. In total, from eleven 'Turks' in the squad, only five were born in Turkey. During one game, a pitch-side microphone picked up Olcay and Gökhan stood over a free-kick, talking about who was to take it. They were debating in German.

'You hear a lot of German,' said Andreas Beck, who played as Beşiktaş fullback from 2015–17. 'You hear a lot of English too. I would say it's 30/30/30 – Turkish, German, English,' he told me. This cosmopolitanism has many benefits, including making the team environment more inclusive of foreigners. Beck said that the number of German Turks at Beşiktaş was a factor in his decision to move from Hoffenheim. It has a positive impact on the football, too. These players are products of the German youth system – one of the best in the world.

But there is a malignant side to this plundering of European-Turkish talent. It is like a sticking plaster for the football system in Turkey.

Investment by the large clubs in their youth set-ups is lamentable.* In the last few years, the number of young players who have gone from youth to first team at Galatasaray, Fenerbahçe or Beşiktaş can be counted on one hand. A culture has arisen of buying in success, especially 'famous' players reaching the end of their careers. The lack of young, home-grown players in the first XI at the top clubs is another way in which the English and Turkish games reflect each other – the main teams are clogged with expensive foreign signings. In England they are usually at the peak of their careers; in Turkey they are often looking for one last payday.

Euro-Turks also keep the Turkish national side afloat. Of the squad of twenty-three for Euro 2016, one third were born abroad. The most exciting talent, Emre Mor, is an eighteen-year-old from Denmark who, if rumours are correct, can barely string a sentence together in Turkish. The over-reliance on football imports worries many in the Turkish footballing world. 'If FIFA pass a law saying players can only play in countries where they were developed, we'll be screwed,' said Ahmet Güvener, who worked in the Turkish Football Federation in the 1990s and 2000s. But there is little sign of serious change.

Most in Turkey see members of the Turkish diaspora not as foreigners but as 'Turks'. Many players also indulge the idea for the benefit of their careers. But this viewpoint is often a projection. So who are these people? And where do they belong?

*

In 1990, Conservative MP Norman Tebbit proposed assessing integration in Britain by applying 'the Cricket Test' to British Asians. 'Which side do they cheer for?' he asked whenever England played India or Pakistan. 'It's an interesting test. Are you still harking back to where you came from, or where you are?'

On this logic, many European Turks would 'fail'. If you happen to be on Stoke Newington High Street in London, or KeupStraße in

* A notable exception is Izmir side Altınordu FK. Playing in the second tier, the club place great pride in developing Turkish talent, captured in their motto: 'a good person, a good citizen, a good footballer'. Recent successes include Cengiz Ünder, who Roma paid €15 million for in July 2017, and defender Çağlar Söyüncü, center-back with Bundesliga outfit SC Freiburg since July 2016.

Cologne at a time coinciding with the end of a Fenerbahçe or Galatasaray match, you'll watch hundreds of people pouring out of bars dressed in the colours of their teams, smoking and debating furiously. 'Turkish boys always support Turkish teams here in Germany,' one Beşiktaş fan told me declaratively. For some, this is evidence of parallel lives and a lack of involvement in mainstream society.

But viewing football support as somehow emblematic of multiculturalism seems, frankly, a rather reductive view of belonging. Pulling on a Beşiktaş shirt and cheering for the side for a few hours is hardly akin to burning your passport in the street. Sports affiliation is not life or death. Indeed, precisely because it's not life or death, people enjoy cultivating a different side of themselves. What seems to evade politicians like Tebbit is that the cocktail of practices, beliefs and actions that we label 'identity' can be poured into containers of many sizes and shapes. And, if you have the ability to do so, every now and then you may want to pour this liquid into a different configuration. Not because you're 'disloyal', a fifth columnist or harbour a great antipathy to the land of your birth, but because it is fun.

I can say this with some authority, as I've spent four years of my life researching fans of Turkish football in Europe. During that period I criss-crossed the Continent, from Portugal to Israel, Lithuania to London, watching Beşiktaş, Galatasaray and Fenerbahçe. I stood with fans on terraces and sat with them in bars as they watched games. I became a member of internet message boards and befriended hundreds of fans on Facebook. I kept people company at work, attended parties, political demonstrations and even weddings, all under the spurious justification of writing a PhD.

I saw that, despite the rhetoric of Turkey as 'homeland', it didn't mean that all fans wished that they lived there. Turkey is a place to feel proud of, to journey to on holiday a few times a year to sightsee, sunbathe and visit relatives – but not to move to or die for.

Football plays a key role in this imagining. In November 2016, while I was queuing up outside the Fenerbahçe ground for my ticket to a Fenerbahçe–Galatasaray game, I noticed that instead of Turkish ID cards, fans were handing over German, Dutch and Swiss passports. They held bags full of club merchandise. Out of their mouths came excited conversation in German or English. At another derby match,

POLICE
ÇARSI
BERLIN
POLICE

I chatted to a man who had flown over from San Francisco.

They would no doubt be offended by me using the term, but these trips to Turkey for games seem a form of heritage tourism, not dissimilar to American sightseers on a tour of Scottish castles. Writing about that group, the anthropologist Paul Basu describes the motivations behind such trips: 'to re-territorialise their identity, become more bounded by place, develop more authentic senses of continuity with their ancestral past, and recover a degree of cultural distinctiveness'. European fans of Turkish football share the same motivations. To my knowledge, no US politician has devised a test of loyalty for North American visitors to Scotland.

Just as these fans shouldn't be seen as unproblematically 'at home' in Turkey, they shouldn't be seen as outsiders in Europe. 'I'm actually more German than Turkish,' one fan confided to me, wearing his Beşiktaş shirt, beer in hand while watching a game on TV in Stuttgart. Disapora fans are part of the rhythms, beliefs and values of the places where they live. They are people like Zeynep, a chain-smoking tri-lingual student from Cologne, who frequently skips lectures and shifts at work to travel to Beşiktaş games. When I chatted to her in English, she used an app on her phone to translate the few words she didn't understand into German – never into Turkish. Another time I met Hakan, a Fenerbahçe fan from London who works in sports science at Crystal Palace FC. He was scathing about the lack of sports scientists in Turkey and vowed never to work there: 'It's just old school – all the managers are old,' he told me in a thick Lahndan drawl. 'They haven't adopted the tactics yet.'

Even those who migrate to Europe as adults, who face greater linguistic and cultural barriers, don't normally want to be viewed as outsiders in their adopted countries. People like Mehdi, who works in a kebab shop in Watford. He beamed with pride when he told me how his two young girls will speak fluent English and have greater opportunities in life than he ever did.

The responses of these fans to the football is rarely a carbon copy of those in Turkey. In May 2013, a Beşiktaş end-of-year celebration in Frankfurt was put on hold for two hours so everyone could watch the Champions League final between Dortmund and Bayern Munich, the crowd dividing into two and the language switching from Turkish to German.

In short, Turkish speakers in Europe are no different from myriad other people whose recent heritage bridges multiple nation states or continents. Any attempt at understanding should not try and 'make' them one thing or the other but accept them for what they are – a dynamic, ever-changing combination of elements.

*

'I was born in England. But I had a Turkish name. I ate pie and mash and watched *Only Fools and Horses*, but I also ate dolma, rolled vine leaves prickled in brine and stuffed with mince meat'.

Muzzy Izzet grew up a half-English, half-Turkish kid in London's East End before making his name playing at Leicester City. I went to meet him on a windy and overcast English 'summer's day'. Izzet now runs a football school in a small town just outside Leicester – less than five miles from where I was born and raised.

When I pulled into the car park I felt a strong sense of déjà vu. I almost certainly played football at the ground as a child, one of many Sunday morning trips to all corners of Leicester, often accompanied by my dutiful dad. Instead of meeting up with team-mates, heading onto the pitch and kicking a ball around, this time I walked across the gravel to a prefabricated cabin and rapped on the door. It opened and out poked the head of Mustafa Izzet. The face was as I remembered him – boyish, alert – but it rested underneath a new hairstyle: a stylish 1950s rocker-style quiff, peppered with grey.

I grew up a Leicester City fan, Izzet was part of my life from an early age. My childhood coincided with Leicester's period of success under Martin O'Neill – two League Cups and top 10 finishes in the Premier League. Izzet was a key part of that famous side, the number 10 able to provide the bit of quality which often led to a win. I had posters of him on my wall. And this was not the first time we had met. He once handed me an award for 'most improved player' at my club's end of season gathering. I was seventeen. I decided against asking him if he remembered.

The inside of the portakabin was furnished like a classroom. The space was dominated by desks arranged into islands of six or eight. On the wall was a whiteboard. To its right, a Turkish flag. We sat down at one of the desks. Izzet's arms were a carpet of tattoos – another addition since his Leicester City days. In retirement he looked

more like a professional footballer then he ever did when he played.

On the surface, Izzet's story is one of success. His performances for Leicester drew the attention in 2000 of the Turkish national side. He ended up playing ten times for Turkey, including in the 2002 World Cup semi-final – the national side's most important football match to date. In his autobiography, Izzet memorably outlined the slightly unusual process by which he was accepted by his new team-mates.

'I remember the other players gathering around me in the changing room, pointing and staring, wanting to know if I'd had it done, if I was "a good Turkish boy". So I showed them. They nodded their approval. And that was that. I can safely say that I've never shown my penis before, or since, to a group of approving young men but, if nothing else, it seemed to help the bonding process.'

But it wasn't all plain sailing. Izzet didn't speak any Turkish. In fact, before he started playing for the national team, he had only been to Turkey once, on holiday to Bodrum in 1996. These barriers were to prove to be an issue. 'I didn't feel quite part of it because I couldn't be their mate,' he said to me. 'I couldn't physically be a friend or make friendships because the language barrier was in the way. I was sort of sitting on the periphery looking in.'

Izzet's account is a fascinating insight into the Turkish national team – the pre-eminent symbol of national pride in Turkey but which, at the playing level, was an uneasy composite of an international cast of characters.

'There were about four or five who came from Germany,' he said. 'Culturally they were different.' Here Izzet paused for a long time, fiddling with his watch and clearly thinking hard about how to phrase his description. 'Turks are quite an intense race of people anyway. They seemed a little bit more laid back, the German Turks. They hadn't been in that culture. There was just something about them, in their body language, they didn't seem as intense and full on.'

Izzet found himself gravitating towards the German Turks, who could speak a bit of English and, like him, enjoyed a drink. But he never fully felt like he belonged. At the World Cup, he would spend all his free time sitting alone in his hotel room, watching endless DVDs and missing home. 'They accepted me and my circumcised Turkish penis . . . But no matter how hard they tried, there was a chasm between this East End boy, a second generation Turk, and them.' As the conversation unwound, I found myself thinking that, in many ways, I am more 'Turkish' than he is. I know the language and have spent far more time in the country. We reflected upon the weirdness of identity – he is supposed to belong in Turkey, while it is expected that I never will.

What struck me most in Izzet's story was the dislocation caused by his upbringing. 'You've got to remember I was brought up in East London with a white-looking face . . . but to be called Mustafa – that was a bit hard at first,' he said. 'You go to a new school and if you were called "Tom" it's fine. But to be called Mustafa Izzet it was a little bit hard back then.'

Indeed, it is dislocation that threads itself through all the stories of these Turkish speakers: players, fans and football agnostics alike. Their lives spill across borders and boundaries that the world tells us are important and sacrosanct.

On a flight back to Istanbul from London one time, I got chatting to the man next to me, who looked Turkish.

'Where you headed?' I asked him.

'Gaziantep for the match,' he replied in a broad cockney accent.

I looked at him blankly. He told me Fenerbahçe were playing there.

'You a big fan then?' I asked.

'Well, I'm fucking flying from London, aren't I?'

It turned out this was Hakan, head of the UK branch of the Fenerbahçe fan club. We chatted as we walked through the airport. He bemoaned the state of Turkish football and the government, before abruptly stopping that line of thought.

'But what do I give a shit? I'm a tourist. The only thing that connects me to here is Fener.'

'Don't you have family here?' I asked.

'No, they're all back at home,' he responded, before realising what he had just called London: 'See, I said "home",' he laughed.

'My dad moved there forty years ago. He drinks his tea with milk!'

As we approached the passport check, I headed in the direction of the 'foreigners' queue, but he pulled up short. 'Unfortunately, I have dual citizenship so . . .' His voice trailed off. We said farewell, and joined our two separate lines.

*

There are plenty of people who complain about integration problems with Turkish speakers in Europe. The European 'Turkish community' (always singular, despite spanning different nations, religions and ethnicities) is often associated with ghettoised, poverty-ridden inner city districts, and frequently the subject of accusatory questions: 'Why do so many Turks seem so attached to their grandparents' homeland?' 'Why are they less successful than other immigrant groups?' 'Is it true that they only ever marry each other?'

Unease and suspicion can easily shade into racism. Utku pins the failure of his short-lived attempt at coaching a local Dutch youth team to his Turkishness. During a bust-up in the clubhouse, the brother of one player ended up blurting out: 'Who the fuck do you think you are, you Turk?' Colin Kazim-Richards, the former Arsenal player who was born to a Turkish-Cypriot mother and a black British father, told an interviewer that he used to hear shouts from the stands of: 'Go back to Turkey, you fucking Turkish kebab.' He said: 'I've faced more racism in England for being Turkish than being black.'

The distancing and othering reaches to the highest levels. On the eve of Euro 2016, Alexander Gauland for the 'Alternative for Germany' party claimed the national football team was 'no longer German', and said of a trip by Özil to Mecca that it was 'hard to get used to'. Such language may push Euro-Turks to associate less with where they are living and more with their perceived 'homeland'.

But the biggest factor inhibiting a sense of belonging for many Turkish speakers in Germany is not rhetoric but citizenship policies. Germany has a strict attitude towards dual citizenship. Until 2014, those holding two passports were forced to renounce one of them before the age of twenty-three.* That year the law was eased slightly, but remaining a

* There is an exception for EU countries and countries that do not recognise dual citizenship, such as Algeria, Iran and Syria.

dual citizen is not automatic. To qualify, children of immigrants must have been born and educated in Germany. In 2002 there were over 2.5 million Turkish speakers in Germany, but only 470,000 with German citizenship (Mesut Özil gave up his Turkish passport in 2006).

The policy is a result of a citizenship model based on a principle known as *jus sanguinis* – right of blood – where citizenship stems not from your country of birth but from where your parents originated. Such a policy has allowed millions of people of German descent living in Eastern Europe to be labelled *Aussiedler*, ethnic German emigrants who have the right to 'return' to Germany and apply for citizenship, despite ancestors living outside German territory for up to five hundred years. By contrast, those born and raised in Germany to Turkish parents – who often speak better German than Turkish – do not automatically have the right to citizenship. The mentality leads to the labelling of Turkish-speakers born and raised in Germany as 'Turks', with no question of how that might be received.

Notions of blood are also at work in Turkey. 'Players like Mesut [Özil] and İlkay [Gündoğan] are genuine Turkish boys who carry the same blood with us in those lands,' wrote Tunç Kayacı in *Fotomaç*. Blood is central to ideas of Turkey and Turkishness. The flag is meant to represent the moon and stars reflected in a pool of blood spilled in battle. And the colour red – symbolising procreation – takes prominent place at many of life's ceremonies: from circumcision to weddings. Turkey and Germany can be as bad as each other with their myths of racial exclusivity. A 2014 book, entitled *Atatürk in the Nazi Imagination*, makes a compelling case that Hitler drew inspiration from the founder of the Turkish republic and his 'prosperous and *völkisch* modern state'.

Turkish election laws, too, have been redesigned to pull Euro-Turks closer to the motherland. Overseas voting was introduced in 2014 by Erdoğan, keen to harness a new constituency in his campaign to become Turkey's first directly elected president. The change has made life more difficult for the Turkish-speaking diaspora. When, in 2017, the results of a referendum in Turkey showed that 63 per cent of overseas voters in Germany backed a highly divisive plan to enhance the president's powers, it prompted howls of outrage from German right-wing political leaders who demanded that this 'fifth column' of Erdoğan supporters 'go home'. A closer look at the numbers tells a less alarming story. Only around half of the roughly 3 million-strong diaspora in Germany was eligible to vote. Turnout was low. So in fact just 14 per cent of Germany's Euro-Turks backed the change.

Indeed, for all the rhetoric about being 'blood brothers', Erdoğan's efforts to cast himself as a leader for the Turkish diaspora frequently alienates its members. On the train to the Turkish Cup final, amid an ongoing war of words between Europe and Turkey, I met a Konyaspor fan from the Netherlands. 'President Erdoğan is making a *big* mistake,' he told me, referring to the president's efforts to claim the diaspora as his own. 'I am very happy in the Netherlands.'

When Euro-Turks journey to Turkey it can also be problematic. They are referred to as *Almancı*, a pejorative term which is something like 'Germany-ones'. People mock their Turkish – sometimes, upon hearing my dodgy grammar, people assume I must be a German-Turk. Visiting the central Anatolian city of Kayseri one August, I was struck by the number of cars with German and Austrian number plates. The restaurants were full of families speaking German. They were bringing money to the region, getting in touch with relatives, but all I got from my local taxi driver was grumbling. 'They build houses in the villages, come for two weeks in the summer, then lock up the door, go back and it's empty for another year.'

It would be wrong to assume that those who moved to Europe are always 'better off' than those who stayed behind. The huge explosion of wealth in modern-day Turkey, combined with the levels of discrimination felt in Europe, means often people who stayed behind (or moved from the countryside to a Turkish city rather than a foreign one) may have more comfortable lives. Though European salaries may sound high to Turkish ears, there is little appreciation of the high cost of living. Utku recently had to take a desk job to keep the family afloat. At the Konyaspor cup match, I met a seventeen-year-old who had just moved *from* Holland to Turkey. When I asked why, he shrugged: 'No opportunities there. My parents preferred to be in Turkey.'

Recent years have seen a growing intolerance towards 'hybrid' identity. 'If you believe you're a citizen of the world, you're a citizen of nowhere,' UK Prime Minister Theresa May said in her speech to the 2016 Conservative Party conference. European Turkish speakers are at the centre of a battle over where they really 'belong'. Erdoğan told

German Turks in 2008 that it was acceptable to integrate but that assimilation was 'a crime against humanity'. They should learn Turkish first, not German, he said. Germany's foreign minister at the time, Guido Westerwelle, hit back, saying that the priority must be for children to learn German. The end result is politicians using ever-tougher language, locking themselves in a dangerous race to the bottom.

If we stop demanding that Euro-Turks choose sides, it becomes glaringly obvious that it is possible to be both Turkish and German, British or Dutch. In 2014, Beşiktaş drew Arsenal in the Champions League qualifying round. The Emirates Stadium sits in a part of north London where many migrants from Turkey settled when they first came to Britain.* Consequently, many London-Turks are Arsenal fans. The game might have been seen as a Turkish Tebbit test in action, but the diverse response of football fans showed why the entire concept is so silly.

Supporters went in all directions. 'Is my heart torn? Don't be stupid,' said a kebab shop owner from Dalston. 'Come on Arsenal, spank 'em!' I met other Beşiktaş-Arsenal fans who were proudly rooting for the Istanbul side. As for London fans of both Tottenham Hotspur and Beşiktaş, they had a double reason to cheer for Arsenal's defeat.

Other Beşiktaş-Arsenal fans were more torn. 'I literally screamed when I saw the draw,' said Volkan Çelik, a fan of both teams who was born less than a mile from the Emirates. Çelik told me he was in two minds about who he wanted to win. But I noticed that he used the pronoun 'we' to refer to Beşiktaş, and pointed this out. 'That's a bit weird,' he admitted, but remained resolute that he was a fan of both teams. His conclusion? 'I'll be happy because whatever team wins, I'll be happy for them.'

Sorry, Norman.

* The rapid gentrification of Highbury has since pushed many Turkish speakers further out, to suburbs such as Edmonton and Enfield.

22
24

12

Trabzon

'In goal, Kasper Schmeichel. On the right: Simpson; at centre back, Huth and Morgan; Fuchs on the left. In the middle is Drinkwater with Kante; on one wing is Schlupp or Albrighton, on the other Mahrez; up front Okazaki and' – he gestures at his T-shirt, grinning – 'Jamie Vardy.'

Semih Öküz is an opera singer and an avid fan of Trabzonspor, a team from Turkey's Black Sea coast. Semih has short hair, glasses, and the type of belly you might expect from a tenor. Stretched across it was a white T-shirt. In the middle, a black and white picture of Jamie Vardy, the star striker for Leicester City. I came to Trabzon, the biggest city on Turkey's Black Sea coast, to talk about its football team – after the Big Three of Istanbul, the largest and most successful in Turkish football. I did not expect to be talking about my own side, Leicester City.

'Leicester City is very similar to Trabzonspor,' stated Semih. We were sitting in a tea garden in the central square in Trabzon, huddled under an awning as the rain pelted down. 'Chelsea, Manchester United, Manchester City, Arsenal, teams with big budgets – also Tottenham – they spend too much money. Leicester City are . . .' He searched for the word. '*Mütevazi*.' Humble. Modest.

It was May 2016, two days after a Chelsea draw with Tottenham handed Leicester their first ever top division championship. I was still slightly fragile when I travelled to Trabzon. As a life-long, largely disappointed Leicester fan, there had been some celebrations. Upon arriving, I had been told that at 6 p.m. there would be a gathering here too for Leicester in the city's main square, a paved and shady space surrounded by busy cobbled roads. But at 5 p.m. a cloudburst erupted and the rain pounded heavily, sending pedestrians searching for cover. When I arrived, the celebration was just Semih and his friend Ali, a statistician with the local council.

'There were thirty or so people, but they went home when the rain started,' Ali told me, his voice a mixture of disappointment and embarrassment. Ali fished around in a couple of carrier bags and produced two home-made Leicester City flags. They comprised fabric cut from a bedsheet attached to blue broom handles. Across the top, 'Leicester City' was scrawled in black pen. Below were three images – a Leicester logo flanked by two Premier League trophies. It was sparingly coloured with a highlighter and blue pen.

I asked Ali why he had gone to all this trouble for Leicester. 'We haven't seen a championship in our entire lives,' he explained. 'We support a team but we really wanted to experience a championship.'

Semih corrected him: 'No, we did – in 2011.'

'Yeah OK, so there was 2011,' Ali conceded. 'But we couldn't celebrate it.'

Officially Trabzonspor won their last league title in 1984. Everyone in Trabzon, however, believes their last championship title was in 2011. That season, the side finished second to Fenerbahçe on goal difference. Six weeks after the season finished, on 3 July 2011, a huge match-fixing scandal erupted with champions Fenerbahçe at the centre. Fenerbahçe were banned from the 2011–12 Champions League. To UEFA the evidence seemed incontrovertible. But domestically no punishment was meted out to the clubs. Fenerbahçe weren't relegated, the title wasn't handed elsewhere. Everyone in Trabzon feels they were on the receiving end of the nation's biggest ever footballing scandal – and that no one apart from them gives a damn.

Also at the table was Levent, a journalist for a local online paper. He used to cover sport in Trabzon for one of the nationals. Levent had been mostly quiet, but suddenly felt the need to speak. 'Do you know the biggest reason why people here are interested in Leicester City?' he thundered. 'They understand that there is justice in the English Premier League. I mean, if a person struggles and works hard, they can win. Here [in Turkey], people say: "No, never."'

I was taken aback by the force of Semih, Ali and Levent's grievance. Five years on, I didn't expect match-fixing to remain so sore a wound. But perhaps I should have been prepared. Trabzon has a reputation as a place where grievance is nurtured to an extreme level – bound up with the inhabitants' infamous hot-headedness and patriotism, bursting out from time to time in the form of intense vendettas and feuds.The match-fixing allegations cast a pall over the whole of Turkish football — but nowhere is it felt more keenly than in Trabzon.

*

In the centre of town stands a museum to Trabzonspor. Built in 2010, it's a huge heft of sand-coloured stone, sticking out among the concrete and granite grey of the rest of the city. But unfortunately it doesn't have any windows. Going in is a bit like walking into a bank vault. Completing the effect, the inside is lit by blue neon strip lighting, making you feel you are entering a giant machine to check the validity of £20 notes.

The museum's director is Hakan, a friendly man who wears a sharp suit and trendy glasses. It is very popular. In the hour or so we chatted, dozens of people came to have a look around. When I went to the main Trabzon museum later on, I was the only visitor. I asked Hakan which of all the artifacts in the large collection was the most important. His answer surprised me. He didn't mention the dozens of Trabzonspor championship cups, or the programmes from matches against Liverpool or Inter Milan. Instead he said they were the amateur things, the documents from the three teams that predated Trabzonspor's emergence in the 1960s. He got up out of his seat at the door and led me to one.

A photograph showed eleven men in trousers and long shirts, sitting, kneeling and standing on a field with their arms crossed. At the back, there was a man in a suit and an old fez hat – presumably the coach. Someone had written their names in black pen onto the image in neat Ottoman script. In Turkish underneath, the caption read: 'Idman Yurdu in 1914: the first football team founded in Trabzon'. That is not strictly true. Football's early years in the city followed those of other ports in the Ottoman empire. It was the foreigners – Russians, French, Britons and Italians – who started playing the game, followed by the Greek Orthodox population. Idman Yurdu are the 'first football team' only if you decide to ignore this history. It was unclear whether the oversight was intentional or not.

As I was looking at the image, Hakan provided a commentary over my shoulder. 'When the First World War came, they were conscripted and all died.'

'What, all of them?' I asked.

'Sadly so', he said. 'They were just the right age for conscription.'

I wondered if he was perhaps exaggerating for dramatic effect. Yet it is true that the First World War wreaked havoc on Trabzon. It was the central trauma in a decade of upheaval, devastation and genocide that transformed the city – and Turkey as a whole. The war and its aftermath sped up the untangling of the multi-ethnic and multireligious communities along the coast, what the historian Charles King has called 'the great unmixing'.

When the Russian army invaded the Ottoman empire from the Caucasus in 1916, some members of the Armenian and Assyrian communities launched an uprising against the Ottoman state. For a government already suspicious about the loyalties of its Christian subjects, the incident explains – but in no way justifies – the response. Throughout the Empire, although concentrated mostly in eastern Anatolia, somewhere between 600,000 and 1.5 million Armenians were killed or died. For many it is unambiguously the first genocide of the twentieth century. The Turkish state still rejects the use of that term, arguing that the massacres were an unfortunate by-product of war and were not pre-meditated.

Less than a decade after the organised killing of Armenians came the Greek Orthodox population exchange – the one that moved many relatives of Lefter Küçükandonyadis. It also affected hundreds of thousands of Rums who had populated Trabzon and its mountain uplands for centuries. Trabzon, the Black Sea region, and Turkey as a whole was emptied of its Christians. Amidst the upheaval of war and revolution, a large influx of Muslims from the Balkans and Caucasus came the other way. But under the ideology of the new Turkish nation, ethno-religious diversity went from something externalised to something repressed – the official narrative cast everyone as a Turk.

Football arrived in Trabzon at this turning point in history. When the game first came to the city, it was arguably a far more important place than it is today, and indisputably more multicultural. Within a decade, the game's role in the social life of the city quickly changed in shape and purpose. No longer a game through which different ethnic and religious minorities jousted with each other; on the surface at least, it was now an exclusively Turkish affair.

Trabzon was an enthusiastic centre of football in the new Turkish republic. It published one of the first books on the game in the Ottoman empire, a 1922 copy of the rules of 'English Association Football', translated by Süleyman Rıza. It had a thriving local amateur league, with teams frequently being invited to play elsewhere in Turkey.

In the 1950s and '60s, two clubs in particular emerged as dominant: İdmangücü and İdmanocağı (something akin to 'athletic power' and 'athletic organisation'). These two teams began to make a name for themselves further afield. In 1963 İdmangücü came second in the regional championship. In 1964, İdmanocağı won the newly formed 'Turkey Amateur Football Championship', much to their neighbour's irritation, no doubt.

The 1960s were a difficult time for the Black Sea region economically. In the binary Cold War logic, Turkey was in the Western camp. Cities like Trabzon – closer to the Soviet Union than Istanbul – found themselves in an economic cul-de-sac. The trade routes that had supplied the city for centuries crossed borders that were now closed. But the city's enthusiasm for football continued unabated. The vibrancy and success of local amateur football in Trabzon – and Turkey more widely – contrasted markedly with the game at the professional level. Despite the introduction of professionalism in the 1950s, it remained limited to football's three traditional centres: Istanbul, Izmir and Ankara. The 'national professional league', established in 1959, only included teams from these three cities. By the mid-1960s, the Turkish government was desperate for the league to be a truly nationwide competition. The TFF announced its desire for all big cities to have professional football. With its vibrant culture and success, Trabzon was high on the list. It was time for football in Trabzon to go professional. Time for Trabzonspor.

*

Özkan Sümer is someone who has seen it all. Born in 1937, he has been involved in football in Trabzon for over six decades. With hollowed eyes and a lugubrious face, Sümer was slouched on a sofa in the office of a local newspaper. Semih – the opera-singing Leicester City fan – had arranged for us to chat. His father, a retired journalist, knew Sümer personally. 'One of the most important people in Turkish football,' said Semih's father, as he introduced us. Sümer wafted away the compliment with his hands, saying: 'Don't exaggerate!' But he probably wasn't. Sümer is a one-man institution, the only person to have been a player, manager and director at Trabzonspor. He has direct experience of the entire sweep of the club's existence.

Sümer began playing football in the 1950s at İdmanocağı. 'The Turkish Football Federation wanted clubs in each region to combine to make a [professional] team,' Sümer told me. In Trabzon, the TFF made İdmanocağı merge with its historical rival, İdmangücü. It was as if Galatasaray suddenly were told to become a club with Fenerbahçe. Unsurprisingly, both were resistant. It took a threat of suspension by the TFF for them to eventually accept. In the autumn of 1967, Sümer stepped on the field to represent the new entity of Trabzonspor, playing in Turkey's second league.

But the past was not easily put to bed. 'The sense of superiority continued at both clubs for years,' Sümer told me. 'There wasn't conflict or uncomfortableness among the players [but] there was among the fans – they [only] wanted to support the players from their old teams.' Across Turkey, fans of sides like İdmanocağı grumbled as their clubs

– organisations representing different elements of the Anatolian patchwork with decades of history – were wiped out. In many places, this centralised, top-down engineering of football simply hastened the stampede of fans to the Big Three. Fortunately this wasn't the case in Trabzon.

These days, Trabzonspor play in a distinctive maroon and sky-blue that earned them the nickname 'the claret and blues'. The city is awash with the colours. The municipal council's logo is a maroon boat on a blue sea. Across the city, blocks of kerb are painted in alternate maroon and blue. It is a shock to hear, then, that this most elemental facet of Trabzonspor identity was chosen just to keep the peace. Sümer explains. 'İdmanocağı played in yellow and red ... İdmangücü played in green and white ... The [Trabzonspor colours] came because they needed a strip that didn't involve any of them.'

Sintered together from four local amateur clubs (the smaller Martıspor and Karadenizgücü were also folded into the new side) and riven by jealousies and rivalries, the great social experiment shouldn't really have worked. But in 1973, five seasons after their foundation, a team that included Sümer himself gained promotion to Turkey's top league. In 1976, they went one better and won the first division championship – the first club outside Istanbul ever to do so. The side repeated the trick the following season.

By this stage, Sümer had made the transition from gangly centre-half to youth team coach, and then assistant manager to Ahmet Suat Özyağıcı. Over the next eight years, the two men alternated management duties, in effect co-managing the side. The results were spectacular. Trabzonspor won three consecutive titles (1979, 1980 and 1981), making them the first team in Turkey ever to do so. The wave of success didn't fully subside until 1984 when Trabzonspor won their sixth – and final – championship. Examined from the vantage point of 2016, when Trabzon finished in twelfth place and thirty-nine points off the title, it felt as if Sümer was describing a completely different club.

Around Trabzon people are uncritically in awe of this period. They love the side. Its success is seen as a triumph of local talent and spirit. The team was completely Turkish, with almost every player hailing from Trabzon. 'We were the sons of every house,' said Şenol Güneş, Trabzonspor's goalkeeper in the 1970s and 1980s, who became coach of Beşiktaş in 2015.

A dissenting view comes from Ali Eroğul, writing in a sober collection of essays entitled *Understanding Trabzon*. Eroğul says it is important to put the championships in perspective. The 1970s was a period when Turkish football was in the doldrums. The national team was a failure and the game was awash with poor-quality foreign imports. At the time, only two points were granted for a win. The system did not encourage attacking football but rewarded those who were defensive; and Trabzon were tight at the back. In the thirty games of the 1978–79 season they conceded only seven goals. They didn't score many either. The following season, their league matches produced only twenty-five goals in total. But both years they topped the league. 'They became champions without adding any innovations to Turkish football,' says Eroğul. Just graft and good defending.

But perhaps it's churlish to dwell on the negatives. Breaking the Istanbul stranglehold was remarkable enough; to repeat the feat six times over was truly amazing. It was the Trabzonspor of the late 1970s and early '80s that earned the side a mention at the top. They almost did it again in the 1995–96 season, leading the table before losing at home to eventual winners Fenerbahçe in the final run-in. Such exploits led to pundits and fans sometimes referring to the Big Four instead of the Big Three. But these days, more often than not, when Trabzonspor make the headlines it is for reasons other than their sporting prowess.

*

Ten days before I was due to head to Trabzon, I woke up to find the football club and its notorious fans plastered across the news.

The team had been hosting Fenerbahçe, but no Fenerbahçe fans were present, so it couldn't have been trouble between rival groups. Nor did there seem to have been any contentious decision or goal.

I found myself watching footage of the game to see for myself what had happened. The trouble occurred in the 89th minute. Trabzonspor were losing 4–0, having been outplayed all match. Just minutes before the referee was due to blow the final whistle, there was movement in the crowd behind one of the goals. The voice of the Turkish commentator – normally so lively and over-the-top – was reduced to sad, doleful descriptions of the commotion.

'There's some disturbance behind one of the goals.'

(Hundreds of fans were yanking down the fence that prevents the ball going into the crowd.)

'Now security are spreading out in front of the stand.'

(Lines of police in riot gear were fanning out along the touchline behind one side of the goal.)

A Fenerbahçe player walked towards the corner flag at that side of the stadium to take the corner. He was forced to retreat under a hail of broken chairs and lighters. Was the fence there to stop the ball going into the crowd or the crowd throwing things onto the pitch? Once it was gone, objects rained down. The referee stood on the edge of the penalty area, a couple of Fenerbahçe players next to him. Only the Trabzon footballers dared to get any closer. The goalkeeper stood between the posts, as if expecting a normal corner kick.

A chant rose out of the whole stadium, clearly audible on the TV footage: 'Fenerbahçe are cunts!'

The camera zoomed in on a tubby middle-aged man in a suit and glasses, running round the goalmouth, picking up the fragments of plastic chairs and throwing them behind the advertising hoarding. The riot police were just standing there. The ball boys helped him out. There was an eerie silence on the TV footage, the commentator clearly unsure what he should be saying.

A Fenerbahçe player called for the ball and headed for the corner flag.

'Diego is heading to the area to take the corner!' The commentator roused himself, relief in his voice that he could get back to describing football. The corner was passed 20 yards back down the line to a Fenerbahçe player. They're 4–0 up and it's the last minute – no need to venture into the penalty area and closer to . . . *that*. The commentator returned to naming the players on the ball as everyone – players, commentator, referee – went through the motions of focusing on the game.

'Fernandao'

'Ozan Tufan'

'Volkan Şen'

'Now Fernando . . .'

Fenerbahçe strung together a few passes and headed into the box. But concentration was no longer on the ball. Eyes were drawn instead to the far edge of the six-yard box, where something was going on. A fan was on the pitch. Security officials ran past the goalkeeper as he was positioning himself ready for the Fener player to shoot. The ball ended up out of play – no one was really sure how, as the game had ceased to occupy people's attention. There was a huge scrum around the fan who ran on. The referee signalled for the players to move away.

'Really ugly. These are images we really don't want to see,' said the commentator glumly.

A replay revealed exactly what happened. Turkey employs two officials on the penalty box as well as linesmen. While the players could avoid the trouble, the assistant referee's role required him to stand directly in front of it, with his back to the stand. Out of nowhere, a boy in a red jacket appeared and walloped him in the back of the head. He had no idea it was coming. He fell to the ground. The fan kicked him in the side and then fell over him, trying to grapple the official in a headlock, before security pulled him off.

The official managed to stagger to his feet. He made a gesture in the direction of the referee with his hand – his palm held out and tilting it from side to side, the kind you make when you're unsure about a decision. Perhaps he was saying 'dunno whether to carry on'. He received his answer when the linesman joined him, grabbing his arm and pulling him as they ran off towards the changing rooms.

The game was abandoned.

It would be extraordinary enough if this was the main upset of Trabzon's season, or that such incidents were limited to rowdy fans, but no. Three months earlier, the club's chairman, İbrahim Hacıosmanoğlu, got so angry at one particular match official that he locked him and his three assistants in a changing room after the match (though he later claimed it was for their own safety). It took a 2 a.m. phonecall from President Erdoğan himself to secure the men's release. Challenged over that incident, the chairman defended his actions by saying that the club and its staff would 'rather die like men than live like women. No one has the power to make us live like women.' He did later apologise, saying he did not intend to offend any women. He added, helpfully, 'My mother is a woman.'

These incidents sadly conform to another stereotype of the city's inhabitants: a machismo that often tips over into sexism, extreme nationalism and intolerance. Turkey's only openly gay referee – Halil İbrahim Dinçdağ – is from near Trabzon. When Dinçdağ came out in 2009, he and his family were harassed and received death threats. He has also been ostracised from the referee community in Turkey; Dinçdağ's only refereeing comes courtesy of the Istanbul *Efendi* league, the gentlemanly league, one of many alternative leagues set up to protest at the aggressive, overly-competitive and macho environment fostered in the mainstream amateur divisions.

The Black Sea's fiery reputation mirrors Adana – both are places where men are supposed to be quick to anger and short on apologies. Most of my prior experience of the Trabzonian brand of machismo came from rubbing shoulders with one of the city's native sons while picking walnuts on a farm in central Anatolia. The farm hands were from Trabzon, despite Trabzon – and indeed the sea – being more than 700 kilometres away. They were a father-and-son duo. The older man – Metin – was impossible to understand. It was to his son, Adem, that I became close. Adem was nineteen. He had pale skin and almost mousy-blond hair. He wore a flat cap and kept a coop of fancy pigeons who could perform somersaults in mid-air. He was loud and extroverted – and would frequently work in a Trabzonspor hoodie. He would point at the badge and loudly proclaim that they were the best team in Turkey. Once he told me proudly how, only a few weeks previously, his friends had beaten up a group of Kurds.

On my first day in Trabzon, I walked past the main museum. Housed in a grand-looking mansion, it was starkly at odds with the 1960s concrete shops all around it. I decided to pop in. I found wooden cabinets standing in the middle of fading, crusty rooms. There was no guide to any of the contents. I wandered through the building, peering into cases. Among a collection of hats and rifles belonging to a former MP, I found a picture dated 1900–1914 and titled: 'A Trabzon *delikanlı*' – a Trabzon lad. The Turkish word has two meanings: it is used to mean 'teenager' or 'youth' but the literal translation is 'mad-blooded' or 'hot-headed'.

In the picture was a young man, late teens or early twenties, with a boyish face. He was dressed all in black, with a cloth wrapped round his head. Around his waist was a thick belt, and dangling off it all manner of weaponry, some knives, a pistol and what looked like a stick grenade. He held a rifle in his right hand and stared blankly at the camera, unsmiling.

I was stopped short in my aimless perusal. He reminded me

instantly of Adem. Physically the resemblance wasn't that great. But there was something about his cheeky, slightly cocky, but also proud expression that felt extremely familiar.

So maybe there has always been something of the '*delikanlı*' about young Trabzon men. But there seems a broader sense that this style of behaviour is becoming increasingly entrenched and condoned. In 2006, a priest called Andrea Santoro was praying in his church – the Catholic Santa Maria in Trabzon – when a sixteen-year-old boy stole in and shot him dead. Less than a year later, Hrant Dink, an Armenian journalist who campaigned for recognition of the killing of Armenians as genocide, was assassinated. A seventeen-year-old ultranationalist from Trabzon was convicted of the murder (Dink's family have long maintained that there was state involvement in his killing). After Dink's death, tens of thousands of people marched in Istanbul chanting, 'We are all Armenians.' In Trabzon, some football fans responded by holding up banners that read, 'We are Turks.'

I can't help but feel this aggression and xenophobia is linked to Trabzon's slide from cosmopolitan entrepôt to nationalistic economic backwater. Centuries of diversity have been written out of history, leaving a particularly macho form of intolerance in their stead. Sometimes, these attitudes manifest in football in the behaviour of players and fans. But football itself has also fuelled the sense of marginalisation and despair.

*

Place yourself in the mindset of Semih. You're in your twenties. Your relatives wax lyrical about how glorious Trabzonspor, the beloved family football team, once were. How they swept all before them. But you have never seen any of this. Your team – supposedly the same one that they laud – seems miles away from even catching a glimpse of the championship. It has become so bad that you start to wonder if larger factors are at work: how can a once-successful team end up so down on their luck? But you brush it away. You go to the games with your mates and try to make the most of the small victories – a win against one of the big clubs, a cracking goal.

So imagine how it felt when, in 2011, something wonderful seemed to be happening. That season was different. Trabzon were not just doing alright, they were top of the league for most of the year. As the season approached its final weeks it was a two-horse race between Trabzonspor and Fenerbahçe. Semih, then a university student in the liberal city of Eskişehir, would be sure to watch each match on TV. In April 2011, Fenerbahçe came to town to play the local side, Eskişehirspor. He went along to watch. While he was at the game, he became convinced that something strange was going on. 'Some Eskişehirspor footballers didn't run, they didn't play,' he says. Fenerbahçe won 3–1.

At this point Semih's friend Ali chipped in to continue the story. Following the match, Fenerbahçe bought Sezer Öztürk, supposedly the best player, on a transfer.

The pair were convinced that the match was rigged and that Öztürk was transferred to Fener as a reward for his complicity. Semih concluded sadly: 'After this game, Fenerbahçe v Eskişehirspor, we understood what match-fixing was.'

So what happened?

On the morning of 3 July, anyone who switched on the TV news in Turkey while enjoying their Sunday brunch would have been greeted with an extraordinary sight: the president of Fenerbahçe, Aziz Yıldırım, being led away in handcuffs. He was the most high-profile target in a co-ordinated police operation that arrested forty-nine people, including Eskişehirspor player Öztürk, in fifteen cities across Turkey.

In the weeks and months that followed, damning allegations emerged, with Fenerbahçe at the centre. In the preceding years, the club had been going through a losing streak, having failed to win the title since 2007. Aziz Yıldırım, the club president, had secured re-election in May 2009 by promising to win the championship three years in a row. But in 2009 they came fourth. In 2010 they finished second. As the mid-point of the 2010–11 season approached in early December, Fener were third in the table, lagging behind Bursaspor and the frontrunners, Trabzon, who were nine points ahead. And so, it is alleged, the club tried to buy the title.

According to prosecutors, a web of club officials, intermediaries, players and their agents were accused of collaborating to enable Fenerbahçe to win their own games and to skew the outcome of key clashes between other clubs. It was claimed that rival strikers were asked not to score. Goalkeepers were told not to save goals. Managers and club officials were also alleged to be in on the act. Prosecutors stated that some players were lured with the promise of a transfer to Fenerbahçe the following season. Others were given cash or expensive gifts. Typically players were offered around $100,000 per game, sometimes less.

After their ropy start, during the second half of the season, Fenerbahçe were transformed. They won all but one match. Among the suspect games was the Eskişehirspor versus Fenerbahçe contest that Semih had been so adamant was rigged. Still, before the final game of the season the two teams were level on points. Following a 4-3 victory against Sivasspor, Fenerbahçe won the league on goal difference. As they bounced up and down on the pitch, leading a call and response chant with thousands of delirious fans in the stands, there was no hint on the faces of the Fener players that they knew of rumours that the victory had been bought for them. But they would soon find out.

Unbeknown to those accused of running the fixing network, they were being watched. Police had set up a huge surveillance operation, tapping the phones of dozens of key figures. They collected hours and hours of phone calls between senior football players and officials, going all the way to the Fenerbahçe president. And, after the arrests, they produced jaw-dropping evidence. In one tragicomic exchange,

İbrahim Akın, a Turkey international who played for Istanbul Büyükşehir Belediyespor, is apparently heard calling up a man who he later described as an imam from Erzurum. He asks whether it would be religiously acceptable to accept an offer from Fenerbahçe of $100,000 not to score in the match against them. The imam put his mind at ease. 'Things like these happen in the football world, don't they?' he replied, soothingly, before suggesting that Akin accept the money and send some of it to the imam's village. (The imam later claimed he thought Akin was talking about a transfer fee).

In total, the indictment claimed ninety-three defendants and eight clubs had been part of the fixing network, with thirteen matches rigged.

Before travelling to Trabzon I had known about the match-fixing allegations, of course. But there is a difference between reading about something online and meeting the fans for whom it remains a painful open wound. In love with the terrace culture of Turkish football — the wild passion and crazy songs — I had chosen not to look too hard at anything that would break the spell. But now the book was forcing my hand.

As I delved into the accusations, I learnt that match-fixing was not unprecedented in Turkey. I came across an old Beşiktaş chant called *sekiz sıfır*, 8–0. It's an angry jibe at Galatasaray, whose unusual score against Ankaragücü in the last game of the 1992–93 season saw them beat the Eagles to the championship on goal difference.

And it wasn't just match-fixing. Turkish football has long been dogged by accusations of broader links to the 'deep state' and criminal underworld, with drug-runners and mobsters often popping up as football club officials or lurking in the back rooms striking shady deals.

I discovered that, in the 1990s, the Malatyaspor chairman was jailed in France for heroin smuggling.* I read that Sedat Peker, a convicted organised-crime boss, had sustained a network of connections in football for decades. Once in my mind's eye, football's unsavoury

* That isn't even the best story about him. In 1988, he brought three members of the Brazilian 1982 World Cup squad to play in sleepy Malatya. They were promised waterside villas in Istanbul, but instead ended up in humble apartments 600 miles from the Bosphorus. It didn't end well.

elements were spreading and infecting, like an ink blot on a sheet of paper.

Even with this murky history, the sheer scale of the allegations that erupted in 2011 plunged Turkish football into an enormous crisis. Prime Minister Erdoğan felt compelled to enter the fray. He initially responded to the wave of arrests by taking a neutral stance. 'I am a Fenerbahçe fan but I must act maturely, I must not interfere,' he said. 'Because the judiciary has made this decision.' But it quickly became entangled with politics. In December 2011, the Turkish parliament voted to amend the law to lower the penalties for match-fixing, with the AKP arguing it was too harsh. By the time he took to the podium to address UEFA's member associations at its annual congress in Istanbul in March 2012, Erdoğan was explicitly trying to shield Fenerbahçe.

'We have to identify a difference between the individual and the legal entity,' he said. 'We should act against individuals who committed the crime. Only they should be given the highest sanctions. If a legal entity is punished for the crime of an individual, millions of people would be punished.'

In April 2012, the TFF altered its disciplinary code to remove a requirement that clubs found guilty of match-fixing be automatically relegated. New chairman Yıldırım Demirören explained the rationale: 'Everybody was of the same opinion that the penalties regarding attempts to influence results were disproportionate.'

The TFF showed scant regard for the fact that a court case was ongoing. In May, the TFF ethics committee issued bans for ten players and officials but failed to punish a single club. Demirören said that, even if there had been fixing, there was no evidence that it had affected the outcomes of the games under investigation.

In July 2012, a year after the original arrests, an Istanbul court found a total of forty-eight club officials, players and coaches guilty of match-fixing, including the Fenerbahçe president, a string of other Fenerbahçe officials and İbrahim Akın, the midfielder who had allegedly sought advice from his imam. Players and officials at Eskişehirspor, Beşiktaş, Istanbul Büyükşehir Belediyespor and Bursaspor were among some of the others who were convicted. İbrahim Akın maintained his innocence but was convicted. Sezer Öztürk, the player my friends were convinced had been bought, was acquitted.

Aziz Yıldırım, who had spent the entire 2011–12 season either attending court hearings or behind bars at Istanbul's Metris prison, was sentenced to six years in jail but was released pending appeal.

To the outside world, it looked like an open-and-shut case. The courts had shown that systemic match-fixing was beyond all doubt. But there was a twist. In Turkey, Fenerbahçe fans and officials had been protesting increasingly loudly that they were the victims of a conspiracy. In his defence statement at the opening of his trial, Aziz Yıldırım argued that the case was the work of a group trying to seize control of football in Turkey. They had singled out Fenerbahçe, he said, because the club was a bastion of support for Atatürk. At the time he did not name the group to which he was referring. But the fans were more explicit. They were convinced that their team was targeted by a powerful Islamic sect known as the Gülen movement, which they believed had infiltrated police and the judiciary. They were bent on seizing control of key institutions across Turkey, they warned, starting with its best-supported football club.

It sounds totally bizarre to people outside Turkey that this theory could be anything more than obfuscation and bluster. For a start, it remains unclear why a religious group would want to seize power of a football team. But later the Gülen movement would be accused of wider wrongdoings that extended far beyond the world of football. The government would turn against them. So too would the majority of the population. Many people came round to the view of Fenerbahçe fans that the Gülenists were behind the match-fixing prosecutions. A retrial was ordered for Yildirim and thirty-five other defendants (including Akın, of imam-phoning fame, who said that the tape of his conversation with the religious figure had been manipulated). In 2015, three years after the initial convictions, all were acquitted and walked free.

We will probably never know whether the allegations were based on a genuine match-fixing ring or not. Kenan Başaran, a sports journalist who wrote an entire book on the debacle, says that he simply does not know what happened. 'If you ask me, "was there match fixing or not?" I can't give an answer,' he said. 'Because saying this has now become a political thing.'

*

When it comes to Trabzonspor, the question of whether or not the allegations are true does not especially matter. For the fans, it is simple: their championship was taken away from them through match-fixing and no one was properly punished. Even today, when the referee gives a contentious decision to Fenerbahçe, rival fans across the country will sing, 'Ah, doing some more match fixing Aziz Yıldırım!' The episode bubbles away, magma under the surface, erupting at the slightest of opportunities.

'Kids here – they start watching at the age we did, twelve, thirteen years old,' said Mehmet Fındıkçı head of Trabzonspor's largest and most fanatical fan club, *Gençl Trabzonlular* – the Trabzon boys. 'When you are a kid growing up, seeing the championship stolen, seeing there's always injustice, injustice doled out to Trabzonspor, well, they fill up, fill up, fill up. In the end, after losing back to back, the anger has to explode.'

When I asked Fındıkçı to explain the pitch invasion, his friend forcefully interrupted to defend the fan. 'That kid was swelling, swelling, getting angrier and angrier – in the Fenerbahçe match, the ball hit the player's hand, but the referee didn't give a penalty. He says, "Why don't you give the penalty? Why don't you give it?" They didn't give it. So he jumps on the pitch. He says, "Why don't you give it?" Then hits him . . . The referees always cheat our team out of their rights. They seize them from us. They steal.'

The lava of indignation keeps pouring, flowing ever outwards, justifying any action. Nor is it just the hardcore fans. The pain, anger and bitterness are on display all around the city, if you know what you are looking for.

On my first night in Trabzon, I went to eat in a pizza bar on the main square. Affixed to a wall at the back, alongside a picture of the team, was a plaque with the heading: 'Our table of honours'. Black text on little bronze squares listed the cups that Trabzon had won and the years that they had done so. Under the title 'Turkish league champions' there was a specially made plaque in red lettering stating 2010–11. A few days later I walked past the Trabzonspor shop. In the window was a T-shirt making the same point. The 2010–11 championship was even listed on an official board above the directors' chairs at the Trabzonspor stadium.

This is why the Leicester story – a 'modern-day fairytale' around the world – has had particular traction in Trabzon. 'Because there's a part missing from their own fandom, that part is filled by Leicester's success,' Levent said to me, on that first night when attending the Leicester celebration.

This sense of injustice is all-pervading. It means fans love anti-heroes. What looks like scandalous behaviour to the rest of Turkey and the world makes Trabzonians proud. Or at least is justified as a cry of pain against a system they believe is stacked against them.

One final example underlines this point. In February 2016 – two months before the 'referee attack' – Trabzonspor were playing away at Galatasaray. It should have been a meaningless league match – both sides had blown their chance to win the title months earlier. But the game was catapulted to fame when the referee Deniz Ateş Bitnel sent off four Trabzonspor players in 27 minutes, reducing the visiting team to seven men and rendering the final minutes a farce. The standout moment came when Salih Dursun, a twenty-four-year old defender whom Galatasaray had loaned to Trabzon, protested at this series of events by snatching the red card out of the referee's hand and brandishing it in his face. Unsurprisingly, he too was sent off. The image went viral around the world, held up as yet another example of the unhinged nature of the Turkish game.

But Trabzon rallied around Dursun. Local newspapers declared him a hero. The club chairman gave a defiant press conference alongside the player. The day after the incident, the central square in Trabzon was filled with fans who proudly held aloft red cards. But the story that most caught my attention was one that emerged a few weeks later. The local authority had decided to name a street after Dursun. Before leaving Trabzon, this was something I had to see.

The street in question is in the district of Yomra, on the outskirts of Trabzon. I took the bus and got off in an unassuming neighbourhood, gouged in two by the main coastal road.

I arrived at the the town hall to meet up with the mayor's assistant who, confusingly, was also called Salih. After a brief but intense 'interview', in which he whipped out a tape recorder and fired questions at me, he suddenly became relaxed. Cheery even. He grabbed his car keys and beckoned me to follow. We drove down a main road for about a kilometre until he pulled off into a small side street.

Salih Dursun Caddesi, Salih Dursun Street, was not exactly the most arresting of places. A sign hung from a decorative pole above little more than a dirt track. After twenty or thirty metres the road petered out, dust swirling over the tarmac, leading down to a small port. The only vehicles were trucks, crawling back and forth with materials for building work. Rather apologetically, Salih explained that the port was being developed. 'It will be a marina with cafes,' he said. I peered down at the dust, trying to imagine it.

Suddenly a shiny black car pulled up and out climbed İbrahim Sağıroğlu, the Yomra mayor. He looked a little impatient.

It was a rather odd place to do an interview but we ploughed ahead. Sağıroğlu told me how proud Dursun was about this honour. He lived not far from here, he said, and told the mayor that – even though he was born and raised in Sakarya province, about 500 miles from Trabzon – he would always be *Trabzonlu* and *Trabzonsporlu*: a Trabzonian and a Trabzonspor fan.

All very touching, I thought, but how does a local authority find itself in the position of lauding a man for what would be seen in most other places as some pretty unsportsmanlike behaviour? Sağıroğlu responded by insisting that Trabzonspor suffered a 'terrible injustice' in that Galatasaray game. He says that the player's actions, far from being rash or excessive, were in fact a 'democratic' response to an out-of-control referee.

'Salih Dursun, at that moment, provided an instant reaction on behalf of Trabzonspor lovers. He said what the people were thinking. He translated their feelings. With the gesture, he said to the referee "On this field you can't direct this game of football. You murdered this match. You invited so many of my friends to leave the pitch by showing them a red card. So now, with this red card, I invite you to leave."'

It was quite a speech, but he wasn't yet finished. Because for the local mayor, the street sign was about more than just that incident. Invoking the arrests at FIFA a year earlier as part of a corruption investigation, Sağıroğlu wove Salih Dursun into the global fight for fairness in football. 'We want to transport the game to a higher level in the world,' he says. 'We wish for all the world to do away with match-fixing. When you look at the earthquakes at UEFA, we see that in football there are lots of scams and bribery. We strongly condemn such actions.'

I inwardly rolled my eyes at yet another instance of condoning the uncondonable. Throughout my time in Trabzon, I kept reminding myself of the wider social factors at play. Wealth and diversity has leached away from the region. Its people are caught up in wider social and economic changes that have left their home desiccated, a resentful husk of what it once was. And when it comes to the events of 2011, there is some justification for their anger. Whether or not match-fixing really did take place, Trabzonspor still narrowly (and quite possibly unfairly) missed out on the title.

But empathy has its limits. Having met many people in Turkey who were stoic in the face of real injustice – poverty, war, displacement and discrimination – listening to people in a relative position of power and authority moan about unfairness was wearing thin. I was tired. I had had my fill. But Sağıroğlu was winding up for his climax.

By brandishing that red card, said Sağıroğlu, Dursun acted not only as 'a translator for the love of Trabzonspor' but as someone who stood up for this team and this city that so many here are convinced has time and again been wronged. Naming the street after him was a small way of marking that. 'We did it as a principle to Turkish sporting history,' Sağıroğlu says. 'To defend the rights of Trabzonspor.'

And with that, he climbed back in the car and was gone.

13

Gezi

Everyone has the right to live in a healthy, balanced environment. It is the duty of the state and citizens to improve the natural environment, and to prevent environmental pollution

— Article 56 of the Turkish constitution

The first thing I glimpsed was the banner. Black lettering sprayed onto a square of red cloth. It wasn't a particularly impressive banner. It was pretty tatty, in fact. But it was causing quite a fuss. From my vantage point on a low wall on the edge of Istanbul's Taksim Square, I could feel an excited murmur rippling through the crowd: 'Çarşı are coming!'

It was June 2013 and I had just arrived in Taksim, where hundreds of thousands of people had set up camp. Istanbul's answer to Trafalgar Square had been transformed into a sea of tents and crowds after a local dispute over plans to demolish a park had snowballed into the biggest political protest of a generation. Gezi Park, as the area is known, had become like a giant party.

Teenagers sat in front of tents chatting excitedly or lay slumped on the ground, catching a few minutes' sleep. Hundreds queued for free food, ladled out with gusto by middle-aged women. In one corner, a mix of children and adults were perusing shelf upon shelf of books, labelled 'the library'. 'We can't have ignorant revolutionaries!' joked an older man as he handed out tomes to the passing crowds. The front of a nearby Starbucks had been turned into a medical centre. Volunteers in high-vis jackets lined up supplies on trestle tables.

Behind them stood a makeshift doctor's cubicle, scrawled with the words 'First aid: we need medicine and rations', adorned with a small Turkish flag.

When the protests started, I was living in Cologne, spending a lot of time in dingy bars with German football fans of Turkish descent. But all anyone could talk about was events in Turkey. Not only was the country gripped by major political convulsion, but football fans were playing a major role. Çarşı, a group of fanatical Beşiktaş supporters, had got stuck in and were making waves.

My contacts in Turkey were bombarding me with messages. Adem, an accountant and obsessive Beşiktaş fan I first met in 2009, wrote to me on Facebook: 'John, these are the worst and best days of my life.' Another Turkish friend who despised football found himself enthralled. 'I have never seen anything like this,' he wrote excitedly. 'Consider coming here for a few days'. I bought a plane ticket, threw some clothes into a bag and headed for the airport. Hours later, I was perched on that wall, trying to get a good view of the procession headed by the tatty red banner.

As it came closer, the sound of chanting became audible. 'Beşiktaş! Beşiktaş!' they cried, along with the team's colours: 'White! Black!' The thousands watching them arrive erupted into a spontaneous response: 'The kings of the universe are coming!'

As the snake filed past me, I reckoned it must have been made up of at least 10,000 people. There were the testosterone-fuelled teenagers, carrying burning flares, shouting and jumping excitedly on each another. Older fans in middle age, football scarves round their neck, lent a seasoned veneer to proceedings. There were also quite a few women, some chanting and jumping with the rest, others more detached, filming boyfriends or brothers from a mobile phone. Most of the crowd wore Beşiktaş tops but dotted among them were the colours of Galatasaray and Fenerbahçe too.

Right at the front I spotted the long grey hair and lithe frame of Ayhan Güner, one of Çarşı's founding members. He was buzzing and, it seemed, rather angry at the direction the cortege seemed to be taking. He pushed his way through the onlookers, shouting and beckoning for the group to follow him. The snake was so large it took ten or fifteen minutes before the tail filed past, the chants now addressing the police. 'Keep on spraying your tear gas!' they cried. 'Why don't you take off your helmet, throw down your truncheon and then let's see who the real man is!'

The bustle in the square had paused while everyone stopped to take in the scene. A sea of camera phones held aloft were generating proof that this was actually, really happening. The songs emanated from the Beşiktaş fans but were percolating quickly through the crowd, gathering force and volume. They seemed to give the spectators a renewed vigour, providing a run-up and a rhythm that they could throw their weight behind.

As dusk approached, the group reached Atatürk Cultural Centre, a former opera house that had also been earmarked for demolition as part of the plans to revamp the area. A vanguard entered the building but the rest held back, joining the regular crowd, milling around, watching, wondering what would happen next. A few minutes later, some figures appeared on the roof, small and stick-like. The Lowry-esque outlines fanned out in a line but the gloaming made it hard to distinguish what exactly they were doing.

Then, with a swoosh, a vast banner was unfurled, tumbling down the side of the building. It bore the words 'The Optical Chief' – the nickname of a Çarşı founding member who had died five years earlier. A cry went up from the crowd as a line of flares turned the lip of the building red. With exquisite timing, another thirty shot up into the air to descend slowly in arcs of light towards the crowd below. This prompted another thunderous round of chanting: 'Everywhere is Taksim, everywhere is resistance!' The square seemed to shake from the intensity.

It was an impressive entrance. The following day, these pyrotechnics would make the front page of every newspaper. The country was in the grip of its largest anti-government uprising in recent memory, and a bunch of football fans had managed to secure centre stage.

*

In the heart of Beşiktaş stands a rather passé 1960s concrete shopping mall. Its name, The Big Beşiktaş Çarşı, is spelt out on the roof in large block capitals. The structure itself is instantly forgettable – all strip lighting and brutalist architecture – but its importance in Turkish football is already assured. It's this building and its surrounds that gives its name to the nation's most famous fan group – Çarşı.

Pronounced *Char-shuh*, the second syllable is forced out of the front of the mouth, the same sound as telling a small child to be quiet. The word means something like 'shopping centre' or 'market'. There are conflicting accounts as to how it became the name of a supporters' collective.

'We said to each other, we are kids of the market, so let's call it Çarşı,' Cem Yakışkan, a founding member, told me. One of his contemporaries, Adnan Bostancıoğlu, said it didn't quite work like that. 'It's not like members of Çarşı just said, "We are called Çarşı from now on." It was just when they go into the stadium, people are like, "Who are these guys?" and the others said, "They're the guys from the Çarşı"'

To grasp its meaning fully, you need to leave Beşiktaş and head to Istanbul's old city. Amid the historic mosques and palaces, you will find what in English is referred to as the 'Grand Bazaar' but which in Turkish is called Kapalı Çarşı – the covered market. Inside are thousands of small stores, selling everything from tea sets to toilet cleaner. The bazaar has become a bit of a touristic pastiche, but ignore the customers and take a look at the shop owners. They sit on stools out the front, ordering teas from the passing boys, cadging cigarettes and mocking each other playfully.

Such a place was at the centre of all Turkish towns: where the business community congregated and shoppers would come for their goods. Historically a male domain, for many men in Turkey the day still involves sitting around in this type of çarşı, hanging out over cups of tea. When you're not working, you sit at your friend's place. When neither of you is working, you sit in the café.

The 1960s concrete lump in Beşiktaş serves the same purpose. Several of Çarşı's more prominent members own stores in the building. Ideas for banners are hatched over long afternoons of tea and backgammon, either there or in the warren of streets around it. On match days the Çarşı is a hive of pre-game activity as fans congregate on its steps to drink, smoke and chant. Once you know this, the name starts to make a bit more sense.

*

Çarşı began life as a group of eight teenagers in Beşiktaş who were willing to attend all the games, sing passionately and throw a few punches if challenged by rival fans. The group's genesis – in the early 1980s – came at a particularly dismal period for Beşiktaş. 'It was a reaction to the failure to win a championship for decades. Beşiktaşlessness!' declared Alen Markaryan, another founding member I went to see. 'Beşiktaş were such a failure – Galatasaray and Fenerbahçe were everywhere.' The Black Eagles had not won the league for almost fifteen years. 'There was a danger of youngsters supporting Galatasaray and Fenerbahçe,' continued Markaryan. 'To forestall, thwart, this threat, something was done.'

What was done was a drive to organise Beşiktaş fans in a more systematic fashion. There was no inaugural meeting, no printing of T-shirts. At that time, construction work at the grounds of Fenerbahçe and Galatasaray meant that all three of the big Istanbul teams were playing at Beşiktaş's İnönü stadium. The kids from the Çarşı were unimpressed: 'It was our neighbourhood and we were obliged to protect it,' said Senem Gülkar, editor of a Beşiktaş fanzine who was there in the early days. In the fights to grab the best place in the stadium, Çarşı took a lead. Still in their teens, the group's members slept outside the stadium, fought the other fans and did everything to ensure they didn't enter 'their' stand. Other Beşiktaş fans started to take notice.

Çarşı spearheaded the role of the 'terrace leader', a responsibility that began to emerge at matches in the 1980s and '90s. At Beşiktaş the terrace leader's default place has always been on the top tier, standing astride the advertising hoarding, arms outstretched, leading the crowd in chants. At his feet stands a coterie of friends, holding tight to stop the leader tumbling over the fifty-foot drop to the pitch.

On long bus-rides to away matches or over tea after a game in Beşiktaş I would be regaled with stories about Çarşı's most famous terrace leaders. 'See him there,' whispered one young fan, pointing at a slightly portly man with a round, jolly face and glasses perched on his nose. 'He was crazy. He used to go around stabbing rival fans.' Another terrace leader is said to have had his arm broken by a police water cannon but would not countenance a trip to hospital until after the match. The tales I was being told were hard to square with the avuncular, greying features of Çarşı's founders I had met. They are referred to deferentially as *abi* (big bro) or *amigo* by other supporters, and they act as the peacemakers and final arbiters, trying to set the tone of the group.

Çarşı has a leftist reputation, but its founders insist that such concerns were always secondary. 'It wasn't politics that brought these people together, it was football,' I was told by Bostancioğlu over wine in his flat. 'But these people were mostly from the same community – the Beşiktaş community, a traditionally leftist neighbourhood.' He leant back in his chair and took a long drag on his cigarette before adding: 'Politics manifested itself in an attitude they took towards contemporary events'.'

These 'contemporary events' were tumultuous. The founders of Çarşı came of age during Turkey's leftist–rightist political violence of the late 1970s that left thousands dead. They witnessed a military coup in 1980 and the subsequent crackdown on free speech. Bostancıoğlu himself was imprisoned in 1980 for three years – one of the hundreds of thousands arrested. 'We had to burn our books at home,' recalled Çarşı member Ayhan Güner. They were eye-opening times for impressionable teens.

When Turkey made the transition back to a civilian government in 1983, society had changed for ever. The first elected civilian prime minister, Turgut Özal, abandoned planned economies and nationalised industries, choosing instead to open the country to world markets. Private businesses multiplied exponentially, Turkish exports increased sevenfold and home ownership exploded.

Çarşı's decision to position itself in opposition to this new wave of capitalism is attributed to one of the group's founders, Mehmet Işıklar, who was known by the nickname 'Optik Başkan' (the 'Optical Chief'), apparently because he wore thick glasses as a boy. Optik possessed a rudimentary understanding of socialism and lefist iconography. He also had an artistic eye, a mischievous streak, and a penchant for subversiveness and rule-breaking. Knowing that a wider group of supporters would appreciate it, Optik encouraged Çarşı to adopt left-wing philosophy and iconography. An anarchist 'A' was incorporated into the group's logo, lending impetus to the idea of Beşiktaş as an anti-establishment club. Optik died in 2007, of a heart attack most likely brought on by drug use. He was thirty-eight years old. His role in shaping the group's image explains why, when Çarşı mounted the roof of the Atatürk Centre during the Gezi Park protests, he was given a starring role.

For all the anti-capitalist rhetoric, Çarşı has benefited from the turn towards neoliberalism in Turkey. With the demolition of state monopolies, a more varied and vibrant public sphere emerged. Gradually, and not without backwards steps, Turkish society opened up. There was an explosion of forums for football discussion as new satellite TV stations, websites, chat rooms and TV shows were created. A cheap and popular tactic for filling airtime or column inches was to give fans the chance to 'have their say'. And if those fans said something controversial or subversive? Well, all the better.

At Beşiktaş a tradition of banners started to flourish, most designed by Erol Özdil, nicknamed 'the Camel'. He and his friends would craft them from spray paint on bedsheets, responding to contemporary issues. After the government reported it would flood the 12,000-year-old settlement of Hasankeyf in south-east Turkey as part of dam construction projects, a Çarşı banner warned: 'Leave Hasankeyf alone!' When Orhan Pamuk, winner of the 2006 Nobel Prize for literature, was prosecuted for 'insulting Turkishness', the group unfurled the spray-painted message: 'We applaud the Nobel [laureate]'. A recurrent theme is that Çarşı frames its protests as a stance against something: 'Çarşı against _____'. The phrasing rhymes in Turkish. *Çarşı her şeye karşı* 'Çarşı is against everything!' is its most famous, capturing the group's contrariness. But they have also protested against racism, war, neo-Nazis, child porn, nuclear energy, destruction of theatres, terrorism, oil wrestling, bombs and even – in an existential head scratcher – themselves.

I first encountered Çarşı in 2009 when I spent a summer with some of its members trying to understand what they were about. It was not straightforward. Most people in Turkey saw Çarşı as hooligans, pure and simple. And, yes, at times I found myself caught up in fights or anxiously looking around while a supporter spray-painted 'Çarşı' on road signs and pavements. Fans frequently admonished me for turning conversations towards politics: 'We don't have a political stance, we're not affiliated with any political parties; our stance is being a Beşiktaş fan,' said one prominent supporter. More of our time was spent goofing around. Having developed a slightly misplaced reputation as being addicted to salted peanuts, before one match I was forced to down three bottles of beer in quick succession before eating an entire bag.

At times the fans I met were politically aware, progressive and bitingly satirical. At others I felt like I was talking to a bunch of new-age hippies. 'I use the pure power, the potential of the terraces to do something for the good of humanity, Child Care Foundations, the Turkish Red Crescent and making oppressed people's voice heard around the whole world,' Alen Markaryan told me. 'We are all the ozone layer!' read a banner at one match. Once, on a taxi ride I found myself watching videos of Michael Jackson with fans on a mobile phone. One had Jacko roaming about in a Brazilian township singing, 'All I'm really saying is they don't really care about us.' My companions looked on quizzically. One leant over and asked: 'Who are "they"?'

I did a half shrug and said 'The government? The West?'

The fan nodded gravely. 'Yes. I agree with this.'

As leftist politics and socialism increasingly wither in mainstream political debate in Turkey, the socialist identity of Çarşı has grown more conspicuous. It has resulted in Çarşı frequently being seen as first and foremost a political pressure group, the football becoming almost incidental. Leftist individuals and groups, many of whom don't even like football, have latched onto Çarşı as their socialist life-raft amid the rising tide of neoliberalism. This irritates the founding members to varying degrees: some like the increased attention, others have recoiled and dropped away, uncomfortable at being turned into spokespeople for a political movement they do not want to lead.

In response, Çarşı has gone the other way, denying having a hierarchy or leaders. 'Çarşı isn't a group – it's a shared spirit,' said Markaryan. Other Beşiktaş fans like to quote or paraphrase a poem, in which the group is likened to all manner of objects, people and emotions, including a madman lover, a seventy-two-year old granny holding a Beşiktaş flag, a form of death, 'graffiti on a New York metro train', and the eagle on the nose-cone of an F16 fighter jet.

Such playfulness is inclusive, a 'distinctive, human way of telling you at once too much and not enough – of multiplying, rather than resolving, contradictions', as author Elif Batuman wrote about the group in 2011. But it also means the collective has less control over its 'message'. The word 'Çarşı' has drifted away from simply referring to a group of football fans. It has become a synonym for dissidence, opposition and political change.

When I first met Çarşı, the shine of the AKP's early years in power was wearing off. The twin ideals of religious conservatism and unrestrained capitalism were making themselves felt. Tighter abortion laws were proposed. Planning regulations were relaxed or just ignored. Buildings sprang up on previously free land; new highways slashed through pristine forest. The government was using an increasingly pliant judiciary to settle political scores, including the conviction of more than 500 military officers, academics, politicians, journalists and human-rights activists on the basis of twisted or fraudulent evidence. Media corporations unsympathetic to the government were handed vast fines or starved of the lifeblood of advertising. Journalists were jailed as Turkey slipped down the world press freedom rankings.

It wasn't only people in Çarşı who opposed this. Among liberal, secular classes there was a brewing unease as Recep Tayyip Erdoğan went from simply saying provocative things to acting on them. In May 2013 he forced through a law regulating alcohol consumption and promotion. Alcohol adverts were banned, as was the purchase of drink from supermarkets after 10 p.m. Beşiktaş fans showed what they thought of the changes before the last home match of the season, when in their thousands in central Beşiktaş they raised their glasses singing: 'Cheers to you, Tayyip!'. But it was gallows humour. There was a sense of helplessness in the face of both growing conservatism and a divisive style of rule. The seeds were sown for a tumultuous summer.

*

Gezi Park translates literally as 'Promenading Park'. But it's not really a destination for an excursion. Originally an Armenian cemetery, fifty years ago it used to be a bona fide green space, before land was nibbled away by new roads and luxury developers eager for this piece of prime real estate. What was left by 2013 was a rump, a rundown scrub of land with more concrete than grass, frequented mostly by drunks, drug addicts and young couples looking for a surreptitious place to rendezvous. Yet even this was deemed an excessive allocation of green space. Developers won permission to demolish the park and turn it into a shopping mall modelled on a military barracks that used to stand on the site.*

This final indignity struck a chord with a small group of environmental protesters. When the bulldozers moved in on 27 May 2013, a few hundred of them gathered and camped in the park to stage a peaceful protest against the demolition. The initial event didn't register with many people – twenty-first-century Istanbul is always being dug up, repaved, rebuilt. But when the small demonstration was met with a heavy show of force from police, it quickly blew up into a much bigger cause.

On the morning of 29 May, police officers torched protesters' tents and blasted their inhabitants with pepper gas. The iniquity of the situation for many was crystallised in one image: Ceyda Sungur, lecturer in urban planning, wearing a simple red dress. She had gone along during her lunchbreak to lend support to the demonstration. A now iconic photograph captures her, passively clutching a canvas

* In the 1920s, the barracks was home to one of Istanbul's first football grounds, Taksim Stadium, which hosted Turkey's first ever international match. On 26 October 1923, three days before the nation of Turkey even existed, the side drew 2–2 against Romania.

bag as a masked policeman blasts her at close range with a powerful jet of pepper spray. The picture, along with news of the police response, went viral. Years of pent-up anger – at heavy-handed law enforcement, at government policy, at a feeling of diminishing public freedom and space – erupted into nationwide protests.

What became known as 'Gezi' served as an umbrella under which anyone and everyone who was unhappy could gather. Lesbian, gay, bisexual and transgender organisations joined in, along with hard-left political parties and far-right Turkish nationalists. So too did ethnic minority groups, most notably members of the large Kurdish population. Across Turkey, hundreds of thousands took to the streets. It quickly became the largest example of civil unrest since the 1970s. When it finally subsided after nineteen days, 8,000 were left injured, eleven were blinded and six people were dead.*

*

Çarşı were a little slow off the mark. 'We were actually followers in the Gezi park protest,' admitted Ayhan Güner, one of the group's founding members. 'When we woke up and saw the scenes on television we were all sad. Sad for the sake of the youth, sad for those people trying to show environmental awareness.' A topic was started on their web forum, quickly gathering interest. Members decided to march to the square and throw their weight behind the protests.

While many people in the Gezi demonstrations had little experience in protest and police battles, Çarşı were experts at both. After the passing of the 6222 anti-violence law, police were given unprecedented powers to control fans. When I travelled with Çarşı to away matches, our bus would frequently be stopped on the outskirts of the city we were visiting. We would be made to wait for hours, frequently missing up to half of the match. I had been teargassed, pushed by police shields, forced to run from water cannon. Fans would be slapped about for no reason. Less than a month before Gezi, officers

* The number of deaths had risen to eight a year later. Nineteen year-old student, Ali Ismael Korkmaz, was beaten by men (including plain clothes police officers) in protests in Eskişehir and died from his injuries in early July 2013. Berkin Evlan, a fourteen year-old left in a coma after being hit by a tear-gas canister, died on 11 March 2014. He had left the house to go and buy bread for his family.

provoked violence before Beşiktaş's last match of the season by firing in the air, starting a massive riot. 'Let me put it like this,' said Ayhan Güner. 'We're a terrace hounded by tear gas.'

For most of the mainly middle-class environmental protesters, being confronted by water cannon and volleys of tear gas was a new experience. For Çarşı it was another day at the office. As police fought to destroy the Gezi Park camp, the fans waded into the fray, surging forward to drive the authorities from the park. They helped to build barricades using bricks, burnt-out cars and several public buses. A few nights into the protests, the group 'borrowed' a JCB digger from a local construction site and used it to go after the police. The image of the yellow bulldozer just metres from the officers' lines instantly secured a place in Çarşı legend.

Due in part to their fearlessness, the protesters scored a massive victory: at about 3.45 p.m. on 1 June, the police withdrew from the park. The central point of Istanbul – an area of a few square kilometres – became completely free of police control. The heart of the city became a people's republic.

As well as their toughness, Çarşı also brought humour to the protests. Feminist and gay groups in Taksim Square objected to an adapted football chant that went *yarağımı ye Erdoğan* – suck my dick Erdoğan. So Çarşı reworked the lyrics into a nonsensical slogan that played on the rhyme between the words for biscuit and dick: *kurabiye Erdoğan*. Biscuit Erdoğan. A day after the bulldozer stunt, a spoof auction appeared on eBay, 'For sale: police armoured vehicle. Second hand.' In all, Çarşı's involvement was so prominent and successful that something strange happened: fans of other Turkish teams started to pitch in.

Çarşı members welcomed their supposed enemies. As one fan explained to me: 'Well, we have to make peace because if you don't make peace and don't come together, we lose Turkey and then we also lose our teams. If we lose Turkey, we would not have a league. No Beşiktaş, no Fenerbahçe, no Galatasaray, right? So now we have to fight against the regime.' He added, 'After that we can be enemies again!'

As news of the co-operation spread, a meme appeared on Facebook, an amalgam of the colours of all three Istanbul teams dubbed 'Istanbul United'. (A film of the same name would be released in 2014, covering the moment of collaboration.) Back in Gezi Park, fans in Fenerbahçe tops would stand in front of the Çarşı stall with signs saying *Teşekkürler Çarşı* – Thanks Çarşı. Fenerbahçe fans circulated letters online warning that, at their upcoming match with Galatasaray, they didn't want any police on the terrace, calling for the fans to be mixed. Only a month before, Burak Yıldırım, a nineteen-year-old Fenerbahçe fan, had been killed in a fracas between supporters of these two teams.

Wherever you looked in the protests, you could see the thread of football. Football shirts and scarves dotted the temporary tables and stalls that sprang up to sell merchandise to the protesters. The burnt-out cars and buses were covered in Çarşı stickers. Graffiti sprayed around the square read: 'Çare Drogba' – The solution is Drogba. The Ivorian international, at the time playing for Galatasaray, had been praised a few months earlier by Erdoğan for his on-field approach. The words were now being thrown back at him, daubed in paint on any available surface.

As the Gezi sit-in continued, life elsewhere in the city carried on. It was easy to feel like all of Turkey had assembled in Gezi Park. But, of course, there were millions more who not only went nowhere near the square, but who believed Erdoğan when he said that the protesters were terrorists and looters.

In the square it was like a parallel world. The Turkey I knew was a deeply polarised place, scored and marked by impassable fault-lines. A 2008 report by the World Values Survey put Turkey third from bottom on a list of sixty countries ranked by levels of trust between citizens. (It was level-pegging with Rwanda, which was still recovering from a genocide that took place little more than a decade earlier.) Even among different groupings opposed to Erdoğan, there was deep suspicion and sometimes all-out hatred. Now feminists were teaching football fans how to be more aware about women's rights. Kurds and Turks held hands and danced.

Walking down the street with friends on those evenings, there was a buzz in the air. It also made me realise how heavily policed Taksim was as a matter of course. I was used to officers with riot shields and helmets, standing in clumps, their radios giving off high-pitched bleeps, turned up less to communicate than to draw attention to their presence: we are here. Do not forget.

Now they were not here, and the threat of violence had not increased but attenuated. Erdoğan, too, had temporarily disappeared, out of the country on a tour of North Africa. A festive atmosphere had descended, like the heady sense of transgression when the teacher steps out of the classroom.

In the evenings, a wider set of Istanbullus would come and promenade around the park. People who were not protesting but were broadly sympathetic strolled amongst the tents and stalls as you would an art exhibition. They would point at the banners that made them laugh and take photos of their kids at the steering wheels of burnt-out buses. Towards midnight, a large queue would form on a road to Gezi's north. People waiting patiently for a dolmuş, one of Istanbul's yellow shared minibus-taxis, to take them home.

The sense of transformative hope was contagious. But, as with the music festivals that the protest often resembled, you couldn't help but wonder what would happen when everyone had to go home.

*

On 7 June 2013, after ten days of protests, Erdoğan returned to Turkey. In a perfectly arranged piece of political theatre, he was greeted by tens of thousands of supporters as he arrived at the airport. 'Give us the word and we will crush Taksim!' they chanted. In a fiery speech, Erdoğan accused the protesters of being vandals and claimed they were being manipulated by foreign media, the US and terrorist groups. 'These protests that are bordering on illegality must come to an end immediately,' he said.

The tide had turned. People who had broken free of the rigid polarisation of life in Turkey were being squeezed back into their boxes. 'Something extraordinary had been born, and was now being throttled and slowly broken down in the acid bath of Turkish politics,' wrote the journalist Alex Christie-Miller, who had been following the protests from the start.

A week later, on 15 June, the police finally cleared Taksim Square with the aid of thousands of tear-gas canisters and water cannon. Both the festival atmosphere and the darker moments were swept away in a matter of hours after a final push ordered by Erdoğan.

Despite the dismantling of the camp, many of those who took part in the Gezi Park movement saw it as a turning point. There was an infusion of energy and hope into a generation of young, largely middle-class, government opponents who usually viewed the political landscape with a mixture of resignation and despair. Meetings were held in parks. Protests rumbled on. They saw Gezi as a resetting of politics, a washing of the stables.

Çarşı were heralded as heroes. No longer a bunch of football hooligans, they were now seen as the movement's muscle – the witty, fearless young men without whom the protesters would have been trounced. Breathless articles were written, praising their intervention and its importance. When the football season kicked off two months later, fans renewing season tickets were forced to sign agreements that they wouldn't engage in political chanting. It made no difference: stadiums would echo to the sound of 'Everywhere is Taksim, Everywhere is resistance'.

But as summer slipped into autumn, the heroism and defiance slowly began to ebb away. In the months and years that followed, it became clear that Gezi was indeed a turning point – just in the wrong direction. Turkey was sliding from troubled democracy into an increasingly authoritarian state, centred on a single man.

*

Three years after the Gezi occupation, I went to visit Sezgin Gülnar, another Çarşı 'amigo'.

A few months after the protests, Gülnar had been arrested along with approximately eighty other football fans from Beşiktaş, Fenerbahçe and Galatasaray. The story of his ordeal unfolded in distracted dribs and drabs, in between puffs on a shisha pipe. 'I didn't expect it at all,' Gülnar said. 'They came to my house at 4 a.m. They took me to the police station. I was there for three days under arrest. They took my telephone but there wasn't anything on it. No pictures. They were listening to my phone already.'

Five days before his arrest, at a match between Beşiktaş and Galatasaray, a pitch invasion in the 90th minute by Beşiktaş fans had caused the game to be abandoned. Gülnar and the other members of Çarşı were being blamed. "That day I wasn't even at the game,' Gülnar snorted.

But everyone knew that wasn't the main reason for the arrests. It emerged that police had been tapping fans' phones for a year as part of an operation against 'organised crime' in Turkish fan clubs. After a few days in detention, Gülnar and most of the others were released. That was not the end of the story, however.

A year later, in September 2014, Istanbul authorities announced that thirty-five Çarşı members would be put on trial for their role in Gezi Park. The charge against them? Plotting to overthrow the government. Prosecutors were seeking sentences ranging from three years in jail all the way up to life imprisonment.

Çarşı responded with a mixture of anger and disbelief. 'I'm not sure whether to laugh or cry,' said Cem Yakışkan, who was accused of being the ringleader, at a press statement delivered in front of the eagle statue in Beşiktaş's central square.

Gülnar insisted that he had barely even been to the protests: 'I went to the park once!' Yakışkan noted drily that Çarşı must be the first football fan group in the world accused of trying to launch an attempted coup.

The allegations centred on the fact that, during the protests, Çarşı members had clashed with police outside the prime minster's Istanbul office. The indictment claimed that they were seeking to occupy the office and 'overthrow the legally established government of the Turkish Republic'. As evidence, it cited flares, gas masks and guns seized from the homes of the fans. It also mentioned intercepted phone calls that showed them encouraging each other to go to the demonstrations, and video footage of them from the park. In a particularly bizarre passage, the indictment pointed to a transaction by one defendant to buy pizza and meatballs for people at the demonstration.

The group's lawyer, Mehmet Derviş Yıldız, complained that twenty-one pages of the thirty-eight-page indictment were taken up by the names and the addresses of the accused. 'It was put together hastily on Word, with spaces of four to five fingers at the top of each page,' he said. Human Rights Watch described the decision to charge Çarşı as a 'blatant misuse of the criminal justice system.'

During the trial, there were moments where Çarşı's trademark humour shone through. Asked by the judge whether the group had planned a coup, Yakışkan replied: 'If we had that kind of power, we would have made Beşiktaş win the league.'

In December 2015 the decision came: all thirty-five fans were acquitted. But others involved in Gezi were not so lucky. The following year, more than 240 other people were handed jail sentences for various charges connected to the protests.

Despite their acquittal, a cloud continued to hang over the Çarşı members, who feared that the decision could still be overturned in higher courts. And the legal case, which had dragged on for more than two years, had taken its toll. 'It was a difficult process,' said Gülnar. 'There were some of us who lost friendships, there were some who developed psychological problems, some who separated from their partners. And the Beşiktaş management didn't give a shred of support.'

Ties between the fans and the club had never been great. 'Both an arse-kisser and a liar' is one of the milder insults I heard used about the Beşiktaş president, Fikret Orman. But Çarşı's role in Gezi Park and the subsequent trial drove a wedge between the supporters and the team administration.

In the winter after the protests, Erdoğan was hit by a huge scandal when police arrested the sons of three ministers, accusing them of corruption. In the months that followed, material was published online purporting to be recordings of phone calls made by Erdoğan and other senior figures in his administration. In one call, Erdoğan appeared to urge his son to hide millions of dollars stashed in the family home. He claimed that the tapes were a montage – cut and spliced to manipulate what he was saying. He described the investigation, eventually quashed, as a coup attempt. Police officers, prosecutors and judges involved in the operation were removed from their jobs.

At the time of the Gezi protests, Beşiktaş president Orman appeared to come out in support of the fans. He described Çarşı as a 'very colourful and very creative' group whose 'chants, placards and jokes all enliven Beşiktaş'. Speaking about Gezi Park, he said that the protests had managed to achieve something that most people couldn't do: they had made even Fenerbahçe and Galatasaray fans support Beşiktaş. 'All the public's sympathy towards Beşiktaş has grown.' He hastily added a few lines about how Beşiktaş's role was not politics, but sport, and condemned any violence or clashes.

The leaked tapes revealed just how much these comments infuriated the ruling party. One recording appeared to show Ahmet Hamdi Çamlı, a former Istanbul councillor, call up a friend, İsmet Yıldırım, a businessman linked to the construction of the new Beşiktaş stadium. Çamlı complains about Orman, whom he calls a 'faggot', a 'bastard' and a 'son of a bitch', and suggests they threaten him with cancelling the stadium construction.

In another tape, Erdoğan himself speaks with Hasan Gürsoy, a former member of the Beşiktaş administration and a close friend of Orman. He asks him to find out whether it is true that the management had put a statement on the team website in support of Çarşı and warns: 'They are behaving disgracefully.' He makes an unspecified threat: 'If the Beşiktaş board does not stop this business then I am sorry, but I will not be able to keep my promise.'

By the end of June 2013, Orman was performing an about-turn. '[Çarşı] made a big mistake in joining the Gezi Park actions,' he said. 'As chairman, I do not approve of them taking part.' This stance understandably enraged the fan group. Çarşı members were also angered by the club's collaboration with AKP allies, men such as Reza Zarrab, an Iranian-Turkish gold trader mired in a corruption scandal, who bought a box in the new stadium. Orman defended the move, saying that Zarrab was a fan who had 'the light of Beşiktaş in his eyes'. Çarşı responded angrily: 'Beşiktaş is not the light in Reza's eyes . . . Beşiktaş has a conscience.' It wasn't until Zarrab was arrested in Miami in 2016 on allegations of US sanctions-busting that the club decided to resell his box.

Paradoxically, Çarşı's role in Gezi may have served to push their club further into the hands of the government. Orman found himself in an unenviable position, teaming up with a pro-government investment bank and kow-towing to politicians in order to support the club's finances – and keep himself in a job. It is little surprise that he felt unable to throw the club's support behind Çarşı members when they were arrested and put on trial. That does not stop the anger. 'No one from Beşiktaş – not the president, the management, nobody – made a statement saying Beşiktaş fans were not organising a coup,' fumed Gülnar. 'Because they were scared. They didn't take ownership – they left us alone.'

The summer of 2013 and its aftermath also took its toll on the dynamics within Çarşı. Alen Markaryan, the group's first terrace leader, began to withdraw. He disagreed with Çarşı's involvement in Gezi, feeling it was not part of the group's founding purpose. 'Because people load Çarşı with their own political views, it is dividing it,' he complained when I met him again in 2016.

Cem Yakışkan, meanwhile, became more of a political figure. He would show up at events in Beşiktaş with the CHP, an opposition party. 'The CHP and Çarşı are arm-in-arm,' said one fan, dismissively. It's not that the grumbling fan was a government supporter – far from it – but he did not like the idea of the group being beholden to politicians.

Çarşı has also suffered from getting old. Some of its original members gradually ran out of patience for the constant politicking, the stress, the anxiety of the games. One older member complained that Çarşı, the group named after a local marketplace, had become 'like a shopping mall', causing a burst of laughter from the group of people we were with. At first I looked a little bemused. But the more I thought about it, the more apt the image seemed. In the same way that everywhere else in Turkey the old is being bulldozed and replaced by gleaming, half-empty shopping malls, so something similar has gone on in Çarşı. The group, the same fan said, has become 'too big, too luxurious', shunted aside by many of the processes of capital in football that has seen the old terrace culture diminish in influence.

The new stadium has not helped. In the scramble to get tickets, the old groups who used to stand together were scattered. Sezgin Gülnar, who had stood in the old Kapalı terrace since 1995, now stands behind the goal. 'Çarşı has dispersed to three stands,' one member told me.

Others complain about the architecture of the Vodafone Park. In the past all eyes would be on the Kapalı as much as the action on the pitch, waiting for the cue for the next chant. At games in the new stadium, it's hard to pinpoint from where in the bowl songs emerge. It can be as loud, but often it feels directionless.

Yet Çarşı's fall in prominence cannot all be blamed on the new stadium, the age of the fans or the internal disputes about the group's direction. Across Turkey there has been a general squeezing of air out of public displays of opposition. Carşı members face continued harassment. When Alen Markaryan turned up at the first game in the Vodafone Park, he went onto the pitch to lead tens of thousands of fans in an *üçlü* – the 'on three' opening chant at every match. Alen had been doing this chant for years. It involves the terrace leader standing in the centre of the pitch. He pushes a finger to his lips and silence falls. He motions: one, two, three, the crowd counting with him, before they begin clapping and jumping arm-in-arm, singing: '*La la la la la la la la laaaah – ooooh Beşiktaaaaaaş!*' According to some fans, a week later he was called in to see the police for having gone onto the playing surface without permission.

The pressure increased with the imposition of a state of emergency after the July 2016 military coup attempt – and was still in place as of early 2018. It gave greater authority to local governors to restrict public gatherings and enhanced the powers of the police. It became ever rarer to see banners in stadiums making social or political statements. The 'Çarşı against ____' banners feel like they belong to a more innocent era. In August 2017, a handful of Beşiktaş fans unfurled a banner supporting Nuri Gülmen and Semih Özakça, an academic and a teacher on hunger strike in protest at being summarily dismissed from their jobs. 'Long live Nuri and Semih!' it declared. They were arrested at their homes and charged with producing terrorist propaganda.

Amid the gathering storm clouds, it is hardly surprising that a new generation has seemed reluctant to take up the mantle. One young fan told me that being part of the group leadership today was simply too risky. 'Anyone can call himself Carşı and do some silly things in the street,' he said. 'You wouldn't want to deal with that mess.' These days, he said, they just sing the chants. 'The group is just a name now, nothing more.'

Stadiums are not yet wholly passive. In response to the increasing government pressure, an old Republican marching song with the refrain, 'Long live Mustafa Kemal!' has found itself turned into an anti-government anthem. It feels as if public expression has been squeezed so much that people have been left stranded on the one shibboleth that the AKP does not feel fully able to challenge: the sacred position of Atatürk.

*

In the summer of 2016, I was at a football conference in Izmir when I bumped into one of the fans who I had seen, three summers previously, snaking his way through Taksim in the Gezi Park cortege. He had changed. I remembered him as a ball of energy, but he seemed distant and distracted. I was eager to catch up, but he was reluctant. 'I'd love to talk to you but I can't at the moment,' he said. 'While the country is in this situation, I can't.'

He said that he felt under pressure. He believed police were tapping his phone. Officers came to his business to check up on him every week or so, he said. Then came a pause. 'If they say I died in a traffic accident, don't believe it. OK? Don't believe it. That's the kind of life we're living.'

My mind wandered back to the square. To the banners, the chanting. Three years had seen unspeakable change. But the fan was not giving up.

'I'm not afraid of anyone. There's stuff I can do. There are scores to be settled. I'll settle my scores with this government. We'll settle our scores with this president.' His focus had expanded beyond his beloved Beşiktaş. 'Football isn't everything, my friend,' he said.

'Until today we devoted our lives to football but when the time comes we'll set football aside. For life, for the sake of living.'

SYRIA
4

14

Gaziantep

'In Syria, when someone says, "Where do you want to go?" and you don't have any idea, you say, "Red hell! Black monkey!"'

— Hamdo

Ever since he left Syria for Turkey, Anas Ammo felt that life had been dull. As he watched the clock in unsatisfying jobs – first as a hotel translator and then manning a family stall – his mind would frequently flick back to his life in Aleppo. A football obsessive, Ammo had been a sports writer on a national newspaper. He had quit long before the 2011 uprising that would send his nation crashing into a spiral of destruction and death, resigning in protest at the government telling journalists what they could and couldn't publish – even on the sports pages. But he yearned to find a way to return to football.

Like the majority of Syrians who have sought refuge in Turkey, Anas is a staunch opponent of Bashar al-Assad, the Syrian dictator whose family have ruled the country since 1971. He watched on with horror in the spring of 2011 as Assad and his army first clamped down violently on peaceful protests then, as conflict morphed into war, mortared houses, dropped barrel bombs on hospitals and used chemical weapons on villages. As a sports-lover, Anas was especially irked by the co-option of Syrian football into Assad's propaganda war and the complicity of international sports bodies in legitimising this effort.

We met in a coffee shop in Ankara on a winter's day, the light outside thin, cold and fading out for the evening. Anas wore a Dennis the Menace red and black striped jumper that added to his air of boyishness as he excitedly zipped through files on his laptop, eager to show me how football in Syria has become disfigured and destroyed by war.

He pulled up a video of Abbasiyyin stadium in Damascus, the capital's main football arena. 'Watch,' he said, as the film showed the stadium on a clear, blue day. Some vehicles were on the pitch. Suddenly there was a huge roar. What looked like a normal truck was actually a missile carrier. A rocket fired into the air. 'That's forbidden by FIFA,' said Anas, totally deadpan.

He clicked the mouse and the video was replaced by pictures of young men. Some wore football kit, others were in battle fatigues. He named each person as he moved through the images, seemingly less for my benefit, and more as part of a litany of grief. Zakariya al Yousef, a player for Al Ittihad, killed in shelling by Syrian regime artillery; Jehad Qassab, a player with al Karama and the national team, tortured to death; Jamal al Refa'ie, who played for the Jabla club, arrested on the Lebanese–Syrian border and never seen since. The names meant nothing to me, but for a Syrian it would have been akin to a British fan hearing a list of English Premier League players whose lives had been shattered by war.

According to Anas, at least thirty-eight footballers from the top two divisions in Syria have been killed in the civil war, with dozens more from lower divisions. Their deaths are part of a larger toll of sports people caught up in the horror, documented by the Syrian Network for Human Rights. A total of 478 Syrian athletes have been arbitrarily arrested; 264 have been killed, 253 of those by the Syrian regime, the others by opposition forces; 15 footballers are currently in prison. 'My life is on here!' Anas had joked when he first pulled out his laptop. As the conversation unfolded I came to realise he was deadly serious. His existence has become tied up with assiduously documenting and cataloguing the tragedy dealt to Syrian sport.

The different sides in the war among Syrians are mirrored in the country's footballers. You find players supporting Bashar al-Assad and players for the opposition, those who are activists and those who are apolitical. Anas told me he knows at least two players who remain part of the national team out of fear that if they refuse, the government will kill their families. Others have sided with the opposition, like Abdul Basset Saroot, a goalkeeper for the Syrian Under-20 national team who became leader of an opposition volunteer brigade. (His story is told in the 2013 documentary *Return to Homs.*) Dozens, like Anas, have fled abroad.

In late 2014, Anas finally had his brainwave. What Syria needed, he decided, was an alternative footballing structure, something that would, through its very existence, discredit the official Assad narrative. When two football federations could claim to represent the Syrian nation and argue with FIFA that they were the rightful heir to Syria's history of participation in international football, then the world would be forced into recognising and condemning the current situation. And it would lift the spirits of the millions of people who dreamed of building a future without Bashar al-Assad.

What Syria needed was an alternative national team.

*

It is hard to overstate the impact of the Syrian war on its neighbour to the north. As the conflict has dragged on, Turkey has found itself grappling more and more with the spillover. The war has damaged trade and disrupted the country's foreign policy. It saw the Turkish government sponsor Syrian rebel groups and, later, send its own troops into battle on Syrian soil. It turned the country into a transit point for international jihadists and triggered a spate of deadly bombings inside Turkey. Perhaps the most profound and long-lasting change, however, is the millions of Syrians who have flocked to Turkey as refugees.

For most of its short modern history, Turkey has been a country of emigrants. The Syrian crisis has turned that pattern on its head. An estimated 11 million Syrians have been forced to leave their homes since 2011 – one of the largest population movements of the twenty-first century. More than three million have ended up in Turkey. No corner of the country has been left unaffected. Syrians can be found working in Istanbul suburbs and Ankara factories, as day labourers on central Anatolian farms and translators at Mediterranean beach resorts. Some held highly skilled jobs back in Syria – as doctors, architects or businessmen. The experience of footballers is no different. Many of the country's top-flight players have ended up destitute after fleeing their homes and being forced to start from scratch.

The first step for Anas as he sought to cobble together his new football team was to find these men. From his home in Mersin on Turkey's southern coast, Anas got in his car and he drove. To Kilis, Gaziantep, Şanlıurfa, Kayseri, Antalya, meeting the ex-professionals that the war had scattered. Finding them wasn't difficult. 'It's like a family,' he recalled with a smile. 'You kind of know where everyone is.'

Their stories were a sad reminder of how far many had fallen. Players for Syria's top teams, some of whom, before 2011, pulled on the national team jersey and ran out to represent their nation, were dotted among dead-end jobs. Ahmet Tit, a former player in the Under-17 Syrian team at the World Cup, was working in a factory in Kayseri, spraying furniture. Abdulrahman Abu Zaid, an attacking midfielder who played for the Aleppo sides Ittihad and Al Hurriye, was in Bursa working for a removals firm.

Whenever Anas found a player, he would deliver the same line: 'I want to make a national team. We don't have any money. But we'll just have a go'.

Everyone he asked to join said yes.

One of his most important approaches was to Firas al-Ali. He was one of Syria's best-known footballers, a tall, lithe defender for the Damascus team al-Shorta who also played for the national side. Al-Ali played in front of crowds of 50,000, had three houses, two cars and national fame. He had no desire to play anywhere else but Syria.

But war changed everything. In August 2012, Firas was staying with the national team in Damascus preparing for a football tournament in India when he received a call. His thirteen-year-old cousin had been killed in a government attack. Immediately after he took the call, the national team gathered for dinner. When one of the players ridiculed the thousands of people protesting, Firas flung a spoon at him. They had to be separated by team-mates. Unable to represent a regime that was responsible for harming its own people, Firas decided to leave. On the 400-kilometre drive to the Turkish border, each time he needed to pass a military checkpoint, Firas only had to poke his head of the window and give the soldiers a grin and the car would be waved straight through.

He, his wife and two children eventually ended up in Karkamış refugee camp, a small site perched on a hill near the Turkish–Syrian border that houses around 7,000 people. I met him in May 2017 in a park nearby the camp. Sitting on a bench, he told me about the family 'home' – a canvas tent just 4 metres wide. 'In the summer it's like a sauna,' he said. 'In the winter it's very cold. You don't have walls to protect you. I've gone from five-star living to half-star living — or no star.'

The majority of refugees in Turkey eventually left the camps in favour of rented houses in towns across the country. But, struggling for money, Firas's family has remained in Karkamış. Though all services are provided free, life is claustrophobic. Residents are allowed to go out to the nearby towns and cities but must be back in the compound by 9 p.m.

Firas took little persuasion when, in the winter of 2014, Anas phoned him up and explained his project. 'He told me: you are a good person. You left the Syria national team for the revolution.' He immediately agreed to take part.

Finding the players, it seemed, was the easy bit. There was a raft of logistics to sort out, first of which was the question of where the players would train and where they would stay.

Help arrived in the form of Farid Ward, a handsome, tall twenty-four-year-old studying for a degree in management and working for an import-export firm. With his fluent Turkish and connections to the sports ministry, Farid became the grease between the Syrian team and its Turkish hosts. He arranged for the team to meet in Kilis – a small town three miles from the border with Syria – where his family lived.

The Syrian footballers were allowed free use of one of the town's two artificial pitches. What the local authorities couldn't offer was money. Kilis had seen its population almost double with the influx of refugees from Syria. Conscious of the risks of community tensions, officials didn't want to be seen to be aiding the new arrivals more than the Turkish population. But the training space was an important first step.

On a sunny day in May 2015, in front of a phalanx of Arab and international media, twenty-three Syrian footballers gathered in Kilis. Fifteen of the players had played in the first division; of those, half were ex-national team players, like Firas. The coach was Marwan Mona, an ex-professional who won the Asia Under-20 cup with Syria in 1994. Six months after conceiving the idea, Anas had created a Free Syrian National Team.

*

The first training session was like a reunion. 'There were guys who were back together again for the first time in four or five years,' recalled Anas. 'It was a very happy atmosphere.' Firas al-Ali related a similar enthusiasm. 'We were excited,' he said. 'We had a lovely feeling inside of us, like we must do something.'

While the players were focused on regaining their touch and fitness levels, Anas was worrying about finances. A tour of local businesses and charitable foundations had proved fruitless, with the exception of a small donation of $3,000. By the time he had rented two flats (cramming fifteen players in each) and bought a kit, balls and medical supplies, those funds were exhausted. Their predicament became so desperate that Anas had to send everyone back to their homes for a week while he scrambled to find a solution. He returned to some of the groups that he had approached before. One – a foundation funded by a Syrian businessman based in the Gulf – had changed its mind.

The organisation, called the Sankari Foundation, offered a grant of $20,000 a month for a period of six months. Anas hired thirty people, including administrators and doctors. He paid every member of staff $500 a month, more than any of them could expect to earn elsewhere. 'I didn't want them to work any other job,' he said. 'I just wanted them to be professionals.' Videos from those halcyon days show players performing group callisthenics under the watchful eye of their coach. They wore smart green and white kits displaying the side's logo — an eagle with the letters SFF, standing for Syrian Football Federation. Nestled in the border were the three red stars that adorn the middle of the Syrian opposition flag.

On 12 August 2015 the side played their first match: a friendly with Akdeniz Beledyesi, a local amateur club. They won 4–0. Just like the early days of the Syrian uprising – when young activists and protesters felt buoyed by a sense that they really could topple Assad – there was a sense of momentum and expectation. Anas recalls the time with excitement and pride: 'After one and a half months my team was professional.'

Then the problems began.

*

By the end of 2016, the Turkish government said it had spent over $12 billion on helping Syrian refugees. It had also sent $520 million worth of humanitarian aid into Syria. All registered Syrians inside Turkey have access to free health care. Schooling, though patchy, is being expanded. I frequently hear grumbles – even racism – from Turks about Syrians in Turkey. They have grown louder the longer the war has dragged on. But given the huge number of people who have come here, there have been remarkably few outbreaks of tension between communities.

At the same time, life for many Syrians in Turkey is hard. Housing and food is expensive. The difficulty of obtaining work permits means that the vast majority of Syrians work illegally, often for low wages and in exploitative arrangements. Many parents have to send their children out to work. Though Turkish families have been generous to neighbours in need, it is not uncommon to hear Syrians complain about hostility or unfriendliness. It does not help that communication is taxing – Turkish and Arabic belong to different language families and are written in different scripts.

It is not a surprise, then, to hear Anas speak with deep ambivalence about the Turkish authorities. 'Nobody wanted to play us,' he said. 'The local government didn't want it.' The fluent Turkish of Farid Ward perhaps bestows him with more understanding. 'I don't want to lie, they did give us some support,' he said. But he felt that Syrians struggled to be taken seriously. 'No one Turkish viewed us as professional . . . even Turkish amateur teams are in a better situation than us. They have pitches, they have kits, they have homes. We have none of that.'

The team's biggest obstacle was gaining permission for the Syrian footballers to play for Turkish clubs. There was never any chance of them reaching the necessary level of fitness for the national side without the rigour of weekly competitive games. But, in order for a foreign footballer to play in the Turkish leagues, the Turkish Football Federation requires a licence from their home FA – or to apply for one if they are not yet registered. This applies to every level of the football pyramid: from Robin Van Persie at Fenerbahçe all the way down to a Syrian wanting to play for his local weekend side. Obtaining a licence may be little trouble for the likes of Van Persie, or even an ordinary footballing Dutchman. But Syria is not the Netherlands. Many Syrian footballers came to Turkey without documentation. The cost of a licence – 3,000 lira (£700) if new or 6,000 lira if they had one in Syria – is out of the reach of both the players and amateur clubs.

Farid and Anas were in discussions with the Turkish Football Federation to try and find another way to allow their players to register for Turkish clubs, but their attempts were rejected. An official at the TFF told me that the Ministry of Labour approached the federation and asked if it wanted to change the system, but the TFF refused, having neither the resources nor compulsion to act as border guard. It was a source of immense frustration. 'We didn't come from Europe,' said Farid. 'We were escaping from war.'

Problems were also brewing within the team. The Sankari Foundation established a 'Free Syrian Football Federation', its remit like any other football association – to govern and monitor the sport in Turkey and rebel-held areas in Syria. But Anas dismissed them as incompetent and 'corrupt'. He believed that the charity was trying to shunt him aside in favour of its own people. He said that some of the players became 'excessively' Islamic. He showed me a picture on his laptop of two men, allegedly players from the team, wearing Salafi clothes. 'I don't have any problem with Islam,' said Anas. 'Just extremists.'

When I went to see the director of the Sankari Foundation, Abdulrahman Dadam, in his Gaziantep office, he rejected Anas's claims as 'lies'. Asked if the charge of interference was fair, his response was robust. 'Of course!' he declared loudly. 'We should know where every dollar is going . . . We can't just give money and let you work on what you want, no. We should have control.' He accused Anas of running the club as his own personal fiefdom, cherry picking who he wanted and failing to account for decisions or budgets.

I found it impossible to decipher the claims and counter-claims, but one thing is clear: by September 2015 it had all become too much for Anas. He decided to walk away.

The football team split into rival camps and factions – one group stayed with the coach while another migrated to the Sankari Foundation and a new side. For a while there were two Free Syrian football teams in Turkey. The Sankari Foundation arranged a 'launch event' for their side, covered in the press, who seemed to have forgotten that something similar happened barely four months previously.

Firas al-Ali was caught in the crossfire. Both teams wanted him. He wished for them to unite but instead found himself tricked by the Sankari team. Feeling used and despondent, he picked up his bag and returned home, seeing life in Karkamış refugee camp as preferable to the machinations and conflict of the football.

The remnants of the original opposition team had no money and the side quickly folded. The Sankari side played just one further match, against the second-string of Gaziantepspor, the local Süper Lig side. They drew the game 2–2. By now, it was approaching the end of 2015. The initial six-month contract would soon be up. The Sankari Foundation was willing to sign a new deal but the players wanted more generous payment. The foundation would not budge. When no agreement could be reached, the side disbanded.

December 2015 marked the end of the Free Syrian National Team. Their record: played 2, won 1, drawn 1.

*

After the collapse, the players and managers went back to their day jobs. Anas returned to working as a football agent. Thanks to his mother – who was born in the city of Mardin in eastern Turkey – he had applied for, and received, Turkish citizenship in 2014. He had all the rights that status entails, including a passport that allowed him to travel the world. When I met him in Ankara, he had just returned from a five-day trip to Senegal to check out some prospective targets and scout for an Iraqi premier division team. In the previous year he had been to Cameroon, Mauritania and Egypt, building contacts and checking on players.

Farid also did well. He was among the lucky few to get a good job in Turkey. He found a role with a company exporting food products to Europe and the Middle East. In 2017, he was close to finishing a degree in management, and had set up a Syrian side in Kilis, called *al-Savra* – restraint.

But the situation for Firas – Syria's former star – was bad. He returned to his two tasks: running training sessions for children in the camp and working as a labourer on nearby farms – fifteen hours a day for 40 Turkish lira, less than £10.

When I met him, Firas told me he had a new plan.

'I've decided to migrate,' he said.

'Where to?'

'Black monkey!' he responded.

I look confused and Hamdo – Anas's friend who was translating – explained. 'In Syria, when someone says, "where do you want to go?" and you don't have any idea, you say, "Red hell! Black monkey!"'

You might expect their views and feelings about Turkey would correspond to their situations, but it was Anas who railed most loudly against his new country of citizenship. 'Turkey did only three things: they let people in, they gave them shelter and let them go to a doctor if they are ill,' he complained.

But at the same time, Anas has made little attempt to fit in. Despite living in Turkey for almost five years, he speaks no Turkish – he says that he does not want to learn. It's hard to know whether his views reflect a long-held ambivalence towards the country of his mother's birth, or whether his experiences with the team – and as a Syrian – have made him bitter towards it.

The Turkish response to Syrian footballers has been equally mixed. In general, schemes to help have focused on Syrian-only initiatives: in 2016 a new league was founded in Hatay, with close to fifty teams. But neither the Syrian teams nor Syrian players take part in Turkish leagues. Syrians play each other in an expat enclave.

Many Turkish coaches see the futility of this situation, and tell rueful stories of having to let talented Syrians go because they could not get permission to play them. 'From amateur to professional – it's impossible for a Syrian to play. In any form,' one told me with exasperation. Ultimately, the wall of citizenship stands in the way. By autumn 2017, Turkey had begun granting nationality to a select group of Syrians but the numbers are very small and the issue highly sensitive among the Turkish population, which was told that the Syrians had come as 'guests' – with the implication that they would be leaving in future.

And so Firas has sat in his camp, watching the opportunities go by. It shouldn't matter that he used to be a wealthy superstar, but the comparison somehow seems to make his situation all the more iniquitous.

Football agents occasionally used to spot him playing, but when they learnt that he was born in 1985, they would back off – no one wants to sign a player over the age of 30. He watched as younger team-mates from his days in Syria were snapped up, such as the striker Omar Al Somah, who now plays for Al Ahli in Saudi Arabia. 'When I used to pass him he would look at the boots I was wearing,' said Firas, more with resigned humour than anger. 'Now he's a famous footballer.'

In 2014, he was offered a three-year contract with a side in Jordan but was stopped at Hatay airport with his family and prevented from travelling on account of not having the right paperwork. 'I only cried twice in my life,' he said. 'The first was when my brother was killed. The second when they didn't let me go to Jordan. I felt I was destroyed.'

In the summer of 2015, when Syrians left for Europe in their thousands, making the perilous crossing to Greece in shoddy lifejackets and rickety boats, the Syrian football team had only just got started. 'I thought I needed to stay here and take part,' said Firas. Now it seems he regrets the decision to stay. In late 2016 he started developing respiratory problems which he attributes to living in a tent for three years.

As our conversation drew to a close, Firas turned to me: 'What about you, can you help?' After my incessant questioning, having Firas ask one back took me by surprise. Can I help? The question cut to the quick. I stammered and stuttered. I felt a rising burning in the cheeks at the words I could hear myself saying: excuses of relative ignorance (an academic rather than an aid worker), the promises to contact some people who might know more. It was all true, but carried the veneer of abdication. I felt helpless.

Firas spoke with determination about his desire to get out of Turkey. 'All the gates are closed in my face here,' he said. It was his friend Hamdo who offered the note of realism. 'He has nothing. No real idea about how to travel. There's no plan. Just a dream.'

*

I thought I had missed my chance to see the Free Syrian National Team play. Then in late May 2017 I received a text message from Farid, the team's fixer.

'Invite: The Free Syrian National Team management invites you to an exhibition match, on 23 May at 17.30 at Kilis 7 December Stadium.'

It is a forty-minute drive between Gaziantep and Kilis, along straight roads lined with pistachio trees. On the journey, Farid explained that the side would be the same as before, but that these days they had no money. 'A potential sponsor will watch this match today,' Farid said, looking a bit nervous.

We pulled into a football complex and killed the engine. Fifteen men appeared and embraced Farid and his friends as they stepped out of the car. Among the crowd I spotted Anas, wearing light-blue jeans and a cap. 'We are starting back from square one,' he said, but with a smile that suggested he wasn't too upset.

The opposition turned up – a mixed team of local footballers from Kilis, none of whom looked over twenty. Then the referee arrived. And then a bus of riot police.

'Is that really necessary?' I asked Ali, a friend of Anas's.

'Unfortunately, relations between Syrians and Turks are not good at the moment,' he said. The police were there for the Syrians' protection.

The game was disjointed. In the 10th minute, Syria took the lead. Ahmet Seyhuni – one who previously played for the national team – ran onto a through ball and looped it over the onrushing keeper.

The crowd of around eighty broke into a cheer. Most watching were Syrian. My eyes tracked Firas al-Ali. He was wearing the captain's armband and playing in a defensive-midfield role. His carriage exuded confidence and experience, his long legs striding all over the pitch, demanding to be involved. He even took the side's corners.

During the second half, I got the chance to ask Anas a bit more about how it was all going. 'Look, I'll be honest with you, things are not OK,' he stated. 'We cannot play any games. I can only pay for the players' bus tickets. And now we'll go to a small restaurant here and then we will go home.' He turned from the game to fix me square on. 'But now I can speak with my friends, maybe in Turkey, out of Turkey. For sponsors.' That irrepressible hope was still there.

The wind rose and the rain which had been threatening finally came. It felt more like a game in Manchester than sunny southern Turkey. The police abandoned their position for the comfort and safety of the dugout nearby, their helmets and riot shields left stacked against the fence, raindrops streaking down their hard surfaces. In the second half, Kilis equalised with a powerful header past the keeper. Fifteen minutes before the end, Syria got the winner – a speculative lob from the edge of the centre circle.

For all their happiness at the result, the match felt more like a nostalgic reunion than the start of something new. It was clear that the team was not going to get the financial or logistical help it needed to get properly off the ground. Anas's side was not the only 'Free Syrian' side. There were reports of Syrian refugees in Lebanon founding a team in 2014, and in spring 2017 Anas had helped to co-ordinate another Free Syrian team in Germany. These sides present themselves as alternatives to the regime's national team. But watching Anas's team labour to victory over a local amateur club, it was impossible to escape the reality of limited resources, of talent attenuated by disruption, poor diets and a lack of competitive football.

The team seem the perfect metaphor for the Syrian rebel groups – divided, abandoned by international backers, dogged by accusations of religious extremism and ultimately unsuccessful. Farid even drew the comparison for me. 'Our situation is connected to the situation in Syria,' he said. 'The opposition with every passing day is losing, so our confidence is decreasing.'

Just as international governments seemed increasingly willing to accept Bashar al-Assad's continued role in Syria, the regime's national side experienced a resurgence. In autumn 2017, it got the closest it has ever been to the World Cup finals, passing all the group stages to reach a play-off with Australia. The country's most famous star – Firas al-Khatib – rejoined the side after five years in exile. 'I want to say that I will never play for the Syria national team as long as there are bombs falling anywhere in Syria,' he said in July 2012 to a packed media, draped in a sash with the colours of the revolution. In October 2017 he ran out in the jersey of the same side in Australia, as Syria lost 2–1 in extra time.

Although the majority of Syrian refugees in Turkey would love to go back home, many of them feel that they can never be safe there while Assad remains in power. It seems likely that millions will stay for many years to come. Their presence presents a huge challenge. Integrating them will be very difficult. But they also represent a huge opportunity. In the future, Turkey will have a young, multilingual population of second- and third-generation Syrians with the potential to contribute their own skills, talents and ambitions. There may never be another Greek-speaking Turkish footballer like Lefter, but perhaps in future decades we will see a young footballer of Syrian origin play for the Turkish national side.

After the final whistle, the Kilis players trooped off, while the

Syrians hugged each other. Firas al-Ali grabbed a Syrian opposition flag while Anas lined up with the rest of the coaching staff for photos, laughing away. The sun came out, the last rays of the day hitting the buildings behind the pitch. And then they were shooed away. Within minutes, Turkish players had come onto the pitch, members of a local side warming up for the next game.

In the darkness we went for dinner, chicken and chips at a Syrian-owned restaurant in town. Thirty men sat at long tables piled high with flatbread. We broke open the skins, scooping out the white flesh in a cloud of steam and laughter.

After dinner, there was a protracted goodbye on the pavement outside, each man cycling round all the others, giving kisses and bear hugs that conveyed real affection. And then the players of the Free Syrian National Team drifted home. Anas Ammo headed back to his football scouting in Mersin. Abulrahman al-Zaid took the nightbus back to his furniture deliveries in Bursa. And Firas al-Ali returned to the Karkamış refugee camp.

EFSANESİN AMED
AMEDSPOR
HERKES SEVER BİZ ÖLÜRÜZ

15

Diyarbakır

Names that are not Turkish, whose pronunciation and structure is incompatible with the vocal harmony of Turkish, which might be confused due to similar pronunciation and which do not have a pleasant meaning and are contrary to the common sense of the people shall be changed.

— *1984 Symposium on Turkish Toponyms*

Fighter jets roared overhead. Tear-gas canisters arced across the sky. In front of me, twenty-two professional footballers ran around trying to ignore it all, playing a game of football. This was Diyarbakır, the de-facto capital of Turkey's Kurdish region.

The day I arrived in February 2016, the city was in its sixtieth consecutive day of being a conflict zone. A quarter of its historical centre had been taken over by Kurdish militants. The Police and Gendarmerie special forces had yet to dislodge them. I was warned not to set foot outside in the evening. That night, as I tried to go to sleep, I kept hearing the sound of gunshots.

I was visiting because the local professional football side, Amedspor, had drawn Fenerbahçe in the quarter-finals of the Turkish Cup. Amedspor were in Turkey's third footballing tier. Their ground held 1,500. But it was not simply the potential for some giant-killing that prompted the trip – the big teams regularly seem to lose in ignominious fashion in the cup. The reason I decided to go was because Amedspor are viewed as a symbol of Kurdish identity in a predominantly Kurdish city. And the game was taking place at a time when Kurdish–Turkish relations were at a particular nadir.

Approximately a fifth of the population of Turkey are ethnically Kurdish. That's over 15 million people. If you add up the populations of Scotland, Wales and all of Ireland, you just about get there. But in truth no one in Turkey knows how many people are Kurdish. The government does not collect data on ethnicity. Like all questions of identity, the warp and weft of what makes someone a 'Kurd' is hard to define. As is the question of what football has to do with all this. But I shall have a go.

*

The city of Diyarbakır was not always named so. For many thousands of years, it was referred to by the name of its Assyrian founders: Amida or Amed. Turks referred to the city as Diyar Bekir, the 'land of the Bakr', an Arab tribe that had settled in the region in the seventh century. On a visit in November 1937, Atatürk changed its name to 'Diyarbakır'. At the time, Turkey was in the grip of the 'Sun-theory' of language, according to which Turkish was the ur-tongue to which all other languages could be traced. 'Bekir' sounded a lot like the Turkish word for copper, *bakır*. This, then, was deemed the original name of the place.

Renaming sat at the heart of the Republican project. A surname law was passed in 1934, requiring citizens to choose a last name. The honorific titles of the Ottoman nobility or the local appellations of peasants were deemed unproper for a new, modern nation. In each area, people rushed to register their favourite moniker before neighbours beat them to it (only one surname was allowed in each district). Officials were armed with a long list of prefixes and suffixes, which disappointed parties could add if they were too late.

The relative newness of the law means that surnames in Turkey have a literalness and immediacy that has mostly been lost in the UK. I worked for two months for a man named 'Mr Earless', either because his ancestors never listened or had their ears cut off for being thieves. I have a friend called 'Mr Unforgettable'. To compound the strangeness to a British ear, Turkish first names are often adjectives or nouns: Sea, Leaf, Indomitable, Rain, Happy. This leads to full-name combinations such as 'Brave Cloud' (a presidential adviser), 'Volcano Iron Hand' (Fenerbahçe's goalkeeper) and 'Saint No Worries' (a forward for Galatasaray).*

But the surname law had more malign consequences. Suffixes from Armenian ('-yan'), Greek ('-is', '-dis', '-pulos', '-aki'), Persian ('-zade') and Arabic ('-veled', '-bin') were not allowed. Non-Turkish letters – Q, X and W – were also banned from use. While Turkish saw them as extraneous, their banning meant that Kurdish speakers were forced to Turkify their names. On identity documents, the name Welat became Velat; Xilas became Klas or Hilas. Such diktats revealed additional motivations behind the law: not simply to standardise and log citizens in the nation-state era, but also to mould society into what academic Senem Aslan calls 'ethnically indistinguishable citizenry' where everybody – at least on paper – was a Turk.

Names of villages and towns were also changed. Between 1920 and 1990, 36 per cent of all villages in Turkey were renamed. Kurdish, Greek, Slavic, Lazuri, Armenian, Aramaic, Syriac and Arabic words for places, natural features, hamlets and provinces were Turkified. In the Kurdish regions of Turkey, up to 91 per cent of place names were changed.

The 'Kurdish question' existed long before Atatürk and the birth of the republic. Kurds in the Ottoman empire were seen as a distinct grouping. They were Muslim, and so coreligionists of Turks, but they also were deeply tribal, with a tendency for rebellion that made them difficult for many a sultan to keep under his suzerainty. During the War of Independence, Atatürk enlisted the help of certain Kurdish tribesmen. 'Kurds and Turks are true brothers and may not be separated,' he said in 1919. He promised them 'all manner of rights and privileges' if they backed his fight.

After the 1923 proclamation of the republic, however, Mustafa Kemal never mentioned the Kurds by name again. 'Within the political and social unity of today's Turkish nation, there are citizens and co-nationals who have been incited to think of themselves as Kurds,

* The Turkish names are Yiğit Bulut, Volkan Demirel and Eren Derdiyok respectively.

Circassians, Laz or Bosnians,' he dictated in 1930 to his adopted daughter Afet. 'But these erroneous appellations – the product of past periods of tyranny – have brought nothing but sorrow to individual members of the nation.'

Thus began a ninety-year systematic denial and repression of Kurdish identity. In the East, Atatürk's aphorism 'Happy is he who says he's a Turk' was written in letters tens of feet high on hills. Teachers would get students to spy and inform on anyone who was speaking Kurdish, resulting in beatings. Army conscripts were given handbooks that explained that the word 'Kurd' came from the sound emitted when these 'mountain Turks' crunched through the snow: *kurt kurt!*

*

Like everywhere in Turkey, football is huge in Diyarbakır, the city having multiple professional sides. Amedspor were always the insignificant one. The club began life in 1972 as amateur side Melikahmet Turanspor. In 1990, the Diyarbakır municipality purchased the team and the club assumed its name. For decades Diyarbakır Büyükşehir Belediyespor inhabited the lower echelons of Turkish football, attracting little attention or support.

The main football club in the city was Diyarbakırspor, created in 1968 as part of the Football Federation's strategy of 'a team for every province'. Mirroring the formation of Trabzonspor, two amateur teams were merged to form one professional side that represented the city. Their emblem is one of my favourites. It depicts the ramparts of Sur – the historic Roman basalt walls that ring Diyarbakır – along with the Tigris river and the city's most famous symbol: a slice of watermelon. Locals are so proud of the local melons that festivals are held whereby the size of the fruit is determined by how large a child you can sit in the hollowed-out shell.

In the early days, all the players came from the local population. 'There wasn't a single transfer from outside of the city,' wrote Faruk Arhan in his history of Diyarbakırspor. Most Kurdish football fans, however, like most people in Turkey, supported Galatasaray, Fenerbahçe or Beşiktaş. Diyarbakırspor were never in the mix for leagues or cups, although by 1977 they had made it into the top division.

The 1970s were restless years, even by Turkish standards. Kurdish politics became entangled in the wider struggles between left- and right-wing groups, which were frequently violent. Kurds ended up battling against one another as often as they did against 'Turks'. Even so, the situation was calm enough for journalist David Hotham to assert in 1972 that: 'There is no sign that Ankara would ever try for anything other than an economic and social solution to the Kurdish problem'. He had not bargained on a man called Abdullah Öcalan.

Öcalan co-founded the Kurdistan Workers' Party, better known by its Turkish acronym PKK, in 1978, while a student of political science at Ankara University. The group started off as one among many leftist Kurdish groups preaching revolution. Quickly, however, the PKK came to dominate the Kurdish nationalist movement in Turkey.

In August 1984, the PKK began using violent means to reach their goals. They launched an assault on a pair of military bases – the first salvo in a long and seemingly intractable conflict that would stretch over almost four decades and cost tens of thousands of lives.

The PKK attacked government institutions: the army, the gendarmerie, sometimes even schools, their Ankara-appointed teachers viewed by the group as equally complicit in the subjugation of the region. The PKK also targeted Kurdish villagers whom they accused of collaborating with the state. But those who sympathised with the group's aims of establishing an autonomous Kurdish entity were impressed by its commitment to armed struggle. By 1992, it had recruited around 10,000 men and women fighters and claimed to have upwards of 60,000 in its network of recruiters and logistics operatives.

Even as they realised the scale of the threat posed by the PKK, Turkish officials refused to see the group's success as rooted in genuine grievances. They were determined to pursue a military solution. The 1990s – the darkest days of the conflict – were marred by a brutal campaign to quash the PKK by force. Thousands were arrested. The army forcibly evacuated and burned hundreds of villages. Security forces and their helpers in the 'deep state' kidnapped, tortured and executed thousands of PKK members, Kurdish activists and intellectuals. Millions were driven out of their homes, ending up in the shanty towns of Diyarbakır, Adana and cities further west. Today, the city with the largest Kurdish population in Turkey is not Diyarbakır but Istanbul.

As the PKK's founder and leader, Öcalan, known as 'Apo', came to personify Kurdish dreams of greater dignity and independence. To this day his portrait – dominated by his bushy black moustache – is held aloft at protests and hung on offices across the Kurdish region. He gained a reputation as a paranoid, fiery leader with no tolerance of internal dissent.

There is a footballing anecdote that illustrates his domineering character and cult of personality. A female PKK veteran described to journalist and author Aliza Marcus the story of a militant tasked with keeping track of Öcalan's goals in a football match played at a camp. The game took place in Syria, from where he directed the insurgency throughout the 1980s and '90s.

Öcalan asked the goal-counter, a PKK member called Mehmet, how many goals he had scored. Mehmet said twelve. Öcalan started shouting, 'You bum, how could you forget four of my goals?' Mehmet apologised, saying he only counted twelve, but Öcalan kept shouting. Later that day, when Öcalan came to give a lecture, the first thing he said was: 'Where is that low-life? How could he forget four of my goals? To forget four goals is like forgetting four fighters. And to forget four fighters is to forget to kill four [Turkish] soldiers and that means to forget the revolution and to forget Kurdistan.'

Apo is said to be a huge Galatasaray fan. Many Kurds apparently support the team as a result, although I have also been told that the reason is that you only need to add green to Galatasaray's yellow and red colours to form the Kurdish flag.*

In 1999, Öcalan was captured in a raid in Kenya by Turkish

* Kurdish support for Galatasaray is proof of the fallacy of viewing Cim Bom as 'the team of the aristocracy', as many try to claim.

intelligence with help from the CIA. He was taken to Turkey and imprisoned on Imralı island in the middle of the Marmara Sea, from where he still commands the organisation today. After his detention, Öcalan reoriented the PKK's aims away from independence and towards greater autonomy. But, as writers Bora and Erdoğan jokingly note, his football allegiances show perhaps that he never wanted full independence: 'Is not PKK leader Apo's "addiction" to Galatasaray a sign of how the Kurdish existence is tied up with Turkey's? Perhaps it's the most obvious and trustworthy sign!'

One of the great tragedies of the conflict between the PKK and the Turkish state is the way that it has eroded the middle ground. The government's harsh tactics pushed many Kurds onto the side of the guerillas, boosting recruitment and support for a more militant approach. At the same time, the PKK's campaign against the armed forces and its attacks on civilian targets fuelled ultranationalist sentiment among the Turkish population, further diminishing the public sympathy for greater Kurdish autonomy and rights.

Emotions spilled into football. In May 1993, thirty-three soldiers were killed by an ambush on a road between the Kurdish towns of Elazığ and Bingöl. That weekend at some football grounds, crowds sang the national anthem. The following week, the Turkish FA decided that all games should start in that manner to commemorate the victims of PKK violence. Today, every league game in Turkey starts with the national anthem – from amateur matches on municipal fields to Galatasaray–Fenerbahçe derbies.

Diyarbakırspor found themselves associated with the militants. At away matches the home crowd would shout, 'Down with the PKK!' Turkish flags would be displayed, and the chant of 'martyrs never die, the nation is indivisible' frequently shouted. This behaviour upset Diyarbakırspor players and management. 'We are a team of Turkey. Diyarbakır is a province of Turkey. Diyarbakırspor is a team associated with the Football Federation . . . As a club it's not associated with any political organisation or party,' said chairman Çetin Sümer. 'We feel like foreigners in our own country,' said Diyarbakırspor press spokesman Suat Önen.

The abuse continued. By 2010 it was starting to take its toll.

Diyarbakırspor were in debt; the chairman had a huge falling out with the club staff and players, who were not being paid; their games were frequently forfeited, unable to finish because of crowd trouble. The rules of the federation stated that if a side forfeited two games in a row, they had to be automatically relegated. But the TFF balked from relegating Diyarbakırspor, worried that it might inflame the situation. They needn't have worried.

In May 2010, Diyarbakırspor fell out of the top division. In 2011 they were put under government ownership because of their debts. The club had to rely on individual donations to raise the funds to travel to away matches. On 17 April 2011, the players for Denizlispor ran out at the Atatürk stadium in Diyarbakır but no home team joined them – the club employees had gone on strike, from the players to the turnstile operators. No one had thought to tell the opposition, or the referee. Diyarbakırspor sank like a stone: four relegations in four consecutive years saw the club fall into the amateur leagues before being wound up in 2013.

*

Whilst Diyarbakıspor's fortunes went from bad to worse, Turkey's Kurds were undergoing a period of change and cautious hope. The emergence of the AKP government in 2002 changed the dynamic of the decades-long conflict. In 2005, Erdoğan travelled to Diyarbakır to make a ground-breaking speech. 'The Kurdish problem is not only a problem for just one part of this nation, it is a problem for all of it,' he declared. 'It is my problem.' The solution, he said, was 'more democracy, more civil rights, more prosperity'.

Already the AKP, with the backing of the European Union, had begun loosening the decades-long programme of denial of Kurdishness. It lifted the state of emergency on the south-east region that had been in place for more than a decade. Compensation was promised to the hundreds of thousands forced from their homes over years of fighting. The government eased restrictions on publishing and broadcasting in Kurdish. Later came the launch of a state-run TV channel and a decision to allow Kurdish-language university departments.

Ministers promised huge investment in the south-east, the country's poorest region. And the party recruited parliamentary candidates such as Mehmet Şimşek, who was born in a village in the eastern province of Batman before going on to become a banker for Merrill Lynch. Kurds have always played a role in Turkish politics (Turgut Özal, prime minister in the 1980s, was part Kurdish) but for many decades ethnicity was the elephant in the room. Under the AKP it became explicitly invoked. 'Think of a family that does not know how to speak Turkish, in which both the mother and father are illiterate,' said Şimşek in 2015. 'But today I am the Finance Minister of the Republic of Turkey . . . this is completely due to meritocracy, equality of opportunities'.

The overtures to the Kurdish minority were motivated at least partly by electoral calculations. When Erdoğan stared down the military in 2007, he enjoyed a massive spike of support in Kurdish regions. Many Kurdish voters felt they had more in common with Erdoğan's openly pious, socially conservative party than Kurdish parties linked to the Marxist-Leninist PKK.

In 2009, the Turkish government began peace talks with the PKK, first in secret, and then with Abdullah Öcalan from his prison on Imralı Island. In 2013, Öcalan ordered the PKK to put down its weapons, calling for 'politics, to come to the fore not arms'. The group's fighters began withdrawing from Turkey.

Although many accusations would later be traded on both sides, it was a time of cautious optimism. For all the criticism of the AKP's motives and tactics, the steps it took towards peace were unprecedented, risky and historic. The change in the climate may not have been enough for some Kurds, but it was real. And I often witnessed it first-hand.

In 2014, on a coach journey to Istanbul I sat next to Sedat, a young man coming back from a football match in Malatya. When the bus conductor was struggling to make himself understood to the old, wizened couple sat behind us, Sedat swung round and spoke to them in Kurdish. Like a wand had been waved, they snapped to attention and responded. Letting out a huge laugh, the conductor also then switched into Kurdish. All three parties chatted together for a few minutes while I surveyed the scene in amazement. When the conductor was done, Sedat told me the couple behind were Syrian Kurds. Talking about the incident to friends later, they agreed that it simply couldn't have happened before the 2000s.

It is in this context that Diyarbakır's other football team, the succinctly-named Diyarbakır Büyükşehir Belediyespor, decided to change their name.

*

'People think the name Amed is Kurdish, but it isn't. . . it's a Farsi-derived word. One of Diyarbakır's names from 900 years ago,' Faruk Erol, sporting director at Amedspor, explained to me. Even five years previously, referring to Diyarbakır as Amed would have been considered a separatist gesture, leading most likely to a court case. In the new climate of openness following the peace process, those at the club felt it possible.

But Erol wafted away suggestions that the change was political: 'Istanbul has old names . . . if you say Constantinopolis, you're directly seen to be Greek because it's a Greek name. But Amed isn't a Kurdish name, it's just an old name.'

This seemed like wilful naivety. Changing a name in Turkey is always a political gesture. Erol seemed to accept this later on when he compared the team to Athletic Bilbao and Barcelona, sides in Spain that represent regions battling for greater recognition of their difference and autonomy. 'The reason I decided to go into this sport business was that we felt this team would grow, that this team would get support from the people,' he told me, eyes shining. It didn't sound as if the change was a passing fancy.

In January 2015, the Turkish Football Federation fined Amedspor 10,000 lira (£2,000) for changing the name, crest and colours of the team without prior approval. The Amedspor chairman, Ihsan Avcı, said that he informed the TFF at the start of the season. Amedspor continued to petition the TFF for the name change, but it was rejected on account of a team already operating under the name 'Amedspor'. The other team – a small amateur side – agreed to change their name and on 7 July 2015, Amedspor tried once more for the name change. This time they were successful. Diyarbakır Municipality Club became Amed Sports Activities Club. But football was about to be overtaken by events off the pitch.

On 20 July 2015 in the town of Suruç on the border with Syria, a twenty-year-old ISIS supporter detonated a backpack of explosives among a group of young people. They were volunteers from the

Federation of Socialist Youth Associations, and were working to send aid to Syrian Kurds. Thirty-three people were killed and over a hundred injured.

The PKK responded to the bombing by killing two policemen. The group said that the murders were revenge against the Turkish government, which it accused of condoning the attack. Ankara responded by ordering the launch of airstrikes against PKK bases in northern Iraq.

The insurgency roared back into life, this time with a devastating twist. For the first time, fighting erupted in urban areas. PKK-linked youth militia dug trenches and built barricades in neighbourhoods of a number of towns and cities, including the Sur district of central Diyarbakır. 'Self-rule' was declared in these zones. The military announced round-the-clock curfews and, in September 2015, began clearing them by force. Towns and cities across the south-east became urban warzones. Huge numbers of civilians were displaced – by some accounts as many as 350,000 – as the government used aircraft, tanks and heavy artillery to try and dislodge the militants.

An important factor leading to the collapse of the peace process was the impact of the war in neighbouring Syria. While Western countries were most alarmed by jihadi fighters, Turkey's primary concern was Kurdish combatants getting weapons and combat experience in Syria. The successes of Kurdish militias, who were winning territory in northern Syria, inspired Turkish Kurds and alarmed the Turkish government in equal measure.

As the conflict on Turkish soil intensified, Erdoğan vowed to continue battling the PKK until every last fighter was 'liquidated'. Heavy clashes continued in south-eastern cities throughout the winter months. One of the worst-hit places was Cizre, a town of around 120,000 people, tucked in the corner where the borders of Turkey, Syria and Iraq all meet. In mid-December, the town was placed under a blanket curfew that would last seventy-nine days. Over that period, sixty-six Cizre residents, including eleven children, were killed by gunfire or mortar explosions according to Human Rights Watch.

In late January 2016, as fierce fighting in the city continued, security forces surrounded three buildings where around 130 unarmed civilians and injured combatants were said to be trapped in basements. For weeks, local politicians and NGO workers tried to negotiate access for ambulances and an evacuation. On the day that medical help was meant to arrive, the basements were stormed by security forces. The Turkish government has claimed that militia were using the civilians as human shields. Human Rights Watch said that the available evidence suggested the Turkish government 'deliberately and unjustifiably killed about 130 people'.

*

While the Cizre basement siege was unfolding, Amedspor played Istanbul Başakşehir in the Turkish Cup. To an almost empty stadium, the Amedspor fans started chants: 'Everywhere is Cizre, everywhere is resistance'; and 'Don't let children die, let them come to matches.'

Bilal Akkalu, a twenty-eight-year-old Amedspor fan, told me about the response they received from the security forces. He described being arrested by the police and beaten, shoved into the back of a van and handcuffed with his hands behind his back. Some of his friends had their legs broken. One had his arm broken. Bilal says he was held for twenty-four hours and wasn't given any water or food for twenty of them. He was released but, when we spoke, he still had a court case outstanding. According to news stories, close to a hundred people in total were detained.

The football federation's disciplinary board ruled that Amedspor's fans had chanted ideological slogans and banned them from attending their club's next game. The club were also fined 25,000 Turkish lira (£6,500). The match finished 2–2. Semih Şenturk, after scoring an equaliser for Başakşehir in the last minute, celebrated by doing a soldier's salute – a gesture that was almost certainly intended to upset the Amedspor fans. It went unpunished.

At an Eskişehirspor–Antalyaspor match a few weeks later, a provocative banner was displayed: *aşk bodrumda yaşanıyor güzelim* – the place for love is Bodrum, my dear – a line from a cheesy pop song by Bülent Serttaş. Bodrum is the name of a popular tourist destination on the south coast of Turkey, a favourite of Kate Moss, among others. But it's also the Turkish word for basement, a clear reference to the events in Cizre. These fans were also unpunished.

The stalemate with Başakşehir was good enough to take Amedspor through to the last-16 of the cup. They were to play Bursaspor, a side known for having a strong seam of Turkish nationalists among its supporters. 'There was a sense as though two different national teams were playing one another,' Faruk Erol told me. Bursa fans hung Turkish flags on the advertising boards. 'The players were announced on the screen. Bursa, which was saying "I'm Turkey's team", had nine foreign players and two Turks. [Whereas] our first XI were completely Turkish.' A smile played across Erol's face. 'We're there in the position of "foreigners", but the team playing nine foreigners is seen as being the "patriotic" home side!'

Amedspor won the match 2–1. The player who powered in the team's second – a stinging rocket from the edge of the area – was their star midfielder, Deniz Naki.

Born in Germany to a Kurdish family, Naki began his career playing for German clubs St Pauli and SC Paderborn (another example of the folly of labelling all Turkish-speakers in Europe as 'Turks'). In a deep baritone voice, he explained what brought him to Amed. 'I had offers from the first and second leagues in Belgium and Holland, but Amedspor is a matter of the heart,' he said. 'I didn't look at the money or the career prospects and came here.'

Naki is fiercely pro-Kurdish. On one forearm he has a tattoo of the Kurdish word for freedom, *azadi*; on the other, the word 'Dersim', the name of the town where his family are from. But if you look on a map you won't be able to find Dersim. In 1937, there was a rebellion there. The Turkish government flew in planes and dropped bombs. Thousands were killed and tens of thousands more forced to leave their homes. And the town was renamed as Tunceli.

After the match against Bursaspor, Naki wrote a post on Facebook about the curfew and siege in Diyarbakır. 'We dedicate this victory to those who have lost their lives and been injured in the fifty days of oppression we face on our lands.' The TFF responded by hitting him with a twelve-match ban, on account of 'unsporting' comments. More seriously, that remark, along with others he had previously made on Facebook, were passed to a prosecutor and a criminal case was opened. Naki was charged with 'terrorist propaganda', 'creating enmity and hate between two different sections of society' and 'presenting security forces as committing massacres against the region's people'. He faced up to five years in prison.

Amedspor fans believed that his arrest was part of an attempt by the state to shut down their club. 'This is being done in a planned, programmatic way by the TFF and the government,' a fan told me. 'They want to destroy us.' Naki was upset about the punishment, but mainly because it meant leaving his team-mates in the lurch. He defended his right to be political. 'The general reaction I receive is "You're a footballer, just play football." But in my opinion, before being a footballer I'm a person. And when I see a war here, I cannot stay silent. I voice my opinions.'

Naki's punishment meant he would follow the rest of Amedspor's cup run from the stands. After beating Bursa and making it to the quarter-finals, the team was rewarded with a date with one of the big boys: Fenerbahçe. But, due to the fans' chants at the Başakşehir match, the TFF ordered Amedspor to play the cup game behind closed doors. Turkey's largest football club would be visiting Diyarbakır. But no one was going to be there to watch.

*

The Amedspor ground stood on a hill. What attracted the eye from the road were the green, yellow and red panels that lined the stadium's exterior. There was a ploughed field around the stadium ringed with temporary police barriers, eight feet high. This is my abiding memory of Diyarbakır, these barriers throughout the city, roping off all available public space. But most of all there were police. Police with tear-gas canisters and police with guns.

When I arrived there were perhaps sixty fans gathered outside, congregating moodily, looking at the security barriers and grumbling. 'If we were Turkish, we could watch this match, but because we are Kurdish, we can't,' Ahmet Aksu, a nineteen-year-old student, told me. 'In England, if you say "Freedom", it's fine, but here, they just send us to jail.'

As sixty fans turned into close to a hundred, that mysterious shift by which small groups become a crowd started to occur. 'I live within these borders. I am a citizen of this country,' one Amedspor fan told me. 'What does it mean when a citizen within these borders can't support their own team? I can't travel to games outside of my own province! I can't go to Istanbul. I can't go to Eskişehir, I can't go to Tarsus . . . I'm not free to speak my own tongue; I'm not free to support my own team.'

Knowing that things could quickly spiral out of control between the frustrated fans and the police, I was glad when the time came for me to move through into the *cordon sanitaire* around the ground. I had managed to tag along with a journalist friend who was writing a story about the game. There was a brief moment of panic when my name was not on 'the list'. Someone went to fetch another list. My name was on that one, much to my relief. We headed inside.

The car park was full of coaches and TV trucks trailing cables the thickness of a leg. Both teams were already here. The Fenerbahçe side flew in that morning and would leave immediately after the game. Even this was not precaution enough. I was handed a sheet with the line-ups. Fenerbahçe was shorn of many household names: no Robin Van Persie, Mehmet Topal, Lazar Marković. Playing in their away kit of light-blue and white hoops, it didn't feel like Fenerbahçe proper.

Nor did it really feel like a 'spectatorless' match. Half the main stand was full of journalists, the other half police in riot gear. With bulky leg pads and chest protectors, they folded themselves uncomfortably into the chairs, knees digging into the back of the person in front.

The teams came out, the Amedspor players holding hands with children carrying white carnations. They also held a banner reading: 'Don't let children die. Let them come to the match'. Later on, in the reports on pro-government news websites, the banner would be pixelated.

The game kicked off but something wasn't right. The Amedspor players were not moving. Instead, they individually stood to attention, arms by their sides, and turned to face the stand. Under a barrage of applause they stood, still as statues. It was a protest – at the officials who banned their star player, fined their club and stopped their supporters from attending. From American footballers kneeling to athletes raising their fists, I was used to sports people protesting in the interludes – the pre-game anthem or medal ceremony. To see them stilled when they should have been in motion was both surreal and effective. The Fenerbahçe players passed the ball idly among themselves, until one of them sliced it into touch. The Amedspor players reanimated and the game began for real.

Watching professionals play in an empty ground is a very strange experience. It made me realise how much of their 'professionalism' stems not from them but from the crowd; without supporters as a prop, they were diminished. I felt like it debased Danish international Simon Kjaer to hear him shouting and ordering around the rest of the Fenerbahçe back four – 'right right right!', 'go go go!' – like a gobby man on a Sunday morning down the park.

Fighter jets flew over every ten minutes or so. It was unclear whether their sorties were related to the game or another engagement – in the south-east, Northern Iraq or in Syria. Their noise was so loud it blotted out all others for the seconds they were overhead. In lulls, you heard the tinkling of teaspoons stirring sugar into tea cups in the directors' box, and the faint drumming and cheering of the fans outside. In the middle in the VIP section sat the directors of Amedspor. They cheered, whooped and hollered at every attack.

In the 13th minute an Amedspor player had a speculative shot from 30 yards. The goalie parried it but only into the path of Şehmus Özer, who scooped the ball in. The directors in the stand cheered. The players hugged. The captain picked up a top from the bench and ran to the halfway line, where he displayed the back right in front of the management section: Deniz Naki. This too was not shown on television.

The dream was on for all of four minutes, before Fener carved open the Amed defence, waltzed through and slotted the ball past the keeper. With half-time approaching, Amedspor won a corner. There was a moment of panic at a bang and the sound of breaking glass in the directors' box. Someone had got so excited at the corner that they knocked over their chair. Upon realising it was nothing serious, a wave of relief and nervous laughter passed over the crowd.

From the corner Fenerbahçe broke away and scored. The Amedspor players trooped off for the break, the 2–1 deficit not reflecting how they had played. My friend came back from the bathroom in hysterics; while he was washing his hands, a security official handed him his holster – complete with loaded handgun – while he buckled his trousers.

The second half saw the pressure crank up further. The Fenerbahçe captain was booked for an agricultural challenge. The Amedspor directors started to lose the patina of detachment. 'Faggot!' someone shouted aggressively.

In the 68th minute Yusuf Yağmur surged into the Fenerbahçe box. He looked like he might shoot but cut back and laid it off. An Amedspor player ran in and stroked the ball into the bottom left corner: 2–2. The small crowd of directors erupted. Less a cheer, more a roar. A minute later Yağmur again burst into the box. This time he didn't square it but drove on, firing the ball across the keeper into the top corner: 3-2!

For a while Fenerbahçe were all at sea. They seemed to have misplaced their central midfield. Could this really happen? As the game careered to a close, it became more raucous. Behind the stand on the other side of the pitch, the tell-tale stream of smoke from a tear-gas canister caught my eye. The noise of fans outside the stadium diminished as they no doubt were forced to scatter.

But Fenerbahçe were not done. A long ball over the top. Volkan Şen turned inside one defender, then hooked it past the keeper. The game finished 3–3. Complete equals.

After the match, there were the standard press conferences. From the Fenerbahçe general secretary were platitudes and thanks: 'Our aim in coming here was sport. Fenerbahçe is one of Anatolia's biggest civil society organisations. But we don't do politics. We are completely focused on sport.' From the Amedspor chairman came a more focused, angry criticism: 'The punishment that the federation gave was unjust. Our club shouldn't be exposed to this sort of racism and discrimination. Today in our protest we had the aim of showing this in a peaceful manner.'

While I waited for a taxi back to the city centre, another football bus pulled in. I could see from a distance that it was painted in the colours of a team. As it flashed by, my eye was drawn to the lettering on the side.

The bus pulled to a halt and a new set of professional footballers from Diyarbakır got off, laughing and joking, strolling into the changing rooms. It was Diyarbekirspor, not the old side that used to be in the Süper Lig, but the other professional team of the city, who play in the fourth and lowest professional tier.

I walked past the bus. Someone had stuck a letter 'E' over the 'A' in Diyarbakır. When the bus was moving you might not notice, but now it was stationary, the addition stood out – the lettering of the E a bit too thin and its green surround not quite the right shade. I realised this must have been the bus of the old Diyarbakırspor, defunct three years ago. No point in letting a good team coach go to waste: here it was, requisitioned to ferry another set of professional footballers in Diyarbakır.

It seemed no one could separate out Diyarbakır's football clubs – Amedspor, Diyarbekirspor and the defunct Diyarbakırspor. Nearly everyone I spoke to thought that Amedspor were a renamed Diyarbakırspor. Even the buses were involved in the conspiracy – Diyarbekir, Diyarbakır ... It seemed a metaphor for the wider fortunes of Turkey's Kurds – that it's perhaps stupid to try and separate them out. When you could be sitting on a bus for five hours chatting to someone in Turkish only to find out they're a Kurd; when a 'Kurdish' team contains more Turkish citizens than its 'Turkish' opposition, it seems redundant to be too strict about labels and definitions.

*

Amedspor lost the return fixture 3–1. I watched the game in a basement café in Kadiköy, less than a kilometre from the Fenerbahçe stadium after Amedspor fans were banned from attending. On the final whistle, the crowd of seventy or so in the café broke into a round of applause. It then separated into smaller groups, which slowly began to drift home – some peeling off their Amedspor shirts, others keeping them on. Everyone studiously ignored the hundred police in riot gear standing five metres from the entrance.

In the months that followed, the grim cycle of conflict continued. Heavy clashes took place in Diyarbakır and other urban centres. The PKK responded with attacks not just in the south-east but also in Western Turkey. In March 2016 a PKK offshoot rammed into a bus and caused a huge explosion in the centre of Ankara. Thirty-seven people were killed, among them a former student at the Ankara school where I had taught. The heads of the largest Kurdish-issue political party, the HDP, were arrested and held in prison, accused of terrorist propaganda. Academics who signed a petition condemning the war were hounded – some arrested, others forced to quit their jobs. 'There is no difference between a terrorist with a gun and bomb in his hand and those who use their position and pen,' said Erdoğan.

Amedspor continued to provoke controversy. At an away match at Anakaragücü, four of their directors were badly beaten in the VIP section in what Faruk Erol told me was an unprovoked attack. Footage from mobile phones shows men in suits throwing punches before the Amedspor press spokesman is picked up and dropped over the side of the stand onto his head. When the team played away in Sivas, their hotel reservation was cancelled and no other place in the city would oblige. The team ended up staying at a thermal spa hotel 40 kilometres outside the city.

*

Ankara spring days are like days nowhere else in the world. The sun is strong but the air is cold. Ice lingers in shadows but pale skin left exposed will redden unexpectedly. On just such a day, a year after the Fenerbahçe match, Amedspor came to town.

I had moved to Ankara months previously to start a new job. The violent clashes in the cities of the south-east had come to an end but the crackdown on Kurdish activism and cultural expression was continuing. I wanted to see how a team from Diyarbakır would fare in the capital, so I went along to watch.

The opposition were Keçiörengücü, a municipality side with no real fanbase. The team's stadium sits on the side of a hill that, thirty years ago, would have been Gecekondu housing and thirty years before that grass and steppe. It now housed three small compact stands, wedged between colourful apartment blocks. Behind two of them were police riot trucks.

Keçiören has a reputation as an AKP stronghold. I asked a young teenager with bad teeth if there were normally so many police. 'No. But the other side is *pis*,' he responded, using the Turkish word for 'dirty'. The police were taking no chances. They did not want a rerun of the trouble at Ankaragücü.

'Amed!' Clap, clap, clap. 'Amed!' rose from behind one of the stands. One hundred and fifty fans were waiting to enter.

A man with a friendly smile called Murat, whom I had never previously met, pulled me into the queue. He had appointed himself Guardian of the Foreigner.

The stadium was new. Players zig-zagged around cones on a uniform green pitch. The terrace concrete was unblemished by chewing gum and tea spillages. Over the air the loudspeakers played the 'Mehter March', the martial tune of Ottoman military campaigns. The Amedspor fans continued singing. The sound system was turned up more loudly. It was unclear whether the soundman was finding his level for the game or trying to drown out the chanting.

Suddenly, the Amedspor fans' drummer struck up a beat, too quick for any chant. There was a rush and the terrace emptied. The fans formed a line at the front, standing side by side, linking little fingers. The boys began shaking their shoulders and clicking their fingers, performing the *halay*, a dance rolled out at parties and weddings. From the stand, the group of four young girls to my left began trilling. I had never seen this at a football match before.

The tribune leader wore a tracksuit. He was around five foot high and fifty years old, but neither fact stopped him leaping on top of the fence at the front of the stand.

'Today is our first away match for twenty-four weeks,' he shouted. 'I don't want to hear a single swear word.' Swearing would mean a ban. Swearing would probably mean a shield in the face from the riot police watching on the left and right. Swearing would mean another twenty-four weeks without football.

'For ninety minutes, let's show Turkey we are the most gentlemanly, the number-one fan club.'

The main stand opened and the Keçiörengücü fans began to filter in. White seats were slowly coloured in by bodies. A few carried Turkey flags. A Turkish flag was hung over the fence onto the pitch. Perhaps 1,000 fans were for the home team, 250 for the away.

The sides came out and lined up for the anthems. The loudspeaker crackled: 'Attention please: our national anthem'. *Our*. Has a pronoun ever carried more weight of assumption? The fans from Amed stood silent as words set to music floated across the pitch.

Don't frown! I beseech you, oh thou coy crescent . . .
But smile upon my heroic race! . . .
Why the anger? Why the rage? . . .
For freedom is the absolute right of my God-worshipping nation.

The game began. Behind the curtain of the pounding drum and the roll of the chants, it felt small and far away. Game and crowd were out of kilter. By half time they still had not come into alignment, the crowd too hyped and assertive for the disjointed, scrappy play. The first half ended scoreless.

The noise of the home supporters poked through in the lulls from the Amed fans. 'Türkiye! Türkiye!' they chanted. It was met by jeers and whistles. The Amedspor fans may not have sung the national anthem, but they felt that they too were a side from Turkey.

The home supporters kept at it, words sharpened into needles then hurled across the pitch in the hope of provoking a reaction: 'Where are you crazies? Where are you, so-called hot-blooded ones?' they screamed. When it elicited no response, the stakes were raised: 'Mother fuckers, Amed!' The Amed tribune leader was like a man with dogs on a leash. 'Listen, the TFF won't do anything to them,' he warned. 'But they will to us. So don't respond. Don't be provoked.' He marshalled his young charges into a reply: '*Amed küfür etmez!*' Amed supporters don't swear! Murat, by my side, turned to me hoarsely: 'My voice has gone.'

Around the hour mark, legs began to tire. Space opened up. The ball trickled the wrong side of the Keçiörengücü post in front of us, causing howls of frustration. At the other end the Amed keeper was saving headers from free-kicks and corners. He was keeping them in the game.

Stationed at the side of the pitch facing the away crowd was a plain-clothes police chief, dressed in a brown leather jacket and aviator shades. Two rows of seated officers were boxing us in. Police in Turkey have a reputation for being highly nationalistic, but after the game, one next to me – all paunch, gilet and sunglasses – would turn to Murat and say: 'I've been watching your terrace and you were great not to be provoked.' He would chat about cars. About women. He would offer us a lift home and – when we politely declined – insist on accompanying us back to Murat's car.

But he was not in charge. The chief in the brown leather jacket argued with a fan over a banner. It read 'Diyarbakır Champions'. He was not allowing the supporter to show it. Fans were getting angry. While I was watching the dispute I heard a roar. Keçiörengücü had scored.

But Amed regrouped and came again. They pushed forward and won a free-kick on the edge of the area. We stood and watched Deniz Naki approach the ball, the late afternoon sun angling into our eyes. The drummer stopped his roll. The ball arced perfectly over the wall and into the top corner.

Fans fell onto the floor. Fans rushed to the front and scaled the fence. Naki sprinted towards our terrace and came to a halt in front. In the months ahead he would go on to face more problems, including a second spell in detention, a lietime ban from football by the TFF and an armed attack on his car in Germany. But for now, he was basking in the adulation.

'You're all sons of bitches!' began the home crowd, but the goal had immunised the Amedspor supporters. They cheered and sang and jubilated. The game ended 1–1.

A wave of relaxation washed over proceedings. We were done. No major problems. All around me, people sat down and began lighting up cigarettes. The Amedspor players gave us their thanks and walked towards the tunnel.

A group of Keçiörengücü supporters gathered around the tunnel entrance. As the Amedspor players filed through they began shouting abuse and pelting them with objects. A few tried to scale the fence onto the pitch. The police were at our end. It was the Amedspor fans whom they had been eying warily. It was the Amedspor fans who were encaged in a box of truncheons and shields.

Suddenly, the officers realised their error. Twenty men in riot gear turned towards the home supporters and began to run.

16

Inferno

That brute which knows no peace
Came ever nearer me and, step by step,
Drove me back down to where the sun is mute

— *Dante,* Inferno, *Canto 1*

I almost slept through the entire event.

Attending a football fan conference in Izmir on 15 July 2016, I arrived back at my hotel late, tired and sweaty, clothes stuck to me like a second skin in the 35-degree heat. I showered, changed and just before collapsing onto the bed had one final check of my phone. There was a text from my wife:

Some strange goings on in Istanbul and Ankara right now.

Two bridges closed by army.

Helicopters overhead.

It looks like a coup . . .

I was instantly awake.

I turned on the television in time to see the prime minister confirm that an attempted coup was underway. My mind raced. I got up, left my room and walked around the hotel. No one was out of their rooms. I could hear the news on televisions, their muffled urgency leaking through doors. Heading down to the reception, the middle-aged man on duty looked completely unbothered. His age meant he had already lived through one military coup – possibly more. I wanted to take my cue from him but couldn't dull my anxiety. Tanks were massing in Istanbul and Ankara. I peered out of the hotel. The road was normal, empty apart from the occasional streak of painted light that signalled a passing car.

On Twitter people were posting about stocking up on food and money. The former wouldn't be an issue – I was in a hotel. But the latter . . . I looked in my wallet and realised I had no cash. The nearest ATM was 400 metres away. I did not especially want to go outside, but my head was playing images on fast forward: of martial law and soldiers stationed on the hotel doors; of electronic payment – all electronic communication – going down; a black economy where everything is paid for in cash; of the 300-mile journey I would need to make to get home.

I headed back into the night.

Walking the streets towards the cash point, nothing seemed untoward. And then I emerged onto the main road to be confronted by three men with automatic weapons.

At the front was a portly bald man with a moustache. His brow was furrowed. He took one hand off his machine gun, lowered it and flicked his wrist, gesturing for me to pass behind them. The men climbed into an unmarked car, checked their weapons and drove off.

I spotted the cash machine 100 metres ahead, marked by people pulling up in cars and taking money out. I ran to the machine and waited my turn, casting anxious looks around. Jabbing the buttons I withdrew an arbitrary amount, shoved it in my wallet and ran back to the hotel.

At this stage it was not clear that the attempt was understrength. I did not know that only certain factions of the military had elected to take part. Events were stirring the mind too quickly to notice the odd elements: why had the internet and phone lines not been shut down? Why did the plotters start at 10 p.m. when every other coup in Turkey had taken place at dawn? (There have been four, a large enough sample for Turkish elders to point out trends and disparities.) In my head I kept returning to the thought that at least 50 per cent of the population – Erdoğan's supporters – would be bitterly opposed. The opposition parties came out almost immediately in condemnation of the attempt, but still I saw uprisings, military rule, civil war. It troubled me to be far from home and my wife, and I wondered how long before I would see either of them again.

I sat in my room. The evening was a flurry of text messages, email,

Twitter and television – assuring friends and family in the UK, checking on friends in Turkey, following developments and worrying about it all. It crescendoed in the early hours with extraordinary scenes: President Erdoğan appearing on FaceTime on the newscaster's phone to call people onto the streets. Fighter jets bombing the Turkish Parliament, tanks mowing down civilians who had joined angry demonstrations. I watched live as soldiers stormed the studio of a major television channel, the camera left pointed at a wall, as the sound of shouts and then gunfire rang out in the background. But then the broadcast resumed. 'It isn't going to work,' I began thinking to myself. 'It's clear it isn't going to work.' The overriding emotion was one of relief – that life wouldn't be turned completely upside down. At 5 a.m., I collapsed onto my bed and fell into a panicked, frenzied sleep.

I awoke to images of the last soldiers surrendering on the Bosphorus bridge under a brilliantly blue July morning sky. The thought that it could ever have worked seemed ridiculous. But such trauma is not easily skirted. Part of me wondered what had been dislodged by the process. Something had irrevocably altered – even in my hotel room I could feel it.

My mind muddled by exhaustion, I decided to go to the second day of the football fan convention. I arrived hours after it was due to start to find the foyer completely empty. I walked around the building and bumped into a Fenerbahçe fan dismantling banners. 'It's cancelled,' he said.

*

When I stepped out of the terminal at Istanbul's Sabhia Gökçen airport, two lorries were parked, jackknifed across the road to prevent any vehicles from entering. Beyond them, traffic was converging – taxis, cars, even the occasional public bus. On the right-hand carriageway there was a row of half a dozen tanks, abandoned in the chaos of the night, each with a policeman standing on top. At their base, curious onlookers were prodding and poking. It was as if the trauma of the past twenty-four hours had caused us all to regress. Like a toddler, our eyes were not enough to comprehend the objects before us. They had to be touched. A man pulled gently at the fabric straps on the tank's side. Men holding a Turkish flag were taking it in turns to peer down the barrel of its gun. Someone had scratched 'no to the coup' on the tank's side – the white of the letters standing out like a spider web over the camouflage.

I got home and gave my wife an enormous hug. My body sloughed off the worry that I had been carrying; into its place rushed a wave of exhaustion and emotion, strong enough to bring tears. I was home. But home no longer felt like it used to.

*

The attempted coup was quickly blamed on a man called Fethullah Gülen and his followers. A Muslim preacher who had lived in the United States since 1999, Gülen was an ally of Erdoğan and his party for many years. But the two sides later fell out spectacularly. The alliance turned out to be one of the biggest mistakes of Erdoğan's political career.

Gülen was born in the eastern city of Erzurum. He began to gain popularity in the 1970s, attracting support through his speeches and his efforts to fill gaps in services provided by the state. Over the subsequent decades, he managed to develop and grow his movement from one among many Muslim orders, into one of the most important actors in Turkish society and politics.

The Gülen movement placed a high importance on education, building schools and study centres across Turkey and overseas. By recruiting bright, often poor, young students and supporting their education and careers, it ended up with a lattice of followers in influential positions throughout the Turkish state – from government ministries to the police, judiciary and army. Members of the movement founded banks, publishing houses, charities, newspapers and television stations. At its height, the organisation is said to have been millions strong.

After the AKP came to power in 2002, it formed an unofficial pact with the Gülen movement. Recep Tayyip Erdoğan was anxious about the threat posed to his fledgling government by the 'deep state', that amorphous structure of actors who have interfered in Turkey's politics and governance throughout its modern history. He feared that the generals and their allies would conspire to overthrow him in a coup d'état – the fate of four democratically elected leaders before him. Erdoğan wanted to take on the old secularist establishment to ensure that could never happen, but he lacked the necessary manpower in Turkey's politicised and factional state apparatus. So he turned to the Gülenists for help. The plan was to team up with Gülen's network of followers in the police and the courts to defang the armed forces. In return, the movement received government favours, securing support for its schools and lucrative tenders for companies owned by sympathisers.

At first the plan seemed to have worked: in 2007, police announced that they had uncovered a plot to overthrow the government. A group of figures in the military, academia, politics, media and criminal underworld were accused of plotting false flag attacks in order to incite chaos and provide the cover for a coup attempt. Over several years of investigations and trials, hundreds were jailed. It seemed that the politicians had finally managed to neuter the over-muscular, shadowy elements within the state. But it would soon all unravel.

In late 2013, the government and the Gülen movement dramatically fell out, and the one-time friendship descended into all-out war. Gülenist police officers launched a corruption probe that went to the heart of Erdoğan's inner circle. They arrested the sons of three of his ministers and released taped conversations that seemed to show him telling his own son to hide millions of dollars stashed in the family home (Erdoğan claimed that the recordings were fabricated).

Erdoğan went on the attack. He described the corruption allegations as an attempt to bring down the government. Those same people who, with the AKP's blessing, conducted the investigations against the deep state were now charged with trying to form their own 'parallel state'. The AKP began to purge those accused of being Gülen supporters from the police and judiciary, cracking down on Gülenist media outlets and seizing an affiliated bank. Gülenists in turn leaked more damaging details throughout 2014. Both sides were trying to obliterate the other.

Years before the coup, then, the government had already blacklisted Gülen's organisation, declaring that it would henceforth be known as the Fethullah Gülen Terrorist Organisation, or FETÖ. So when, on the night of the attempted coup, Erdoğan declared that the nation was under attack from a 'parallel structure', this did not come out of the blue. Many Turkish citizens found it easy to believe that the Gülenists were behind the attempt.

*

What on earth has all of this got to do with football? The answer is quite a lot.

As well as building up a network of supporters in the bureaucracy, business and politics, Fethullah Gülen also cultivated influence within Turkey's favourite sport. Between 2008 and 2012, The 1. Lig, the division below the Süper Lig, was sponsored by Bank Asya, an Islamic bank with close links to the movement. The construction firm Dumankaya, later seized by the government for allegedly financing the Gülen movement, was shirt sponsor for Galatasaray. And Gülen counted some of the country's top footballers among his acolytes, the most famous being Galatasaray striker Hakan Şükür.

The story of Şükür's life mirrors the rise and fall of the movement. When Şükür got married in 1995, the ceremony was led by Erdoğan, then mayor of Istanbul. Sitting at the ceremony table at Şükür's left-hand, was a bald man in glasses acting as a witness – none other than Fethuallah Gülen himself. In 2002, when a TV interviewer asked his views on Gülen, the footballer replied: 'To tell the truth, I am a sympathiser.' Four months later, the AKP came to power and the era of co-operation began. Şükür and Erdoğan frequently appeared in public together. When Queen Elizabeth visited Turkey in 2008, he was brought out for a kickabout with Erdoğan and foreign secretary David Miliband. In 2011, Şükür became an AKP member of parliament. But two years later, amid a growing rift between the ruling party and the Gülen movement, Şükür resigned from the AKP.

When the ruling party fell out with the movement and declared that it was operating a parallel state, many in Turkey rushed to say: we told you so. Among them was Aziz Yıldırım, the Fenerbahçe president who had spent a year in jail for his alleged role in the 2011 match fixing scandal.

'This is what I have been saying to the courts, to UEFA . . . in short, to everyone,' he said in December 2013. 'We said there is a structure within. We said they are playing with us, targeting us. The court didn't listen. Nor did the judges. Now the government is saying the same thing.'

From the outset, Yıldırım had insisted that the accusations that he and other officials had cheated and bribed their way to the 2011 Süper

Lig championship was a conspiracy. He said the 'evidence' against him was manipulated and fabricated. This is the other key way that football intersects with the Gülen movement. Here, the Gülenist connection was not through footballers, but followers of the movement in law enforcement agencies and the judiciary, who were accused of launching a politically or ideologically motivated prosecution to take over one of Turkey's most important clubs.

At first, I was completely dismissive of Yıldırım's claims. They seemed a poor attempt to cast him and Fenerbahçe as victims when phone recordings, CCTV footage and suspect match results appeared to show them to be, in fact, guilty as hell. But, as I looked deeper into the Gülen movement, the coup attempt and the match-fixing case, doubts began to creep in.

It is very difficult to prove that something is the work of the Gülen movement. There is no formal system of membership. The group's followers are secretive and rarely declare their affiliation. James Jeffrey, a former US ambassador to Turkey, wrote in a 2009 cable from Ankara: 'The assertion that the [Turkish National Police] is controlled by Gülenists is impossible to confirm but we have found no one who disputes it.' Gareth Jenkins, a leading authority on the Gülen movement, describes trying to pin down the actions of the group as like 'trying to interact with shadows'. He compares them to the wind that shapes the trees on an exposed headland. You cannot see the wind but you can see that all the trees have grown in the same direction.

That is why it is important not to look at the 2011 match-fixing allegations in isolation. Instead, the case needs to be placed side-by-side with the military show trials – those prosecutions of the 'deep state' – that took place a few years earlier. When this is done, some intriguing parallels start to emerge.

At the time of the court case against the military, Turkish liberals and foreign governments applauded. The way they saw it, an elected government was finally strong enough to stand up to the deep state's meddling with democratically elected governments. A few lone voices looked at the evidence and weren't so sure. The case relied heavily on wiretaps, and many of the defendants claimed that the recordings had been edited and spliced to incriminate them. One of the turning points came when a digital document supposedly setting out the plans of the 2003 coup plot turned out to have been produced on a version of Microsoft Office not available until 2007. Later it was shown definitively that much of the evidence was either tampered with or totally fabricated.

Two years later came the match-fixing allegations. Like the military cases, the football operation also depended on wiretaps. Individuals who featured in them claimed that the recordings had been manipulated or taken out of context. The match-fixing probe was launched by Zekeriya Öz, the same Istanbul state prosecutor who had spearheaded the military trials. Jenkins, who wrote about the case in 2012, noted also that prosecutors seemed to be selectively going after Fenerbahçe president Aziz Yıldırım. He noted that 'several other suspects would appear to be much more seriously implicated than Yıldırım. Yet they are free while Yıldırım remains in prison.'

The first response of an outsider – if they are still managing to keep up – is normally 'so what'? The proof that the case was a conspiracy is circumstantial, unclear and unresolved. Empiricists, keen on 'facts', like to simply scoop up this theory and dump it in the bin. A prominent international expert on match-fixing threatened to hang up on me when I raised the question that the evidence might have been tampered with. I have sympathy for that position – it would certainly make life a lot easier to just discount the Fenerbahçe claims.

But as is known by anyone who has spent prolonged time in Turkey, questions about complex, disputed events rarely end with definitive answers. Turkey has a history of shady sub-groups within the state dating back more than a century. Elected governments have always been only one half of the state's power structure, coexisting uneasily with guardian state actors, from the military to mafia. Turkish political history is the story of politicians powerful enough to keep the deep state at bay, those who openly colluded with it and those who were overthrown by it. As the academic Kerem Öktem has noted, 'only an understanding of [the deep state's] manipulative capacity begins to explain the counter-intuitive twists and turns in Turkey's history.'

Şekip Mosturoğlu, the Fenerbahçe vice-president who was imprisoned on match-fixing charges, later overturned, conveyed to me his frustration at trying to explain his and Yıldırım's theory to officials at UEFA's Swiss headquarters. 'People in Switzerland have very monotone, ordered lives,' he told me with a grin. 'They ask: [sceptically]

"Would the police set a trap for ordinary citizens?" When you look at Switzerland of course the police won't set a trap . . . sadly, in Turkey, they do.'

*

In the days and weeks following the attempted coup, life in Turkey developed a wild, mercurial streak. Like a soldier who has just had a bullet graze his head, both exhilarated and enraged by the near miss, the government responded with immediate retribution.

Thousands of people were rounded up as a whirlwind of anti-Gülen sentiment ripped through Turkish society. Organisations scrambled to prove their loyalty to the government. Those who were slow, insufficiently harsh or dared to question the official narrative were harassed by pro-government media, accused of being 'traitors'. The Sports Writers Association was trolled because its anti-coup statement was seen as being too short. Çarşı were criticised for taking four days to comment. At the headquarters of the football federation, all mention of Hakan Şükür was removed. The unsurpassed leading goalscorer for the national team, one of the country's most famous footballers, was overnight exorcised from the national memory.

Erdoğan and his associates warned of the danger of another coup attempt. Along with every other mobile phone user, I received a text message from 'RT ERDOGAN', urging me 'onto the streets to defend your nation'. Democracy vigils were organised, large rallies held in the centre of cities from sunset until sunrise. One of the largest was in Taksim square.

On the steps of Gezi Park, where three years earlier I had watched Çarşı, Kurds and Turkish nationalists dance together in protest, a stage had been erected. From its screens videos of the president were broadcast, interspersed with graphic footage from the coup attempt and thunderous music. A huge board listed the names of some of the 248 people who had lost their lives on the night of the coup. The talk of martyrdom, with its emphasis on the celebration of sacrifice rather than the sadness of death, has always made me uncomfortable, whether it came out of Kemalist or religious mouths. Now martyrdom had jumped from the soldiers to the citizens. 'We gave you our martyrs for the continuation of a democratic country and a humane, honourable life,' the board told me. On the screen were images of

Erdoğan praying over citizens' graves. On the side of the Atatürk Kültür centre a banner was displayed: 'The mongrels of Satan, FETÖ, we will hang you and your dogs by your chains.'

As a foreigner in Turkey, I had always felt a certain ability to shape-shift. Like a cat squeezing itself through an impossible space, I believed I could wriggle out of most awkward or dangerous spots by selecting a hat favourable for the circumstance: English or Scottish, Turkish-speaking, Beşiktaş-Leicester City supporting, Ankara-denizen academic, man, human. If that didn't work, I could always throw them all up at once and, while my interlocutor puzzled over them, beat a retreat. But now I felt I was being pushed back to my side: foreign. My act of seeming to have a foot on both the boat and shore was starting to wear thin. I didn't have long enough legs.

That I felt unwelcome was by the by. What was much sadder was that most of my Turkish friends felt the same way. For a short window, there was the chance to build a common legend out of the crisis. All sides of the political spectrum condemned it. It could have been used to colour back in some of the middle ground that was vanishing all around. Instead, it deepened Turkey's gaping social divisions. My friends thought the president was leveraging the trauma of the coup for political gain. They didn't feel comfortable at the nightly 'democracy watches', which were dominated by AKP supporters.

The country felt like it had sloughed off all the elements I liked: the hospitality, the easygoingness. Turkish-speaking foreigners – always seen as spies – were now being increasingly vilified. Given that Gülen had been living in America for close to two decades, most Turks were convinced that the USA had played some role in the coup attempt. Anti-Americanism soared, while European nations were criticised for what was seen as their slow and lacklustre condemnation.

The atmosphere was angry and vengeful. One day, when going to get a ferry, I bumped my toe on a piece of metal. Cursing, I looked around to see a man carrying a mock scaffold with a noose. At night as I tried to sleep, I could hear the sound of the local democracy vigil floating through the window. Car horns mixed with shouts of *Allahu akbar* – God is great – and chants demanding the reinstatement of the death penalty. All of it awed me, in the original sense of the word. I was scared by it.

*

Kandırıldık. We were deceived. This became the favourite phrase of Erdoğan and his ministers in the months following the attempted coup. Like a body rejecting a donor organ, the government violently purged the state of the 'traitors'.

Erdoğan declared a state of emergency and began ruling by executive decree. These decrees were often released at night, always without prior warning. They banned protests, seized businesses, closed down newspapers and civil-society organisations and listed the thousands of public servants to be sacked. The government said that the purges, though difficult, were essential to ensure that the nation never again faced a threat as grave as the night of 15 July. But those who lost their jobs complained that they faced no due process – there were no disciplinary hearings, no chance for the accused to defend themselves. They learnt of their fate through being on one of the public 'lists', tarnished for ever as terrorist supporters.

The crackdown saw 71,000 people taken into detention. Of these, 50,000 were jailed pending trial. A total of 150,000 people were sacked from their jobs. Their passports were cancelled to prevent them from leaving the country. Those dismissed included 4,000 judges, 24,000 policemen and security personnel, and 200 governors and their staff. At the TFF, 300 people were investigated, dozens sacked, and the head of the referee's commission (MHK) forced to resign. The former national-team goalkeeper Ömer Çaktıç, the Konyaspor chairman Ahmet Şan and ex-Başakşehir defender Bekir Irtegün were all arrested, accused of collusion and involvement.

Conspicuously absent from these lists and purges were the many AKP politicians and officials known to have enjoyed close links with the Gülen movement. Sons of prominent politicians were arrested but released a few days later, while teachers or doctors who made the mistake of opening an account with the wrong bank lost everything. 'We were deceived,' said Erdoğan. But only Erdoğan and those close to him were allowed the luxury of deception. For everyone else it was dismissal or prison.

Some sportsmen had already laid their cards on the table. When he resigned from the AKP, Şükür said that for more than twenty years he had known and loved 'the venerable *hoca efendi*' (Gülen) and his movement. 'Treating these sincere people, who supported the government on every issue . . . as if they are enemies, is nothing but unfaithfulness,' he lamented in 2013, as the row with the ruling party began to snowball. Two years later, Şükür sold his house, withdrew his savings and moved to California, seemingly aware which way the wind was blowing. Enes Kanter, an NBA basketball player, went further. 'I swear to God, I will give up neither the *hoca efendi* nor the movement,' he posted after the coup attempt. Living abroad, Kanter and Şükür were safe from the arrest warrants subsequently issued for them. Their parents, however, were not – Kanter's father was arrested and then released on bail. Şükür's spent four months in jail before being transferred to house arrest.

For the sports stars still in Turkey who had come into contact with – or been part of – the Gülen movement, there was some serious explaining to do. Following the coup attempt, a new trend emerged: the television confessional. Turkish TV shows were filled with footballers performing a very public *mea culpa* to explain their encounters with the group.

One of the people to phone in was Hakan Ünsal, Turkey's most famous left-back. He described being recruited to the movement after joining Galatasaray in 1994, aged twenty-one. 'My family were far away in Sinop,' he said over a crackly line piped into the studio of CNN Türk. 'I was young. I didn't know Istanbul and I needed someone to show me the way.'

Ünsal said that he was asked to join the group by 'Brother Ismail' – fellow Galatasaray left-back Ismail Demiriz, who was eleven years older than him. The younger players respected him, Ünsal said, and he was convinced by Demiriz to come along to meetings 'in order to learn our religion, to keep us on the straight and narrow, to ensure we stayed away from bad habits'. Ünsal attended *sohbets* – discussions where players talked about religion. On several occasions he went to meetings led by Fethullah Gülen himself, who was still living in Turkey in those days.

The pattern was repeated by Gülenists across Turkey's social landscape. Older 'brothers' and 'sisters' would approach promising young students in their early teenage years and encourage them to attend meetings. At first these would be study sessions aimed at boosting their scores at school but, gradually, they would be introduced to the ideas of Fethullah Gülen and then, finally, his speeches and his name.

Supporters of the movement say it gave them succour, providing faith and meaning in their lives. Many say that they never knew — and do not believe — that the group has or ever had a malign side that it kept concealed from the world.

Gülen has repeatedly and vehemently denied being involved in the coup. He has also denied involvement in the military trials and the match-fixing case. Some European governments are sceptical of the Turkish government's claims that he and his followers were solely responsible for the putsch. There are questions about how a septuagenarian living in Pennsylvania could plan and organise such an elaborate and vast operation, secretly plotted over a period of decades. Such arguments, however, carried little weight in Turkey, where the majority of the population was convinced of the movement's malevolence. Even if the attempted coup was the work of Gülenists, it seemed hard to believe that the group's ordinary sympathisers - the teachers and doctors who made up the rank and file - could have known about it. But this did not seem to matter in the aftermath. It was denounce or be denounced.

The names of footballers who had encountered the movement kept flooding in. Mustafa Kocabey, a journeyman footballer, confessed to giving Gülenists money. Cihat Arslan and Cafer Aydın, both coaches, claimed that their careers had been stunted due to the influence of the group: 'One day I argued with one of those from FETÖ,' said Aydın. 'Two days later my duty as a coach at Malatyaspor was brought to an end.'

The most-regular figure on television wasn't a footballer at all, but a man called Said Alpsoy. Between 1999 and 2003, Alpsoy says he acted as Gülen's primary recruiter in football, earning the nickname the 'football imam'. 'Turkey's popular and beloved players were used as a vehicle for advertising the community,' Alpsoy explained. He gave examples of how connections with Galatasaray players would be leveraged with local governors ('Look, do you see? We placed a call and now footballers from UEFA Cup champions Galatasaray are coming. We're that powerful') and he explained how the players would work to extract cash from the owners of large corporations who were Galatasaray fans.

Through the numerous testimonies and confessions, a picture of

Gülen's influence in football started to emerge, and it didn't look good for Galatasaray. It became clear that Turkey's most successful club included many footballers who had supported Gülen. The players in question were not on the fringes but the nucleus of Galatasaray's most successful ever side, the winners of the 2000 UEFA Cup. Players such as Hakan Şükür, the club's second-top scorer, midfielder Arif Erdem, Hakan Ünsal and its young rising star, the combative midfielder Emre Belozoğlu, were among those who had visited the cleric or donated money to his causes.

As Galatasaray were the most successful Turkish club of the period, their players also made up the spine of the national team. When Turkey finished third at the 2002 World Cup, the 'football imam' claims to have convinced a string of players to donate their bonuses to the movement. 'Emre Belozoğlu, Okan Burak, Hakan Şükür, Hakan Ünsal, Arif Erdem collected among themselves $250,000 or $500,000,' said Alpsoy.

The involvement of Gülenists in the national team continued into the next decade. A former senior official at the TFF told me that when Turkey played several friendly matches in the USA in 2010, some players made use of the hire cars and drivers laid on by the federation to visit Gülen in Pennsylvania. As late as 2013, Gülenists had an influence in football. But how far did it go? And what was their ultimate aim?

*

The attempted coup caused Gülen's influence in football to be spun into increasingly elaborate theories of influence and sabotage. In May 2012, after Galatasaray won the league at Fenerbahçe's ground, a huge riot erupted. At the time many thought it was fans angry at losing out to their rivals on their home turf. Wrong, I was told: the riot was stirred up by Gülenist police officers. 'They wanted a stampede, for people to die, for the state to be responsible, and the government to fall. Do you understand?' a member of the Genç Fenerbahçeliler fan club told me. A dramatic armed attack in April 2015 on the Fenerbahçe team bus – not far from Trabzon – had been blamed on enmity between the two teams. But after the coup attempt, it was claimed that the attack was also the work of FETÖ police officers.

Events on the pitch were also sucked into this logic. 'I want research into the goalkeepers of rival teams in the years in which Hakan Şükür won the golden boot,' demanded retired footballer Mustafa Kocabay. 'Those goalkeepers could be FETÖ. They could have let those goals in knowingly.' Such insinuations didn't feel like dramatic revelation of 'the truth'. They instead carried the whiff of smear attempts. Like the blaming of Snowball in Orwell's *Animal Farm*, an opportunity had arisen for articulation of long-nurtured resentments and settling of scores – be that between fans and the police, or unremarkable footballers and the superstars who had always beaten them to the limelight.

The stance on Gülen's involvement in football varied from fan to fan, according to their biases and allegiances. For Fenerbahçe supporters, Gülenists were everywhere. 'The Turkish Football Federation is in their hands,' one Fenerbahçe fan told me more than a year after the coup. 'Galatasaray and Beşiktaş, the two clubs are being robbed from within.' Some Fener supporters assert that every trophy won by Galatasaray back to the 1990s was fixed by Gülenists, overlooking the inconvenient fact that a side containing world-class players such as Gheorghe Hagi, Cláudio Taffarel and Hakan Şükür might actually be alright at football.

Galatasaray fans were furious that they were viewed as a 'Gülenist' club because of the actions of a few players. The ferocity of fans' responses can be explained by the gravity of the situation: Galatasaray and Fenerbahçe, organisations that have been around longer than Turkey itself, with their comforting rhythms of weekly matches and communities of millions of fans, now seemed to be under attack. One of the few patches of stable ground had become wobbly and unsafe.

History became distorted. In the aftermath of the coup attempt, complex issues that had been subject to decades of twists and turns were ironed out, chopped up and assigned simplistic causality: either Gülen was involved in everything bad in Turkey, or nothing. Gülenists were blamed for the 2011 killing of a group of three dozen Kurdish smugglers and for the downing in November 2015 of a Russian fighter jet that sparked a diplomatic crisis between Moscow and Ankara. They were blamed for the harsh police response to the 2013 Gezi Park protests and for causing the 2014 Soma mining disaster. One Erdoğan adviser even floated the idea of a 'deep connection' between the Gülen movement and the 9/11 attacks.

On the specific issue of match-fixing, this polarisation resulted in two main positions: either there had been match-fixing in 2011 or the whole thing had been the work of treacherous Gülenists. Amid the clamour, many seemed to have lost sight of one important fact – the two positions were not mutually exclusive.

Match-fixing undoubtedly takes place in Turkey, as it does across the world. Senior officials admit this in private. 'These kinds of events always happen in countries where football is commercialized,' an executive from a top club once told me. 'To say otherwise is naivety and fantasy.' Likewise, few football fans, even those from Galatasaray, try to argue that football was free of Gülenist involvement.

It is possible that match-fixing did take place in 2011 *and* that Gülenist elements within the state tried to use that to their advantage (although it remains unclear exactly why the Gülen movement might want to sabotage or take over a football club). It is also possible that neither is true. We will almost certainly never know what really happened. The same applies to the coup attempt. While the government – along with the majority of Turkish citizens – believe that Gülenists were behind the putsch, there are still many questions about what happened on the night of 15 July. Given that there has been no truly independent inquiry, they are likely to remain unanswered.

*

Like many of history's great purges, the Turkish one took on a life of its own, spreading wider and wider, the denunciations rippling out through a society slowly eating itself. The clampdown was expanded to include tens of thousands who had no apparent link to the Gülen movement or the coup attempt. Using the powers bestowed by the state of emergency, thousands of Kurdish activists and politicians were detained. Leftist academics were sacked from their university jobs. Critical journalists were locked up, accused of collaborating with or supporting the aims of terrorist organisations. Among them was investigative journalist Ahmet Şık, first arrested and imprisoned in 2011 *by* Gülenist prosecutors after they discovered that he was working to expose the group's influence within the state. This time, absurdly, he was accused of helping them.

Boats that smuggled Syrian refugees to Greek Islands were now being used to transport Leftists, Kurdish activists and fugitive

Gülenists – people who took one look at the executive orders, the skewed judicial system, the years of social exclusion and decided to take their chance with the sea. One of the judges in the match-fixing case, now wanted for arrest himself, was caught trying to cross the Greek–Turkish border with a judge from the military show trials and a pair of Pakistani migrants.

Ever since moving to Turkey in October 2015, I had felt like the country was sliding further and further down the rabbit hole; following 15 July 2016, I felt it had reached the point of total melt-down. Innocent people were imprisoned for being in possession of a one-dollar bill (said to be the secret sign of Gülenist sympathisers), whereas those known to be close to the movement would walk free. Conventional ideas of enemy and foe were tipped on their head. For decades, the 'deep state' had been the threat to the government, but now the 'parallel state' cultivated to go after the deep state had become the danger. The government's bogeyman shifted from the army to the Gülenists, but on 15 July we were told the Gülenists *were* the army and that 248 citizens had lost their lives standing up to them. The precarious handholds that I had worked to identify suddenly disappeared. I had no idea what I believed or who I trusted. The result was a sense of both weightlessness and falling, as my doubts spread and infected more elements of life.

At times like this, it would have been nice if football could have been an escape and a distraction. But football was an increasing part of the madness. Five months after the coup attempt, shortly before Christmas, I was on my way to the pub to watch Gençlerbirliği away at Fenerbahçe. I had images in my mind of a quiet Monday night, a beer or two shared with friends while lamenting Gençlerbirliği's inevitable defeat. As I crested the hill on the final stretch, I saw a cluster of emergency vehicles at the bottom. It didn't fully register at first. I turned into a side street and carried on. But then came more sirens – an ambulance and a police car passed me in the opposite direction. These tipped the balance. I took out my phone. 'Russian ambassador shot in Ankara'. Oh shit.

I started walking back in that direction before pausing. What was I doing? I didn't need to be there. My next thought was whether I should still be going to watch the football. The bar was 500 metres from the scene. It felt a bit . . . perverse.

But I carried on to the pub. Just like everyone in Turkey, I was getting better at screening out these events. All the same, this attack felt the most personal of the lot. Five nights previously, I had been sitting in the same building where he had been shot, listening to a colleague give a lecture on housing and climate change in the city of Mardin. Now it was surrounded by SWAT teams, the very same atrium where we had been now had a body on the floor.

My mind rehashed all the old worries, adding some new ones for good measure: was it really mental strength and fortitude to carry on in the face of this? Would any right-minded individual not be so disgusted, so sickened by the frequency of violence – physical or otherwise – that they would be unable to do anything else but campaign tirelessly against it . . . or run? Was this what Hell looked like? Not unbearable tragedy all the time, but the gradual drip-drip erosion of humanity, until one day you turn around and realise you've lost sight of what it means to be an empathetic human.

I got to the pub. The owner was outside, wearing a Gençler scarf and hat. He greeted me with the words: 'Get out while you can'. He went on: 'Seriously. You should get out. I will be. Before it's too late.'

I had last seen him only a month previously, when he was phlegmatic about everything that was happening in Turkey. He'd told me the current events were nothing like the 1990s, when he'd have to hide his student ID when coming into downtown Ankara in case the police would find it and slap him about. Tonight, though, I was confronted by a more pessimistic person.

'We have the example of two countries – Iraq and Syria. I have a ninety-day visa for Europe. I can just go . . .' His voice trailed off before he found it again. 'Plan. Everyone needs a plan.'

He became distracted by greeting somebody else and I moved into the bar. The scene inside was as before any football match anywhere – the sound muted on the big screen, people having their beers and chatting with friends.

With this exception: the images they were showing each other on their phones were of a dying ambassador, his police officer assassin stood over him snarling; the Twitter feeds they were updating were filled with bile, pointing the finger at others – of rightists blaming

FETÖ, leftists blaming Islamists, Russians blaming NATO. So much hatred, anger, injustice, all bubbling away. *And yet we watched the game.*

'Look at it,' said my friend when I found him. He was gesturing at the television and the player line-ups, which had been swelled by the addition of twenty or so police officers. The tribute was not in response to today's incident but to commemorate fourteen soldiers who had been killed three days earlier in a bombing in Kayseri. Or was it to remember the bomb ten days previously after the Beşiktaş match, the one that killed forty-six? It was all beginning to blur into one.

'Everything used to be cancelled out of respect. Now we just get on with it!' he added. But what else were we to do? I found myself resenting the entire apparatus: the government; the useless opposition; individuals electioneering before the blood was dry; the geopolitics that had brought us to the point where, by engaging in normal sports fan behaviour, we were slowly encouraging our reserves of humanity to evaporate. How else to describe newsfeeds boomeranging from posts of tonight's line-up to a picture of an ambassador lying in his own blood? We were being forced to compartmentalise attention and emotion, to switch from sad to happy, from death to football, in the swipe of a finger. Perverse was the word; in its literal meaning – turned away from what was right and good.

The game itself was a strange affair. Gençlerbirliği were better than Fenerbahçe. They had more possession, generated better chances and looked the more capable of scoring. Then came a Fenerbahçe breakaway. The ball found its way to Moussa Sow, who slotted it into the corner of the net. Completely against the run of play, and just before half-time, Gençler found themselves behind.

We assumed that would be it but it wasn't. In the second half Gençler continued to be the better side. They hit the woodwork twice and forced the Fenerbahçe goalkeeper, Volkan Demirel, into a host of top-notch saves. It felt as if the equalising goal was only minutes away. And then in the 87th minute there was another Fenerbahçe breakaway. A shot past the keeper. 2–0. Game over.

'Fuck's sake. They could go on and lose 4–0 for all I care,' said my friend, getting up to go the toilet. By the time he got back, Gençler were halfway there, conceding a third in injury time. The final whistle went. It was one of the strangest disparities between performance and goals that I could remember.

'This was perfect Gençlerbirliği,' said the bar owner, eyes shining, as we made our way out. In Turkish football circles there's an expression: 'Don't look at Hatice, look at the result.' Hatice is a girl's name, the statement a version of the perennial 'the result is more important than the performance' line of thinking. The bar owner was almost delirious with laughter as he explained that Gençlerbirliği fans have always inverted the wisdom.

'We are into Hatice! We're not interested in the score. And today was *exactly* that – everybody's smiling! HAH HAH! Because we like Hatice! We love Hatice!'

He seemed slightly unhinged. We inched past him and into the car waiting to pick us up. I feared for everyone's mental health, including my own. I was surrounded by 80 million people whose sinews were fraying. The gap between what people wanted to do and what life was allowing them seemed to be growing and growing. Football fell completely into perspective. Suddenly, it didn't matter one jot.

Postscript

Almost a year after that strange and violent night, I am back watching Gençlerbirliği, this time on the terrace. The opponents are Beşiktaş. Ankara's night air is yet to take on a wintry chill. The stand is fuller than usual, swelled, no doubt, by fifth columnists like me – away fans in the home end.

The ghosts of previous games at the 19 May stadium are with me. I was at the same fixture eight years previously, my first-ever away match, in the visitors' end with Özgür, my first footballing friend in Turkey. Since then, the games and friends have multiplied, memories accruing to the point where I can cycle through them: the same fixture last season, the loss to Fenerbahçe the week before, the Ankaragücü matches in the same stadium. Football matches are my way of archiving Turkey. Ninety-minute blocks – date, time and location fixed – around which wider recollections cluster. And football matches are also my way of forgetting Turkey. A scheduled weekly window when I can switch off my brain and lose myself in the crowd.

After the madness of 2016 – with its urban clashes, coup attempts and assassinations – 2017 has been a calmer year, for me at least. Elsewhere the screws have continued to tighten. There have been more arrests (journalists, human rights defenders, opposition politicians), more elections (Erdoğan won a referendum giving the presidency more power) and more extensions of the state of emergency (eighteen months and counting). It feels less like a corner has been turned and more an interlude, a pause before the floor crashes out again.

In the 16th minute Gençler take a deserved lead – a cross bundled in at the back post. I do not cheer but nor do I curse.

One of our usual attendees has brought along two friends from the Malaysian embassy. I spot them looking around excitedly. As the game progresses, I keep stealing glances at them. They are spending as long casting their eyes over the fans as they are watching the action on the pitch.

Turkish football for them doesn't mean match-fixing, mafia, Leeds United and hooliganism. The thought arrives unprompted, as does the envy and annoyance that follows in its wake. I find myself wanting to share with them, in a mean-spirited huff, the darker side of Turkish football: to play them the match-fixing tapes, take them to an Amedspor away match, troop them out of the stadium and up to the police, standing with their riot shields and tear gas, and show them what happens if they open a banner saying 'Peace Now'. I want to shatter their enjoyment, to sully the experience, just like it has been tainted for me.

And then the malevolence is chased away by calmer thoughts: that was me eight years previously, before I decided to dig deeper into Turkish football. I always believed that Turkish fans were the best in the world. I still maintain that is the case. Only now I know the extent to which they are let down by their game. Their administrators. Their politicians. Their clubs.

In the 48th minute, Beşiktaş winger Ryan Babel is sent off three minutes after coming on. It looks a routine, innocuous challenge. In my mind the conspiracies spool out unprompted: 'Now he won't play against Başakşehir next week, they're a government-backed team . . .'

'Could the referee have been paid?'

While I'm gathering them up and putting them away, the game continues, like a television set left on in an empty cafeteria.

It is the crowd that shocks me back into the present. The bodies standing in front and behind are not touching me but still I feel them, focused and taut, watching the game. Through the crowd I can feel the match. In their shouts and gasps, I sense Gençlerbirliği growing in strength and confidence. I can sense a goal is coming.

The Beşiktaş left-back has pushed too far forward. On a Gençler counter-attack, a midfielder finds one of their forwards in oceans of space. He tries to play in a colleague. The ball spoons up off a Beşiktaş defender, generating a confused convergence of attacker, defender and keeper. There is a touch from somewhere and the ball loops up invitingly for an onrushing attacker. It has the kindest of trajectories, like an underarm throw to a child learning to swing a racket. The player makes no mistake.

This time I cannot hold back a cheer. I am hugged from behind by a stranger. My arm is being pulled by my friend's son. I do not stop to think of betrayed loyalties to Beşiktaş but hug and pull back, joining in with the rush of noise and movement that engulfs the stand. Beşiktaş have been awful: no bite, no passion. And anyway, I have ceased to be me. Individuality has been traded in for the intensity and warmth of the herd.

My friend yanks me closer. The plastic chairs squeak under the transfer of weight. The floodlights draw outlines around the players. As I watch Beşiktaş stretch and strain to get back into the match, I realise everyone in the stadium is experiencing what I am – being pulled into the drama.

This is the remedy to the cynicism and anger kicked up by my search for Turkish football's heart: being on the terrace with the fans. Scenes play in my memory, fast and sharp like slides on a projector. I think of the Fenerbahçe fans waiting at the airport to greet that season's latest *yabancı* (unless he's a defender). I picture Adana Demirspor, founded by leftists, owned by an ultranationalist and supported by both Kurds and Turks who can shrug off the contradictions when they are squashed into the stadium, arm-in-arm, watching like we are now. And I think of the dancing Amedspor fans, running the risk of a beating or arrest to cheer on their team away from home. Everywhere I go in Turkey I find the same intensity, the same passion and the same earth-shatteringly stupid, crazy, lovesick obsession that keeps drawing me back in.

Beşiktaş pull a goal back with a few minutes remaining: 2–1. The party atmosphere evaporates, replaced by a steaming tension. For the first time since kick-off, the 2,000-odd Beşiktaş fans in the corner of the stadium are audible.

We are deep into injury time. The Gençlerbirliği terrace is raked by nerves, bodies jangling and jumping impatiently, ears stung and scoured by whistles. I want it to stop. How can the referee not also want it to stop? Before I know it, the game will be over. I imagine myself back home, preparing for work the next day. This moment will be reduced to the pulsing of blood in my ringing ears as I try to sleep. The annals will fix the game as a 2–1 home win, traceable for time immemorial. Gençlerbirliği will still remain bottom and probably be relegated; Beşiktaş will probably win the league. But none of these points matter. They are not the reason that we attend games.

I put my left arm around that of the stranger next to me, and the right one around my friend. We are pushed together so I can feel their ribs digging into mine. I keep my eyes on the terrace leader at the front, who has his fingers to his lips, telling us to hold still and be ready for what is about to happen.

And then in a flash he drops his arm. Around us, the terrace moves as bodies, arms and voices meld into one to cheer the side home. And we jump and bounce and sing and laugh.

Select Bibliography

For the sake of space, full notes to the text have been omitted from the print edition. Comprehensive references can be found online at: www.johnmcmanus.co.uk. The purpose of this section is to offer the reader a sense of the key sources used.

BOOKS AND PERIODICALS

Abadan-Unat, Nermin, *Turks in Europe: From Guestworker to Transnational Citizen*, Oxford: Berghahn, 2011

Ahıska, Meltem 'Occidentalism: The Historical Fantasy of the Modern', *The South Atlantic Quarterly* 102, no. 2/3, 2003

Ahıska, Meltem and Zafer Yenal, *The Person You Have Called Cannot Be Reached at the Moment: Representations of Lifestyles in Turkey 1980–2005*, Istanbul: Ottoman Bank Archive and Research Centre, 2006

Akçam, Taner, *The Young Turks' Crime against Humanity: The Armenian Genocide and Ethnic Cleansing in the Ottoman Empire*, Princeton, NJ: Princeton University Press, 2012

Akın, Yiğit, 'Not Just A Game: The Kayseri vs. Sivas Football Disaster', *Soccer and Society* 5, no. 2, 2004

Altınay, Ayşe Gül, *The Myth of the Military-Nation: Militarism, Gender, and Education in Turkey*, London: Palgrave MacMillan, 2004

Arhan, Faruk, *Diyarbakırspor: Düğünde Kalabalık, Taziyede Yalnız*

[Diyarbakırspor: Popular at the Wedding, Alone at the Wake], Istanbul: Iletişim Yayınları, 2012

Arjomand, Noah, 'Every Turk Is Born a Soldier', *Public Culture* 29, no. 3, 2017, pp. 418–32

Aslan, Senem, 'Incoherent State: The Controversy over Kurdish Naming in Turkey', *European Journal of Turkish Studies* 10, 2009

Başaran, Kenan, *Arkadan Müdahale: 3 Temmuz Şike Davası Süreci* [Intervention From Behind: The Story of the 3 July Match Fixing Case] Istanbul: İletişim Yayınları, 2013

Basu, Paul, *Highland Homecomings: Genealogy and Heritage Tourism in the Scottish Diaspora*, London: Routledge, 2007

Batuman, Elif, 'The View from the Stands', *The New Yorker*, 7 March 2011

Bora, Tanıl, *Ankara Rüzgarı: Gençlerbirliği Tarihi* [The Winds of Ankara: A History of Gençlerbirliği] Ankara: Gençlerbirliği, 2003

---., 'Adımız Çıkmış Futbolcuya' [Once a Footballer, Always a Footballer], *Socrates*, August 2017

Bora, Tanıl and Necmi Erdoğan, 'Dur Tarih, Vur Türkiye: Türk Milletinin Milli Sporu Olarak Futbol' [Stop History, Shoot Turkey: Football as the sport of the Turkish Nation], in *Futbol ve Kültürü: Takımlar, Taraftalar, Endüstri, Efsaneler* [Football and Culture: Teams Fans, Commercialism, Legends], edited by Roman Horak, Wolfgang Reiter, and Tanıl Bora, Istanbul: Iletişim Yayınları, 1993

Bozdoğan, Sibel, *Modernism and Nation Building*, Seattle: University of Washington Press, 2001

Brink-Denan, Marcy, 'Names That Show Time: Turkish Jews as "Strangers" and the Semiotics of Reclassification', *American Anthropologist* 112, no. 3, 2010, pp. 384–96

Brotton, Jerry, *This Orient Isle: Elizabethan England and the Islamic World*, London: Penguin, 2017

Buğra, Ayşe, and Osman Savaşkan, *New Capitalism in Turkey: The Relationship between Politics, Religion and Business*, London: Edward Elgar, 2014

Çakır, Ruşen, and Fehmi Çalmuk, *Recep Tayyip Erdoğan: bir dönüşüm öyküsü* [Recep Tayyip Erdoğan: A Tale of Transformation], Istanbul: Metis, 2001

Cameron, Alan, *Circus Factions: Blues and Greens at Rome and Byzantium*, Oxford: Clarendon Press, 1976

Canefe, Nergis, 'The Legacy of Forced Migrations in Modern Turkish Society: Remembrance of the Things Past?' *Balkanologie* 5, no. 1–2, 2001

Çarşı and Forza Beşiktaş, *Çarşı Geliyooor! Tribünün Asi Çocuklarından Türkiye'yi Sarsan Haziranın Hikayesi* [Çarşı Is Coming! From the Rebel Kids of the Terrace, the Story of the June that Shook Turkey], Istanbul: Okuyanus, 2013

Cengiz, Firat and Lars Hoffmann, *Turkey and the European Union: Facing New Challenges and Opportunities*, London: Routledge, 2013

Christie-Miller, Alexander, 'Occupy Gezi: From the Fringes to the Centre, and Back Again', *The White Review*, July 2013

---., 'War Is Easy, Peace Is Hard', *The White Review*, October 2015

Clark, Bruce, *Twice a Stranger: How Mass Expulsion Forged Modern Greece and Turkey*, London: Granta, 2006

De Bellaigue, Christopher, *Rebel Land: Among Turkey's Forgotten Peoples*, London: Bloomsbury Publishing, 2009

Delaney, Carol, *The Seed and the Soil: Gender and Cosmology in Turkish Village Society*, Berkeley: University of California Press, 1991

Dikici, Sema Tuğçe, *Çarşı: Bir Başka Taraftarlık* [Çarşı: Another Kind of Fandom], Ankara: Dipnot Yayınları, 2009

Emrence, Cem, 'Playing With Global City: The Rise and Fall of a Turkish Soccer Team', *The Journal of Popular Culture* 40, no. 4, 2007, pp. 630–42

Erhart, Itır, 'Women, Islamic Feminism and Children Only Soccer in Erdoğan's Turkey: Empowerment or Discrimination', in *Sport in Islam and in Muslim Communities*, Alberto Testa and Mahfoud Amara (eds.), London: Routledge, 2016, pp. 66–80.

---., 'Ladies of Besiktas: A Dismantling of Male Hegemony at Inönü Stadium', *International Review for the Sociology of Sport* 48, no. 1, 2011, pp. 83–98

Eroğul, Ali, 'Trabzonspor Tarihi Üzerine Bir Deneme'[an essay on Trabzonspor history], in *Trabzon'u Anlamak* [Understanding Trabzon], Güven Bakırezer and Yücel Demirer (eds.), Istanbul: Iletişim Yayınları, 2009, pp. 337–360

Fainaru, Steve, 'The Dictator's Team', *ESPN*, 11 May 2017

Finkel, Andrew, *Turkey: What Everyone Needs to Know*, Oxford: Oxford University Press, 2012

---., 'Captured News Media: The Case of Turkey', *Center for International Media Assistance (CIMA) and National Endowment for Democracy*, October 2015

Finkel, Caroline, *Osman's Dream: The Story of the Ottoman Empire 1300–1923*, London: John Murray, 2005

Garrido, Juan E. Rodriguez, *Arda Turan: Bayrampaşa'nın Dahisi* [Arda Turan: Bayrampaşa's Genius], translated by M. Özgür Sancar, Istanbul: Altın Kitaplar, 2014

Gingeras, Ryan, 'Last Rites for a "Pure Bandit": Clandestine service, historiography and the origins of the Turkish "Deep State"', *Past & Present*, no. 206, 2010, pp. 151–74

---., *Heroin, Organized Crime, and the Making of Modern Turkey*, Oxford: Oxford University Press, 2014

Gökaçti, Mehmet Ali *'Bizim İçin Oyna': Türkiye'de Futbol ve Siyaset* ['Play For Us': Football and Politics in Turkey], Istanbul: Iletişim Yayınları, 2008

Goldblatt, David, *The Ball is Round*, London: Penguin, 2007

Güneş, Günver, 'İzmir'de Futbol' [Football in Izmir], *Toplumsal Tarih*, October 2005

Gürbilek, Nurdan, *The New Cultural Climate in Turkey: Living in a Shop Window*, London and New York: Zed Books, 2011

Güven, Dilek, 'Riots against the Non-Muslims of Turkey: 6/7 September 1955 in the Context of Demographic Engineering', *European Journal of Turkish Studies* 12, 2011

Hansen, Suzy, 'Inside Turkey's Purge', *New York Times*, 13 April 2017

Hasdemir, Haci, *Aman Babam Görmesin* [Please don't Let My Father See], Istanbul: Zaman, 2005

Hatıpoğlu Duygu, and M. Berkay Aydın, *Bastır Ankaragücü: Kent, Kimlik, Endüstriyel Futbol ve Taraftarlık* [Attack Ankaragücü: City, Identity, Commercialised Football and Fandom], Ankara: Epos Yayınları, 2007

Hergün, Haluk, *Lefter: Futbolun Ordinaryüsü* [Lefter, Football's Professor], Istanbul: NTV yayınları, 2012

Hoş, Mustafa, *Big Boss: neoTürkiye'nin panzehiri hafizadir* [Big Boss: Memory Is the Antidote to neo-Turkey], Istanbul: Destek, 2014

Hotham, David, *The Turks*, London: John Murray, 1972

Ihrig, Stefan, *Atatürk in the Nazi Imagination*, London: Belknap, 2014

Izzet, Muzzy, *Muzzy: My Story*, Liverpool: Sport Media, 2015

Jenkins, Gareth, 'Between Fact and Fantasy: Turkey's Ergenekon Investigation', *Central Asia-Caucasus Institute Silk Road Studies Program*, August 2009

---., 'Football and Fethullah: The Gulen Movement's New Goals?', *The Turkey Analyst* 5, no. 11, 28 May 2012

---., 'The Ergenekon Verdicts: Chronicle of an Injustice Foretold', *The Turkey Analyst* 6, no. 14, 13 August 2013

Karakaş, Burcu, and Bawer Çakır, *Erkeklik Ofsayta Düşünce: Futbol, Eşcinsellik ve Halil İbrahim Dinçdağ'ın Hikayesi* [Masculinity Offside: Football, Homosexuality and the Story of Halil İbrahim Dinçdağ], Istanbul: İletişim Yayınları, 2013

Kılıç, Behram, *İstanbul'un 100 Spor Olayı* [Istanbul's (top) 100 Sporting Moments], Istanbul: IBB Kültür A.Ş. Yayınları, 2010

Kılıç, Ecevit, *Futbol ve Mafya: Kirli Kramponlar* [Football and Mafia: Dirty Boots], Istanbul: Bilgi Karınca, 2004

King, Charles, *The Black Sea: A History*, Oxford: Oxford University Press, 2004

---., *Midnight at the Pera Palace: The Birth of Modern Istanbul*, London: W. W. Norton & Company, 2015

Kurt, Richard, *United! Despatches from Old Trafford*, Edinburgh: Mainstream Publishing, 1999

Kuper, Simon, and Stefan Szymanski. *Soccernomics: Why Transfers Fail, Why Spain Rule the World and Other Curious Football Phenomena Explained*, London: HarperSport, 2012

Lewis, Geoffrey, *The Turkish Language Reform: A Catastrophic Success*, Oxford: Oxford University Press, 1999

Mandel, Ruth, *Cosmopolitan Anxieties: Turkish Challenges to Citizenship and Belonging in Germany*, London: Duke University Press, 2008

Mango, Andrew, *Atatürk*, London: John Murray, 1999

---., 'Atatürk and the Kurds', *Middle Eastern Studies* 35, no. 4, 1999, pp. 1–25

Mansel, Philip, *Levant: Splendour and Catastrophe on the Mediterranean*, New Haven and London: Yale University Press, 2010

Marcus, Aliza, *Blood and Belief: The PKK and the Kurdish Fight for Independence*, London and New York: New York University Press, 2007

Mayor, Adrienne, *The Amazons: Lives and Legends of Warrior Women Across the Ancient World*, Princeton and Oxford: Princeton University Press, 2014

Morris, Chris, *The New Turkey: The Quiet Revolution on the Edge of Europe*, London: Granta, 2005

Morton, Giles, *Paradise Lost: Smyrna 1922: The Destruction of Islam's City of Tolerance*, London: Sceptre, 2009

Mutlu, Dilek Kaya, 'The Midnight Express (1978) Phenomenon and the Image of Turkey', *Historical Journal of Film, Radio and Television* 25, no. 3, 2005, pp. 475–96

Nuhrat, Yağmur, *Fair Enough? Negotiating Ethics in Turkish Football*, PhD thesis, Brown University, 2013

---., 'Fair to Swear? Gendered Formulations of Fairness in Football in Turkey', *Journal of Middle East Women's Studies* 13, no. 1, 2017, pp. 25–46

Okay, Cüneyd, 'The Introduction, Early Development and Historiography of Soccer in Turkey: 1890–1914', *Soccer and Society* 3, no. 3, 2002, pp. 1–10

Öktem, Kerem, 'The Nation's Imprint: Demographic Engineering and the Change of Toponymes in Republican Turkey', *European Journal of Turkish Studies* 7, 2008

---., *Angry Nation: Turkey since 1989*, London: Zed Books, 2011

Özdil, Erol, *Çarşı: 35 Yılın Pankartları Eski Tribün Kavgaları Deplasman Anıları* [Çarşı: 35 Years of Banners, Old Terrace Scraps and Away Match Memories], Istanbul: Siyah Beyaz Kitap, 2015

Özyeğin, Gül, *New Desires, New Selves: Sex, Love, and Piety among Turkish Youth*, New York: New York University Press, 2015

Parla, Ayşe, 'The "Honor" of the State: Virginity Examinations in Turkey', *Feminist Studies* 27, no. 1, 2001, pp. 65–88

Parla, Ayşe and Ceren Özgül, 'Property, Dispossession, and Citizenship in Turkey; Or, the History of the Gezi Uprising Starts in the Surp Hagop

Armenian Cemetery', *Public Culture* 28, no. 3, 2016, pp. 617–53

Pirlo, Andrea, *I Think Therefore I Play*, London: Backpage, 2004

Pope, Nicole and Hugh Pope, *Turkey Unveiled: A History of Modern Turkey*, London and New York: Overlook Duckworth, 2011

Poulton, Hugh, *Top Hat, Grey Wolf and Crescent: Turkish Nationalism and the Turkish Republic*, London: Hurst & Company, 1997

Ridsdale, Peter, *United We Fall: Boardroom truths about the beautiful game*, London: Pan Books, 2008

Rogan, Eugene, *The Fall of the Ottomans: The Great War in the Middle East*, London: Penguin, 2015

Said, Edward W, *Orientalism*, London: Penguin, 2003

Saunders, Doug, *Arrival City: How the Largest Migration in History Is Reshaping Our World*, London: Windmill, 2011

Stokes, Martin, *The Arabesk Debate: Music and Musicians in Modern Turkey*, Oxford: Oxford University Press, 1992

---., '"Strong as a Turk": Power, Performance and Representation in Turkish Wrestling', *Sport, Identity and Ethnicity*, Jeremy MacClancy (ed.), Oxford: Berg, 1996, pp. 21–42

Süldür, Fahrettin, *Türk Futbol (Tepük)* [Turkish Football (Tepük)], Ankara: Kısmet Matbaası, 1977

Tee, Caroline, *The Gülen Movement in Turkey: The Politics of Islam and Modernity*, London: I.B. Tauris, 2016

Temelkuran, Ece, *Turkey: The Insane and the Melancholy*, London: Zed Books, 2016

Tunç, Sevecen, *Mektepliler, Münevverler, Meraklılar: Trabzon'da Futbolun Toplumsal Tarihi* [Students, Intellectuals, Aficionados: The Social History of Football in Trabzon], Istanbul: İletişim Yayınları, 2011

Türköz, Meltem, 'Surname Narratives and the State-Society Boundary: Memories of Turkey's Family Name Law of 1934', *Middle Eastern Studies* 43, no. 6, 2007, pp. 893–908

van den Niuewenhof, Frans, *Hiddink: Dit Is Mijn Wereld* [Hiddink: This is My World], Eindhoven: De Boekenmakers, 2006

Vassell, Darius, *The Road to Persia*, Glasgow: Inama Enterprise, 2017

Waldman, Simon A., and Emre Caliskan, *The New Turkey and Its*

Discontents, London: Hurst & Company, 2016

Wheatcroft, Andrew, *The Ottomans*, London: Viking, 1993

White, Jenny, *Islamist Mobilization in Turkey: A Study in Vernacular Politics*, Seattle: University of Washington Press, 2002

---., *Muslim Nationalism and the New Turks*, Princeton and Oxford: Princeton University Press, 2013

---., 'The Turkish Complex', *The American Interest* 10, no. 4, 2 February 2015

Yalçın, Soner, *Kayıp Sicil: Erdoğan'ın Çalınan Dosyası* [Lost Record: Erdoğan's Stolen Dossier], Istanbul: Kırmızı Kedi, 2014

Yeğen, Mesut, 'The Kurdish Peace Process in Turkey: Genesis, evolution and prospects', Working Paper, Istanbul Şehir University, Stiftung Mercator, *Istanbul Policy Center*, May 2015

Yüce, Mehmet, *Osmanlı Melekleri: Futbol Tarihimizin Kadim Devreleri* [Ottoman Angels: The Old Periods of Our Football History], İstanbul: İletişim Yayınları, 2014

---., *İdmancı Ruhlar: Futbol Tarihimizin Klasik Devreleri: 1923–1952* [Haard-Working Souls: Our Football History's Classic Period: 1923–1952] Istanbul: İletişim Yayınları, 2015

Zürcher, Erik J., *Turkey: A Modern History*, London: I.B. Tauris, 2004

FILMS

Derki, Talal (dir.), *Return to Homs*, Proaction Film, 2013

Eslam, Farid and Oliver Waldhauer (dirs.), *Istanbul United*, Mind Riot Media, 2014

Kana, Ersin (dir.), *Asi Ruh* [Rebel Soul], Pancard Kalan, 2008

Özgentürk, Nebil (dir), *Lefter: Futbolun Ordinaryüsü* [Lefter: Football's Professor], NTV Spor, 2012

Parker, Alan (dir.), *Midnight Express*, Columbia, 1978

REPORTS

'Most Notable Violations against Syrian Athletes', *Syrian Network for Human Rights*, 29 March 2017

'The Human Cost of the PKK Conflict in Turkey: The Case of Sur',

International Crisis Group, 17 March 2016

'Turkey: State Blocks Probes of Southeast Killings', *Human Rights Watch*, 11 July 2016

ADDITIONAL SOURCES

Blasing, John, 'Goodbye Izmir Alsancak Stadium: The Past and Present of a Country as Seen Through the Eyes of a Football Stadium', *Thisisfootballislife* (blog), August 9, 2015. https://thisisfootballislife.com/2015/08/09/goodbye-izmir-alsancak-stadium-the-past-and-present-of-a-country-as-seen-through-the-eyes-of-a-football-stadium/

Bora, Tanıl, *Ankara Futbolu: Bazen Karakter Oyuncusu, Bazen Figüran* [Ankara Football: Sometimes a Main Character, Sometimes a Bit Part Player], copy given to author

Levantine Heritage Foundation (*www.levantineheritage.com*)

Mirza, Salmaan, 'Football in the Ottoman Empire', unpublished paper

Rodrik, Dani, 'The Plot Against the Generals', June 2014: http://drodrik.scholar.harvard.edu/files/dani-rodrik/files/plot-against-the-generals.pdf

Acknowledgements

This book would not exist without the support and generosity of hundreds of people. To those who are named in the book, my debt is obvious. But there are many more whose names I do not know or cannot use. I thank all the fans who welcomed me onto their terraces and into their lives. Special gratitude is due to Özgür, Çağrı and their Beşiktaş gang; without their first embrace, the rest would not have followed.

The research and writing was made possible through the generous support of the British Institute at Ankara. I am enormously grateful to Lutgarde Vandeput and the rest of the council for the award of their postdoctoral fellowship, and to Leo, Işılay, Gülgün, Nihal, Burçak, Ender, Pete, Kezban and Mustafa for their support and camaraderie.

The following people also gave time and help: Murat Arpaç, Tanıl Bora, Devrim Cem, Craig Encer, Can Evren, Burcu Gül, Funja Güler, Gareth Jenkins, Utku Kaya, Tan Morgul, Andrew Norfolk, Kerem Öktem, Mehul Srivastava, Mehmet Şenol, Özgehan Şenyuva, Alp Ulagay and Leen van Broeck. Bağış Erten was especially wonderful – a seemingly limitless source of phone numbers and ideas.

My thanks to Simon Kuper, for listening while I rattled on about my idea at a football conference and then introducing me to my agents, David Luxton and Nick Walters, both of whom have offered a calm steer through my first book. The messy, difficult process of book writing was admirably marshalled by my editor at Weidenfeld & Nicolson, Paul Murphy.

Sean Singer, İbrahim Altınsay, Peter Cherry, Hannah Lucinda Smith, Salmaan Mirza, John Angliss, Alex McManus, Emre Deliveli, Ertan Keskinsoy and Emre Peker were all good enough to offer their feedback on sections of the manuscript. Any errors are mine alone.

I have had a wealth of support from friends and family. Thanks to Ekin Can Genç and Emrah Serdar – for their friendship and help over the years with all things Turkish – and Tom Hodgson for being a good source of distraction. Işılay Gürsu helped with more than her fair share of phone calls and translations of Fatih Terim speeches. Renaissance man Leonidas Karakatsanis provided ideas, corrections, image advice and camaraderie throughout. The first and last chapters owe huge support to Ed Posnett, who in book writing has been the best comrade-in-arms I could have hoped for. Yağmur Nuhrat has provided thoughts, help and support not just throughout the book but over many years of friendship.

My parents, Alex and Gerry, helped me undertake the master's programme that lit the fuse with my first foray into Turkish football. I'm not sure any of us thought it would still be burning a decade on.

But most of all to Laura Pitel, whose red pen and wells of patience were, by the end, definitely overused. There would be no book, and nothing to acknowledge, without her ideas, encouragement and love.

Picture Credits

Pages 14, 74, 132, 184, 237, 250, 334 Getty Images; 18 PA Images; 53, 102 Levantine Heritage Foundation; 66 İETT Archive; 90 Philipa Threadwell (courtesy of the Levantine Heritage Foundation); 99 Enrichetta Micaleff (courtesy of the Levantine Heritage Foundation); 148, 151 Haluk Hergün personal archive; 168, 216 Rex Features; 172 Erol Abasız; 188 Cengiz Hoşfikirer; 204 Blick Magazine, 11 June 2008; 224 Zeki Günen, Konak Belediyesi; 262 (left) Trabzon Müze Müdürlüğü; 272 Levent Kulu; 294 Omar Alkhani; all other images courtesy of the author.

Index

7 December Stadium, Kilis 305
7 Eylül Gençlikspor 228
6222 law 79, 81, 117

Ağar, Mehmet 206
Abbasiyyin stadium, Damascus 296
Abdulaziz, Sultan 48
Abdülhamid II, Sultan 21, 40, 97
AC Milan 34, 201
ACF Fiorentina 152, 201
Adana 186
Adana Demirspor 186, 188–9, 193–4, 195–8, 200–1
Adanaspor 84, 186, 200–1
Adem (Beşiktaş fan) 274
Adem (Trabzonspor fan) 261
advertisements 71–2
airports 75, 77
Akbaş,İlker 138–9
Akçaabat Sebatspor 71
Akgül, Ceyhun 18, 19, 20, 203
Akin, Fatih 235
Akın, İbrahim 265, 266
Akkalu, Bilal 322
AKP (Justice and Development Party)
  beginnings 6–7, 70–2
  civil unrest 338–40
  new teams 85
  in power 212–13, 318
  supporters 80, 344
Aksu, Ahmet 324
Aksu, Fulya 191
Aktif Bank 82, 84
Alanç, Ali 224
Albayrak, Berat 83
Ali (Demirspor general manager) 186–7
Ali, Firas al- 298–300, 304–5, 307, 309
Ali Sami Yen stadium 18, 49
Ali (Trabzonspor fan) 252
Alsancak arena, Izmir 102–3
Altay S.K. 74, 95, 97, 103
Altınordu 103
Altınordu FK 239
Altınsay, İbrahim 33
Altıntepsi S.K. 137–8, 144
Amedspor
  beginnings 314
  name 320
  stadium 324
  v. Anakaragücü 329
  v. Bursaspor 323
  v. Fenerbahçe 311, 324–8
  v. Istanbul Başakşehir 322–3
Ammo, Anas 295–7, 298–304, 306–9

Anakaragücü 329
Anelka, Nicholas 179–80
ANFA (private security firm) 125
Ankara 7, 12, 109–26, 128–31, 329
Ankara 19 May Stadium 115–16
Ankara cup 110–11
Antalyaspor 322
Arda Turan Street, Bayrampaşa 133, 135
Armitage, Horace 53
Arsenal FC 249
Article 56, Turkish Constitution 273
Asian side, of Istanbul 38, 48, 51, 52
Aslan, Senem 313
Assad, Bashar al- 295, 296, 308
Ataca, Rabia 228
Atatürk Cultural Centre, Istanbul 275, 344
Atatürk, Mustafa Kemal
  and AKP 293
  birthplace 154
  daughters 122–3, 313–14
  and Fenerbahçe 267
  leader 111–12
  and population 7
  reforms of 212, 312
  support for 156
  Turkey's founder 70, 72
Atatürk Olympic stadium 34, 103, 128, 224
Ateş, Deniz 269
Athletic Bilbao 320
Atlético Madrid 139, 140–1
Aurélio, Marco 176, 177
Australia 308
Avcı, Ihsan 320
away fans, Turkish 231
Aydoğdu, Selahattin 205–6
Azzurri S.K. 104

Başaran, Kenan 267
Balkan wars 98
Bank Asya 340
banners
  and British views 11
  ideas for 71, 176, 262, 273, 275, 276
  making of 9, 279
  title winners 60
Barış (Fenerbahçe fan) 176
Basu, Paul 242
Batuman, Elif 281
Bayraktar, Köksal 30, 31
Bayraktar, Ömer 31
Bayrampaşa 133, 137
Beck, Andreas 180, 238
Beşer, Hayri 69
Beşiktaş 39, 275
Beşiktaş J.K.
  Inönü stadium 11, 38–9, 42
  background 6, 9
  chants and songs 55–7, 214, 225, 265
  crest 40
  fans 7–8, 42, 43–4, 277
  kit 6
  league title 2016 60, 238
  Les Ferdinand at 27
  match-fixing 266
  'middle-classification' of football 49–50
  and Milne 163–4
  nickname 6
  and Nouma 170
  penalties 9
  scouts 237
  success 44, 164, 217
  tickets 83
  v. Arsenal FC 249
  v. Dynamo Kiev 180, 182
  v. Galatasaray S.K. 288
  v. Leeds Utd 33
  v. Man. Utd 231–2
  v. Napoli 96
  Vodafone Park Arena 43, 85, 86–7, 292
  women's team 219
beleştepe (freebie hill), Beşiktaş 43
Bellaigue, Christopher de 114
Belözoğlu, Emre 156
Bereket Gymnastics Club 40
Bey, Kenan 61–2
Beyazit II, Sultan 46
Biçer, Ilhan 82
'Big Three' (*üç büyükler*) 54–60
  card system 83
  and civil unrest 284–5, 288

domination 10, 37–8
love of the crest 225
sharing stadium 277
sociological definition 316
Bilal (Ankaragücü fan) 118
Bilgili, Serdar 33
Birol (Azzurri player) 105
Black Stockings FC 52
Blatter, Sepp 203
Bodrum 322
Boloğlu, Nezih Ali 19
Bora, Tanıl 80, 109, 121, 167, 173
Bornova Football Club 93, 94, 98, 100
Bosphorus 15, 27, 38
Bostancıoğlu, Adnan 276
Bruce, Steve 18
Bulgaria 181
Bull, John 21
Bulut, Yiğit 313
Bursa 10
Bursaspor
kit 9
match-fixing 266
success 10, 110
v. Amedspor 323
v. Beşiktaş J.K. 86
v. Manchester Utd FC 88
Busbeq, Ogier de 20
Butt, Nicky 18
Byzantium *see* Sultanahmet, Istanbul

Cadi-Keuy (Kadiköy) FC 53, 100
Çakar, Ahmet 143
Çağlaoğlu, Hakan 22
Çalık, Ahmet 83
Çalık Holding 77, 82–3
Çalışkan, Birol 133–5
Çamlı, Ahmet Hamdi 290
Campbell, Sol 183
Cantona, Eric 19, 171
Çapa 68
çapulcu (looter, vandal) 80
Çarşı (Beşiktaş J.K. fans) 274–92
background 7
fundraising 59
leaders 42, 60
logo 9
supporters 194
and Şükür 343
Carlos, Roberto 164
Ceferin, Aleksander 182
Çelik, Volkan 249
Çeviköz, Ünal 32, 34
cfcuk (Chelsea fanzine) 34
chairmen, club 58
Chalcedon *see* Kadıköy, Istanbul
Champions League 1, 26, 242
chants
Amedspor 322, 324, 330
Beşiktaş J.K. 8, 43, 52, 217–18, 225
Fenerbahçe 39, 52
Gençlerbirliği S.K. 116
militant 123
MKE Ankaragücü 118–19
sekiz sıfır, 8–0 265
Sivasspor 81–2
Takism Square 284
Trabzonspor 259
Chelsea FC
cfcuk fanzine 34
fans 182
CHP (Republican People's Party) 81, 103, 291
Christie-Miller, Alex 287
Çırağan Palace 48
citizenship, dual 246
civil unrest 116, 282–3
Cizre, war in 321–2
Clark, Edwin 98
Clark, Joe 98
Clash, The 115, 169
Constantinople 109, 198
Constantinople Association Football League 100, 101
corruption 271, 289–90
Council for Workers' Health and Work Safety 79
coups 12, 114, 292, 335–44
Cumberbatch family 92–3
Cumhuriyet (newspaper) 142, 213

Curry, Steve 20
Cyprus 155

Dadam, Abdulrahman 302
Daily Record (newspaper) 182
Davala, Umit 199
Delivelli, Emre (Beşikta fan) 206
Demir, Ali Umit 30, 31
Demir, Turgay 181
Demirel, Volkan 156, 313
Demirkol, Mehmet 180
Demirören, Yildirim 72, 84, 85, 142, 266
Denizli, Mustafa 166–7
derbies
  Inönü stadium 42
  Adana 186, 200–1
  Big Three 4, 39, 52–5, 217–18, 240–2
Derdiyok, Eren 313
derin devlet (deep state) 25
dernek (foundation) 58
Derwall, Jupp 166, 192
Díaz, Picu 141
Didi, Waldyr Pereira 69
Dinçdağ, Halil İbrahim 260–1
Dink, Hrant 262
Diyarbakır 311–12
Diyarbakırspor 314–15, 317–18, 329–33
Diyarbekirspor 328
Dişli, Davut 202
Doğan, Hasan 203
Dolmabahçe Palace, Istanbul 39
Drogba, Didier 285
Dudulluspor 226, 228
Dumankaya (construction firm) 340
Dursun, Salih 269–71
Dynamo Kiev 180, 182

Ecevit, Bülent 155
Edwards, Gary 26–7, 33, 35
Egemenoğlu, Yunus 80
election laws 247–8
elections 115
Elizabeth I, Queen 35
emigration, to Western Europe 232–4
employment rate, female 227
Emrence, Cem 198
England, national team of 151
English teams 165
Enrique, Luis 143
Erdoğan, Ahmet 67–8
Erdoğan, Esra 83
Erdoğan family 289–90
Erdoğan, Necmi 173
Erdoğan, President Tayyip 67–81
  and Ankara 128–9
  and attempted coups 337, 343
  and Çalık 83
  and citizens 344
  and civil unrest 286–7
  enforcing laws 281
  and Fenerbahçe 265
  and German Turks 248–9
  and Gülen movement 338–9
  and Kurd support 319
  and Lefter 156
  and national flag 31
  palace 104
  roots 121
  and Trabzonspor 260
  and Turan 142
  and UN 163
  and Vodafone Arena 85–6, 89
Erhart, Itir 214
Erol, Faruk 320, 323, 329
Eroğul, Ali, *Understanding Trabzon* 258
Ersoy, Şükrü 154
Erten, Bağış 28
Erzik, Şenes 192
Eskişehirspor 263, 266, 322
Eto'o, Samuel 9, 179
EU membership 72, 163, 177–8, 182
Europa League 124
European Championship 12
European clubs, Turkish footballers at 140
Evlan, Berkin 283
Evren, General Kenan 123–4
Eyüboğlu, Bedri Rahmi 152

Eyüp Sultan Mosque 68

'fan', Turkish definition 4
'fanatic', English definition 4
Fanatik (newspaper) 180, 228–9
fans 17, 167–70, 232–3, 236, 242
Father Gül 46
FC Barcelona 133, 139, 141, 143, 320
FC Schalke 04 2, 26
Federation of Socialist Youth Associations 321
female teams 218
Fenerbahçe
  Şükrü Saracoğlu stadium 156
  2008 Champions League 2
  'all-female' crowd 215
  beginnings 101
  Champions League ban 253
  in Europe 52
  famous players 52, 148–56
  fans 5, 27, 42–4, 154, 156, 245
  and Hiddink 173
  kit 4
  league title 20161 252–3
  match-fixing 253, 263–5, 340–3
  modern 52
  nickname 4
  signings 68
  songs 55–7
  stadium 48
  tickets 83
  titles 54
  Ülker Stadium 156
  unbeaten 217
  v. Amedspor 311, 324–8
  v. Beşiktaş J.K. 2013 39
  v. Eskişehirspor 263–4
  v. Trabzonspor 258–60
Ferdinand, Les 26, 27
Ferguson, Sir Alex 182
Fernandes, Manuel 39
FETÖ (Fethullah Gülen Terrorist Organisation) *see* Gülen movement (Islamic sect)
FIFA 182, 202–3
fines, club 54, 103, 218, 320, 322
Finkel, Caroline 134
First World War 22, 53, 150, 254
flag, national 247
flags, club 60–3, 153, 159
flags, national 330
Fındıkçı,Mehmet (Trabzonspor fan club leader) 268
football, Turkish 71
footballing style 136–7
foreign players 164–5, 170–1, 174–7, 178–9
Fotomaç (newspaper) 22, 179, 180, 182, 209–10
France 181
Free Syrian National Team 298–303, 305–8
Frer Mektebi (elite school) 51–2
Frisk, Anders 182
fundraising 59

Galata, Istanbul 38
Galatasaray High School 46–8
Galatasaray Island 15, 26
Galatasaray S.K.
  Ali Sami Yen stadium 18, 49, 76, 78
  Atatürk Olympic stadium 34, 77, 77–8
  banned in Europe 58
  beginnings 47, 101
  club magazine 195
  debts 58
  fans 3, 5, 23–4, 42, 43–4
  Istanbul League winners 107
  kit 4
  Kurdish support 316
  nickname 4, 18
  Passolig card sales 84
  players 47, 173
  songs 55–7
  and Souness 171–2
  Super Cup winners 2000 47
  tactics 199
  and Terim 185–95
  titles 54, 194
  and Turan 139
  Turk Telekom Arena 49

Galatasaray S.K.—*condt.*
UEFA Cup winners 2000 17, 47, 162, 198–9
v. Ankaragücü 1993 265
v. Arsenal 198
v. Beşiktaş 288
v. Konyaspor 49–50
v. Leeds Utd 15, 23–5, 29–30
v. Manchester Utd FC 17–18, 22, 34
v. Trabzonspor 269
Garrido, Juan Rodríguez 141
Gauland, Alexander 246
Gaziantepspor 303
Gecekondu (MKE Ankaragücü fan club) 120
Gençl Trabzonlular (Trabzonspor fan club) 268
Gençlerbirliği S.K. 83, 110–16, 118, 130
Germany 204, 235–6, 240, 247–8
Gezi Park 273, 282–5, 287–90, 293, 343
Gezmiş, Deniz 114
Giggs, Ryan 18
Giley, Vesyel 24–5, 59, 85
Giraud, Brian 98–100, 106
Giraud, Edwin 98
Giraud family 98–100
Giuliano (Azzurri captain) 104–6
Gökçek, Ahmet 127
Gökçek, Melih 126–9, 176
Gökçek, Osman 128
Gökçen, Sabhia 123
Göktürk, Erdem 226
Gomez, Mario 88, 179
Gori, Cecchi 201
government, Turkish 25–6, 301
Göztepe S.K. 10, 102, 192
graffiti 37, 124
'Grand Bazaar', Istanbul 276
Greek Orthodox community 94
Grichthing, Stephane 202
Guerra, Iñako Diaz 141
Gül, Abdullah 212–13
Gül, Hayrünnisa 212
Gülen, Fethullah 338, 344
Gülen movement (Islamic sect) 232, 267, 338–44
Gülkar, Senem 277
Gülmen, Nuri 292
Gülnar, Sezgin 287–9, 291
Gültiken, Ali 44
Gündoğan, Ilkay 235, 247
Gündüz, Yüksel 151
Güneş, Şenol 257
Güneş, Günver 4
Günen, Zeki 224, 227
Güner, Ayhan 42, 274, 278, 284
Güner, Ayhan Beşiktaş Çarşı's leader) 60
Güngör, Necla 210–11, 226, 228
Gürbelik, Nurden 162
Gürsoy, Hasan 290
Güvener, Ahmet 239

Hacıosmanoğlu, İbrahim 260
Hagi, Gheorghe 30, 139, 199
Hakan (Fenerbahçe fan) 242, 245
Hakan (Trabzonspor museum director) 253–4
Hakan, Şükür 30
Halil (Demirspor employee) 187, 189–90
Hamilton, Fabian 32, 34
Harington Cup 53
Hasan, Ulubatlı 172
hate crimes 25, 28
Hector, Michael 238
Heysel disaster (1985) 22
Hiddink, Guus 173–4
Hikmet, Nazim 115, 197
Hillsborough disaster (1989) 27, 76
Hoş, Mustafa 69
homosexuality 215, 221, 260–1
hooliganism 27–8, 85, 163, 200, 258–60
Hotham, David 129, 232, 315
Huggel, Benjamin 202
humour 57
Hungary, national team of 151–2
Hunt, Peter 28–9
Hürriyet (newspaper) 28
Hüsametin 54
Hüsnü, Fuat 52, 53

Idman Yurdu 254
İdmangücü 255, 256
İdmanocağı 255, 256
Ihrig, Stefan, *Atatürk in the Nazi Imagination* 247
Işıklar, Mehmet 278–9
Işılak, Uğur 73
Imam Hatip college 68
Imdat, Ali 120–2
Imalat-ı Harbiye 111, 122
immigration 297, 301
Infantino, Giani 182
Iniesta, Andres 142
Inönü, Mevhibe 220
Inönü stadium 11, 38–9, 42
International Women's Day (IWD) 209–10
Iraq 321
ISIS 181, 320
Istanbul 30, 37, 38
Istanbul Başakşehir F.K. 77, 85–6
Istanbul Büyüksehir Belediyesi S.K 265, 266, 322
Istanbul League 47
Istanbul transport authority (İETT) football team 68
Istanbul United 284
Istanbulspor A.S. 153
Istiklal Caddesi (Independence Avenue), Beyoglu 45–6, 60
Izmir 92–5, 95, 97–9, 102–3
Izzet, Mustafa ('Muzzy') 7, 35, 243–5

Jeffrey, James 341
Jenkins, Gareth 23, 24, 341, 342
Johnson, Boris 181
Johnstone, Dave 34

kabadayı (gangsters) 62, 191, 202
Kadiköy 51, 92
Kaloperović, Tomislav 68, 69
Kalyon Group 77, 83
kapalı tribün (covered terrace) 42, 292
Karadenizgücü 257
Karakızıl, (Gençler fan group) 115
Karalić, Suad 191
Karşıyaka S.K. 74, 97, 103, 224
Kasapoğlu, Koço 153
Kasımpaşa S.K. 69
Kastamonuspor 1966 224
Kaya, Utku 234, 236–8, 246, 248
Kayacı, Tunç 247
Kayseri 123
Kayseri S.K. 76
Kazancı, Ceyhun 76, 81–2
Kazim-Richards, Colin 176, 246
Keçiören 128
Keçiörengücü 329–33
Kemal, Mustafa *see* Atatürk, Mustafa Kemal
Kemalism 128, 228
Keremoğlu, Tugay 140
Kewell, Harry 28
Khatib, Firas al- 308
Kilis Belediyespor 299, 305–8
King, Charles 254
Kılıç, Suat 218
Kırşehir, Anatolia 31
Kızılyalın, Arif 142–3
Kjaer, Simon 326
Klose, Miroslav 236
Kocaman, Aykut 166
Köksal, Ebru 47
Konak Belediyespor 223–5, 227
Konya 12
Konyaspor 49–50, 77, 248
Korkmaz, Ali Ismael 283
Kırşehir, Anatolia 31
Küçükandonyadis, Lefter 'Ordinaryüs' 148–59
Kuneralp, Sinan 181
Kuper, Simon 130
Kurdistan Freedom Falcons 43
Kurdistan Workers' Party (PKK) 43
Kurds 311–12, 315–16, 318
Kurt, Richard 20

La Fontaine, James 100–1
language, Turkish 232

Leeds Utd FC
and Muzzy Izzet 35
v. Beşiktaş J.K. 33
v. Galatasaray S.K. 15, 23–5, 29–30
leftism 113–15, 278, 280
Leicester City FC 175–6, 243–5, 251–2, 268–9
Levant United FC 95–6, 107
Levantines 93, 94–5, 102, 104–7, 105
Levent (journalist) 253, 269
Liverpool FC 22, 34
Loftus, Andy 31–2
Loftus, Christopher 16, 23, 27–8, 30, 34
Loftus, Darren 16
Loftus, Pam 31–2, 34
Lonfat, Johann 202
Lowe, Sid 141
Lucescu, Mircea 143

Maç için Sabahlayan (Galatasaray) 23–4
Macheda, Federico 231
Mahalles (neighbourhood) 62
managers 166
Manchester United FC
and Turkish police 19–20
v. Beşiktaş 231–2
v. Galatasaray S.K 17–18, 22, 34
Manisaspor 215
Mansel, Mansel 98
Marcus, Aliza 316
Markaryan, Alen 59, 277, 280, 281, 291, 292
marriage, Turkish 217
Martıspor 257
martyrdom 222
Martyrs' Hill, Beşiktaş 43
match-fixing 58, 263–5, 266–7, 340–3
Matthews, Stanley 151
May, Theresa 248
Mecidiye köyü, Istanbul 48–9
Medeiros, Wederson Luiz da Silva 176
media reporting
British 20
Dutch 178
Spanish 143
Turan and 141
Turkish 22, 28, 77, 172, 174–5, 180, 269
Meşe, Bilal 142
Mehmet (barber) 189–90
Mehmet (communist) 113
Mehmet the Conquerer 198
Meier, Urs 183
Melikahmet Turanspor *see* Amedspor
'Melikyan *efendi*' 97
Menderes, Adnan 74, 120, 128
Mendes, Tiago 141
Metin-Ali-Feyyaz 44
Metin (Trabzonspor fan) 261
Metro Inşaat 103
MHP (Nationalist Movement Party) 186, 189, 194
Midnight Express (film) 21
migration 120, 121, 232–4, 242
military service 123
Millî Selâmet Partisi (National Salvation Party) 70
Milliyet (newspaper) 68
Milne, Gordon 44, 163, 166, 173
misafir (guest) 26–7, 33
Mithatpaşa stadium *see* Inönü stadium
MKE Ankaragücü 118–24, 126–8, 130, 192
modern 54
Mona, Marwan 299
Moore, Richard 181
Mor, Emre 239
mosques 128
Mosturoğlu, Şekip 342–3
motherhood 222
Murat (Adanaspor fan) 84
Murat (Amedspor fan) 330, 332
Murat (Galatasaray fan leader) 23–4

Naki, Deniz 323–4, 326, 332
Nani, Luis 168
national anthem 202, 317, 331
nationalism 101–2, 163
Netherlands 234
Neville, Gary 17
Niang, Mamadou 39
Nouma, Pascal 170–1

Nuhrat, Yağmur 80

Öcalan, Abdullah 'Apo' 315, 316–17, 319
OGC Nice 152
Okechukwu, Uche 176
Oktay, Metin 47, 140
Öktem, Kerem, *Angry Nation* 25, 342
Öküz, Semih (Trabzonspor fan) 251–2, 256, 263
Olympic Games, 1906 94, 99
Olympique Lyonnais, France 219
Onazi, Ogenyi 173
O'Neill, Martin 243
Or, Erdan 218–20, 228
Oriental Carpet Manufacturers 99–100
Orientalism 20
Orman, Fikret 85, 289, 290
O'Rourke, Jessica 57
Osmanlıspor (Ankaraspor) 85, 125–6, 128–30
Ottoman Empire
  background 20–1
  and Britain 35
  control of Europe 134
  loss of territory 98
  Russian invasion 254
  and surnames 312
  and wars 102
  wealth 38, 91
Öz, Zekeriya 342
Özakça, Semih 292
Özal, Turgut 278, 319
Özalan, Alpay 202
Ozan (Fenerbahçe fan) 169
Özçeri, Tugay 111
Özdelik, Mehmet 202
Özdemir, Cem 235
Özdil, Erol 279
Özel, Özge 222–3, 227
Özer, Şehmus 326
Özgentürk, Nebil 156, 157
Özgür (friend and guide) 8
Özil, Mesut 235–7, 246, 247
Özoğuz, Aydan 235
Öztin, Tahsiz 155
Öztürk, Sezer 263–4, 266
Özyağıcı, Ahmet Suat 257

Pamuk, Orhan 279
Panionios FC 94
Park, Ji-sung 231
Park protests (2013) 116
Parker, Alan 21
Parla, Ayşe 220
parliamentary laws 79, 213, 312
Parlour, Ray 199
Pasha, Grand Vizier Ali 93–4
Passolig football ID cards 81–2, 83–4, 116–17, 200
Paxer FC 98
Pears, Henry 100, 101
Pekdaş, Şema 223–4
Penbe, Ergün 199
Petit, Emmanuel 199
Piontek, Sepp 192
PKK (Kurdistan Workers' Party) 315–17, 319, 321, 328–9
Podolski, Lucas 179, 236
poetry 152
pogroms 154
political summits 31
politics, football and 59–60, 77
Popescu, George 199
Portugal 203
Pozzo, Vittorio 151
Princes Islands 147
professional football 110, 256
protests, political 273–5
Puddefoot, Sydney 54
Puskás, Ferenc 152
Putin, Vladimir 74

Qassab, Jehad 296
Quaresma, Ricardo 85, 88

Ramírez, Fabricio Agosto ('Fabri') 180
RB Leipzig 8
Reçber, Rüştü 231
Refa'ie, Jamal al 296
referees 163, 191, 260, 269, 270

religion 70, 150, 154, 157–8, 212, 255
Return to Homs (2013 documentary) 297
Revolutionary People's Liberation Party-Front (DHKP-C) 114
Ridsdale, Peter 15–16, 29, 33
rioting 154
rivalry 54
Romania 282
Rönesans Holding 103
Röthlisberger, Kurt 19
Rums (Turkish citizens of Greek ethnicity) 149–50, 154–6, 157, 255
Russia/USSR 162
Rıza, Süleyman 255

Sabhia Gökçen airport 337
Şahan, Olcay 39
Şahin, Mehmet Ali 203
Şahin, Nuri 235
Said, Edward 20
Salih Dursun Street, Trabzon 269
Sankari Foundation 300, 302–3
Santoro, Andrea 262
Saracoğlu, Şükrü 156–7
Sariyer SK 27
Sağıroğlu, İbrahim 270, 271
Saroot, Abdul Basset 297
Saunders, Dean 171
Seaman, David 199
season tickets 50
Sedat (football fan) 319
'Self-rule' 321
Şen, Volkan 327
Şenes Erzik 180
Senol Günes Stadium 75
Şenol, Mehmet 195
Şenturk, Semih 322
Şeraffettin, Ahmed 40
Şeref Stadium 48
Serttaş, Bülent 322
Seyhuni, Ahmet 306
SFF (Syrian Football Federation) 300
Simeone, Diego 140, 141
Simes, Andrew 95–7, 105, 106, 107
Şimşek, Mehmet 319
Sivas Belediyespor 76
Sivasspor 82, 264
Skibbe, Michael 137
Škrtel, Martin 74, 168–9, 178
Smyrna 91–2, 93
Sneijder, Wesley 50, 173, 178
Socialist Workers Party 113
Socrates (magazine) 138–9
Somah, Omar Al 305
songs 55, 214, 293
Sosa, José 178–9
Souness, Graeme 171–2
Souza, Alexsandro de ('Alex') 176
Söyüncü, Çağlar 239
Speight family 32
Speight, Kevin 16, 23, 27–8, 30
sponsorship 58, 76, 84, 138, 156, 229
Sporel, Zeki Riza 53
sports facilities 75
sports, Turkish 161
Sports Writers Association 343
stadiums 75–6, 215
stampedes 39, 76
Star (newspaper) 28
Streller, Marco 202
Strummer, Joe 115
Şükür, Hakan 199, 340
Süldür, Fahrettin, *Turkish Football* 161
Sultanahmet, Istanbul 37
Sultanbekov, Arslanbek 73
Sümer, Çetin 317
Sümer, Özkan 256–7
Sun (newspaper) 183
Sungur, Ceyda 282–3
Süper Lig 31, 44, 166, 174–5
'Supporter', English definition 4
surname law 312–13
Suruç, war in 320
swearing
  British fans 23
  match bans 82, 231
  and rivalry 119
  in Turkey 179, 193, 214–15
  warning against 330
  and women 218

Switzerland 202–4
Syria 10–11, 295
Syrian, national team 308
Szymanksi, Stefan 130

Taffarel, Cláudio 30
Taksim square, Istanbul 30, 273–5, 287
Tanin (newspaper) 106
TarafDer (supporters' rights association) 117
taraftar ('fan') 3–4
Tarde, Gabriel 122
taxation 174–5
Taylor Report (1990) 79
Tebbit, Norman 239, 240, 242
techniques, training 165
Tekin, Metin 44
Telat (Adana Demirspor fan group president) 193–4, 196
Temulkuran, Ece 220
Terim, Fatih 143, 185–95, 198–9, 201–7
'terrace leader' conception 277–8
terrorist attacks
  Ankara 12
  'deep state' 25
  Istanbul 48
  'Martyrs' Hill' 43
  Paris 181
  PKK and 328–9
  soldiers and 317
  Suruç 321
Thomson, Craig 180–1, 182
tickets 118
  Tiryakioğlu, Sarp 139, 140
Tit, Ahmet 298
TOKI (housing agency) 76, 78
Tore, Gökhan 222
Toroğlu, Erman 175
Torun, Aziz 78
Torun Center 78–9
Torunlar Construction 78
Trabzon 255–6, 257
Trabzonspor 251–4, 256–71
  fans 261, 269
  kit 257
  stadium 75
  titles 10, 110, 257
  v. Fenerbahçe 258–60, 268
  v. Galatasaray S.K. 269
Traverso, Andrea 58
Turan, Arda 133–45
Turan, Okan 139
Türel, Metin 165
Turgay, Turkan 29
Türk, Egemen 139
Turkey
  development of 120
  economy 102
  Euro 1996 192
  history 37, 38
  national flag 31
  and Syria 297
Turkey, national team of
  Euro 1992 192
  Euro 2012 174
  Euro 2016 22, 141–2
  success 162
  v. Germany 2010 236
  v. Greece 1948 156
  v. Hungary 1956 151
  v. Iceland 2015 12
  v. Romania 1923 282
  World Cup 2006 202, 203
Turkish army 25
Turkish Football Federation (TFF)
  and Ankaraspor 127
  and Diyarbakırspor 318
  expansion 256
  and fans 81
  and Fenerbahçe 58
  fines from 54, 102, 218, 320, 322
  licences 301–2
  match-fixing 266
  and women 215–16, 219, 227
'Turkish history thesis' 162
tutmak (football support) 10

Uçar, Feyyaz 44
UEFA 29, 58, 181–2, 219–20, 226–7, 271
Ülgen, Hayri 68

UltrAslan (Galatasaray supporters' club) 24, 26, 59, 85
Uluğ, Yiğiter 203
Ulugay, Alp 203
Ulusoy, Kemal 111, 117–18
UN Security Council 163
Ünder, Cengiz 239
underworld, football and the 265–7
Üsküdar, Istanbul 38

Valverde, Ernesto 143
Van Persie, Robin 168, 175
Vardar, Sinan 175
Vartanyan FC 94
Vassell, Darius 127, 168
Viera, Patrick 199
villages and towns, Turkish 313
violence, street 114, 154

War of Independence (1919–23) 123, 124, 155, 313
Ward, Farid 299, 301, 302, 303, 305–8
watermelon festivals 314
Welfare Party 70
Werner, Timo 8
West Germany, national team of 151
Westerwelle, Guido 249
White, Jenny 72, 114
Whittall, Herbert Octavius 94
Wilkinson, Steve 28
women, Turkish 210–29
workplace accidents 78–9
World Values Survey (2008) 286

Yaşar, Ahmet ('Fatty Ahmet') 187–8
Yakın, Hakan 204
Yakın, Murat 203
Yakışkan, Cem 276, 288, 291
Yalçın, Hakkı 175
Yalçın, Soner 69
Yağmur, Yusuf 327
Yarımoğlu, (Gençler fan) 110, 111, 115–17
Yelkovan, Banu 31, 213
Yen, Ali Sami 47, 52
Yeni Malatyaspor 265
Yenikent, Aksaray Province 125
Yiğit, Orcan 116, 117
Yıldırım, Aziz 52, 170, 263–4, 267, 340–2
Yıldırım, Burak 285
Yıldız Holding 84
Yıldız, Mehmet Derviş 289
Yörük (Galatasaray S.K. fan) 49–50
Young Turks 40, 97–8, 107
Yousef, Zakariya al 296
youth teams 239
Yüce, Mehmet, *Ottoman Angels* 54, 100
Yusuf (gardener) 148, 152–4, 157–9

Zafer (journalist) 233
Zaid, Abdulrahman Abu 298
Zaid, Abulrahman al- 309
Zaman (newspaper) 69
Zarrab, Reza 290
Zavotçu, Mutlu Can 221
Zazaistan 196